MW01009788

Pakistan's Enduring Challenges

Pakistan's Enduring Challenges

Edited by

C. Christine Fair and Sarah J. Watson

PENN

UNIVERSITY OF PENNSYLVANIA PRESS

PHILADELPHIA

Published by

University of Pennsylvania Press

Philadelphia, Pennsylvania 19104-4112

Printed in the United States of America

on acid-free paper

10 9 8 7 6 5 4 3 2 1

Library of Congress Cataloging-in-Publication Data

Pakistan's Enduring Challenges / edited by C. Christine Fair and Sarah J. Watson.—1st ed.

    p. cm.

  ISBN 978-0-8122-4690-2 (hardcover : alk. paper)

    1. Pakistan—Politics and government—21st century. 2. Pakistan—Economic conditions—21st century. 3. Pakistan—Foreign relations—21st century. 4. Political stability—Pakistan—21st century. 5. Internal security—Pakistan—21st century. 6. Religious militants—Pakistan—21st century. 7. Democracy—Pakistan—21st century. 8. Military assistance, American—Pakistan—21st century. 9. Pakistan—Military relations—United States. 10. United States—Military relations—Pakistan. I. Fair, C. Christine. II. Watson, Sarah J.

DS389.A73 2015

954.9105'3—dc23

                                     2014029616

Contents

Introduction: Pakistan's Enduring Challenges   1
  C. Christine Fair and Sarah J. Watson

PART I. SECURITY CHALLENGES

Chapter 1. Pakistani Militancy in the Shadow of the U.S. Withdrawal   27
  Stephen Tankel

Chapter 2. A Cooperative Jihad? The Religious Logic of Hafiz Muhammad
Saeed and the Limits of Pan-Sunni Cooperation in Pakistan   55
  Joshua T. White

Chapter 3. The Future of the American Drone Program in Pakistan   72
  Sarah J. Watson and C. Christine Fair

Chapter 4. The Safety and Security of the Pakistani Nuclear Arsenal   98
  Christopher Clary

PART II. DOMESTIC POLITICAL AND ECONOMIC ISSUES

Chapter 5. Democracy on the Leash in Pakistan   131
  C. Christine Fair

Chapter 6. New Media in Naya Pakistan: Technologies
of Transformation or Control?   156
  Huma Yusuf

Chapter 7. Pakistan's Self-Inflicted Economic Crises   178
Feisal Khan

PART III. FOREIGN RELATIONS

Chapter 8. America and Pakistan After 2014: Toward Strategic
Breathing Space   205
Paul Staniland

Chapter 9. Partner or Enemy? The Sources of Attitudes
Toward the United States in Pakistan   227
Karl Kaltenthaler and William J. Miller

Chapter 10. Friends of Last Resort: Pakistan's Relations
with China and Saudi Arabia   256
Aparna Pande

Chapter 11. Violent Nonstate Actors in the Afghanistan-Pakistan
Relationship: Historical Context and Future Prospects   278
Daveed Gartenstein-Ross and Tara Vassefi

List of Contributors   297

Index   303

Acknowledgments   311

Introduction: Pakistan's Enduring Challenges

C. Christine Fair and Sarah J. Watson

Pakistan on 9/11: From Pariah to Paladin

On September 10, 2001, Pakistan was virtually a pariah state. It was encumbered by layers of sanctions meant to punish it for, inter alia, nuclear and missile proliferation, its May 1998 nuclear tests (conducted almost immediately after those of India), and the 1999 bloodless coup in which Chief of Army Staff Pervez Musharraf overthrew the democratically elected government of Prime Minister Nawaz Sharif. The U.S. Department of State had even considered placing Pakistan on its list of countries that support terrorism. While Pakistan narrowly escaped designation as a state sponsor of terrorism, it did in fact support a vast fleet of Islamist militants waging a terror campaign throughout India, particularly in Indian-administered Kashmir, and it was providing key military, political, diplomatic, and other support to the Taliban regime in Afghanistan.[1] When then U.S. President Bill Clinton visited the subcontinent in 2000, he spent several days in India, but in contrast, only a few hours in Pakistan. He took the opportunity to lecture Pakistani leaders on their reckless policies and even refused to shake the hand of General Musharraf, the country's fourth military dictator. Prior to 9/11, the George W. Bush administration had embarked on a serious effort to reconfigure its relations with India and Pakistan. Whereas the United States sought to engage India in a significant strategic partnership, it was trying to prepare Pakistan to accept its unequal position in South Asia and diminished importance to the United States (Fair 2004; Tellis 2001: 88; Tellis 2008).

The tragic events of September 11, 2001, afforded Pakistan the opportunity to regain its standing among the community of nations and to force the United States to modify its plans to forge an entirely new policy in South Asia, one predicated upon moving boldly forward with India while helping Pakistan to accept its unequal and indeed inferior position in South Asia. Almost immediately, the United States had to find some way of releasing Pakistan from its burden of sanctions, both in order to secure the necessary Pakistani political will to support the looming war effort in Afghanistan and also to arm Pakistan, which would—once again—become a frontline state in an American war. Virtually overnight, President Musharraf was transformed from yet another "mango republic" dictator into a much-feted partner of the free world and an intrepid cobelligerent in what became known as "the war on terror."

Pakistan's assistance was critical to the U.S. war in Afghanistan, launched on October 7, 2001, under the name "Operation Enduring Freedom." Pakistan provided the United States with unprecedented access to ports, military bases, airspace, and ground lines of control, and Pakistani security forces also provided highly necessary security for U.S. assets positioned in Pakistan (Fair 2004). As the United States and NATO developed the Afghan theater, they freed themselves somewhat from their dependence on Pakistan. But Pakistan remained a crucial player in the war effort because the United States was unable to find a cost-effective alternative to trucking supplies into Afghanistan over Pakistani territory. Goods were off-loaded at the Karachi port and then transferred onto thousands of privately owned local transport trucks for the trip into Afghanistan, either through the pass at Chaman (in Baluchistan) or through Torkham (in Khyber Pakhtunkhwa). As the war in Afghanistan drew on, Pakistan also became an indispensable partner in the drone program, which targeted al-Qaeda, the Taliban, and (ostensibly) their "allied forces" in Pakistan and Afghanistan.

President Musharraf benefited politically from his role in the war effort. Even as he became a greater and greater liability for the Pakistan army and as his policies vexed and alienated ever more Pakistanis, the United States redoubled its commitment to securing his place in Pakistan's politics (Markey 2007). In order to keep him on as president while quieting critics of U.S. hypocrisy, the United States, working with the United Kingdom, helped broker a deal in 2007 that would allow Benazir Bhutto to return to Pakistan. The legislation that came about, the National Reconciliation Ordinance, offered her and her associates amnesty for any crimes committed during their previous spells in power, thus allowing them to contest elections. Musharraf would remain the president, with Benazir Bhutto as prime minister. The deal faltered when Bhutto was tragically assassinated in late 2007. Musharraf's career could not be resuscitated, and by the end of 2008, he had resigned from the position of the presidency and from the military (Wright and Kessler 2007; Sehbai 2011). Even though the 2008 elections ushered in a civilian government led by the Pakistan Peoples Party, the United States focused instead on Ashfaq Parvez Kayani, Musharraf's successor as chief of army staff.

For the first five or six years of the war, Washington was relatively pleased with Pakistan's cooperation. President Bush would frequently cite the various al-Qaeda operatives who had been captured with Pakistani help as proof of Musharraf's dedication to the war. When al-Qaeda began targeting President Musharraf in 2004 for this very cooperation, Washington worked even harder to support him and his army (Vandehei and Lancaster 2006). Between fiscal years 2002 and 2008, the United States provided Pakistan some $2.2 billion in security-related assistance and $3.2 billion in economic aid. These figures paled, however, in comparison to the $6.7 billion that the United States transferred to Pakistan under the Coalition Support Funds (CSF) program, under which the United States reimbursed Pakistan for its expenditures on the war on terror in the same period (Congressional Research Service 2014). The terms of reimbursement under this program were absurdly favorable and subject to very little oversight (GAO 2008a).

By 2007, tensions between the two countries were apparent. The Bush administration had slowly come to the realization that, while Pakistan had aided the U.S. war on al-Qaeda, it had also continued supporting its clients in Afghanistan, most importantly Mullah Omar's Taliban and the North Waziristan-based network run by Jalaluddin Haqqani. This realization was all the more troubling because the United States and its NATO partners were finally convinced that they were fighting an insurgency in Afghanistan, led by the very same groups patronized by Pakistan. Prior to 2007, the international community had assumed that the military operations in Afghanistan would soon begin winding down, as the Taliban had long been vanquished and even al-Qaeda no longer operated in Afghanistan (Jones 2007a; Jones 2007b).

From Pakistan's perspective, on the other hand, the United States had fallen short on many counts. First, in late 2001, the United States was unable to prevent the Northern Alliance from taking Kabul. The Northern Alliance was the only remaining source of resistance to the Taliban and it received assistance from India, as well as Iran, Russia, Tajikistan, and the

United States, among others. From the point of view of Pakistan's military and intelligence agencies, the United States had handed the keys of Kabul to India's proxy. Second, the December 2001 Bonn Conference, which excluded the Taliban, was a convention of the conquerors of a government long-sponsored by Pakistan. Third, India slowly rebuilt its presence in Afghanistan under the U.S./NATO security umbrella. Pakistan saw every Indian gain in Afghanistan as a direct threat to its own interests and believed that India—in connivance with the anti-Pakistan Afghan government—was using its strongholds in Afghanistan to support insurgency and terrorism in Pakistan.

Worse yet, in 2005 the United States announced its support for a civilian nuclear program in India, explicitly embracing the objective of assisting India's ability to develop nuclear weapons (Tellis 2005: 35–37). Additionally, Pakistan's military support for the U.S.-led coalition that routed the Taliban and destroyed al-Qaeda prompted a lethal rebellion among some of Pakistan's erstwhile militant assets. By 2007, several militant commanders—all of whom were associated with the Deobandi interpretive tradition—had grouped themselves under the umbrella of the Tehreek-e-Taliban-e-Pakistan (Pakistani Taliban Movement, or TTP). These Deobandi commanders had long-standing connections to the Afghan Taliban through a shared architecture of Deobandi madrassas, mosques, ulema, and political leadership. Because of the colocation of al-Qaeda and the Taliban in Afghanistan, many of these Pakistani groups also had ties to and sympathies with al-Qaeda. At first, Pakistan's military, paramilitary, police, and intelligence agencies bore the brunt of the TTP's onslaught. However, by 2008, the TTP began savagely attacking civilians far beyond the tribal areas and in Pakistan's important cities of Islamabad, Lahore, Peshawar, Karachi, and Quetta, among others (Fair 2013).

From the army's point of view, this sequence of events was all the more troubling. While the American and Pakistani publics routinely cited the ever-higher amounts of military assistance poured into the Pakistan army's coffers, and while Americans increasingly complained that their government was not getting what it paid for, the Pakistan army had its own complaints. The monies that the United States gave to Pakistan did not go to the army directly but rather to the Ministry of Finance, and the Pakistan army claimed that it was not receiving the stipulated reimbursement. General Kayani, Pakistan's army chief at the time, told American interlocutors that in fact only 40 percent of CSF funds went to the military. Kayani requested changes in the way in which CSF funds were distributed to prevent the impression that the Pakistan military was "for hire" (U.S. Embassy Islamabad 2011). Unfortunately, that impression had long settled in, and, in a final blow, the Pakistani public began viewing the army with contempt. Pakistanis did not like the perception that the Pakistan army had become a mercenary army operating at the behest of Washington. Nor did they support the bloody operations being conducted against their own countrymen.

Things Fall Apart—Rapidly

When Barack Obama campaigned for the U.S. presidency in 2008, he spoke strongly about the need to end the "wrong war" in Iraq and rededicate American efforts to the "right war" in Afghanistan. Obama chastised the Bush administration for failing to develop a policy toward Pakistan, which was necessary for any kind of victory in Afghanistan. Obama was not alone. The nonpartisan U.S. Government Accountability Office issued a scathing criticism of the U.S. failures in Pakistan (GAO 2008b). In response, the Bush administration commissioned numerous assessments in the final months of its tenure. Upon assuming the presidency, Obama asked Bruce Riedel, a long-time Central Intelligence Agency (CIA) official who advised several U.S. presidents on issues pertaining to South Asia and the Middle East, to conduct an assessment of the assessments and proffer a way forward (Riedel 2012).

The first document to emerge from this process was a white paper that declared that "the core goal of the United States must be to disrupt, dismantle, and defeat al Qaeda and its safe havens in Pakistan, and to prevent their return to Pakistan or Afghanistan" (Office of the President 2009: 1). To achieve this core goal, the white paper laid out numerous "realistic and achievable objectives," which included disrupting terrorist networks in Afghanistan and Pakistan, promoting better government in Afghanistan, developing the Afghan National Security Forces, assisting the civilian government of Pakistan to better economic growth, and enlisting the involvement of the international community in all of these endeavors—all formulaic bromides. What the study did not address forthrightly was the fact that, while Pakistan had been an important partner in aspects of the war, it was in fact the biggest hindrance to ensuring that the Taliban did not return.

While the Obama administration, under Riedel's guidance, considered the best course for the United States in Afghanistan and Pakistan, the August 30, 2009 initial assessment report of General Stanley McChrystal, commander of the International Security Assessment Force (ISAF) in Afghanistan, was leaked to the public. While the report acknowledged the need for a better partner in Afghanistan, most analysts and policy makers focused upon the other key element of his conclusions: the need for some 40,000 more troops (Commander ISAF 2009). Obama did not immediately consent to the military's calls for more troops, but on December 1, 2009, he announced a "way forward" in Afghanistan, which included a so-called "surge" of an additional 30,000 U.S. troops along with an ironclad commitment to begin wrapping up the war, transferring all security duties to the Afghans, and withdrawing troops. This plan focused upon military objectives in Afghanistan and presented a scaled-back version of the nation-building goals announced in March 2009. Obama stated clearly that "we will remove our combat brigades from Afghanistan by the end of next summer, and all of our troops by the end of 2011" (Obama 2009: n.p.). That deadline came under immediate fire. Obama's political foes cried that he had given the Taliban an incentive to wait out the American withdrawal and argued that such a declaratory position assured a Taliban victory. However, Obama was also under considerable domestic pressure to end a war that had become deeply unpopular. Trying to navigate between the opposing positions, Obama eventually announced that "by 2014, this process of transition will be complete, and the Afghan people will be responsible for their own security" (Obama 2011: n.p.).

The Obama administration repeatedly stated that it understood that American "success in Afghanistan is inextricably linked to our partnership with Pakistan" (Obama 2009: n.p.). However, the Obama administration—like the Bush administration before it—was never able to formulate a coherent policy toward Pakistan that would enhance the likelihood of achieving any of its goals in Afghanistan. Unlike the Bush administration, however, the Obama administration did not view Pakistan as an indefatigable collaborator in the U.S. efforts in South Asia. Instead, policy makers understood that Pakistan's military and intelligence agencies were working assiduously to undermine many of the gains in Afghanistan and in South Asia for which the Americans and their allies had sacrificed much blood and treasure. Yet despite this very different view of Pakistan, the United States under Obama became even more dependent upon Pakistan than it had been under Bush. With an expanded number of troops in Afghanistan, Pakistan became ever more important as a logistical lifeline to sustain the war. Thus, ironically, the very troop surge that was intended to help defeat the Taliban rendered the United States ever more dependent upon the one country dedicated to restoring some version of the group to power in Afghanistan. The United States had no strategy for addressing this fundamental conundrum.

As suggested above, the Obama administration was not ignorant of the paradoxical position in which it found itself. By the time Obama assumed the presidency, Pakistan fatigue had begun to set in across the departments of Defense and State, in the intelligence community, within the White House, throughout the members of Congress, and among the American people. The South Asia analytical community largely understood that it was Pakistan—not Afghanistan—where the most salient U.S. national security interests resided. But with troops in Afghanistan, sustaining the expanding military presence in Afghanistan took up almost all America's attention. The "Pakistan problem set" was just too hard to solve. Thus, Obama— much like Bush before him—continued a policy of pushing on core issues while deferring punitive or coercive measures, fearing that Pakistan would further undermine the war effort in Afghanistan. Using less delicate phraseology, all understood that the Americans were "simply kicking the can down the road," hoping that someone would deal with the problem later.

While the United States continued to fund Pakistan—ultimately providing some $28 billion between fiscal years 2002 and 2014 (Congressional Research Service 2014)—these disbursements became increasingly controversial as more information became available about the extent to which Pakistan was continuing to invest in the Taliban, the Haqqani Network, and terrorist groups like Lashkar-e-Taiba, while also expanding its rapidly growing nuclear arsenal (Joscelyn 2011). Despite knowledge that Pakistan was still pursuing policies that were antithetical to U.S. interests and that by law precluded Pakistan from obtaining U.S. security assistance, in March 2011 the U.S. secretary of state declared that Pakistan was in full compliance with all security assistance conditionalities. In August 2012, Hillary Clinton, then secretary of state, formally notified Congress that the administration would seek to continue funding Pakistan by requesting that those conditionalities be waived.[2] In doing so the administration conceded that Pakistan was not in compliance but argued that to cease funding would be damaging to the national security interests of the United States. This was the first time that the Obama administration waived aid sanctions on Pakistan.

At the time of writing, all key American decision makers agree that the Pakistan of late 2014, at the end of the war in Afghanistan, is likely to be a greater danger to itself, its neighbors, and the United States than it was on September 10, 2001.

Escaping Afghanistan's Pull

With the United States resolved to wind down major military operations in Afghanistan by 2014, tension between the United States and Pakistan intensified. On the one hand, Pakistan became ever more committed to waiting out Washington and attempting to secure the best possible future for itself in Afghanistan. At the same time, Washington was ever more anxious to wrap up the war while still saving face. The patience of both countries has worn thin.

American legislators, who write the checks to Pakistan, are wary of continuing to fund Pakistan while it in turn continues to fund U.S. enemies (not just the Taliban but also the Islamist militant groups, such as Lashkar-e-Taiba, which Pakistan uses to harass India). At the same time, as Karl Kaltenthaler and William J. Miller show in this volume (Chapter 9), Pakistani civilian and military leaders alike have been pushed to the breaking point by U.S. policies that Washington pursues with indifference to Pakistani sentiment. The entire country, it seems, is fed up with the United States.

The list of *recent* Pakistani grievances is long. In January 2011, Raymond Davis, a CIA contractor, shot and killed two armed men he claimed were menacing him and brandishing their weapons in Lahore. An American rescue vehicle raced to the scene to extract Davis and in doing so hit and killed a third person. There has been some speculation that the two men killed by Davis were themselves contractors for Pakistan's Inter-Services Intelligence Directorate, the ISI (Waraich 2011). The Davis affair helped bring to light the expanding U.S. intelligence presence in Pakistan, which was undertaking operations beyond the purview of the ISI. Some of these operations targeted Pakistan's prized militant assets such as the Lashkar-e-Taiba. This impasse over Davis was only resolved when the two governments came up with a plausible solution: the United States would pay blood money to the victims' families, who would then drop the charges (Miller and Constable 2010).

Just as the two countries were struggling to reestablish some degree of equilibrium, in May 2011 the United States launched a unilateral raid upon Osama bin Laden's Pakistani hiding place. The United States learned that bin Laden had been living for years in Abbottabad, home to the esteemed Pakistan Military Academy. The raid was conducted using stealth helicopters and a large Navy SEAL team. The Pakistan military was humiliated by the U.S. ability to conduct a raid of this sort, undetected, in a sensitive area. Pakistanis' outrage tended to focus on the unilateral nature of the raid, rather than the disturbing fact that bin Laden had been in Pakistan all along, despite repeated Pakistani claims to the contrary. Many Pakistanis felt confronted with a choice: should they believe that their government had been complicit in harboring the world's most notorious terrorist? Or was it simply incompetent? In November 2011, yet another upheaval jarred the U.S.-Pakistan relationship when U.S. forces, operating as part of the NATO coalition in Afghanistan, erroneously attacked and killed numerous Pakistani armed forces personnel at a border outpost in Salala. The United States refused to offer a formal apology.

Combined with the CIA's escalation of drone strikes in the tribal areas, 2011 was a tipping point in the fraught history of U.S.-Pakistan relations. In the wake of the bin Laden raid, Pakistan's national assembly convened a Parliamentary Committee on National Security, which sought to redefine Pakistan's relations with the United States. While Pakistan's defense and security policy remain firmly in the hands of the army, this move was an important step. Not only were civilian politicians inserting themselves into the army's domain, the Pakistani people began to grow accustomed to seeing elected officials in this arena. After Salala, Pakistan closed down the NATO ground supply routes through Pakistan (although not Pakistani airspace), forcing the United States to develop more expensive ground routes through Central Asia and to fly in more cargo. Pakistan also forced the United States to vacate a drone base in Shamsi. (It is not clear if the United States is still using other bases in Pakistan for drone strikes.)

At the time of writing, the United States and Pakistan are still struggling to recalibrate their relations. Each country adheres to its own narrative of defeated expectations. Pakistan deploys a highly stylized account of its relations with the United States since the mid-1950s as proof that the Americans have never honored their commitments to Pakistan. Pakistanis cite the failure of the United States to support Pakistan in its 1965 war with India; the inadequate support Pakistan received in the 1971 war with India; and the U.S. arming of India during the latter's 1962 war with China. All of these actions (or inactions) are seen as flouting U.S. treaty obligations to Pakistan. Yet as Husain Haqqani, among others, has long noted, these criticisms are invalid. The treaties that bound the Americans and the Pakistanis specifically excluded any conflict with India and only promised U.S. support in the case of communist aggression (Haqqani 2013).

The Americans, for their part, continue to pursue the same (failed) policy toward Pakistan, one of transformation through economic and military assistance. As Haqqani (2013) also notes, during previous periods of engagement the Americans have tended to assume that there is a level of assistance that will suffice to transform Pakistan into the partner the Americans desire—or that will at least obtain needed amenities. While Americans are continually shocked at Pakistan's ingratitude, Pakistanis lament that the United States gives only when doing so is in its strategic interests. While neither side much likes the other, there appears to be no exit for either (Markey 2013).

As 2014 begins, Pakistan seems better set to achieve its objectives in Afghanistan than does the United States. The United States has been unable to conclude a so-called bilateral security agreement (BSA) with the government of the outgoing Afghan President, Hamid Karzai. This agreement would specify the number of U.S. troops that would remain in Afghanistan and the roles that they would serve. It would also lay out the terms of a long-term economic support package to Afghanistan. While Pakistan's goal of resurrecting some variant of the Taliban in Afghanistan is still far off, the lack of a BSA can only improve the Taliban's prospects.

Not All Bad?

While it is easy to inventory the vast swamp of problems in which Pakistan is mired, it should be remembered that in recent years Pakistan has taken a few meaningful, positive strides. Most significantly, the past several years have witnessed the slow consolidation of democracy, and a corresponding growth in civil society, within Pakistan. The 2013 general elections were an important and unprecedented milestone: they marked the first time in Pakistan's history that a democratically elected government carried out a constitutional transfer of power to another such government under an entirely civilian dispensation. But these gains are far from secure. The internal security crisis has taken a particular toll on Pakistan's neglected minority populations and on its increasingly embattled liberals. The threat of terrorist attacks hobbled liberal parties during the 2013 campaign season, and, even more disturbing, Pakistan's sectarian terrorist organizations appear to be waging a campaign of ethnic cleansing against Pakistan's Shia population. Prime Minister Nawaz Sharif has yet to exhibit a vision or policy agenda to contend with Pakistan's myriad security challenges, economic stagnation, or the widening gaps between its citizens' various visions of Pakistan's future.

While civilians have made important gains, these are limited. Civilians still have precious little input into Pakistan's foreign or national security policies, the bailiwicks of the army and its associated intelligence agencies. Pakistan's security establishment continues to be primarily focused on India and to see the conflict in Afghanistan as an extension of its decades-long rivalry with its far larger eastern neighbor. This strategic perspective has governed its actions in Afghanistan and the tribal areas and will continue to determine its responses to the postwithdrawal political situation in Afghanistan.

After 2014, the Deluge?

Pakistani politicians have publicly urged the United States to leave Afghanistan, and indeed America's departure from the region will present Pakistan with opportunities as well as challenges. In May 2014, Obama announced that 9,800 U.S. troops would remain in Afghanistan "for one year following the end of combat operations in December [2014]. That number will be cut in half at the end of 2015, and reduced at the end of 2016 to a small military presence at the U.S. Embassy" (De Young 2014). While this is a serious revision of the "zero option," it is still safe to assume that the United States will begin to take a more hands-off approach to Pakistan as troop levels in Afghanistan continue to decline. To the extent that American outreach to Pakistan is currently disproportionately aimed at the military establishment, a shift to a more traditional diplomatic relationship may help Pakistan's civilian leaders continue to claw back the military's power over foreign affairs and security policy. Pakistan's military establishment, in contrast, likely believes that it will have a freer hand in its quest to control Afghanistan's future.

But Pakistanis who believe that the U.S. presence in Afghanistan is the cause of their country's problems are likely to be disappointed. The U.S. withdrawal from Afghanistan will leave turmoil in its wake, and there is no doubt that the resulting chaos will spill over into Pakistan (as it has for the past ten years). A power vacuum in Afghanistan will also mean fertile new ground for the Indo-Pak rivalry. A deep insecurity regarding India has dictated Pakistan's actions since independence and will continue to do so as long as Pakistan's security establishment escapes civilian control. Furthermore, Pakistan faces a host of economic and governance challenges, none of which have an easy solution. In the end, Pakistan alone can take control of its destiny.

For years, Pakistani and American analysts have wondered what will happen to this problematic relationship after 2014 when the United States has less need for Pakistan. Will the United States reorient its policies away from appeasing Pakistan and toward more punitive policies such as coercion or even containment? Without a BSA with Afghanistan and with a diminished presence in Pakistan, how will the United States be able to sustain its counterterrorism initiatives centered on al-Qaeda, Lashkar-e-Taiba, and other terrorist groups based in and from Pakistan? Other analysts counter that such a deliberate effort to abandon Pakistan is impossible, if for no other reason than the threat posed by Pakistan's ever-expanding nuclear program.

Some Pakistanis have also long sought to restructure, if not dismantle, Pakistan's dependence upon the United States. Yet not only has the United States supplied enormous financial and military assistance through grants, debt relief, and military sales on favorable terms, it has also been an important voice at multilateral institutions such as the International Monetary Fund, the World Bank, and the Asian Development Bank. While some Pakistanis may dismiss the actual amount of U.S. development assistance, only the foolish would dismiss the important role that Washington plays in ensuring that multilateral organizations continue investing in Pakistan despite Pakistan's repeated failures to fulfill its side of the bargain.

Pakistani media and political and military elites often reassure its citizens that should Washington again abandon Pakistan, China will step in to the fill the void. China, however, has not been so willing to play this game. China's record of relations with Pakistan is not so different from that of the United States. China encourages Pakistan to formalize the status quo with India in Kashmir, urges Pakistan to take its domestic Islamist terrorism seriously, and chides Pakistan for supporting international Islamist terrorist groups. While China does provide military equipment and even nuclear technology to Pakistan, it does not wish to see Pakistan and India go to war. Nor does China want to encourage a complete break between Washington and Islamabad, as it has no interest in taking over America's expensive role in propping up Pakistan.

While Pakistanis and Americans alike would like to find some way of unlocking what Bruce Riedel has called a "deadly embrace," the essays in this volume suggest that this may be more easily said than done. There is little evidence that the two estranged "frenemies" can simply walk away from each other. Yet there is also little evidence that this relationship will become more palatable to domestic elites and ordinary citizens on either side.

This Volume

The contributors to this edited volume hope to cast light on several interrelated issues that will contribute to Pakistan's post-2014 trajectory. One cluster of concerns pertains most closely to Pakistan's domestic security situation. The internal security threats to Pakistan are numerous and stem in part from the long history of the deep state's patronage of Islamist terrorist groups to achieve foreign policy goals in India and Kashmir.[3] This policy commitment enabled the rise of an armada of Islamist militant groups, some of whom have turned their guns and bombs against their erstwhile Pakistani patrons. The domestic security situation is also related to the state's inability to resolve persistent debates, not just about the role of Islam in the state but also over what kind of Islam Pakistan should hold up as the banderole of the Islamic state. Pakistan has long failed to manage the sectarian differences between Sunni and Shia and even among Sunni Muslims. Needless to say, Pakistan's religious minorities have long been treated as second-class citizens. A third set of events that has influenced the rapidly degrading security environment is at least partially exogenous: the U.S. war in Afghanistan and Iraq, antagonistic U.S. policies such as the drone campaign, and fluctuations in the Indo-Pakistan competition.

Part I of this volume thus focuses on these security challenges. In Chapter 1, Stephen Tankel explores the evolution of the militant nexus in

Pakistan and assesses the implications for domestic and regional security. Tankel argues that Pakistani militancy has become a buyer's market, the fluidity of which decreases the utility of separating pro-state from anti-state militants, thwarting even committed counterterrorism efforts. Factors such as the U.S. drawdown in Afghanistan and continued India-Pakistan competition could exacerbate tensions among militants, while also granting them greater maneuverability and making it more difficult for Pakistan to manage even "pro-state" entities. In the short term, the fluid nature of the militant milieu makes it more difficult for Pakistani militants to unite behind any single cause and less likely that they can overthrow the state. Over the medium term, however, the creeping expansion of jihadist influence will have a pernicious impact on the health of Pakistan's society, and the militant infrastructure in Pakistan will remain a persistent threat to regional stability.

As Tankel makes clear, the diversity of Pakistan's militant groups tends to prevent them from effectively uniting their forces. The same is true of Pakistan's Islamist movements, which emerged out of a diverse set of ideological traditions, yet nonetheless have managed at times to join their efforts in the political domain.

In Chapter 2 Joshua White discusses these efforts at collaboration among various Sunni Islamic movements, and the ways in which they might shape the contours of post-2014 Pakistan and the security of the wider region. One striking and representative example of such collaboration has been the formation of the Difa-e-Pakistan Council—an ad hoc pan-Sunni collective that has brought together the Jamaat-ud-Dawa (i.e., Lashkar-e-Taiba) of the Ahl-e-Hadith tradition, the Jamaat-e-Islami of the modernist tradition, and the Jamiat Ulema-e-Islam (Sami ul-Haq faction) of the Deobandi tradition. By comparing recently published Quranic commentary from Lashkar-e-Taiba founder Hafiz Muhammad Saeed to parallel commentaries from other Sunni traditions, White explores both the potential and limits of Sunni cooperation in matters relating to jihad and the state. He finds that, particularly in a post-2014 environment in Pakistan in which market pressures are likely to drive Islamist groups to differentiate themselves, the existing ideological divides between Sunni groups may preclude certain forms of joint mobilization for jihad within Pakistan itself. The analysis also points, however, to the relative ease by which broad-based Sunni coalitions will find it possible to forge substantive cooperation targeting already-vulnerable minority groups inside Pakistan, or working together on a case-by-case basis to support jihadi projects outside of Pakistan's borders.

In the third chapter Sarah J. Watson and C. Christine Fair turn their attention to the U.S. armed drone campaign. The American-operated drone campaign against militants in Pakistan's northwest is not obviously an internal security issue for Pakistan. But the authors argue that the program is in fact a crucial element in Pakistan's internal security landscape. This is so whether, as critics charge, the drone program fuels terrorism or, as its proponents counter, it is the only realistic method of targeting Pakistan's militants, whose redoubts in the tribal areas are beyond the reach of Pakistani law enforcement agencies. While the program's foes denounce the strikes as emblematic of an American effort to secure its global and regional security objectives at the expense of Pakistan, Watson and Fair argue that American drones have increasingly targeted Pakistan's enemies, rather than those of the United States. In fact, the Americans launched the drone campaign in 2004 with a "goodwill kill" of a wanted Pakistani terrorist. The United States certainly wanted to gain Pakistan's consent to strikes in the tribal areas. But it also has a direct interest in securing the Pakistani state due to fears that militants will gain access to Pakistan's nuclear materials or know-how. Furthermore, given the complex and fluid alliances among militants operating in this area, Pakistan and American interests may often converge.

In this chapter, the authors argue that the drone program is in fact conducted with the consent of Pakistan's establishment, and that in fact the Pakistani military has a crucial stake in the program's continued success. When seen in this light, it becomes clear that much of the legal and moral opposition to the program is based on mistaken assumptions about Pakistan's consent to the program, as well as on dubious reports of high civilian casualty rates. When evaluating the drone war in Pakistan, they argue that while drones certainly have their drawbacks, they are superior to Pakistan's other options for combating its increasingly severe internal security crisis. Recognizing the strikes' utility naturally gives rise to questions about Pakistan's ability to manage its internal security issues should the drone strikes cease with the U.S. withdrawal from Afghanistan.

As noted above, Pakistan's troubled internal security picture has important consequences for its (in)famous nuclear program. As Christopher Clary points out in Chapter 4, while Pakistanis often find U.S. concerns for the safety of the arsenal insulting, the nuclear program faces real dangers.

Clary identifies four command and control threats to Pakistan's program: Pakistan's relationship with nonstate militants, the insider threat from Pakistani army officers or nuclear scientists, the external threat posed by antistate militants (who have long targeted Pakistani military installations), and the risk that ongoing tensions with India will escalate into full-scale conflict, causing Pakistan to relax the protocols in place for protecting its nuclear warheads. While Pakistan has taken many steps to secure its arsenal, its inherent instability means that the risk of a command and control failure will remain small, but real. Clary's analysis is not likely to reassure American policy makers. Pakistan's fragile internal security, coupled with fears of nuclear proliferation, will no doubt help drive American policy well beyond 2014, and fears about the security of the arsenal will make it difficult for the United States to ever fully end American involvement in Pakistan.

Part II of this volume focuses on Pakistani domestic politics and political economy. While the first part of this volume lays out the risks to Pakistan's internal security, and the implications of these doomsday scenarios for the United States and the international community, the chapters in the second part will exposit domestic movements that can either exacerbate or mitigate the problems addressed in Part I.

One of the most important developments of the last decade in Pakistan has been the rebirth of democratic institutions. Historically, internal security and foreign policy have been the sole responsibility of the Pakistan army. But, as C. Christine Fair shows in Chapter 5, the balance of power between Pakistan's military and civilian rulers may finally be shifting. In the spring of 2013 Pakistan witnessed a historic peaceful transfer of power. The outgoing Pakistan Peoples Party (PPP) government, despite its limitations, made real progress toward institutionalizing democracy, including making considerable efforts to take responsibility for foreign and defense policy making. President Asif Ali Zardari is the first sitting Pakistani president to have ever devolved extensive presidential powers to the prime minister and has also made unprecedented strides to pass power to the provinces. The PPP's replacement, Nawaz Sharif's Pakistan Muslim League-Nawaz (PML-N), won a sufficient parliamentary majority to enable him to rule without the constant fear for his political base that dogged the previous government. This does not mean, of course, that Pakistan's democracy is in the clear. While civilian agency is emerging within Pakistan's government, it is still fragile. While the army remains restricted in freedoms of movement and tainted by Musharraf-era policies, it has developed new tools to keep Pakistan's democracy on a tight leash.

One of President Musharraf's most important contributions to Pakistan, ironically, was the legal space for private media. Over the last decade, Pakistan's media has developed into a lively and raucous terrain, which has certainly helped shape Pakistani views toward domestic and foreign policy—for better or for worse. As elsewhere, social media has become an important factor in Pakistan's domestic politics. Pakistan's 2013 general elections were the first such contests in which social media played a significant role, particularly in the unprecedented success of Imran Khan's Pakistan Tehreek-e-Insaf (PTI). In Chapter 6 Huma Yusuf explores Pakistan's new media landscape, with particular attention to the social networking platforms, such as Facebook, that are becoming an increasingly large part of middle-class Pakistani life. Some believe that social networking technologies, which offer an alternative to Pakistan's corrupt and state-controlled mainstream media, have the potential to transform Pakistani politics. Yet the reach of these technologies is still small and class bound, and Pakistan's authorities are taking steps to control the Internet, just as they have successfully harnessed Pakistan's other media platforms. It remains to be seen whether social media in Pakistan can expand beyond its current middle-class base and achieve the impact they have had in countries such as Egypt.

Chapter 7 turns to Pakistan's economic challenges. In this chapter Feisal Khan addresses the two main problems that have hobbled Pakistan's economic growth: the inability of the country's energy sector to produce enough power to keep Pakistan running; and the dismal performance of Pakistan's taxation system, which is one of the most inefficient and inequitable in the world. Khan shows how a series of shady backroom deals tied Pakistan to an inefficient and overpriced power generation system in the 1990s. The decision to allow the development of private power plants, although championed by international institutions such as the World Bank, has resulted in Pakistan paying far more for its power than it would have done if it had built the plants itself. Exacerbating the problem is the country's massive "circular debt"—a huge, and still growing, imbalance of payments that prevents the existing utilities from investing in infrastructure, making power generation even more expensive. Pakistan's taxation system is equally shambolic, being marked by rampant income tax evasion at even the highest levels of government. Politically motivated decisions to exempt certain sectors from taxation have shrunk the tax base even further, making

Pakistan dependent on loans from multilateral institutions and on the financial support of the United States. Although the government of Nawaz Sharif was elected on a platform of fiscal responsibility, it has shown itself unable to truly confront these issues. In the absence of bold and concerted action, Pakistan's economic outlook is dark and getting darker.

Part III of the volume looks beyond Pakistan's domestic affairs to examine its foreign relations both within the region and beyond. The first two chapters in this part are devoted to Pakistan's most contentious alliance: that with the United States. This focus is warranted for several reasons. First, whether Washington wants to admit it or not, it cannot afford to walk away from Pakistan. Pakistan will remain the single most important producer of insecurity in the region. Similarly, while Pakistanis may wish they could walk away from the Americans, they too know that they will require American diplomatic and economic support. At a minimum, Pakistan would like to prevent the Americans from declaring it to be a state sponsor of terrorism or from undertaking a punitive campaign that would further undermine Pakistan's economic prospects.

In Chapter 8, Paul Staniland argues that the drawdown from Afghanistan provides the United States with an opportunity to create strategic breathing space. The United States and Pakistan have had a particularly dysfunctional relationship since 9/11, characterized by resentment and suspicion despite huge flows of U.S. money and supportive public euphemisms. The U.S. drawdown will reduce American reliance on Pakistan and its military, giving America a freer hand in the region. Over the long run, India will be more strategically important than Pakistan, and a reduced U.S. commitment in Afghanistan allows the United States to move beyond the debilitating paralysis that afflicts its current strategy on the subcontinent. In turn, a more distant American role may benefit Pakistan as well. It may reduce its civilian leaders' vulnerability to being accused of acting as a puppet for America and limit, if only on the margins, the military's domestic power. Eventually, a more "normal" relationship between the United States and Pakistan may emerge that avoids the costly and unproductive dynamics of the last decade.

Much has been made of the importance of anti-Americanism as a factor in U.S.-Pakistani relations, but relatively little has been done to explore the sources and correlates of Pakistani attitudes. In Chapter 9, Karl Kaltenthaler and Will Miller explore the Pakistani mass public's attitudes toward the

United States. They argue that at least two different strains of anti-Americanism are present in Pakistan: one is driven by concerns about Pakistan's sovereignty and the other is colored by a religious discourse that paints the United States as the enemy of Muslims. While the majority of Pakistanis express only a passive anti-Americanism, a small minority hold a militant view that is primarily the product of a radical Islamist discourse in Pakistan.

With the future of U.S.-Pakistan ties in question, Pakistan has sought to cultivate China ever more. As Aparna Pande shows in Chapter 10, Pakistan, never fully certain of American aid, has over the years looked to countries with which its leaders feel an affinity, either ideological or strategic, in order to diversify its avenues of support. China has been a source of military assistance, while Saudi Arabia is an ideological and economic collaborator. Between them, the two countries are seen as Pakistan's friends of last resort. The 2014 American withdrawal from Afghanistan will result in a lessening of U.S. interest in Pakistan and Afghanistan. In order to compensate for lack of American interest, Pakistan's leaders may attempt to make Pakistan relevant and critical to countries they believe will be able to provide them economic and military support. In this context, Pakistan may be tempted to seek security and economic strength by turning even further toward Saudi Arabia and China, even if that means providing an assurance of military security to Saudi Arabia and hoping China will use Pakistan for deterrence against India.

Finally, Part III turns to Pakistan's endgame in Afghanistan. In Chapter 11, Daveed Gartenstein-Ross and Tara Vassefi examine the legacy of the extraordinarily strained relationship between Afghanistan and Pakistan and how it will continue to influence Pakistan's policies as the United States draws down. Gartenstein-Ross and Vassefi show that a critical factor that first drove Pakistan's support for Islamic militant groups in Afghanistan is Afghanistan's historical demand that an independent "Pashtunistan" should be carved out of the Pashtun-majority areas of Pakistan. Afghanistan's aggressive military actions in support of Pashtunistan look much like Pakistan's support for violent Islamist groups in Afghanistan today. A potent mix of factors now driving Pakistani support for these violent groups in Afghanistan virtually guarantees that this support will continue as the United States draws down. However, Gartenstein-Ross and Vassefi perceive a paradox in Pakistan's strong position in Afghanistan and argue that the more Pakistan presses its advantage in Afghanistan, the more likely it is that Pakistan's adversaries will similarly sponsor violent nonstate actors operating in Pakistan's own territory. In that way, Pakistan's advantage in Afghanistan may in the longer run help to destabilize the country that currently appears to have such a strong hand.

Looking to the Future

The chapters in this volume identify several issues that will continue to confront Pakistan. Pakistan's elected government will struggle to assert its writ, not only over the army but also over an activist Supreme Court that has sought to intrude upon legislative powers. The courts and the military are likely to fight just as hard to preserve their prerogatives. While Prime Minister Nawaz Sharif has secured a strong electoral mandate from his wins in the May 2013 election, Pakistan is thoroughly hobbled by economic malaise, a persistent shortage of power (which only worsens its economic challenges), decrepit human development, and rampant Islamist and ethnic insurgency. Navigating this suite of problems would be daunting for any leader. Sharif's problems are rendered all the more difficult because Pakistan's electorate is deeply divided about the path forward on virtually every domestic and foreign policy question.

Events in Afghanistan will certainly have enormous impact on Pakistan's domestic security and foreign policy concerns. Pakistan likely wants some kind of a stable Afghanistan—as long as the government there is hostile to India and friendly to Pakistan. Owing to long-standing bilateral disputes, Pakistan has never accepted Afghanistan as a neighbor; since the 1950s Pakistan has invested heavily in rendering Afghanistan into a client state. Some Pakistanis recall that on the eve of 9/11, many in Pakistan were ready to jettison their problematic Taliban allies, who had brought such international disgrace upon Pakistan. With the passage of time, however, most Pakistanis nostalgically recall the Taliban era as a relative golden age in which the Indians were at least kept in check, even if the Taliban did not deliver on Pakistan's hope that they would accept the validity of the Durand Line.

The Afghan Taliban as it has evolved over the last decade is also problematic for Pakistan. Many members of the group resent the fact that Pakistan continues to orchestrate events in Afghanistan, at the expense of

Afghans. While Pakistan hopes that some kind of Taliban representation can be achieved at the provincial and subprovincial levels, and maybe even in federal cabinet positions, Pakistan surely does not want the Taliban to control Afghanistan as it did before 9/11. To achieve an optimal result in Afghanistan, Pakistan has to achieve multiple outcomes simultaneously.

The Pakistani army likely wants the United States to remain engaged in Afghanistan at some level. (This is at odds with the public positions of most civilian leaders.) The reasons for this are twofold. One, the U.S. presence in Afghanistan will ensure that Pakistan retains its salience for U.S. regional policy. Second, American support is likely critical to maintaining some form of central government in Kabul in the near-term. This will ensure a steady tension between the central government and the Taliban—necessary to minimize the chance that the Afghan Taliban may turn its guns and suicide bombers against the Pakistani state or offer sanctuary to the Pakistani Taliban. Ideally, with such tension between Taliban and non-Taliban forces in Afghanistan, Pakistan's varied militant groups can reengage themselves in Afghanistan rather than Pakistan.

But the Pakistan military does not want such a robust U.S. or international military presence in Afghanistan that Washington puts pressure on Pakistan to facilitate these operations. The Pakistan army hopes that when it is no longer seen as collaborating with the Americans some of the anti-Pakistan militants can be rehabilitated to once again focus their efforts in Afghanistan or in India. Equally important, the Pakistan army assesses that once the heavy American security presence is gone, India will also have to retrench from some of its most provocative positions in Afghanistan. The Indians have relied on the American security umbrella to prosecute India's various political and development projects in Afghanistan and possibly to engage in covert operations to aid separatists in Pakistan's restive provinces (Fair 2011).

While both Pakistan and the United States may hope to find some way of prosecuting their interests irrespective of the other, neither has very attractive options. Pakistan often threatens to embrace China or Saudi Arabia ever-more tightly, but neither of these states seems willing to pick up the tab. In fact, both prefer that the United States continue to shoulder the heavy burden of keeping Pakistan afloat. While many American policy makers, legislators, and ordinary citizens would like to write off Pakistan for good, this is likely not feasible, due to the enduring threats terrorist groups based in Pakistan pose to regional and international security and the related specter of such militants obtaining nuclear weapons. It seems that Daniel Markey may have put it best: there is "no exit" for either the United States or Pakistan (Markey 2013).

Notes

1. Pakistan had also supported non-Islamist militants in India, including providing extensive support for Sikh militants waging a war of secession in India's orthern Punjab state.

2. The conditionalities were imposed by the Enhanced Partnership with Pakistan Act of 2009 (Epstein and Kronstadt 2013).

3. In recent years, analysts have begun using the expression "deep state" for Pakistan to reflect the fact that a cotterie of current and retired military and intelligence officers essentially run the state irrespective of the policy preferences of Pakistan's civilian leaders. An implication of this is that the civilians exert virtually no control of these elements.

Works Cited

Commander ISAF (NATO International Security Assistance Force, Afghanistan U.S. Forces, Afghanistan). 2009. *Afghanistan, Commander's Initial Assessment.* August 30. Redacted version available at http://media.washingtonpost.com/wp-srv/politics/documents/Assessment_Redacted_092109.pdf.

CRS (U.S. Congressional Research Service). 2014 *Direct Overt U.S. Aid Appropriations for and Military Reimbursements to Pakistan, FY2002–FY2015.* March 26. http://www.fas.org/sgp/crs/row/pakaid.pdf.

DeYoung, Karen. 2014. "Obama to Leave 9,800 U.S. Troops in Afghanistan." *Washington Post.* May 27. http://www.washingtonpost.com/world/national-security/obama-to-leave-9800-us-troops-in-afghanistan-senior-official-says/2014/05/27/57f37e72-e5b2-11e3-a86b-362fd5443d19_story.html.

Epstein, Susan B., and K. Alan Kronstadt. 2013. *Pakistan: U.S. Foreign Assistance.* Washington, D.C.: Congressional Research Service. https://www.fas.org/sgp/crs/row/R41856.pdf?.

Fair, C. Christine. 2004. *The Counterterror Coalitions: Cooperation with Pakistan and India.* Santa Monica, Calif.: RAND.

———. 2011. "Under the Shrinking U.S. Security Umbrella: India's End Game in Afghanistan?" *Washington Quarterly* 34 (2): 179–192.

———. 2013. "Pakistan: Perfidious Ally in the War on Terror." In *Assessing the War on Terror,* ed. Mohammed Ayoob and Etga Ugur, 71–92. Boulder, Colo.: Lynne Rienner Publishers.

GAO (U.S. Government Accountability Office). 2008a. *Combating Terrorism: Increased Oversight and Accountability Needed over Pakistan Reimbursement Claims for Coalition Support Funds*. Washington, D.C.: GAO. http://www.gao.gov/new.items/d08806.pdf.

———. 2008b. *Combating Terrorism: The United States Lacks Comprehensive Plan to Destroy Terrorist Threat and Close the Safe Haven in Pakistan's Federally Administered Tribal Areas*. Washington, D.C.: GAO. http://www.gao.gov/new.items/d08622.pdf.

Haqqani, Husain. 2013. *Magnificent Delusions: Pakistan, the United States, and an Epic History of Misunderstanding*. New York: PublicAffairs.

Jones, Seth G. 2007a. *"Pakistan's Dangerous Game." Survival* 49 (1): 15–32.

———. 2007b. "The State of the Afghan Insurgency." Testimony presented before the Canadian Senate National Security and Defence Committee on December 10, 2007. http://www.rand.org/pubs/testimonies/CT296.html.

Joscelyn, Thomas. 2011. "Admiral Mullen: Pakistani ISI Sponsoring Haqqani Attacks." *Long War Journal*, September 22.

Markey, Daniel. 2007. "A False Choice in Pakistan." *Foreign Affairs*, July–August. http://www.foreignaffairs.com/articles/62648/daniel-markey/a-false-choice-in-pakistan.

———. 2013. *No Exit from Pakistan: America's Tortured Relationship with Islamabad*. New York: Cambridge University Press.

Miller, Greg and Pamela Constable. 2011. "CIA Contractor Raymond Davis Freed After 'Blood Money' Payment." *Washington Post*, March 16. http://www.washingtonpost.com/cia-contractor-raymond-davis-freed-after-blood-money-payment/2010/08/19/AByVJ1d_story.html.

Obama, Barack. 2009. "Remarks by the President in Address to the Nation on the Way Forward in Afghanistan and Pakistan." December 1. http://www.whitehouse.gov/the-press-office/remarks-president-addess-nation-way-forward-afghanistan-and-pakistan.

———. 2011. "Remarks by the President on the Way Forward in Afghanistan." June 22. http://www.whitehouse.gov/the-press-office/2011/06/22/remarks-president-way forward afghanistan.

Office of the President. 2009. *White Paper of the Interagency Policy Group's Report on U.S. Policy Toward Afghanistan and Pakistan*. http://www.whitehouse.gov/assets/documents/Afghanistan-Pakistan_White_Paper.pdf.

Riedel, Bruce. 2012. *Deadly Embrace: Pakistan, America, and the Future of Global Jihad*. Washington, D.C.: Brookings Institution.

Sehbai, Shaheen. 2011. "Rice Reveals All About Benazir-Musharraf NRO Deal." *News* (Pakistan), December 15. http://www.thenews.com.pk/TodaysPrintDetail.aspx?ID = 10996&Cat = 13.

Tellis, Ashley J. 2001. "South Asia: U.S. Policy Choices." In *Taking Charge: A Bipartisan Report to the President-Elect on Foreign Policy and National Security*, Discussion

Papers, ed. Frank Carlucci, Robert Hunter, and Zalmay Khalilzad, 99–109. Santa Monica, Calif.: RAND.

———. 2005. *India as a New Global Power: An Action Agenda for the United States.* Washington, D.C.: Carnegie Endowment for International Peace.

———. 2008. "The Merits of Dehyphenation: Explaining U.S. Success in Engaging India and Pakistan." *Washington Quarterly* 31 (4): 21–42.

U.S. Embassy Islamabad. 2011. "2009: Gen. Kayani Wanted to Avoid Impression That Military Was 'For Hire.'" Embassy cable no. 188670, January 24, 2009. *Dawn* (Karachi, Pakistan), July 2. http://www.dawn.com/news/640985/2009-gen-kayani-wanted-to-avoid-impression-that-military-was-for-hire.

Vandehei, Jim, and John Lancaster. 2006. "Bush Offers Praise to Pakistani Leader." *Washington Post*, March 5. http://www.washingtonpost.com/wp-dyn/content/article/2006/03/04/A R2006030400467.html.

Waraich, Omar. 2011. "U.S. Diplomat Could Bring Down Pakistan Gov't." *Time*, February 9. http://content.time.com/time/world/article/0,8599,2047149,00.html.

Wright, Robin, and Glenn Kessler. 2007. "U.S. Brokered Bhutto's Return to Pakistan." *Washington Post*, December 28. http://www.washingtonpost.com/wp-dyn/content/article/2007/12/27/AR2007122701481.html.

Security Challenges

Chapter 1

Pakistani Militancy in the Shadow of the U.S. Withdrawal

Stephen Tankel

On June 18, 2013, the Afghan Taliban opened an office in Qatar to conduct negotiations with the United States. Eight days later, the insurgent movement launched a brazen assault on the Afghan presidential compound in Kabul (Nordland and Rubin 2013). During the same week, militants fired on a military convey in Srinagar, the summer capital of Indian-administered Kashmir, killing five Indian soldiers and wounding seven more in an assault (Associated Press 2013). The technically indigenous Hizbul Mujahideen claimed credit, but many in India and elsewhere suspected that the Pakistani Lashkar-e-Taiba (LeT) was behind the attack, as it has been behind others during the previous year. The Kashmir front has been torpid for several years, but LeT is promising a renewed jihad once U.S. troops draw down in Afghanistan (Wani 2013). Meanwhile, the jihadist insurgency that erupted in Pakistan shows no signs of abating. Marked by attacks against the state and by sectarian violence, especially directed toward Pakistan's minority Shia community, it damages the country's cohesion and threatens its stability.

Pakistan's militants are fighting on multiple fronts, and the 2014 U.S. drawdown in Afghanistan could contribute to further atomization among them (for more on current ideological fissures between militant groups, see White in this volume). Such a process could rob the collective jihadist movement in South Asia of some of its critical mass, but also fuel mutually reinforcing tensions in Pakistan's militant milieu and in the region. The current peace between India and Pakistan is fragile, and the drawdown could also create conditions under which increased tensions in Afghanistan spill over into heightened violence throughout the region. Pakistan's main political parties are less wedded to a policy of maintaining proxies than the military writ large or its Directorate for Inter-Services Intelligence (ISI). However, they are also more anxious to make peace with antistate militants than is the military, which has spent much blood and treasure waging Pakistan's own war on terror. It is unclear whether the military leadership agrees on the extent and nature of the internal threat or what to do about it. Nor has the Pakistani establishment evinced any indication it is ready to dismantle the militant infrastructure or cease its practice of using jihadist proxies to achieve security objectives. Instead, it continues to selectively support some militants and to counter others, in some cases utilizing pro-state militants to do so. Pakistan's approach is predicated on the utility that groups provide externally and internally, as well as on whether they threaten the state and the level of perceived influence over them. This modus operandi is informed by and contributes to the dynamic and increasingly interconnected nature of Pakistani militancy.

Even given best-case scenarios geopolitically, militants in Pakistan will continue to threaten that country and stability in the region. This chapter explores the evolving dynamics of Pakistani militancy, the Pakistani state's approach to it and some of the developments that could eventuate as and after the U.S. and NATO forces draw down in Afghanistan.

Situating Pakistan's Militants

Pakistan has supported militant proxies since partition and played host to indigenous militant groups since the 1980s. Their numbers proliferated in the 1990s. There are various ways to classify Pakistan's militants, two of which are detailed here. (White, in this volume, presents an alternative understanding of the differences between the groups.) One way to understand the Pakistani militant milieu at the time is to divide groups based on their sectarian affiliation (Fair 2009). Most of Pakistan's militant groups belong to the Deobandi sect, which follows the Hanafi school of Islamic jurisprudence.[1] The major ones emerged from or were tied to the Deobandi Jamiat Ulema-e-Islam (Assembly of Islamic Clergy, or JUI) as well as the robust madrassa (religious school) system associated with it. The largest and most notable of them included:

- Harkat-ul-Jihad-al-Islami (HuJI)
- Harkat-ul-Mujahideen (HuM), which splintered from HuJI[2]
- Jaish-e-Mohammed (JeM), which broke from HuM
- Sipah-e-Sahaba Pakistan (SSP)
- Lashkar-e-Jhangvi (LeJ), initially formed as the militant wing of SSP before (nominally) splitting from it

Separately, Lashkar-e-Taiba (LeT) was the biggest and most significant group to emerge from the Ahl-e-Hadith movement, which is Salafist in orientation.[3] Strong divisions existed between LeT and the Deobandi outfits, but they are collectively known as Punjabi militant groups, a moniker that derives from the fact that they were headquartered and enjoyed their strongest support base in Punjab, Pakistan's most populous and powerful province.[4] Elsewhere, Tehreek-e-Nafaz-e-Shariat-e-Mohammadi (TNSM), formed by a dissident member of Jamaat-e-Islami named Sufi Muhammad in the 1989, was based in Malakand (White 2008a: 35).

Another way of comprehending the militant milieu at the time is to categorize groups based on their activities in one of three loci (Fair 2009). During the 1990s the Pakistani security apparatus backed a welter of proxies against Indian security forces in Indian-administered Kashmir. These included the Deobandi HuM, HuJI, and JeM, as well as the Ahl-e-Hadith LeT. This was in addition to support for indigenous Kashmiri groups, most notably Hizbul Mujahideen (HM). The SSP and LeJ, which benefited directly and indirectly from state support at various times, were engaged in sectarian attacks against Pakistan's minority Shia population. Shia groups mobilized in response, and the country experienced escalating sectarian conflict. After its formation, JeM occasionally involved itself in sectarian violence as well.

Pakistan also supported the Taliban in Afghanistan, and after the latter group swept to power many of the Deobandi groups that focused primarily on Kashmir or sectarian violence in Pakistan used Afghanistan as a base for operational support and training (*9/11 Commission Report*; Tankel 2011: 106–110). In 1994, TNSM fomented an insurrection in Malakand Division in a bid to institute sharia there. Ultimately, an accommodation was reached whereby the state adopted a "hands-off approach to the areas around Malakand" (White 2008a: 35). After the Pakistan military quashed this uprising, Sufi Muhammad turned his attention to supporting the Taliban in Afghanistan, and TNSM mobilized men to fight there during the latter 1990s (Lieven 2011: 465). Jalaludin Haqqani, who hails from southeastern Afghanistan and rose to prominence as a military commander during the anti-Soviet jihad in the 1980s, accepted an appointment in the Taliban government as minister of tribal affairs. The Haqqani Network—Deobandi and Pashtun like the Taliban—was always both an Afghan and a Pakistani organization. It had a significant infrastructure in Loya Paktia, in Afghanistan and in the Pakistani tribal agency of North Waziristan. During the 1990s, the Haqqanis administered their own training camps in the Loya Paktia region.[5] Although located in Taliban-controlled territory, the Haqqanis enjoyed a significant degree of autonomy, hosting al-Qaeda when that group's relations with the Taliban government were strained and protecting LeJ militants on the run from the authorities in Pakistan (Brown and Rassler 2013: 109–111; "Request for Extradition" n.d.). The major India-centric Deobandi groups also benefited from the training infrastructure in Haqqani territory, which strengthened the ties between them and al-Qaeda (Brown and Rassler 2013: 109). Thus, all of the major Deobandi Punjabi groups shared a common ancestry and increased their ties to one another as well as to the Taliban, the Haqqani Network, TNSM, and al-Qaeda during the 1990s.[6] Connections often were diffuse, stemming from time spent at various madrassas, training camps, or fighting side by side (Abou Zahab 2012: 370–372).

Pakistani Militancy Post-9/11

The Deobandi/Ahl-e-Hadith divide shrank after 9/11, but did not disappear, and the number of militant loci increased and blurred.

The India Locus

When Musharraf agreed to support the U.S. invasion, he did so in large part to keep India from gaining a "golden opportunity with regard to Kashmir" (Musharraf 2006: 201–202; *Dawn* 2001). No evidence suggests the United States gave the Musharraf regime any guarantees with regard to the Kashmir jihad at the time. However, the cooperation Pakistan agreed to provide the United States did not include action against those militants focused on fighting in Indian-administered Kashmir or attacking India, save to keep them from traveling to Afghanistan to support the Taliban (*9/11 Commission Report* 2004: 331). After 9/11, LeT, JeM, and HuM, as well as a host of smaller India-centric groups remained active in Kashmir, though violence, measured in terms of fatalities and the number of violent incidents, declined after 2002 (Ministry of Home Affairs 2013: 5). Indian and international pressure contributed to this decline, as did the splintering of HuM and JeM, which saw some militants head to Afghanistan and others turn against the state. The normalizing of politics in Kashmir and introduction of fencing along the Line of Control also contributed to a decline in violence.

Following the launch of the peace process with India in early 2004, known as the Composite Dialogue, and accompanying back-channel negotiations, Kashmir-centric groups were directed to reduce their militant activities (Tankel 2011: 128; Coll 2009). These groups were curtailed further in response to international pressure the following year (Tankel 2011: 176–177). The ISI reportedly paid militant leaders to temper their activities and keep their cadre in line, while seeking to confine many of those no longer active in Kashmir to their training camps. These men were provided food, board, and, in some cases, a stipend. In other words, they were paid not to fight. Many were kept in reserve (author interviews December 2008–July 2011; Haqqani 2005: 306). Positive inducements were coupled with threat of retribution against those militants who disobeyed the directive to reduce their activities (Tankel 2011: 177–180; Amir 2006). The aim was to rein in, not dismantle, militant groups and hold their members in reserve to be either demobilized or reengaged depending on regional developments. By 2006–2007 there was a serious decline in militant activity on the Kashmir front.[7] Diminished support for militancy in Indian-administered Kashmir did not extend to decreased assistance for terrorist strikes against India, which witnessed a rise in attacks by LeT and by indigenous jihadists who benefited from Pakistani support (Tankel 2011: 140–145).

By the time of the 9/11 attacks, it was becoming clear the guerrilla war in Indian-administered Kashmir was not bearing fruit. Some Pakistani militant groups, most notably LeT, began escalating involvement in attacks against the Indian hinterland (Tankel 2011: 140). The 9/11 attacks, followed by the December 2001 assault on India's parliament by JeM, also may have triggered a realization within the ISI that an overreliance on Pakistan proxies risked provoking international ire. These factors likely contributed to

LeT's decision to expand its recruitment efforts in India and terrorist operations there (Tankel 2011). In early 2002, riots in the Indian state of Gujarat claimed the lives of 790 Muslims and 254 Hindus.[8] The riots mobilized a section of India's Muslim population already prone to radicalization at a time when LeT and the inchoate network that would become the Indian Mujahideen (IM) were increasing recruitment efforts (Bedi 2003; Swami 2008b; Gupta 2011: 4). India had banned the Student Islamist Movement of Indian (SIMI) in 2001, driving many of its members underground and triggering a cleavage within it between those who, while extreme, were not prepared to take up arms and hardliners looking to launch a terrorist campaign (author interview June 2012; Fair 2010). A small number of SIMI activists who split from the organization went on to form the core of the IM, a network of militant modules and cells that activated in 2006 and began claiming credit for attacks in 2007 (Swami 2010). A loosely networked leadership operating from Pakistan and the Persian Gulf leads the IM. Their presence in Pakistan has fueled suspicion that the ISI is not only supporting the IM, but also seeking to exert influence over its direction (Tankel 2013b). Clear connections between LeT and IM exist, and the former is widely suspected of supporting the latter (Fair 2010).[9] Since the 2008 Mumbai attacks Pakistan appears to be restraining LeT from launching major terrorist strikes against India, leaving it to work in concert with or support sporadic IM operations.

The Afghanistan Locus

Militants from all of Pakistan's major Deobandi groups joined the Taliban to fight against the U.S. counterattack in the wake of 9/11 (Tankel 2011: 110). Thousands of pro-Taliban Pashtun tribesman streamed across the border as well, with the TNSM leading thousands of them to battle American forces in Afghanistan. After the small number of U.S. forces, fighting alongside the Northern Alliance, routed the Taliban, most of its leaders fled across the border. Musharraf's decision to side with the United States in the wake of the 9/11 attacks did not extend to vigorously pursuing the movement in Pakistan, where Taliban leaders resettled after their government was toppled in December 2001.[10] The Afghan front remained reasonably quiet for the next eighteen months, as Taliban leaders in Pakistan regrouped (Strick van Linschoten and Kuehn 2012: 244, 257). Jalaludin

Haqqani moved across the border to North Waziristan after the U.S. invasion. Initially inactive and possibly even open to a settlement with the Karzai government, Haqqani ultimately decided to fight under the Taliban banner once they launched an insurgency in Afghanistan.[11] However, the Haqqani Network retained a significant degree of operational autonomy as well as strong ties to both al-Qaeda and the Pakistani state (Brown and Rassler 2013: 121–122, 133–134).

From their base in Pakistan, the Taliban began an assassination campaign in Afghanistan in spring 2003 and announced a leadership council that summer (Giustozzi 2009: 1, 34; Strick van Linschoten and Kuehn 2012: 252–253). Training camps for Taliban fighters were operating in Pakistan by this time and the movement began a recruitment drive. This included dispatching Mullah Dadullah, reportedly accompanied by Pakistani authorities, to madrassas in Baluchistan and Karachi (Strick van Linschoten and Kuehn 2012: 253). Significant recruiting efforts directed toward Pakistani volunteers increased in 2004, and these recruits were playing an important role in the Afghan insurgency by 2005 (Giustozzi 2009: 34–35). Rather than remain inactive, Deobandi militants whose activities in Kashmir had been curtailed and who had been confined to their camps migrated toward the Afghan front via the Federally Administered Tribal Areas (FATA), tapping into Afghan-centric militant infrastructure that had risen there (Abbas 2009). The destruction of portions of the training infrastructure in Pakistan-administered Kashmir during the 2005 South Asia earthquake increased the militant migration.[12] This reinforced existing ties among the Deobandi groups, the Taliban, the Haqqani Network, and a raft of Pashtun militants who grew in number and prominence. The Ahl-e-Hadith LeT also opened up a second front in Afghanistan during this time, bringing its militants into closer contact with some of those from these other organizations.

Attempts to reign in historically Kashmir-centric groups in the mid-2000s contrasted with rising Pakistani state support for Afghan-centric proxies, most notably the Quetta Shura Taliban and the Haqqani Network.[13] The overriding primacy the United States gave to al-Qaeda allowed the Taliban-led insurgency space to regenerate, while concerns about American staying power in the region led Islamabad to increase significantly its active support for the Taliban and Haqqani Network from roughly 2005 onward (Barno 2011; Armitage 2009; Mazzetti et al. 2010). Attacks against coalition forces in Afghanistan jumped to over five thousand in 2006, more than a threefold increase from the previous year (Wood 2007). The Afghan insurgency gained momentum over the next few years and was going from strength to strength by 2008, by which time it was interconnected with the revolutionary and sectarian jihads that had exploded in Pakistan.

Revolutionary and Sectarian Loci

President Pervez Musharraf's decision to support the U.S. invasion of Afghanistan after 9/11 strained Pakistan's relations with all of its militant proxies to varying degrees. As early as October 2001, JeM gunmen were targeting Westerners and Christians inside Pakistan in retaliation for the U.S. counterattack in Afghanistan (Iqbal 2001). JeM's leader, Maulana Masood Azhar, is believed to have expelled some of those who were involved in the October 2001 attacks in order to avoid his own arrest (Mir 2003). In response to this action, as well as Azhar's general willingness to continue working with the army and ISI, a number of Jaish members left and joined those who were expelled to form the splinter group Jamaat ul-Furqan. HuM split too, with some members leaving to form Harkat-ul-Mujahideen-al-Alami (*alami* means "global") in response to the leadership's unwillingness to break ties with the state. Despite these incidents, active support continued for Pakistan's India-centric proxies, and no consistent efforts were made to degrade the various indigenous militant groups extant at the time, with the exception of LeJ. This last group was able to regenerate in part thanks to its ability to tap into the legitimate aboveground organizations connected to SSP and JeM, but the early targeting of LeJ members contributed to their subsequent disproportionate involvement in antistate violence (Abou Zahab 2012: 371).

Pakistan made notable efforts to capture or kill al-Qaeda operatives and other foreign fighters, but these tapered off after 2005 (Jones 2011). Initial efforts included launching Operation Al Mizan, a military incursion into the South Waziristan Agency of the FATA in 2002, following the arrival of foreign fighters fleeing Afghanistan earlier that year.[14] Resistance there was prompt (Burke 2011: 175; M. I. Khan 2004; Z. A. Khan 2012). A series of Pakistani military incursions into FATA—followed by peace deals that empowered pro-Taliban Pashtun militants—ensued, contributing to the spread of Talibanization in the tribal areas. Developments outside FATA contributed to the proto-insurgency brewing in Pakistan and strengthened the nexus between Pashtun militants, their brethren from various Punjabi groups who fled to FATA during the ensuing years, and those Afghan militants and al-Qaeda members who sought sanctuary there following the U.S. invasion.

In December 2003, members of the Pakistan air force—inspired by Maulana Azhar, JeM's amir—attempted to blow up President Musharraf's motorcade. Two weeks later, a Jaish member, who, the leadership later maintained, had split from the group by this time, made a similar attempt not far from where the first attack took place. Concerns about the involvement of low-level military personnel and police officers in jihadist activities contributed to a crackdown in which the authorities detained more than a thousand individuals and held many without trial (Mir 2009: 110). This practice of executing mass arrests (and later releasing many of those detained) in tandem with efforts to eliminate specific militants (often through extrajudicial means) constituted the extent of Pakistan's counterterrorism efforts during the early and mid-2000s. Some of those who escaped the crackdown remained in Punjab, but others took shelter in Pakistan-administered Kashmir, FATA, and the North-West Frontier Province (NWFP), known since 2009 as Khyber Pakhtunkhwa (KPK) (Mir 2009: 110; Abou Zahab 2012: 373–374). Many of those who traveled to FATA linked up with Punjabi militants, particularly from SSP, LeJ, and various splinter groups, who had fled there following the aforementioned crackdowns and had since strengthened their ties with al-Qaeda and pro-Taliban Pashtun tribesmen (Abbas 2009; Abou Zahab 2012: 373–374).

Pakistan's failed military incursions and subsequent peace agreements had emboldened pro-Taliban militants, and by 2006 the insurgency against the state was accelerating swiftly (Gul 2009: 12; Ghufran 2009; Fair 2009). In July 2007, Pakistani security forces launched an assault against the Lal Masjid (Red Mosque) in Islamabad and the two madrassas attached to it. The Lal Masjid had been a well-established ISI asset, and one of its madrassas, Jamia Fareedia, historically attracted students from NWFP and FATA, many of whom were sympathetic to militancy (Abbas 2007; Pardesi 2008: 97). The Ghazi brothers, who led the mosque and madrassas, had issued an edict in 2004 that military personnel killed fighting in FATA were not martyrs, and the Ghazis had been arrested that year for stockpiling weapons and planning terrorist attacks in Pakistan.[15] Militants from JeM, HuJI, and LeT were holed up in the complex prior to the raid, and many remained there when it commenced (Pardesi 2008: 103; Asghar and Azeem 2007; Dawn 2007). The raid turned a primarily FATA-based proto-insurgency into a full-blown insurgency that soon threatened to envelop the country. It also transformed the debate for Pakistan's religious parties, some of which had struggled with how closely to embrace the Ghazi brothers' exhortations toward vigilante Islamism. With one of the Ghazi brothers dead and the other under arrest, the religious parties were free to embrace them as martyrs (White 2008b). In so doing, they threw rhetorical fuel on the jihadist fire that soon engulfed parts of the country.

By this time, the Talibanization that had begun in South Waziristan in 2004 spread to other agencies in FATA and was expanding into frontier areas such as Bannu, Tank, Kohat, Lakki Marwat, Dera Ismail Khan, Swat, and Buner. Many of these men, who shared the aim of establishing "local spheres of sharia" in their respective areas of influence, officially united in December 2007 to form the Tehreek-e-Taliban-e-Pakistan (TTP), or Pakistani Taliban (Fair 2009). The TTP quickly became the face of the insurgency but never cohered into a homogeneous entity with firm command and control, instead becoming instead an umbrella organization for many antistate militants. Al-Qaeda provided ideological and operational support for the insurgency in Pakistan, and over time some Pakistani militants joined al-Qaeda's ranks directly.[16] LeJ members are also overrepresented in antistate violence, giving the antistate insurgency a sectarian cast. (Given the harsh crackdowns LeJ suffered after 9/11, its antistate animus is understandable.) LeJ militants, and some of those associated with SSP and JeM as well, exploited Talibanization in FATA and KPK to turn those areas into safe havens (Abbas 2009; Abou Zahab 2012: 376). This dynamic was compounded by TTP commanders' historical connections to LeJ and SSP.[17]

In 2009, following a military incursion (Operation Rah-e-Haq, or "Path of Truth") into Swat, Pakistan reached a peace agreement with TNSM, better known as the Swat Taliban. The agreement institutionalized sharia in Malakand Division and the Kohistan district of Hazara Division.[18] Emboldened, the TNSM—along with other militants operating in the area—began to occupy areas of Swat before expanding to the districts of Shangla and Buner. The proximity of these districts to Islamabad helped catalyze Pakistani public opinion against these militants and paved the way for a major military offensive (Rah-e-Rast) in May 2009 in Swat. The military launched another major campaign against the TTP in South Waziristan—Operation Rah-e-Nijat—the following month. Punjabi militants provided power projection capabilities for an escalation of high-profile terrorist attacks against sensitive targets in cities such as Islamabad, Lahore, and

Rawalpindi intended to punish the state for these incursions (Abou Zahab 2012: 376; Abbas 2009). On the one hand, these incursions achieved a degree of success in the frontier. On the other hand, they also served as an object lesson in the high costs of such actions. Nevertheless, they marked an escalation of Pakistan's efforts to confront the threat.

Confronting the Threat

Pakistan's security policy has always been India-centric. Thus the value of groups like LeT and the Haqqani Network resides primarily, though hardly exclusively, in the leverage they provide against India and in Afghanistan respectively. Pakistan's geopolitical compulsions, however, are informed by worries stemming from external influences on internal stability as well. Although the security establishment was not blind to internal threats, its approach in the initial years after 9/11 remained overwhelmingly India-centric. When confronted with a proto-insurgency in FATA, the Musharraf regime opted for a strategy of appeasement, aimed at halting the spread of militancy into the settled areas of Pakistan. Meanwhile, the state's escalating support for the Quetta Shura Taliban and Haqqani Network in Afghanistan meant that the military deliberately spared significant militant infrastructure in FATA. Moreover, although it did rein in pro-state groups fighting in Kashmir, the Musharraf regime chose not to dismantle them. Instead, using the combination of inducements and coercive mechanisms described above, the ISI reduced the activities of some (LeT) and essentially held others in reserve. The attempt to "bench" these groups occurred at roughly the same time Pakistan was escalating support for the Afghan insurgency, but there is little evidence to suggest that it sought to control the flow of fighters from the east to the west. Nor was the de-escalation of the Kashmir front accompanied by a heightened focus on counterterrorism.

In November 2007, President Musharraf, who had taken power in a coup and remained the head of the army, resigned his command as chief of army staff, making way for General Ashfaq Parvez Kayani. During the Musharraf era, the military made no sustained effort in the areas of counterinsurgency. On the one hand, the internal security threat had not yet manifested. On the other, these lackluster efforts created conditions for that threat to mature. Upon assuming his command Kayani took steps to increase the army's "ownership of and commitment to Pakistan's internal security duties" (Fair 2011b). In 2008 and 2009, the security establishment started making more sustained counterinsurgency and counterterrorism efforts against antistate militants inside and outside FATA. Pakistan launched Operation Sher Dil in Bajaur Agency in 2008 and in 2009 followed with Operations Rah-e-Rast (Swat) and Rah-e-Nijat (South Waziristan) in 2009. Years of experience operating in FATA coupled with training assistance and capacity building provided by the United States meant Pakistan's security forces were better prepared to clear and hold territory (Jones and Fair 2010: 65–74). These campaigns weakened the TTP infrastructure in various areas, most notably Bajaur, Swat, and South Waziristan, and led to the capture or killing of Pakistani militants involved in plotting, supporting, and executing attacks against the state as well as some foreign fighters (Jones and Fair 2010; Pak Institute for Peace Studies 2011: 27).

Military incursions drove some TTP and TNSM militants across the border into eastern Afghanistan, primarily the Korengal Valley, and from there they began to launch cross-border raids into Pakistan.[19] These actors appear to benefit at least from benign neglect by the Afghan security forces, though Pakistan alleges they receive active support from Afghanistan's intelligence agency (Khan and Hussain 2011; Rehman 2013; Tankel 2013c). It is an article of faith among many in the Pakistani security establishment that India uses its Afghan consulates as listening posts to gather intelligence and to equip the TTP and other antistate militants. American forces withdrew from the Korengal Valley in mid-2010, turning an already troubled region into a militant safe haven for Afghan-centric *and* Pakistan-centric militants. Pakistani officials equate the situation, inaccurately, to the safe haven in FATA and accuse the United States of not doing enough to curb militants basing there. When taken to the extreme, this feeds conspiracy theories that the United States supports cross-border TTP strikes.[20] In short, elements within the Pakistani security establishment believe their country is the victim of a proxy war. Coupled with a strategic culture of relying on nonstate actors, this has led the Pakistani military to rely on some militant groups to counter others.

When Pakistan was forced to further rein in LeT following the 2008 Mumbai attacks, the ISI facilitated a pathway for an increased presence in eastern Afghanistan, where the group's fighters began appearing in greater numbers in late 2009 and early 2010. (This chronology has been confirmed both by author interviews conducted in July 2011 and by the statements of American officials during briefings provided to them by the author.) This was partly a means of creating a pressure-release valve for the group. However, it also may have been intended as a means of using a trusted proxy to gather intelligence on the other militants operating in the area, particularly those belonging to the TTP and TNSM (Williams 2008; Gannon 2008). The security establishment also encouraged LeT to carry out a propaganda campaign against al-Qaeda and the TTP, demonizing them ideologically for launching attacks in Pakistan.[21] In some instances, LeT or associated groups acting under its umbrella have even attacked the TTP in the tribal areas. In June 2013, LeT militants in concert with those from Ansar-ul-Islam, a Barelvi group formed in Khyber Agency, launched a cross-border offensive from Kunar Province against the TTP in the Mohmand Agency. They also reportedly struck TTP elements on the Afghan side of the border who had fled Mohmand during previous military operations (T. Khan 2013b). Although LeT is the main group on which the security services rely, the military also gave the Taliban commander Mullah Nazir covert support to attack Uzbek militants who enjoyed the protection of then TTP amir Baitullah Mehsud during Operation Zalzala (Jones and Fair 2010: 57).

On numerous occasions the military also attempted to use the Quetta Shura Taliban and Haqqani Network to temper the TTP and reorient its focus toward Afghanistan. For example, in February 2009, leaders from the Haqqani Network helped create the Shura Ittihad-ul-Mujahidin (SIM). This umbrella group consisted of Afghan and Pakistani militants, including those involved in antistate violence. Mullah Omar publicly reiterated his instructions that SIM, like all militant entities, focuses on fighting in Afghanistan rather than attacking Pakistan (Brown and Rassler 2013: 160). It is generally believed that initiatives such as these were undertaken at the ISI's behest (Brown and Rassler 2013: 161). The Pakistani military made efforts to prevail on other FATA-based militants to withhold support from those actors attacking Pakistan and remain focused on Afghanistan. In exchange, these entities were not targeted during military campaigns in FATA.[22]

To be sure, the geopolitical utility some groups offer is the most compelling reason Pakistan continues to provide them with active support, defined here as providing money and matériel, assistance with training, operations, and logistics, organizational assistance, ideological direction (where possible), and, of course, sanctuary as well as other protection from external enemies (for example, intelligence sharing) (Byman 2005: 59).

However, amid an insurgency, it also has become important for maintaining influence over proxies that, as an organizational policy, eschew attacks against the state. For example, the ISI has provided infusions of money and other goods to LeT to keep current members in line and induce former members who might be assisting antistate militants to return to the fold (author interviews July–October 2011; Tankel 2013a). As part of this effort, LeT leaders reindoctrinated former and current members against launching attacks in Pakistan and encouraged its local clerics to deliver the message that jihad in Pakistan was against Islam (author interviews; Fair 2011a). (For more on this point, see White in this volume.) The Pakistani security establishment also encouraged the involvement of LeT's licit front organization, Jamaat-ud-Dawa (JuD), as well as of other militants groups like SSP, in the Difa-e-Pakistan Council (DPC). The DPC is a coalition of more than forty "politico-religious parties." It serves as a stalking horse for the security establishment and thus fits squarely in the tradition of the military-mullah-militant nexus that has existed for many years (Siddiqui 2012). Consolidating leaders from various militant groups into a single political platform may be a way for the security establishment to increase influence over aspects of their behavior and provide an incentive to keep their cadres in line.[23] At the same time, however, this opportunity amplifies militant voices and provides them with political clout, which can act as a barrier to action against them.

These efforts are part of a broader bid to regain control over the militant infrastructure, rather than to dismantle it. Despite the nuanced fluidity of treatment, this approach is predicated on a straw man: the assumption that the country faces two choices, "tolerate some militants" or "take on every group at once." This belief informs a willingness to accept a persistent level of violence in the hope of avoiding a conflagration, as long as the groups receiving state support have utility either abroad or at home. This approach has also contributed to the integration of militant loci, purposefully in some instances and inadvertently in others.

The Dynamics of Pakistani Militancy

Militant attention to India decreased after 9/11, relatively speaking, though its perceived malevolent involvement in Afghanistan fueled Pakistani support for proxies fighting there and contributed to the integration of these two loci. This was evident from the escalation of attacks against Indian targets in Afghanistan by Pakistani proxies, in some cases with clear army or ISI support, from 2008 onward (Swami 2008a; Mazzetti and Schmitt 2008; O'Donnell 2009; Brulliard 2010; Rubin 2010; Motlagh 2010). Over time, Afghanistan became a focal point for every major militant outfit as well as for a host of smaller networks and splinter groups. It also emerged as a safe haven from which the TTP and its allies could attack the Pakistani state. This reinforces the Pakistani military's support for Afghan-centric proxies and contributes to cross-border clashes between pro-state groups like LeT and antistate ones like the TTP. In short, the Afghan locus has integrated with the insurgency in Pakistan. What began as a reaction to military efforts in FATA and state crackdowns against select militants cohered into this new locus of activity: revolutionary jihad to topple the apostate government in Islamabad and institute an extreme interpretation of Islamic law throughout the country. Sectarian violence became intertwined with this revolutionary jihad. It also expanded, as Deobandi jihadist groups increasingly targeted Barelvis and Ahmadis as well as the Shia (see, e.g., Waraich 2011).

The acceptability of waging war against the state is a major ideological division within the jihadi universe, but the line is permeable. Because separateness and togetherness coexist among and within groups, militants who disagreed with one another over activity in one locus might cooperate (or compete) in another. This creates ideological confusion and discord while simultaneously providing ideological sanction for any one of a number of targets. Cumulatively, this contributes to increased integration and atomization of the various entities within the militant milieu. Historical connections among groups coupled with the fact that many new outfits were born as a result of splintering or fragmentation enabled greater integration and coordination.

Interaction, integration, and competition are most pronounced in FATA. For example, the Haqqani Network is Pakistan's most reliable proxy in Afghanistan and, as a policy, abjures attacks in Pakistan. However, it is also an essential enabler for the TTP as well as for a host of smaller antistate entities (including many Punjabi group splinters) and al-Qaeda (Brown and Rassler 2013). Although it has worked to limit any public association with the insurgency in Pakistan, it actively benefits from TTP manpower. In return, the Haqqani Network acts as a "platform for operational development and force projection" for segments of the TTP and other antistate entities (Rassler and Brown 2011: 46). This includes providing access to training, expertise, resources, and the prestige that comes from participating in certain operations in Afghanistan (Rassler and Brown 2011: 47; "Attack on Sri Lankan Cricket Team" 2009; "Interrogation of Amanullah" n.d.). Moreover, the Haqqani Network has been al-Qaeda's main enabler in the region for more than two decades and is thus more responsible than any other ally for its resiliency (Brown and Rassler 2013). Connections also exist in Pakistan's settled areas, where they enable insurgents to leverage the infrastructure belonging to groups still tolerated, or supported, by the state. Many of the attacks that take place in Punjab, for example, involve at least some measure of coordination with current or former members of tolerated organizations such as SSP, JeM, and, in some cases, even LeT (author interviews July 2011; Abbas 2009; Abou Zahab 2011: 377).

Looking ahead to 2014 and beyond, events in Afghanistan and developments regarding Pakistan's inchoate rapprochement with India could help determine the scope, scale, and direction of Pakistani militancy. However, it is unlikely that sectarian attacks or the revolutionary jihad against Pakistan will abate in the short-term regardless of what happens on either front.

Eyeing the U.S. Withdrawal

The drawdown of Western forces could contribute to further atomization within the militant milieu, not least because foreign troops represent the one target on which all the different entities—whether pro- or antistate—can agree. If so, this might rob the collective jihadist movement in South Asia of some of its critical mass, as various entities refocus on other targets. At the least, it could reduce the propaganda windfall some militants realize from waging jihad against foreign forces. Escalating debates within and between militant organizations over whether to focus violence externally or internally might undercut Pakistani efforts to rein in or hold in reserve some proxies. At the command level, this is likely to create tensions within and between various entities, while integration at the operational level can be expected to continue.

A status quo insurgency or escalating conflict would mean continued Pakistani support for its proxies, with the attendant operational consequences outlined in the previous section. Even given a regional settlement, Pakistan could be expected to maintain ties and perhaps some level of support to its proxies for both geopolitical and internal purposes. Pakistan has significant concerns about the impact of the U.S. and NATO drawdown on its internal security. This has informed its outreach to former Northern Alliance members in Afghanistan and its willingness to help facilitate negotiations between the United States and Afghan Taliban. At the same time, the Pakistani security establishment also worries that a march to power by the Afghan Taliban would invite a massive influx of Indian assistance to the former Northern Alliance.

Islamabad has insisted that negotiations designed to reach a settlement must ultimately include the Haqqani Network. This raises the possibility that the ISI may seek to play one faction against another rather than allow the Quetta Shura Taliban to act as the sole representative of the insurgency. Even absent external efforts to sow division, significant questions exist regarding how much control Quetta Shura Taliban leaders have over their own foot soldiers, much less those operating under the banner of the Haqqani Network or the Pakistani Taliban. Hence it is far from certain that all of the militants currently fighting in Afghanistan would buy into a settlement. Some could be expected to fight on and, depending on the posture of the Pakistani state, might assist the TTP in launching cross-border attacks as well. Additionally, the Quetta Shura Taliban have no love for their sponsors in Pakistan and, if freed from reliance on the Pakistani state, could facilitate support for the TTP.

Looking to the east, despite their increased focus on Afghanistan, groups like Lashkar-e-Taiba have yet to abandon the Kashmir cause or the jihad against India more broadly. LeT is unlikely to vacate the Afghan front; it is a sufficiently elastic group to maintain a presence there while also refocusing on India. The Kashmir front is quiescent and regenerating it would be difficult, though recent events, including several militant attacks and cross-border firing, suggest attempts by groups including LeT to do just that (BBC 2013; Akhter 2013). Hizbul Mujahideen claimed most of the major operations on this front in 2013. Although its leadership is based in Pakistan-administered Kashmir, HM is an indigenous Kashmiri group. Evidence suggests it is working with LeT to slowly reignite the conflict and make increased violence appear organic. Kashmir is unlikely to see a return to the bad old days when roughly two thousand militants were chalking up attacks on a daily basis. There were 192 violent incidents in 2012, the last year for which data is available from the Indian Ministry of Home Affairs (Ministry of Home Affairs 2013: 5). Contrast that with 2,565 in 2004, when the insurgency was already flagging, or the 1990s when whole cities were "liberated" by the insurgents. While returning to that level of conflict is highly unlikely, real grievances remain. Because violent incidents are now the exception, not the rule, and there are so few militants in Kashmir, even a relatively modest uptick can have a disproportionate impact.

Pakistani prime minister Nawaz Sharif has indicated his intention to promote ties with India. This is to be commended and encouraged. The army and ISI have kept LeT from launching any major attacks against India since Mumbai in 2008, but the group is allowed to maintain low-level activities and is unlikely to be dismantled as long as major geopolitical disputes with New Delhi persist. Indeed, modestly improved diplomatic and economic relations with New Delhi have not precluded Pakistan's ongoing development of tactical nuclear weapons intended to deter the type of Indian invasion that might result from another spectacular terrorist attack by Pakistan-supported militant groups. As long as Pakistan maintains militant proxies any Indo-Pakistani rapprochement will remain incomplete and at risk of disruption. If the ISI intends to keep LeT reined in, it could compensate the group's leaders by continuing to facilitate involvement in domestic politics and policy as an offset, while also using coercive mechanisms to keep members in line. However, not all militants would remain idle. Some could attempt unsanctioned attacks against India and others might turn on the state.

The Indian Mujahideen is a notable wildcard. Its existence provides the ISI and LeT, collectively, with another means of striking India. Yet it also presents a potential source of tension between them. The ISI could attempt to exert greater control over the Indian Mujahideen network as an indigenous proxy, thus increasing the level of plausible deniability for any attacks, while also showing "progress" by reining in groups like LeT. Conversely, LeT could attempt to use the IM to circumvent ISI constraints on its own actions.

It is unlikely that sectarian violence or the revolutionary jihad against Pakistan will abate, regardless of what happens vis-à-vis India or in Afghanistan, where the TTP and other antistate insurgents already operate. The TTP and its associates have shown no willingness to part with their maximalist agenda, including the withdrawal of Pakistani military forces from FATA and adjacent territories and the right to institute sharia in those areas, with the eventual aim of imposing it throughout the country. Almost twenty-seven hundred people were killed in more than eleven hundred acts of political violence in Pakistan between January and April 2013. Casualties from jihadist violence constitute a significant number of those killed (S. Khan 2013). This included another spate of mass terrorist attacks against the Shia in Pakistan and the TTP's blistering series of attacks against the Awami National Party, Pakistan Peoples Party, and Muttahida Quami Movement in the run-up to the 2013 elections. These parties were singled out for their "secular doctrine" and because they were "responsible" for the incursions into FATA (T. Khan 2013a).

At the time of writing, the PML-N-led government of Nawaz Sharif has taken steps toward beginning peace negotiations with the TTP, but talks, if they do occur, will face serious obstacles. The military, which has expended much blood and treasure waging Pakistan's own war on terror, opposes negotiating, at least in the short term. However, it is unclear whether the military leadership agrees on the extent and nature of the internal threat or what to do about it. In the meantime, antistate militants launched another spate of attacks throughout Pakistan after the elections. Whether this was part of a strategy by the TTP and its allies to position themselves for peace negotiations with the government is unclear, but at the time of writing they certainly appear to have the initiative. Conversely, beyond the geopolitical utility proxies provide, the security establishment is unlikely to take any action that could draw them into the antistate insurgency. Hence no incursion into North Waziristan, where the Haqqani Network is headquartered, was in the offing at the time of writing. Moreover, any action in the tribal areas is likely to be accompanied by terrorist strikes elsewhere in Pakistan. The TTP is already gaining ground in Karachi and emerging as a new force to be reckoned with in that troubled metropolis. LeJ continues to operate reasonably freely and its networks and connections to SSP mean it can do so throughout the country. In short, even given best-case scenarios geopolitically, Pakistan appears to face a durable jihadist threat. Counterintuitively, this raises the perceived costs of dismantling pro-state groups.

The Amplifying Effect: Safe Haven in Afghanistan

Discourse in the West regarding safe haven in Afghanistan often fixates on al-Qaeda Central (AQC) and its potential to regenerate and launch transnational attacks. Although AQC may be able to carve out small pieces of territory from which to operate, the group is unlikely to enjoy much more freedom of movement than it presently does in Pakistan. Any residual U.S.

force will almost certainly contain a heavy concentration of Special Forces operators who, backed by air power, should be able to continue targeting AQC. In some respects, were AQC to once more cross the border into Afghanistan, targeting its members would be even easier than if they remained in Pakistan.

In contrast to the attention given the future of AQC, the possible consequences of the U.S. drawdown in Afghanistan for Pakistani and Afghan militants are little understood. Antistate militants already launch cross-border strikes from Afghanistan, but the presence of American and NATO forces has limited their prospects for growth. The looming drawdown brings with it the opportunity for the TTP and associated antistate elements to expand and take greater advantage of cross-border sanctuaries in Afghanistan to attack Pakistan. These havens could become essential should the Pakistan military launch an incursion into North Waziristan. (Pakistan's decision to launch such a campaign will be based on the future utility of the Haqqani Network, as well as the ease with which the group can be displaced across the border.)

Afghanistan and Pakistan already are engaged in a cold border war that includes exchanges of artillery. In the absence of a settlement, bilateral relations could deteriorate further, leading Kabul to in fact provide the TTP and associated anti-Pakistan elements with the type of support Islamabad already suspects such groups are receiving. Escalating violence that draws in regional actors, including India, could exacerbate this dynamic. As a result, Pakistan could face not only an internal jihadist insurgency, but also the sort of cross-border jihadist violence that it has long supported against its own neighbors. The inevitable impact of such a conflict on the Pashtun population on both sides of the border would also lead to greater instability in FATA and KPK.

Pro-state Pakistani groups also operate in Afghanistan, and their access to safe haven there will have other consequences. To begin with, the prospect of continued (and perhaps rising) cross-border strikes by the TTP and its ilk makes it unlikely that Pakistan will take steps to demobilize its proxies. Not only could doing so result in blowback, but members of pro-state groups based in Afghanistan could gather intelligence on antistate elements and even launch direct strikes against them. At the same time, access to safe haven in Afghanistan reduces ISI's situational awareness, at least theoretically, of what pro-state groups are doing. This is most worrying in the case of LeT, given its likely intention of escalating attacks against India. LeT's presence in eastern Afghanistan ensures plausible deniability for different factions within the group, for its leaders, and, ironically, for the Pakistani state. Each could conceivably claim they did not sanction plots orchestrated against India from across the border, even if planned in Pakistan, with the result being a heightened likelihood that such attacks will occur. Depending on the state of the insurgency in Afghanistan, it is possible that other militants with a significant presence there will provide at least a modicum of assistance to India-centric groups as well.

Conclusion

Over the medium to long term, Pakistan's triage approach constrains its policy options, further locking the establishment into a reactive as opposed to forward-leaning posture and making it more difficult for the country to face either its geopolitical or domestic challenges. The cumulative creeping expansion of jihadist influence also contributes to an identity crisis that threatens to corrode Pakistan's cohesion. Sectarian violence cuts particularly deep in this regard and threatens to draw in perpetrators who presently have no involvement in militancy. It strikes a sensitive nerve within the military, whose members value their institution's nonsectarian identity. Some military personnel understandably worry about the impact of ongoing sectarian violence on that identity. Barring a cataclysmic event, however, and despite the negative trends, extreme outcomes such as fragmentation, the breakaway of discontented provinces, or total state failure are unlikely in the near to medium term. Instead, Pakistan is likely to continue muddling through. As one scholar observed, however, there are "several kinds of muddling through"; and if current trends continue, Pakistan may face "more extreme and unpleasant futures," with destabilizing consequences for the entire region (Cohen 2011: xiv).

Notes

This chapter is informed throughout by fieldwork performed by the author, including numerous interviews conducted between 2008 and 2012. Interview subjects include Pakistani, Indian, and American security professionals and diplomats, as well as members of militant groups, who spoke on the condition of anonymity. Interviews are cited as a group when necessary. Please contact the author for more information.

1. Adherents to Barelvi Islam also follow the Hanafi school of thought. They historically constituted the largest Sunni bloc, but no reliable recent census data is available to confirm that this remains the case or to determine their percentage of the population relative to other schools of thought within Sunni Islam.

2. The two briefly reunited to form Harkat-ul-Ansar (HuA), or "Movement of Partisans," and then separated again.

3. Salafis adhere to a strict interpretation of the Quran and hadith and reject the various schools of Islamic jurisprudence and the learned men who interpreted them. They believe Muslims must return to a pure form of Islam and advocate emulating the Prophet and his companions in all areas of life.

4. This is not an exhaustive list and accounts only for the largest Punjabi groups extant prior to 9/11. Numerous other smaller groups existed as well, as did front organizations and splinter groups in the Kashmir theater. Nevertheless, prior to 9/11 these entities constituted the major Punjabi organizations.

5. The "Haqqani Network" was not known as such at the time. The appellation was first used in 2006 (Rassler and Brown 2011: 1 n. 2).

6. Thousands of students from Deobandi madrassas in Pakistan, many of whom belonged to various Pashtun tribes that straddled the Afghanistan-Pakistan border, took leave to fight on behalf of the Taliban.

7. Improved Indian counterinsurgency efforts, fencing along the Line of Control, and a reduced appetite for conflict in Indian-administered Kashmir contributed as well.

8. Unofficial estimates put the death toll as high as two thousand. It was widely alleged that officials from the Bharatiya Janata Party (BJP) who led the state government encouraged and assisted Hindus who were involved in violence. For official casualty figures, see BBC 2005. For unofficial casualty figures, see Human Rights Watch 2002. In 2012, a state legislator and former state education minister was one of thirty-two people convicted for their role in the riots (Harris and Kumar 2012).

9. Syed Zabiuddin Ansari (a.k.a. Abu Jundal), an Indian Lashkar operative who played a pivotal role in 2008 Mumbai attacks and was deported from Saudi Arabia in July 2012, reportedly told the Indian authorities he had moved from Pakistan to Saudi Arabia in order to oversee joint LeT-IM operations. He alleged that LeT had set up joint bases with the IM in various locations in India to plan conduct operations there. Mirza Himayat Baig, an LeT operative convicted in India for his role in the 2010 Pune bombing, also acted as a key link with the IM in India. Baig cooperated with the IM to execute the 2010 Pune attack in which other LeT operatives are alleged to have collaborated along with several IM leaders (Nanjappa 2012; Chauhan 2012; Haygunde 2013; Express News Service 2013).

10. After 9/11 the ISI advised Mullah Mohammad Omar, head of the Taliban government, to find a safe haven and later provided him one in Pakistan (Zaeef 2010: 152).

11. Haqqani made overtures to the newly formed Karzai government between 2001 and 2003, only to see his brother who traveled to Kabul as an envoy detained and beaten before being sent back across the border (Brown and Rassler 2013: 123).

12. Most headed to Waziristan, but the sectarian groups also had a presence in Lower Kurram and Orakzai. LeT began reclaiming a foothold in Bajaur and Mohmand where it had historical connections (Abou Zahab 2011: 373–74; Tankel 2011: 197).

13. Gulbuddin Hekmatyar's Hizb-e-Islami (HiG) also benefited from Pakistani support.

14. Although several top al-Qaeda operatives were captured in Pakistan's cities in the first few years following 9/11, many of AQ's lower ranks as well as those who had trained in AQ camps sought sanctuary in South Waziristan.

15. The Ghazi brothers were released after the Pakistani minister for religious affairs Ijaz ul-Haq (General Zia ul-Haq's son) intervened on their behalf (Pardesi 2008: 98).

16. Prominent examples include Ilyas Kashmiri and Badr Mansoor.

17. Hakimullah Mehsud, the TTP amir killed in November 2013, was previously the group's leader for Orakzai, the area where a tribal leader affiliated with SSP first raised a Taliban force using the name Tehreek-e-Taliban in 1999. His relative Qari Hussain Mehsud (known as Ustad-e-Fedayin, or "trainer of the suicide bombers"), who is also deceased, was a member of the SSP and LeJ before joining the TTP. The local TTP commander in Darra Adam Khel, Tariq Afridi, was another former SSP member. He was also affiliated with LeJ, helping it to become one of the most active groups in the area. Darra Adam Khel is strategically located on the highway connecting Peshawar with Karachi, which is used by NATO supply convoys headed into Afghanistan via Torkham. The area also provided a jumping-off point for SSP/LeJ and JeM militants participating in operations in Upper Orakzai, where some militants fled following military incursions into South Waziristan in 2004. For a rich discussion of the sectarian influence on the insurgency in Pakistan, see Abou Zahab 2012.

18. For a copy of the Nizam e Adl Regulation, 2009, see BBC 2009.

19. Each side has lobbed artillery shells at the other, with both typically claiming such actions are in response to a corresponding provocation or to cross-border militant traffic.

20. These tensions played out when American military and intelligence officials confirmed Mullah Fazlullah, the Swat Taliban leader, was operating from northeast Afghanistan. One of their number said he was an "other-side-of-the-border problem." A spokesman for the International Security Assistance Force in Kabul countered this explanation, saying Fazlullah "remains a person of interest" and that coalition forces would attempt to take him out if they received actionable intelligence (Priest 2012).

21. LeT has published books and produced a number of audiocassettes criticizing al-Qaeda and the TTP and labeling their members apostates, a message that its leaders also deliver during sermons. Its leaders assert (in writings such as the sermon "The Schism of Excommunication") that accusing another Muslim of apostasy, as al-Qaeda

and the TTP have done to the Pakistani authorities, is a dangerous practice and that if there is any reason to doubt the accusation then the accuser has sinned gravely (Rabbani n.d.). To defend the Pakistani state's cooperation with America, LeT leaders and clerics argue that cooperating with non-Muslims for worldly profit (in this case foreign aid) makes a Muslim misguided, but not an apostate. Indeed, Muslims are only apostates if they actively fight against other Muslims, and LeT leaders argue that operations in the tribal areas do not count because this is done to protect the Pakistani population. Further, they aver that those who murder Muslims instead fighting the true enemy—that is, Christians, Jews, and Hindus—are apostates (author interview July 2011; Fair 2011a). Al-Qaeda refuted points from "The Schism of Excommunication" in the book titled *Knowledgeable Judgment on the Mujrites of the (Present) Age*. For further consideration of ideological divisions among militant groups, see White in this volume.

22. For example, during Operation Rah-e-Nijat (2009–2010), Pakistan brokered deals with Mullah Nazir's group in South Waziristan and Hafiz Gul Bahadur in North Waziristan in which both were asked to refuse to sanctuary or safe passage to TTP militants in exchange for aid and a ceasefire agreement (Jones and Fair 2010: 73).

23. LeT/JuD has been attempting to become an important player in Pakistan's political landscape, launching mass protests against international issues like Danish cartoons and domestic ones such as Pakistan's women's protection bill. In addition to playing a leading role on the Difa-e-Pakistan Council, some of its members have run for office, albeit not on the JuD line (author interview; Green 2012; MacDonald 2012; Rana 2012).

Works Cited

Abbas, Hassan. 2007. "The Road to Lal Masjid and Its Aftermath," *Terrorism Monitor* 5 (14): 4–7.
———. 2009. "Defining the Punjabi Taliban Network." *CTC Sentinel* 2 (4).
Abou Zahab, Mariam. 2012 "Pashtun and Punjabi Taliban: The Jihadi-Sectarian Nexus." In *Contextualising Jihadi Thought*, ed. Jeevan Deol and Zaheer Kazmi, 369–383. London: Hurst.
Akhter, Zainab. 2013. "Kashmir: Protests and the Return of the Fidayeen." Institute of Peace and Conflict Studies, March 25. http://www.ipcs.org/article/terrorism-in-jammu-kashmir/kashmir-protests-and-the-return-of-the-fidayeen-3855.html.
Amir, Intikhab. 2006. "The Waiting Game." *Herald*, August.
Armitage, Richard. 2009. "An Interview with Richard L. Armitage." *Prism: A Journal of the Center for Complex Operations* 1 (1): 103–112.
Asghar, Mohammad, and Munawer Azeem. 2007. "Late-Night Round." *Dawn*, July 6.
Associated Press. 2013. "Five Soldiers Killed in Kashmir," *New York Times*, June 24.
"Attack on Sri Lankan Cricket Team at Lahore." 2009. Police report, case FIR no. 252, March 3. On file with author.

Barno, David. 2011. Testimony before the House Foreign Affairs Committee, Subcommittee on the Middle East and South Asia, November 3. Washington, D.C.: Government Printing Office. http://www.gpo.gov/fdsys/pkg/CHRG-112hhrg71039/pdf/CHRG-112hhrg71039.pdf.

BBC. 2005. "Gujarat Riot Death Toll Revealed." BBC.co.uk, May 11. http://news.bbc.co.uk/2/hi/south_asia/4536199.stm.

———. 2009. "Text of Pakistan's Shari'ah Law 2009." *BBC Monitoring South Asia*, April 14.

———. 2013. "India Says Pakistan 'Beheaded' Kashmir Soldier." BBC.co.uk, January 9. http://www.bbc.co.uk/news/world-asia-india-20954975.

Bedi, Rahul. 2003. "Bombay Bombings Fuel Tension." *Jane's Terrorism and Security Monitor*, September 12.

Brown, Vahid, and Don Rassler. 2013. *Fountainhead of Jihad: The Haqqani Nexus, 1973–2012*. London: Hurst.

Brulliard, Karin. 2010. "Afghan Intelligence Ties Pakistani Group Lashkar-i-Taiba to Recent Kabul Attack." *Washington Post*, March 3.

Burke, Jason. 2011. *The 9/11 Wars*. London: Penguin.

Byman, Dan. 2005. *Deadly Connections*. New York: Cambridge University Press.

Chauhan, Neeraj. 2012. "Lashkar, IM Have Set up Joint Bases, Says Jundal." *Times of India*, July 6.

Cohen, Stephen P. 2011. "Preface." In *The Future of Pakistan*, ed. Stephen P. Cohen, xi–xv. Washington, D.C.: Brookings Institution Press.

Coll, Steve. 2009. "The Back Channel: India and Pakistan's Secret Kashmir Talks." *New Yorker*, March 2.

Dawn. 2001. "Wrong Step Can Spell Disaster: Musharraf." September 19.

———. 2007. "Who Are These Militants?" July 9.

Express News Service. 2013. "Himayat Baig, Only Man Arrested for German Bakery Blast, Found Guilty." *Indian Express*, April 15.

Fair, C. Christine. 2009. "Pakistan's Own War on Terror: What the Pakistani Public Thinks." *Journal of International Affairs* 63 (1): 39–55.

———. 2010. "Students Islamic Movement of India and the Indian Mujahideen: An Assessment." *Asia Policy* 9 (January): 101–119.

———. 2011a. "Lashkar-e-Tayiba and the Pakistani State." *Survival* 53 (4): 29–52.

———. 2011b. "Why the Pakistan Army Is Here to Stay: Prospects for Civilian Governance?" *International Affairs* 87 (3): 571–588.

Gannon, Kathy. 2008. "Pakistan Militants Focus on Afghanistan." Associated Press, July 13.

Ghufran, Nasreen. 2009. "Pushtun Ethnonationalism and the Taliban Insurgency in the North West Frontier Province of Pakistan." *Asian Survey* 49 (6): 1092–1114.

Giustozzi, Antonio. 2009. *Koran, Kalashnikov, and Laptop: The Neo-Taliban Insurgency in Afghanistan*. London: Hurst.

Green, Matthew. 2012. "Mullahs, Militants and Military—Pakistan's Shadowy Coalition." *Financial Times*, January 23.

Gul, Imtiaz. 2009. *The Al Qaeda Connection: The Taliban and Terror in Pakistan's Tribal Areas.* New Delhi: Penguin.

Gupta, Shishir. 2011. *Indian Mujahideen: The Enemy Within.* New Delhi: Hachette.

Haqqani, Husain. 2005. *Pakistan: Between Mosque and Military.* Washington, D.C.: Carnegie Endowment for International Peace.

Harris, Gardiner, and Hari Kumar. 2012. "32 People Convicted for Roles in Gujarat Riots." *New York Times*, August 29.

Haygunde, Chandan. 2013. "Aspiring Teacher to Terror Accused." *Indian Express*, April 19. http://archive.indianexpress.com/news/aspiring-teacher-to-terror-accused/1104742/.

Human Rights Watch. 2002. *We Have No Orders to Save You: State Participation and Complicity in Communal Violence in Gujarat.* New York: Human Rights Watch.

Iqbal, Anwar. 2001. "Militants See Christians as Easy Target." United Press International, October 31.

"Interrogation of Amanullah (a.k.a. Asadullah, a.k.a. Kashif)." n.d. Police report. Copy on file with author.

Jones, Seth. 2011. Testimony before the House Committee on Foreign Affairs, Subcommittee on Terrorism, Nonproliferation, and Trade, May 24. Washington, D.C.: Government Printing Office. http://www.gpo.gov/fdsys/pkg/CHRG-112hhrg66532/html/CHRG-112hhrg66532.htm.

Jones, Seth, and C. Christine Fair. 2010. *Counterinsurgency in Pakistan.* Santa Monica, Calif.: RAND Corporation.

Khan, M. Ilyas. 2004. "Descent into Anarchy." *Herald*, March.

Khan, Sumera. 2013. "Political Violence Claims 2,670 Lives: Report." *Express Tribune*, May 7.

Khan, Tahir. 2013a. "Deadly Mandate: Liberal Parties Targeted for Their Ideology, Says TTP." *Express Tribune*, April 29.

———. 2013b. "Militants Infighting: Rivals Launch Attack Against the TTP." *Express Tribune*, June 27.

Khan, Zahid Ali. 2012. *Military Operations in FATA and PATA: Implications for Pakistan.* Islamabad: Institute of Strategic Studies.

Khan, Zia, and Naveed Hussain. 2011. "Border Incursions: Suspicions Grow About Afghan Support for TTP." *Express Tribune*, September 11.

Lieven, Anatol. 2011. *Pakistan: A Hard Country.* New York: PublicAffairs.MacDonald, Myra. 2012. "Difa-e-Pakistan: What We Know and Do Not Want to Hear." Reuters, February 16.

Mazzetti, Mark, Jane Perlez, Eric Schmitt, and Andrew W. Lehren. 2010. "Pakistan Aids Insurgency in Afghanistan, Reports Assert." *New York Times*, July 25.

Mazzetti, Mark, and Eric Schmitt. 2008. "C.I.A. Outlines Pakistan Links with Militants." *New York Times*, July 30.

Ministry of Home Affairs. 2013. *Annual Report, 2012–13*. New Delhi: Government of India. http://mha.nic.in/sites/upload_files/mha/files/AR(E)1213.pdf.

Mir, Amir. 2003. "The Maulana's Scattered Beads." *Outlook India*, September 1.

———. 2009. *Talibanization of Pakistan: From 9/11 to 26/11*. New Delhi: Pentagon Security International.

Motlagh, Jason. 2010. "Pakistani Insurgent Group Expands in Afghanistan." *Time*, September 10.

Musharraf, Pervez. 2006. *In the Line of Fire: A Memior*. New York: Free Press.

Nanjappa, Vicky. 2012. "IM's Saudi Hub—Fayaz Kagzai Is the Man We Need." October 15. http://vickynanjappa.com/2012/10/15/ims-saudi-hub-fayaz-kagzai-is-the-man-we-need/.

National Commission on Terrorist Attacks upon the United States. 2004. *The 9/11 Commission Report*. New York: W. W. Norton.

Nordland, Rod, and Alissa Rubin. 2013. "Taliban's Divided Tactics Raise Doubts over Talks." *New York Times*, June 25.

O'Donnell, Lynne. 2009. "Eight Killed in Suicide Attack near Kabul Hotel." Agence France-Presse, December 14.

Pak Institute for Peace Studies. 2011. *Pakistan Security Report, 2010*. Islamabad: Pak Institute for Peace Studies.

Pardesi, Manjeet. 2008. "The Battle for the Soul of Pakistan at Islamabad's Red Mosque." In *Treading on Hallowed Ground: Counterinsurgency Operations in Sacred Spaces*, ed. C. Christine Fair and Sumit Ganguly, 88–116. New York: Oxford University Press.

Priest, Dana. 2012. "Pakistani Militants Hiding in Afghanistan." *Washington Post*, November 6.

Rabbani, Mubashir Ahmad. n.d. "The Schism of Excommunication." Unpublished sermon; copy on file with author.

Rana, Mohammad Amir. 2012. "The Case of JuD." *Dawn*, March 25.

Rassler, Don, and Vahid Brown. 2011. *The Haqqani Nexus and the Evolution of al-Qa'ida*. West Point, N.Y.: Combating Terrorism Center.

Raza, Syed Irfan. 2007. "1,100 Students Surrender." *Dawn*, July 5.

Rehman, Fakhar. 2013. "Pakistan Intelligence Agency Claims Afghanistan Supports Taliban Splinter Groups." NBCNews.com, March 27. http://worldnews.nbcnews.com/_news/2013/03/27/17474913-pakistan-intelligence-agency-claims-afghanistan-supports-taliban-splinter-groups?lite.

"Request for Extradition of Pakistani 'Terrorists.'" n.d. U.S. Military Academy, West Point, N.Y., Combating Terrorism Center, Harmony Database no. AFGP-2002–000079. https://www.ctc.usma.edu/wp-content/uploads/2013/09/Request-for-Extradition-of-Pakistani-Terrorists-Translation.pdf. Document from the Government of Pakistan to the Taliban leadership in Afghanistan appealing for the extradition of nine wanted Pakistani "terrorists."

Rubin, Alissa. 2010. "Militant Group Expands Attacks in Afghanistan." *New York Times*, June 15.

Siddiqui, Taha. 2012. "Difa-e-Pakistan Part 2/2: Who Is Aiding the Jihadis' Resurgence?" *Express Tribune*, February 12.

Strick van Linschoten, Alex, and Felix Kuehn. 2012. *An Enemy We Created: The Myth of the Taliban–Al Qaeda Merger in Afghanistan.* Oxford: Oxford University Press.

Swami, Praveen. 2008a. "Kabul Attack: U.S. Warning Was Accurate." *The Hindu*, August 2.

———. 2008b. "The Well-Tempered Jihad: The Politics and Practice of Post-2002 Islamist Terrorism in India." *Contemporary South Asia* 16 (3): 303–322.

———. 2010. "Riyaz Bhatkal and the Origins of the Indian Mujahideen." *CTC Sentinel* 3 (5): 1–5.

Tankel, Stephen. 2011. *Storming the World Stage: The Story of Lashkar-e-Taiba.* New York: Columbia University Press.

———. 2013a. *Domestic Barriers to Dismantling the Militant Infrastructure in Pakistan.* Washington, D.C.: United States Institute of Peace.

———. 2013b. *Jihadist Violence: The Indian Threat.* Washington, D.C.: Wilson International Center for Scholars.

———. 2013c. "The Militants Next Door." *Foreign Policy*, April 24.

Waraich, Omar. 2011. "Why Pakistan's Taliban Target the Muslim Majority." *Time*, April 7.

Wani, Riyaz. 2013. "Hurriyat Delegation Meets Hafiz Saeed and Salahuddin." *Tehelka*, January 11.

White, Joshua T. 2008a. *Pakistan's Islamist Frontier: Islamic Politics and U.S. Policy in Pakistan's North-West Frontier.* Arlington, Va.: Center on Faith and International Affairs at the Institute for Global Engagement.

———. 2008b. "Vigilante Islamism in Pakistan: Religious Party Responses to the Lal Masjid Crisis." *Current Trends in Islamist Ideology* 7 (Autumn): 50–65.

Williams, Brian Glyn. 2008. "Afghanistan's Heart of Darkness: Fighting the Taliban in Kunar Province." *CTC Sentinel* 1 (12).

Wood, David. 2007. "Commanders Seek More Forces in Afghanistan: Taliban Prepare Offensive Against US, NATO Troops." *Baltimore Sun*, January 8.

Zaeef, Abdul Salam. 2010. *My Life with the Taliban.* Ed. and trans. Alex Strick van Linschoten and Felix Kuehn. New York: Columbia University Press.

Chapter 2

A Cooperative Jihad? The Religious Logic of Hafiz Muhammad Saeed and the Limits of Pan-Sunni Cooperation in Pakistan

Joshua T. White

Two competing organizational trends at work within Pakistani Islamic movements are likely to shape the contours of post-2014 Pakistan, and by extension the security of the wider region. The first, as explored in depth by Stephen Tankel in this volume, is the trend toward atomization within the Pakistani militant milieu. While militant groups may uniformly celebrate the drawdown of Western forces in Afghanistan, the end of a significant foreign military footprint is bound to reveal differences rather than commonalities among these groups. Each will be forced to articulate afresh its core mission, its priorities for recruitment and operations, and its comparative advantages within the militant firmament. With a wealth of potential targets—in Afghanistan, Pakistan, India, and further afield—there is more than enough space for militant groups to develop new areas of expertise or, as in the case of Kashmir, return to old stomping grounds once the United States and coalition presence in Afghanistan no longer provides a compelling shared narrative for jihad.

At the same time, there is a trend toward collaboration among Islamic movements. This is already in evidence among militants, as seen by the growing cooperation between Hizbul Mujahideen and Lashkar-e-Taiba, as well as Pakistani sectarian groups and the Tehrik-e-Taliban-e-Pakistan. This trend is equally striking among Islamic parties and other movements that operate in the formal political space and technically (though not always practically) eschew violence in their pursuit of an Islamic political vision. Perhaps the most striking recent example of this phenomenon has been the emergence of the pan-Sunni movement known as the Difa-e-Pakistan Council (DPC), which challenged the civilian government by agitating for Pakistani sovereignty, publicly condemning cooperation with the United States, and calling for the Islamization of the state.

Although the DPC was structured as an umbrella of dozens of distinct groups, its main constituent organizations were Jamaat-ud-Dawa, the reincarnation of the banned terrorist organization Lashkar-e-Taiba, representing the Ahl-e-Hadith tradition (see Tankel 2010; Fair 2011); Jamaat-e-Islami (JI), Pakistan's largest and best-organized Islamic political party, of the modernist tradition; and Jamiat Ulema-e-Islam [Sami ul-Haq faction] (JUI-S), a small clerical party with long-standing ties to the Afghan Taliban movement, of the Deobandi tradition.[1] The public profile of the DPC has ebbed and flowed since its founding in late 2011, and few expect it to become a permanent and institutionalized feature of the Pakistani political scene. It is, however, precisely this ad hoc nature that makes it interesting, suggesting the possibility of new post-2014 political configurations that encompass traditional Islamic parties like the Jamaat-e-Islami and militant organizations such as Jamaat-ud-Dawa.

Clearly, the dual trends of atomization and collaboration among Islamic movements are not mutually exclusive. If anything, the likely rearticulation by these movements of their unique goals and advantages in the post-2014 era raises the specter of new pan-Islamic configurations of convenience. Regardless of whether these take the form of episodic collaborations between militant groups or arrangements like the DPC that bridge political parties and militant outfits, it is worth considering both their limits and potential to shape Pakistan's security environment. For example, can we expect to see the solidification of long-term Sunni collaboration in Pakistan, particularly with respect to issues of jihad and the state? Will a diverse group of Sunni organizations such as the DPC ever prove coherent enough to contest elections, to turn against the Pakistani state, to target religious minorities, or to collectively mobilize its members for jihad outside of Pakistan? And more generally, which types of groups might we anticipate forming partnerships in an era in which the presence of Western forces in Afghanistan no longer drives the logic of cooperation?

There are many ways to answer these questions. One approach would be to undertake a rigorous examination of pan-Sunni collaborations and their histories and look for ways to extrapolate to the post-2014 environment. Another would be to look for structural conditions under which political incentives for the constituent organizations might align to allow for certain joint activities.

This chapter will take a different tack. Setting aside structural political incentives, I will examine instead the political theologies of several representative organizations that have already begun to collaborate—the key DPC constituent groups—and what they have communicated to the public and to their own members about jihad and the state. This approach rests on several assumptions. First, that while the articulation of religious ideology in the public square is often politically instrumental, it is not always merely a handmaiden to politics. Belief is often legitimately held and earnestly communicated to the community. Second, that by putting down markers on certain theological points in public documents, the leaders of these constituent organizations have consciously socialized certain religious and political norms, and that those norms have an organizational power all their own. (This is particularly true if, as in the case of Hafiz Saeed's commentary analyzed below, they are used as instructional texts for structured cadre training programs.) While it is not impossible for a leader to walk back public statements, such discourse creates organizational expectations that can be difficult to overturn. The third and final assumption that undergirds this approach is that any analysis that relies solely on comparative theological reasoning cannot be comprehensive or conclusive, but at best suggestive of the normative and ideological constraints in which leaders and organizations operate and the likely bounds of interorganizational cooperation.

With these caveats in mind, we will take as our primary text a remarkable book written by Hafiz Muhammad Saeed, founder of Lashkar-e-Taiba and the current leader of its successor organization Jamaat-ud-Dawa, entitled *Tafseer Surah at-Taubah*. The book is a commentary on one particular chapter of the Quran, Surah at-Taubah. Originally compiled from Saeed's lectures at the Lashkar-e-Taiba summer 2004 training session, the material was first published in Urdu in late 2006 while Saeed was in jail, and then translated into English by the organization's in-house press Dar-ul-Andlus two or three years later. For purposes of comparison, I will examine *Tafseer*

Surah at-Taubah alongside commentaries on the same surah by Maulana Maududi, the founder of the Jamaat-e-Islami; and by Mufti Muhammad Shafi', perhaps Pakistan's most respected Deobandi scholar, and one who remains widely read by students in Sami ul-Haq's faction of the Jamiat Ulema-e Islam. (I will also occasionally reference a more recent commentary by Shafi's son, the renowned jurist Muhammad Taqi Usmani, which updates his father's work.)

I will begin with a look at Surah at-Taubah itself, and its significance for Lashkar-e-Taiba and other Islamic organizations that privilege the mission of jihad.[2] I will then compare the ways in which the Ahl-e-Hadith, Jamaat-e-Islami, and Deobandi scholars deal with three broad categories of issues that appear in Surah at-Taubah and have modern-day resonance— the Muslims' proper posture toward non-Muslims; the legitimacy of the state; and the sacrifices that are to be made in the pursuit of jihad. I will conclude with a discussion of what these commentaries suggest about the prospect of collaboration among Sunni organizations in Pakistan in a post-2014 environment that is likely to be both newly atomized and newly collaborative.

Surah at-Taubah in the Lashkar-e-Taiba Hermeneutic

Surah at-Taubah, "the Repentance," contains three major discourses. The first, covering verses 1–37, recounts instructions for the faithful as to how they are to deal with the polytheists among them. This first discourse is often believed to have been revealed after the later discourses in the surah (Maududi 2011: 2:161). The second discourse, verses 38–72, narrates preparations for the Tabuk campaign, an expedition led by Muhammad in response to a reported advance of the Byzantines in northern Arabia, collaborating with Christian Arab tribes; the Byzantines, as it happened, failed to materialize and the campaign was reduced to a "moral victory" linked to the Muslims' show of force (Maududi 2011: 2:168). The third and final discourse, covering verses 73–129, was ostensibly revealed after the return from Tabuk, and both warns hypocrites among the Muslim community and rebukes those who failed to join the jihad.

At-Taubah attracts considerable interest from those Muslims who champion armed jihad against nonbelievers. According to one recent quantitative study, it is the most frequently cited surah by Islamic extremists

(Halverson, Furlow, and Corman 2012: 6–8) and contains one of the most famous exhortations to target nonbelievers, known as the "verse of the sword":

> Then when the sacred months have passed, then kill the *mushrikun* [polytheists] wherever you find them, and capture them and besiege them, and lie in wait for them in each and every ambush. But if they repent and perform *as-Salat* [prayers], and give *Zakat* [alms], then leave their way free. Verily, Allah is oft-forgiving, most merciful. (Quran 9:5, quoted from Saeed n.d.: 61)

Since Surah at-Taubah is widely believed to be one of the last chapters of the Quran to be revealed, harsh exhortations such as this one are said to abrogate earlier Meccan surahs that encourage a more accommodating posture toward nonbelievers.

It should therefore come as no surprise that at-Taubah appears to hold an important place in the ideology of Lashkar-e-Taiba. Hafiz Saeed's commentary on the surah was the very first work of long-form Quranic interpretation published as a book by the Lashkar-affiliated publishing house, and the first to be translated into English. The book's preface praises at-Taubah as "the guiding light for Muslims of the modern world and an explicit admonition to the non-Muslims and polytheists of the world," and laments that the surah was "ousted" from Pakistan's academic curriculum after September 11, 2001 (Saeed n.d.: 24).[3] Hafiz Saeed himself, in introducing the book, frames the importance of the surah and the questions it answers:

> The subject matter of Surah Taubah is "Qital-Fi-Sabccl-illah"[*sic*]— holy war in the way of Allah. What are the aims and objectives of the Islamic jihad? What qualities should go with the holy warriors of Islam? Who are to be fought against? This surah encompasses all these issues. This surah offers us the etiquette of jihad and enlivens before us the golden era of the dominance of Islam. . . . The lesson of the surah is that the Muslims are to dominate the world being the rightful representatives and vice-regents of Allah on earth and that the non-Muslims are to play the second fiddle. (Saeed n.d.: 31, 36)

Insofar as Lashkar-e-Taiba understands Surah at-Taubah as a textbook of jihadi practice, its commentary highlights three particular themes. The first is Muslims' proper posture toward non-Muslims, a subject on which at-Taubah without question provides one of the most polemical Quranic texts. Even more than other interpreters, Hafiz Saeed seems intent on using at-Taubah to delimit clear rules about which groups of people do and do not qualify as legitimate targets of jihad. The second theme is the legitimacy of the state. Here Hafiz Saeed extrapolates significantly from the text in commenting on India, Pakistan, and the legitimacy of democratic governance. Third, the commentary dwells at great length on the sacrifices that are to be made in the pursuit of jihad. Hafiz Saeed uses the Tabuk story as both a metanarrative for modern-day jihad—for example, emphasizing how a show of force against an external enemy can bolster the religious community and weed out hypocrites—and a sourcebook for modern-day jihad, answering a host of quotidian concerns about the modalities of war.

Muslims and Non-Muslims

Drawing on the first few verses of the surah, Hafiz Saeed delimits four categories of people. The first are the "infidels and polytheists." Under the terms laid out in the surah, these nonbelievers living in Muslim lands were to have their peace treaties abrogated, but only after advance notice was given. Ultimately, they were to be given a choice to convert, flee, or be killed. Drawing a modern analogue, Saeed is quick to label Hindus as the modern-day infidels ("It goes without saying that Hindus are the worst polytheists of the world") who have been abusing Muslims and deserve jihad (n.d.: 38).

Surprisingly, the second group of people, Jews and Christians, come in for even harsher criticism than the Hindus. The text explains "beyond any ambiguity" that the people of the scriptures had "mutilated the Shariah" and "devoured others' wealth and property as a right," and that these activities were continuing "even today" (Saeed n.d.: 37–38). At least in this particular commentary, the Jews and Christians are intimated to be the preeminent threat to the Muslim community. In his commentary on 9:29, Saeed easily pivots to the present tense: "Allah has ordered the believers to continue killing the people of the scripture, Ahl-e-Kitab. Such killing is not at all unreasonable and unlawful" (n.d.: 155).

The third group are the true believers, who predictably have been given "divine directions to wage jihad against the enemies of Allah" (Saeed n.d.: 38). The fourth and final group, in stark contrast, are the hypocrites (*munāfiqīn*), who pretend to be Muslims but succumb to greed or worldliness (Saeed 2006: 30ff). Surah at-Taubah speaks at great length about hypocrisy, and Hafiz Saeed draws from this one key judgment: that "it is jihad alone (out of all the practices of Islam) which demarcates true believers from hypocrites" (2006: 40). He later goes on to argue that jihad not only exposes, but also weakens, the hypocrites who are residing among the community of believers.

Thus far, this commentary may appear unremarkable. And indeed, it bears close resemblance to other Sunni commentaries on the same surah. Nonetheless some distinguishing features are worth noting. In the first place, it presents a relatively unqualified interpretation of the famous "verse of the sword." Whereas the staid Deobandi commentary of Mufti Muhammad Shafi' gives only cursory treatment of the verse, and goes on to argue that the "driving objective [of jihad] should be compassion for the enemy" (Shafi' 2004: 4:321), Hafiz Saeed applies the requirements of jihad liberally to polytheists, Jews, and Christians. And whereas Shafi's son, the contemporary Deobandi jurist Muhammad Taqi Usmani, notes carefully that the rules about expunging non-Muslims "are restricted only to the Arabian Peninsula" (Usmani 2010: 347), Saeed suggests no such geographic constraints.

If Saeed appears more zealous than the Deobandi establishment in his rationale for jihad against polytheists, Jews, and Christians, he is nonetheless more cautious than al-Qaeda's ideologues in his vision of jihad against hypocrites. Simply put, he views jihad as a tool by which to winnow the true believers from the hypocrites—thus pressuring and marginalizing those who are wavering or worldly—but admonishes his readers to follow Muhammad's example and "not wage any war or action against those Muslims who were otherwise quite weak in faith" and who were within the fold of Islam (Saeed n.d.: 56). "We must," he cautions, "eschew mutual quarrels" (57). Hypocrites, in other words, are a category off-limits to the regular exercise of jihad.

The Pakistani State

Hafiz Saeed uses his commentary on Surah at-Taubah to address two political questions related to the Pakistani state: (1) is participation in Pakistan's elected institutions legitimate? (2) are there conditions under which Muslims should target the Pakistani state for jihad? On both counts, Saeed is unambiguous. Commenting on verse 34, which lists the many faults of the Jews and Christians in listening to their rabbis and monks instead of to God, he laments that Muslims have followed their lead in adopting parliaments that "come into being through the unnatural process of votes and elections," in which "the majority decides the laws of whatsoever nature." This system of majority decision making is, he argues, "one of the evils of the modern times among Muslims" (Saeed n.d.: 162)

He is no more charitable to Muslims who choose to embrace Pakistan's democratic institutions as the lesser of two evils. In a thinly veiled swipe at the Jamaat-e-Islami, he dismisses attempts by "some religious groups" to seek elected office:

> Some people do believe that the Western democracy is quite un-Islamic but they also take an active part in politics . . . [saying that if] we are not there to combat the irreligious pack of rulers, these people would come up with anti-Islamic legislation. . . . The plea adopted by these brothers is not at all acceptable. (Saeed n.d.: 163)

Although the text of Surah at-Taubah says little about political leadership or representational politics, Hafiz Saeed chooses to take a passage on Jews and Christians and make a point about the illegitimate participation of Pakistan's Islamic parties in the democratic system.

More striking even than this is Saeed's firm rejection of taking up arms against the Pakistani state. Drawing on the four-category framework constructed from the early verses of the chapter, he considers Pakistan to be run by hypocrites, and thus disqualified as a target for legitimate jihad. Addressing this issue directly, he writes:

> Some ignorant people venture to say today: "What need is there to wage jihad against Hindus in Kashmir? There is much room for jihad within Pakistan. There are many centers of polytheism in Pakistan. The very government of Pakistan is anti-Islamic. There is a wholesale waywardliness and secularism here. Why not wage jihad against these evils first. Let's usurp the throne in Islamabad first. Then we would start jihad."

These are all lousy and baseless excuses. . . . Not only with the clans of pagans and polytheists, the Holy Prophet did not wage any war or action against those Muslims who were otherwise quite weak in the faith. (Saeed n.d.: 55–58)

It follows for Saeed that the proper posture toward "tyrant rulers" who are Muslim is to speak truth regarding their misdeeds, press them to reform, and leave to Allah their punishment in the hereafter (Saeed n.d.: 328ff).

Saeed devotes a lengthy section of his commentary to answering those who take a harsher view of dealing with hypocrites. He quotes a hadith from Sahih Bukhari in which Muhammad refused to behead a hypocrite, lest he be accused of killing his own companions (Bukhari 4905, quoted in Saeed n.d.: 323). Later, he bemoans the fact that in challenging Muslim rulers, Islamic revolutionary movements have often brought upon themselves "unpleasant consequences," and that, however hypocritical the state may be, it is counterproductive to invite its enmity (Saeed n.d.: 330).

The rules for dealing with *individual* hypocrites, who presumably pose a lesser risk to the Muslim community, are somewhat harsher. While arguing for leniency in principle, he nonetheless instructs his readers to follow a set of rules when interacting with these wayward believers. The faithful are not to pray for them, stand at their graves, visit their mosques, develop rapport or friendship with them, or allow them to participate in jihad (Saeed n.d.: 324–325). This set of restrictions apparently applies to followers of the Sunni Barelvi sect as well, whom he castigates for their belief that Muhammad is *nūr* (light) and somehow stands above mortals (158).

Hafiz Saeed's treatment of the hypocrites in his commentary on at-Taubah reflects continuity with a long line of Sunni interpretation within Pakistani intellectual circles. Maulana Maududi, in his still-popular commentary on the Quran, read at-Taubah to signal "the change of policy toward the hypocrites. Up to this time [in the life of the Muslim community], leniency was being shown to them. . . . And now it had become possible to crush them" (Maududi 2011: 2:218). He quickly clarifies that the end of leniency toward such hypocrites should not involve an active jihad of the sword, but rather a rigorous social boycott and the exclusion of legal privileges ("their evidence in the courts of law should be regarded as untrustworthy") (2:219).

Maududi's interpretation of at-Taubah's discussion of hypocrites, published in the late 1970s, was likely informed by the heated debates that he himself had been instigating in Pakistan for over twenty years regarding the treatment of the heterodox Ahmadi sect (see Maududi 2006, first published in 1953). His early works on the Ahmadis suggest that he categorized them as *kufr* (infidel) rather than *mushrik* (hypocrite), but his proposed treatment was similar—social exclusion, legal and political sanction, and repeated attempts to demonstrate their subservience to the Muslim majority.

The Deobandi commentaries by Shafi' and Usmani are conservatively drawn and, unlike that of Hafiz Saeed, do not explicitly equate the hypocrites with any political body, much less the state itself. Shafi' counsels his readers to pursue a "vocal" (that is, verbal) jihad against the hypocrites in order to press them to sincerity (Shafi' 2004: 4:427). Usmani echoes his father in claiming that, according to at-Taubah, jihad cannot take the form of armed struggle with hypocrites, only "an oration or debate to convince them to the truth" (Usmani 2010: 366). Although Shafi' and Usmani do not here address the question of challenging the state, the Deobandi ulema throughout the subcontinent have—with rare exception—traditionally been reticent to endorse challenges to the state-as-*kufr*, calling at most for reform of state institutions, much as Hafiz Saeed did in his commentary.

The Pursuit of Jihad

Much of Surah at-Taubah is devoted to discussion of preparations for the Tabuk campaign or denunciations of those hypocrites who refused to participate. As such, the surah provides ample grist to Hafiz Saeed for commentary on the modalities of jihad. The first important lesson that Saeed draws from the Tabuk narrative is that jihad cannot be justified simply on the basis of its outcomes, or even its ultimate political objective. Rather, its value also lies in how it shapes the religious community, winnowing true believers from the hypocrites among them. The Tabuk campaign was, politically speaking, a nonevent; Muhammad and his forces never confronted the Byzantines, and, at best, the entire exercise could be rationalized as a modest show of force.

For Saeed, this makes the story all the more compelling as an archetype for modern-day struggle. Just as the Tabuk campaign—with all its hardships, sacrifices, and disappointments—separated the true followers from the morally weak, so jihad in the modern context has value as a continuous process of purification. "Of course," Saeed writes, one goal of jihad is "the establishment of an Islamic state." But jihad also is Allah's way for revealing who is "patient, resolute, and steadfast" (Saeed n.d.: 213–214). At times, he suggests, Allah even sends his servants on missions that appear fruitless, so as to test and prepare them to fight against "Christians, Jews, Hindus and all other [tyrants] and aggressive disbelievers" (197).

The vision of jihad as a social and religious process has, for somewhat different reasons, generally been shared by the Deobandi clerics, who are cautious of condoning armed struggle, but see the Tabuk narrative as one that endorses in general terms the religiously purifying power of struggle for Allah's cause. Maulana Maududi too acknowledged the value of jihad as a process, but—even in quoting at-Taubah in his famous work *Jihad in Islam*, puts considerably more sustained emphasis on the political outcomes associated with that struggle than social or religious ones (Maududi n.d.: 17–19). For Maududi, jihad was explicitly linked to the pursuit of power, in service of a particular political vision. Hafiz Saeed's logic of jihad, by contrast, seems from the at-Taubah commentary to be less conditional on movement toward a political project and more easily justified in general terms as a devotion that can be shared by the community in all times and all places.

The second lesson that Saeed takes from at-Taubah is that jihad is obligatory. This may seem to be an obvious interpretive point, but in fact the precise nature of the obligation to jihad has long been debated by scholars. Saeed wrestles in particular with one of the last verses of at-Taubah, which counsels that "it is not [proper] for the believers to go out to fight [jihad] all together," and instead a subset should go forth and the rest should remain to study their faith (Quran 9:122, quoted in Saeed n.d.: 473). Coming at the end of a long chapter that has repeatedly called the faithful to participate in jihad, this verse is puzzling. One classic interpretation, shared by many Deobandi scholars, is that jihad only qualifies as an individual obligation (*farḍ al-'ain*) when there is "a general call for jihad from the ruler of an Islamic state" (Usmani 2010: 378). When that condition does not obtain, jihad is considered a collective obligation (farḍ *al-kiyāyah*). This means that, so long as the number of Muslims engaging in jihad are sufficient for the maintenance of the struggle, the "rest of the Muslims stand absolved of the obligation" (Shafi' 2004: 4:493).

Hafiz Saeed does not directly dispute this interpretation, but nor does he entirely embrace it. Whereas Taqi Usmani seems to envision a more or less stable "division of work" between those who were on jihad and the rest of society, Saeed suggests what might be called a "rotational jihad," in which all Muslims are encouraged to take a turn at armed struggle (Usmani 2010: 379; Saeed n.d.: 477). This is consistent with his view that jihad is a perpetual condition, and one that benefits the Muslim community at large. In his commentary on this particular verse, he goes into great detail about what seems to be an obscure issue of jihadi human resource management: how to deal with those returning from the fight? His solution is consistent with the vision for a rotational jihad; he proposes to make them recruiters, pursuing the next group of faithful recruits.

Saeed also elides the implicit question addressed by many other scholars commenting on this passage: who decides when there is an individual obligation for jihad? The traditional Deobandi view is that such a determination requires the intervention of a legitimate political authority. Maulana Maududi also held this view, going so far as to argue that even when there was a public proclamation by a leader, only a subset of Muslims need engage in jihad. Saeed makes no such claim, and in fact does not explain the conditions under which jihad is incumbent on *all* believers.

The third and final lesson that Saeed draws from at-Taubah is that jihad should be maximally facilitated by a Muslim society. Not surprisingly, his interpretation of the permissible use of funds in support of jihad is expansive. Drawing on the text of the surah itself and the hadith literature, he concludes that funds given for *zakat* can properly be directed to buy ammunition and weapons, outfit the needs of the mujahideen (even those who are wealthy), pay off infidels "at a modest rate" to conduct espionage, provide for ransoms, and engage in public relations activities (Saeed n.d.: 262–268).

In urging the direction of *zakat* funds to directly support armed jihad, Saeed is not straying far from traditional interpretations. Shafi' in his commentary endorses the use of funds for such purposes—surprisingly, Saeed even quotes him approvingly—so long as they are not used to pay for the regular provision of public welfare or ordinary religious education (Shafi' 2004: 4:413). Maududi too saw in this text few if any encumbrances in directing charitable funds toward armed jihad. On the contrary, he went even further than Shafi' in arguing that Muslims could freely use their *zakat* funds to "win over to Islam those who might be engaged in anti-Islamic activities"—even if that had the effect at times of channeling money to infidels.

Conclusion

What might these commentaries of Surah at-Taubah suggest about the prospects for pan-Sunni collaboration in Pakistan? More specifically, what might religiously heterogeneous Sunni movements such as the Difa-e-Pakistan Council choose to do jointly that they cannot do separately? Again, we must lead with the caveat that public theology is at best only suggestive of a group's behavior and agenda. That said, we can draw several preliminary conclusions from these texts.

First, it is evident that these three Sunni traditions share strikingly similar views on a number of core objectives. They all seek an Islamic state; they all believe that jihad is an essential vehicle for realizing that state; and they all see value in mobilizing the public to engage in that struggle. These commonalities alone suggest wide scope for cooperation. Comparing their respective commentaries, however, also hints at possible tensions. The Jamaat-e-Islami is considerably more focused on the political outcomes of jihad than on its utility as a tool for refining the Muslim community.[4] For his part, Hafiz Saeed appears entirely comfortable with a perpetual jihad that, like the Tabuk expedition, is rendered valuable by its demonstration effect to enemies and its transformative ability to winnow the truly faithful from the hypocrites. This subtle teleological divergence could easily manifest as disagreement in the day-to-day operations of a pan-Sunni collaboration like the Difa-e-Pakistan Council, with Lashkar-e-Taiba pushing for the DPC to act as a permanent public campaign for jihad, and the Jamaat-e-Islami hoping to leverage it for near-term political objectives.

Second, the three traditions generally embrace similar interpretations of the first discourse of at-Taubah that differentiates between polytheists, people of the book, the faithful, and hypocrites. All take a disparaging view toward polytheists (particularly Hindus), and emphasize that non-Muslims living in a Muslim state must pay a tax that accords with their status as subjects of Muslim rule. Hafiz Saeed goes somewhat further than many Deobandi or Jamaat-e-Islami commentaries by exhorting his readers to continue an active jihad against Jews and Christians. In retrospect, we might observe that Lashkar-e-Taiba's 2008 attack on the Chabad House in Mumbai reflects in practice Hafiz Saeed's normative reading of at-Taubah, which renders Jews and Christians high-priority targets for an armed jihad. Further, we might expect that any pan-Sunni organization in which Lashkar has a prominent role may well choose to prioritize jihad against Christians and Jews in the coming years.

Third, all three traditions hold the view that a state run by hypocrites is not a legitimate target for armed jihad, but should rather be subject to criticism and reform efforts. It is not unexpected that Lashkar-e-Taiba, which from its early days has had a symbiotic relationship with the Pakistani military, would hold this view. It is, however, somewhat surprising that Hafiz Saeed goes to such great lengths in his commentary on at-Taubah to make this point explicitly, repeatedly, and conclusively about the Pakistani state. Indeed, his argument against attacking Pakistan is one of the central themes of his commentary and sends a clear signal to his own organization and to the public that Pakistan must—for theological reasons— remain off-limits as a target of armed jihad. In this, Saeed's views comport with those of the Jamaat-e-Islami and the Deobandi political parties, but directly challenge the *takfiri* ideologies of al-Qaeda (AQ) and the Tehrik-e-Taliban-e-Pakistan (TTP).

Fourth, while each tradition rejects the targeting of a hypocrite state, the commentaries reveal a fundamental difference regarding the legitimacy of democratic institutions. The Jamaat-e-Islami and Jamiat Ulema-e-Islam, by virtue of their status as political parties, have long embraced Pakistan's electoral process (though they are frequently critical of Pakistan's political leaders). Hafiz Saeed in his commentary does not mince words about Pakistani democracy. Dilating on a passage from at-Taubah that has little to do with political leadership, he rebukes those Muslims who take part in elections and reserves special criticism for religious parties such as JI and JUI. In doing so, he situates Lashkar-e-Taiba in an uncomfortable middle ground between the religious parties who accept the legitimacy of the state and its electoral processes, and groups such as AQ and TTP who accept neither. His argument, moreover, is not that the current leadership in Pakistan is too corrupt to collaborate with, but that the very institutions of electoral politics that Pakistan has adopted are borrowed from Jews and Christians, and are thus illegitimate. Absent a wholesale and public revision of this position, it is difficult to imagine Lashkar-e-Taiba or its affiliates joining with religious parties such as the JI or JUI to stand for elections in Pakistan.

Fifth, the commentaries point to significant commonalities regarding the means by which jihad can and should be promoted. All of the writers agree that *zakat* funds can legitimately be used in almost any manner in support of armed jihad. The differences emerge more in theory than in practice, with Hafiz Saeed expressing enthusiasm for rotational recruitment of volunteers, and less concern for the role of the state in declaring the parameters for a general jihad that prompts an individual Muslim's obligation to serve.

Taken together, these observations suggest that pan-Sunni groupings such as the DPC may have limited potential beyond their current use as platforms for intermittent and ad hoc public rallies. Any collective movement to use the group to mobilize for electoral political purposes would likely meet with resistance by Lashkar-e-Taiba or its affiliates. Moreover, any movement to challenge Pakistani state institutions by force or embrace those who do so would be highly suspect—at least on ideological grounds—to Lashkar and the religious parties alike. Given the explicit body of teaching in each of these traditions regarding politics and the state, shifts in either direction would require at least one organization to walk back a very public aspect of its ideological platform.

Those limitations notwithstanding, it is possible to imagine the DPC or another pan-Sunni group like it evolving beyond a loose knit confederation into something that involves more substantive collaboration but remains within the boundaries articulated by its leading ideologues. One model, taking into account the groups' congruent views of fund-raising, could be joint mobilization for a jihad outside of Pakistan proper—for example, in Afghanistan, Kashmir, or farther afield. Although organizational politics might interfere, there is nothing ideological that would preclude these groups working closely to jointly fund-raise, recruit, publicly advocate, and provide political protection for an armed jihad taking place outside of Pakistan.

An alternate but related model could be joint activity targeting Hindus, Jews, or Christians—either within Pakistan or more likely elsewhere in the region. While all three traditions sanction armed jihad against these nonbelievers in certain circumstances, Lashkar-e-Taiba's ideology is the most permissive in its emphasis on continuing an active jihad against them and in dismissing the need for legitimate state authority to weigh in on the targets of such a jihad. If Lashkar continues to take the lead in groups such as the DPC, it may be able to convince the other participant organizations to adopt this more focused mandate. (In view of the rising tide of sectarianism in Pakistan, joint activity by these Sunni organizations against Shia is not outside the realm of possibility; the Jamaat-e-Islami, however, has historically been wary of anti-Shia agitation, and Hafiz Saeed in his commentary on at-Taubah passed up numerous opportunities to label the Shia as infidels—or even hypocrites.)

It would be hopelessly naive to consider these commentaries authoritative in their ability to predict the bounds of future behavior by Islamic organizations in Pakistan. The last thirty years have amply demonstrated that such organizations frequently adapt their tactics and even their objectives. They splinter in disputes over both leadership and ideology. And they operate in a dynamic political environment in which survival is often dependent upon staking out a niche in the political and religious marketplace. These "market pressures" are only likely to intensify after 2014.

These commentaries can, nonetheless, point to the real challenges that a diverse body of Sunni organizations might reasonably face in trying to collaborate more substantively in Pakistan. By choosing to expound publicly and at length on its ideology of jihad and the state, Lashkar-e-Taiba in particular has perhaps precluded opportunities to collaborate both with religious parties and with more radical organizations that challenge the Pakistani state by force. Lashkar too may well adapt, choosing to leave behind the religious logic of the at-Taubah commentary or wait until a new generation of leadership has the opportunity to quietly reinterpret it. Until then, the organization may find itself in the uncomfortable position of leading an awkward coalition that has a great deal to say, but can find very little agreement about what it might actually do.

This analysis suggests that Lashkar-e-Taiba, one of the region's most technically proficient militant organizations, is likely to remain favorably disposed toward the Pakistani state post-2014 and that attempts to fashion a big-tent, pan-Sunni anti-Pakistan coalition with membership wider than the existing Deobandi-oriented Tehrik-e-Taliban-e-Pakistan would face serious organizational challenges. That is perhaps good news for those concerned about Pakistan's internal stability. But while pan-Sunni cooperation may indeed be restrained in the coming years by groups' particular ideological and theological commitments, this analysis also points to the relative ease by which broad-based Sunni coalitions may forge substantive cooperation targeting already-vulnerable minority groups inside Pakistan or working together on a case-by-case basis to support jihadi projects outside of Pakistan's borders. Those targets sadly remain easy ground for pan-Sunni collaboration after 2014 and are ones against which the Pakistani state is likely to remain supportive, or at best indifferent, as it seeks to displace Islamic militant challenges to its own legitimacy.

Notes

1. Most of the organizational energy and funding behind the DPC comes from Lashkar-e-Taiba and not the Jamaat-e-Islami. Author interview with a senior Jamaat-e-Islami leader, Lahore, August 2012.

2. This chapter will regularly refer to Lashkar-e-Taiba instead of Jamaat-ud-Dawa, as the latter is widely recognized to be merely a front organization for the former.

3. This trope regarding at-Taubah's removal from the curriculum is a frequent topic for sermons by Lashkar ideologues (e.g., Abdus Salam bin Muhammad, a.k.a. Bhutwi Sahab), as found on extremist websites.

4. Although Maududi's commentary on at-Taubah dates to the 1970s, research by the author into the party's more recent writings suggests that this observation continues to hold.

Works Cited

Fair, C. Christine. 2011. "Lashkar-e-Tayiba and the Pakistani State." *Survival* 53 (4): 29–52.

Halverson, Jeffry R., R. Bennett Furlow, and Steven R. Corman. 2012. *How Islamist Extremists Quote the Qur'an.* Tempe: Center for Strategic Communication, Arizona State University.

Maududi, S. Abul A'la. 2011. *The Meaning of the Qur'ān.* Ed. A. A. Kamal. Trans. Ch. Muhammad Akbar. Rev. ed. Vol. 2. 6 vols. Lahore: Islamic Publications.

———. 2006. *The Qadiani Problem.* 4th ed. Lahore: Islamic Publications.

———. n.d. *Jihad in Islam.* Trans. Abdul Waheed Khan. Lahore: Islamic Publications.

Saeed, Hafiz Muhammad. 2006. *Tafsīr Sūrah At-Taubah.* Lahore: Dar-ul-Andlus.

———. n.d. *Tafseer Surah At-Taubah.* Trans. M. Saleem Ahsan. Lahore: Dar-ul-Andlus.

Shafi', Muhammad. 2004. *Ma'ariful-Qur'an.* Ed. Muhammad Taqi Usmani. Trans. Muhammad Hasan Askari and Muhammad Shamim. Vol. 4. 8 vols.

Tankel, Stephen. 2010. *Lashkar-e-Taiba in Perspective: An Evolving Threat.* Counterterrorism Strategy Initiative Policy Paper. Washington, D.C.: New America Foundation.

Usmani, Muhammad Taqi. 2010. *The Meanings of the Noble Qur'ān.* Karachi: Maktaba Ma'ariful Quran.

Chapter 3

The Future of the American Drone Program in Pakistan

Sarah J. Watson and C. Christine Fair

The Obama administration's effort to conclude the U.S. military commitment in Afghanistan motivated it to act aggressively to eliminate al-Qaeda and Afghan Taliban personnel from their Pakistani sanctuaries. The Americans' weapon of choice has been strikes carried out by armed drones (otherwise known as unmanned aerial vehicles, or UAVs) under the operational control of the Central Intelligence Agency (CIA). As is now well known, according to a deal struck in 2004 by then U.S. president George W. Bush and Pakistani president General Pervez Musharraf, Pakistan allowed the United States to prosecute its drone campaign in Pakistan's Federally Administered Tribal Areas (FATA), provided that Washington also use the drones to eliminate those militants who are hardened and incorrigible enemies of the Pakistani state (Miller and Woodward 2013). When the last American soldier leaves Afghanistan, rendering the United States less dependent upon Pakistan, Washington will have to make some serious choices about its relations with Pakistan and how (or whether) the vexed, ostensible allies will cooperate in the future. The outcome of that process will likely have significant impacts on Pakistan's internal security situation.

Presumably, as the U.S. need for Pakistani counterterrorism and counterinsurgency cooperation diminishes, so may the need for the continued use of American armed drones in the FATA. Indeed, the Pakistani general public is looking forward to a drone-free future: despite important pockets of support for the program, it is widely despised. We argue in this chapter that drones are not likely to disappear entirely from the Pakistani skies for one fundamental reason: the stability of Pakistan will remain a key American security interest for the indefinite future. However, these drone operations are likely to increasingly focus upon Pakistani security targets rather than on individuals who threaten American security.

Irrespective of its impacts upon security of Pakistan or the United States, the program has taken a heavy toll on the legitimacy of Pakistan's civilian government. As we discuss below, the program has the sanction of the country's military and intelligence agencies, despite the loud protests of various civilian political actors. As it is currently run (by both the United States and Pakistan's military), the drone program has three negative consequences for Pakistan's polity. First, the army and intelligence agencies derive much of the direct benefit of the program—after all, American drones can eliminate foes that Pakistan's armed forces could not confront without significant collateral damage (and subsequent public uproar). Yet these agencies shoulder no responsibility for the program. Second, this dynamic fundamentally undermines civilian officials' effort to insert themselves into the country's national security and foreign policy making (see Fair in this volume). With every strike, the protestations of Pakistan's elected governments become ever more risible in the eyes of their constituents. Equally problematic, American reliance upon the military and intelligence agencies as key partners further diminishes any prospects for effective civilian control over Pakistan's military. Finally, this modus operandi is not sustainable over the long term, because neither Pakistan nor the United States understands the costs and benefits of the program. Continued drone strikes on these terms further enable Pakistan to defer taking responsibility for its own security—a reasonable expectation of a sovereign state. For all of these reasons and more, sustaining this program after the United States withdraws from Afghanistan will be a challenge for both American and Pakistani governments.

This chapter examines America's covert armed drone program in Pakistan and discusses its potential futures. The chapter is organized as follows. First, we present and evaluate the most recent and reliable information about the covert drone program and attempt to dispel a number of common misconceptions. This provides an important empirical baseline for discussing the program and aims to provide an important corrective to popular accounts (both American and Pakistani) that are not supported by the available evidence. We contend that the program has been widely

misunderstood in the Western press: instead of marking a criminal infringement of Pakistan's sovereignty, one which has caused the death of
thousands of innocent Pakistani civilians, we maintain that drone strikes
are performed with Pakistan's consent and often at its government's behest.
Despite the unpopularity of the program, Pakistani demand for counterterrorism outcomes will be an important driver of its future.

Next, we discuss the program's legality under the various legal regimes
—American, Pakistani, and international—which govern it. Some consensus about the legality of the program is a necessary, if insufficient, condition
for the program's continued existence. In the third and fourth sections, we
discuss the unique form of governance in the tribal areas in light of Pakistan's current internal security crisis. Fifth, we exposit some of the Pakistani
government's current options for confronting militancy in the tribal areas.
When the unique legal, cultural, and security environment in FATA is
understood, it becomes clear that there are few better (or at least less bad)
alternatives to the use of armed drones. We conclude with a discussion of
possible futures for the Pakistani drone program following the U.S. drawdown in Afghanistan in 2014 and a consideration of Pakistan's domestic
security futures.

Background to the Armed Drone Program in Pakistan

The Pakistani drone program began in 2004 with the targeted killing of
Pashtun militant Nek Muhammad in South Waziristan. In a sign that the
program is more complex than either its supporters or detractors allow,
Muhammad, although he had once fought with the Taliban in Afghanistan,
posed little threat to coalition forces there; his primary target was the Pakistani state. We now know that his death was part of a secret deal between
the United States and General Pervez Musharraf's military regime, under
which the United States used drones to kill targets identified by the Pakistani government in return for Pakistan's consent to the program as a
whole (Mazzetti 2013a).

Despite Pakistani cooperation, drone strikes remained rare occurrences
at first, never rising above four per year. It was not until 2008 that the
strikes reached double digits (36). The following years show a rapid increase
in the number of strikes, which reached a peak of 122 in 2010 (see Figure
3.1). According to the New America Foundation, which offers the most

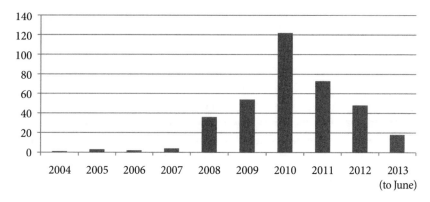

Figure 3.1. Drone strikes in Pakistan, 2004–June 2013. Source: New America Foundation.

widely cited database of drone strikes and related casualties, the 370 strikes conducted under the program have resulted in between 2,080 and 3,428 deaths, of which between 258 and 307 are believed to have been civilians (New America Foundation 2013).

It is important to note that estimates of civilian casualty rates vary dramatically. The Bureau of Investigative Journalism (BIJ, 2014) puts the number of strikes slightly higher (383) and assesses that between 2,296 and 3,719 persons have been killed in these strikes, of whom between 416 and 957 were civilians.. In 2009 Amir Mir, a Pakistani security analyst, put civilian casualty rates at 98 percent (Plaw 2013: 128).[1] At the other end of the spectrum, U.S. intelligence reports for the period between September 2010 and September 2011 identify a single civilian casualty out of 482 killed (Landay 2013).[2] This absurdly low number is reflective of the fact that the United States conveniently defines any military-age male killed in a strike as a militant unless there is explicit evidence to the contrary (Becker and Shane 2012).

Given the lack of reliable reporting from the area, however, all public databases must rely on the same set of media accounts, many of them produced by actors who are biased in either direction. The higher figures from the BIJ, for instance, are likely the result of favoring reports that identify victims as civilians over equally plausible (or implausible) accounts that identify all the victims as militants (Braun 2012). Some inhabitants of FATA even argue that no media account of casualties can be relied upon:

"after every attack the Taliban terrorists cordon off the area and no one, including the local villagers, is allowed to come near the targeted place. The militants themselves collect the bodies, bury the dead and then issue the statement that all of them were innocent civilians" (Taj 2010: 530).

Even critics of the drone program, however, admit that the accuracy of the strikes has improved over time. The New America Foundation found that of the 222–361 victims of drone strikes in 2012, only 5 could definitely be identified as civilians, while 23–39 were "unknown," giving a civilian casualty rate that ranges between 12 and 20 percent (assuming that all the unknowns were civilians and depending upon when you use 222 or 361 as the denominator). In 2008, in contrast, between 24 and 29 percent of those killed were listed as either civilians or "unknowns" (New America Foundation 2008). Even as dedicated a critic of the program as Woods of the BIJ admits that civilian casualty rates are falling even faster than the absolute number of strikes, indicating that drone operators are exercising greater care to avoid civilian casualties (M. Cohen 2013). It is equally undeniable that the number of strikes is falling; 2013 had the lowest number of strikes of any year after 2007 (New America Foundation 2014).

But while the drone program is likely killing fewer civilians than its critics claim, recent reporting has shown that the militants targeted by the strikes come from a far greater variety of groups than U.S. officials have admitted. In April 2012, for instance, White House counterterrorism adviser John Brennan stated that the United States "conducts targeted strikes against specific al-Qaeda terrorists" (Miller 2012). Barack Obama, in a May 2013 speech, referred to strikes against "al Qaeda and its associated forces" (Obama 2013). But al-Qaeda targets make up only a small minority (by one estimate, roughly 8 percent) of militants targeted under Obama (down from 25 percent under Bush). Members of the Taliban (whose relationship to al-Qaeda, always complex, has become increasingly murky) make up 50 percent of targets (Bergen 2012).

Classified intelligence documents obtained by journalist Jonathan Landay show that, in a one-year period ending in September 2011, less than half of the ninety-five strikes targeted al-Qaeda members and that only six al-Qaeda leaders were killed during the same period. The strikes killed not just lower-level al-Qaeda militants but also members of groups—such as the Pakistani Taliban and Lashkar-e-Jhangvi, a Pakistani sectarian terrorist group—that have never targeted the U.S. homeland and that devote the vast majority of their energy to staging attacks within Pakistan (Landay

2013). Landay also revealed that the United States conducts so-called "signature strikes" in the Pakistani tribal areas—strikes on targets whose exact identity is not known but whose patterns of behavior make it highly probable that they are militants.

There have long been rumors that, contrary to the protestations of Pakistani politicians, Pakistan in fact condoned, or even supported, the drone strikes. Recent revelations confirmed this rumor almost beyond all doubt. Former president Musharraf has admitted that he authorized the strikes in the early years of the program, although he maintained that he did so "only on a few occasions, when a target was absolutely isolated and [there was] no chance of collateral damage" (Robertson and Botelho 2013). In late 2008, shortly after his election to the presidency, Asif Ali Zardari, chairman of the Pakistan Peoples Party, allegedly told CIA director Michael Hayden to "kill the seniors. Collateral damage worries you Americans. It does not worry me" (Stein 2010). That said, given the reality of the Pakistani military's firm control over the country's foreign and security policy, from a practical standpoint Pakistan's civilian politicians' support for the program matters far less than that of the Pakistan army and intelligence services (Haqqani 2005). Evidence of direct military-to-military cooperation surfaced in late 2013, when the CIA released a dossier showing that Pakistani officials "received classified briefings on strikes and casualty counts" as a matter of routine (Miller and Woodward 2013). In early 2014 the United States acceded to Pakistan's request for a near freeze on strikes as the government of Prime Minister Nawaz Sharif began serious negotiations with the Pakistani Taliban (DeYoung and Miller 2014). All of these revelations point to an uneasy but high-functioning partnership, in which the United States does not explicitly ask permission for the strikes and Pakistan does not explicitly refuse to grant it.

This cooperation benefits both sides: the drone program (particularly as conducted during Obama's first administration) is clearly in line with the Pakistan army's priorities. Since the inaugural strike against Nek Muhammad, the United States appears to have pursued a policy of (roughly) "one for them, one for us"—killing militants who threaten the Pakistani state in order to be allowed to operate in Pakistani airspace and strike Pakistani citizens who pose a threat to American troops in Afghanistan. Landay's reporting on the high number of Pakistani Taliban killed in the attacks buttresses this view, as do reports in the Pakistani media that Pakistan is seeking not an end to the drone strikes but greater control over targeting. During talks between Pakistan and the United States in mid-2012, for instance, Pakistan demanded control over the human intelligence that guides the drone program in return for reopening NATO supply routes into Afghanistan (Khan 2012). Controlling human intelligence would help the Pakistan military to target its perceived enemies rather than its clients, such as the Haqqani Network. Even the popular outcry over the program may serve the Pakistan army's goal of shoring up public support: by raising the costs to Pakistani politicians of continuing to acquiesce to the strikes, it thus strengthens the military's position vis-à-vis its civilian rivals. And the United States is a useful whipping boy: in March 2013, nine militants were killed in two air strikes that the United States specifically (if informally) disavowed, leading to speculation in American media that the Pakistan army had carried out the strikes and then blamed them on the United States in order to avoid a backlash among Pakistani citizens (Walsh 2013a).

One recent example of this dynamic is the death of Tehreek-e-Taliban-e-Pakistan (TTP) deputy chief Wali ur Rehman in a drone strike on May 29, 2013. Rehman, a member of the powerful Mehsud tribe, had left the Haqqani Network, which focuses on attacking the United States, to join the TTP in 2008. Rehman regularly feuded with TTP leaders Baitullah and Hakimullah Mehsud, and toward the end of his life he is believed to have led a faction of the TTP that was pushing for peace talks with the Pakistani government, a move that Hakimullah Mehsud strongly opposed (*Express Tribune* 2013). Rehman's death had significant repercussions for both the TTP and the nascent peace negotiations. He was perhaps the most dynamic and respected leader of the TTP, and one of the few with the prestige necessary to bring a large faction of the group to the table for peace talks (Agence France-Presse 2013). Following his death, the group, facing a leadership vacuum, announced that it was withdrawing from the much-hyped talks, dealing a sharp blow to the newly elected prime minister Nawaz Sharif's agenda (Fazl-e-Haider 2013).

Although Rehman was linked to the 2009 suicide bombing of a CIA base in Khost, Afghanistan (Hussain and Landay 2013), his association with the Pakistani Taliban makes him an unlikely target for the U.S. drone program, which, in President Barack Obama's words, targets "high-value al Qaeda targets" and "forces that are massing to support attacks on coalition" troops (Obama 2013). The TTP, by contrast, primarily targets Pakistan army forces (at the time of Rehman's death, the army was in fact engaged in military operations in FATA against another branch of the TTP).

And while Pakistan's civilian politicians have widely embraced peace talks with the militants, casting Rehman as a valuable interlocutor, the military has been less enthusiastic, specifying, among other conditions, that the TTP "unconditionally submit to the state" before talks can begin (Agence France-Presse 2013). The two consequences of Rehman's death—division within the TTP and an end to talk of negotiations—were thus both desirable from the Pakistan army's standpoint, leading to speculation that the army collaborated with the United States on the strike that killed Rehman (Hussain and Landay 2013; Saeed Shah 2013).

Despite the mutually beneficial aspects of the strikes, there are signs that the program, at least in its current form, may soon be coming to an end. In May 2013 President Obama, in a speech at the National Defense University, indicated that the strikes would continue until the U.S. withdrawal from Afghanistan in 2014. But he also implied that, following the withdrawal, the need for, and thus the frequency of, strikes would decrease until they were no longer necessary (Obama 2013). This position was reinforced by reports that surfaced in early 2014 that the CIA had informed its Pakistani counterparts that it would no longer add to its list of twenty high-priority targets (previously, when a target was killed, a new one would be added to the list, so that the CIA always had twenty more kills to go) and that it would aim to end the drone program by the end of Prime Minister Nawaz Sharif's tenure in office (that is, in 2017) (Entous, Gorman, and Shah 2014).[3]

Legal Aspects of the Drone Wars

For many Pakistani and non-Pakistani academics, lawyers, and human rights activists alike, the drone program violates international law and the law of armed conflict (LOAC), results in the deaths of hundreds, perhaps thousands, of Pakistani civilians, and summons up a deeply troubling vision of a future in which governments can kill their own citizens or the citizens of other countries from the safety of an air base deep within their own territory. A full treatment of the debate over the legality of such strikes would require its own volume, but we shall attempt to briefly summarize it here.[4] Most legal analyses of the program are based on three assumptions: that the Pakistani government opposes the strikes, that the targets of the strikes are almost entirely high-level leaders of al-Qaeda or the Afghan Taliban, and that the ratio of civilian to militant casualties in the strikes is as high as forty-nine to one. As the previous section showed, none of these assumptions are correct.

As laid out in the joint Stanford and New York University law schools' report *Living Under Drones* (Stanford 2012: 103–104), any legal analysis of the program must assess it on three main levels:

- *Jus ad bellum*: the legality of America's use of force within Pakistani territory. If Pakistan has not consented to the strikes, then the United States must (under the United Nations Charter) be able to make the case that it is acting in self-defense.
- *Jus in bello*: U.S. conformity with international law governing conduct in war, such as the requirements of proportionality and distinction of civilians from noncombatants; the rights of both the targets and the unintentional casualties of the strikes under either the Geneva Conventions (if they are lawful combatants) or international human rights law.
- American domestic law governing the balance between the executive and legislative branches when it comes to the use of military force.

We add a fourth category to these three areas of assessment:

- Pakistani domestic law, particularly the constitutional division of power between the elected government and the military and the *lex specialis* governing FATA.

Table 3.1 presents a brief breakdown of these questions for each type of strike (depending on the target).

Jus in bello considerations, technically the second step in any law of war analysis, are the easiest to dispose of in this case, and thus we will deal with them first. The international law of war demands that belligerents in an armed conflict observe the three principles of necessity, proportionality, and distinction. These principles demand that any military action (1) fulfill a military purpose (no wanton destruction); (2) achieve a military goal proportionate to the harm it does (particularly to civilians; you can't kill one hundred civilians to get one combatant); and (3) observe the distinction between civilians and combatants, most importantly by not taking any

Table 3.1. International and Domestic Legal Considerations

	Target of the strike	
	Enemy of the Pakistani state	Enemy of the United States
Jus ad bellum justification	Pakistan, which is involved in a non-international armed conflict, has requested that the United States, its ally, carry out the strikes.	Unclear. Perhaps derived from posited U.S. armed conflict with al-Qaeda and associated forces.
Jus in bello justification	Strong, in either scenario. Best available evidence suggests that drone strikes have a high militant to civilian casualty rate and that drone operators carefully observe principles of proportionality and distinction. An increase in signature strikes is a troubling sign, however.	
Domestic law, United States	Very shaky. Unlikely that 2001 Authorization for Use of Military Force covers strikes against groups which postdate its passage.	Strong for some groups (al-Qaeda and Afghan Taliban), provided that the targets are acting against U.S. interests. Weak for Haqqani Network and other groups.
Domestic law, Pakistan	Fairly strong. Pakistan is clearly waging a major counterinsurgency campaign. There is evidence that both civilian and military leaders support strikes against the TTP. Death of male civilians is in accord with Frontier Crimes Regulations provisions for collective punishment.	Murky. Pakistan's constitution vests all authority in its elected representatives. While the Pakistani military may have consented to strikes as part of a quid pro quo, it is not clear that Pakistan's civilian leaders have consented to non-TTP strikes or that they could say no if they wanted.

actions that primarily target civilians, even if they have an indirect effect on the military (you can't target a nation's farmers because they are feeding its troops) (Walzer 2006).

Most of the debate regarding drone strikes focuses on the latter two principles, but it is unfortunately marred, as discussed above, by the use of spurious statistics regarding civilian casualties. We would argue that unmanned aerial vehicles provide one of the best opportunities in modern military history to observe the demands of proportionality and distinction. With no threat to himself, a drone operator can hover above a target for hours, even days, waiting until the target is alone or surrounded only by fellow militants. In some cases, of course, the operator will decide to strike even though he or she knows civilians will be killed. Adherence to proportionality and distinction does not require perfection, however, and the remarkably low number of civilian casualties over the last year suggests that the Obama administration has been utilizing the drones' capabilities to their utmost.

The greatest current challenge to this judgment is the American use of signature strikes in the tribal areas. The principle of distinction certainly does not require that a belligerent know the names of his targets (if it did, adherence would make modern warfare, of any kind, impossible). But it does require that he know them to be combatants. Without transparency regarding the criteria for a signature strike, it is difficult to say with any certainty whether the United States will maintain the recent improvement in civilian casualty rates.

The question of *jus ad bellum* presents a thornier challenge, but not an insurmountable one. Most analyses of the question begin with the assumption that Pakistan strongly objects to the strikes. But, as discussed above, there is a great deal of evidence that Pakistani military and civilian leaders directly, if unofficially, consented to the strikes in the past, and very little evidence that all elements of the Pakistani state have withdrawn their consent.[5]

Assuming, as the evidence suggests, that Pakistan has consented to the drone strikes does not end the discussion, however: Pakistan's invitation does not necessarily free the United States to kill Pakistanis. Determining whether it is legally able to do so requires determining whether Pakistan's fight against militancy rises to the level of an armed conflict (in which case international humanitarian law, as codified in the Geneva Conventions, applies) or whether it is merely a law and order situation, in which case human rights law such as the International Convention on Civilian and

Political Rights (with its absolute prohibition on assassination except in cases of imminent danger) applies (Radsan 2012).

It would be difficult to describe Pakistan's internal conflict as anything other than a noninternational armed conflict (NIAC). Between January 1, 2003 and June 1, 2014, terrorist attacks have killed 18,946 civilians and 5,751 security force personnel (South Asia Terrorism Portal 2014).[6] In response to the challenge militancy and terrorism pose to the integrity of the state, the Pakistan army has launched a number of full-scale offensives in the tribal areas (Khattak 2011). Since 2008, these operations, aspects of which will be discussed at greater length below, have resulted in the deaths of over 15,000 members of the security forces, not to mention thousands of militants (Raja 2013). No one seriously challenges Pakistan's right to conduct such operations, although they have been criticized on other grounds. To the extent that it acts, with Pakistani consent, to kill militants who threaten the Pakistani state, the United States is clearly on the right side of the law.

Of course this does not cover all of the strikes, many of which are aimed at members of al-Qaeda, the Haqqani Network, and other terrorist groups that target the United States. Pakistan may even oppose such strikes, particularly those against the Haqqani Network, which is widely seen as a Pakistan government proxy (Bumiller and Perlez 2011). Thus most analyses of the legal aspects of the conflict focus on the status of the U.S. war on terror, arguing that it is (or is not) an armed conflict as defined in international humanitarian law; a further subset of this debate is concerned with whether members of al-Qaeda who are not directly implicated in imminent attacks on the United States can be killed anywhere in the world, at any time. The war on terror, which is well into its thirteenth year, raises important questions about how long an armed conflict can last, what it takes to elevate a criminal activity (terrorism) to the level of an armed conflict, and how we know when such an unusual war is over. Furthermore, since almost all of the intelligence surrounding strikes is secret, it is impossible for observers to independently determine whether the targets of the strikes did indeed pose the sort of imminent threat to the United States or U.S. interests that would justify the United States acting in self-defense. These questions are too extensive to deal with here; the debate is still very much alive and has been waged in a number of important books and articles.[7]

Ironically, where President Obama is strongest under international law he may be weakest under American domestic laws governing the executive's use of force abroad. Recent reporting has shown that the United States consistently strikes members of terrorist groups that did not exist in 2001, when Congress passed the Authorization for the Use of Military Force (AUMF),[8] the legal basis of the drone campaign (Landay 2013). Many of these strikes, we argue, are carried out with the consent (and even upon the request) of the Pakistani government, minimizing their international law implications. But under U.S. law, the consent of a foreign country to the United States' use of force within its borders does not in itself authorize the president to use such force.

It is even more difficult to speak with any authority about the legality of the drone strikes under Pakistani law, largely because the hierarchy, and actual responsibilities, of Pakistan's elite are so unclear and vary so widely from their official powers. Article 243 of Pakistan's 1973 constitution vests control over the military solely in the federal government (the prime minister and federal ministers), with the president as commander in chief (National Assembly of Pakistan 2010). In reality, however, the Pakistani military brooks no interference with its self-appointed role as defender of Pakistan—which means it views the civilian government as holding power by sufferance (see, e.g., S. P. Cohen 2004). Although civilian leaders have been shoring up their control of other areas of government, the military still largely dictates Pakistan's foreign and security policies (See Fair in this volume). Thus it is not clear that Pakistan's civilian leadership has the freedom to withdraw its consent to the drone strikes—an important consideration for anyone who supports the development of constitutional governance in Pakistan.

Looking beyond 2014, Pakistan may seek to continue the armed drone program by developing or purchasing its own armed drones. The legality of the program under these circumstances remains a serious question and a difficult one to resolve. As we note below, a different legal regime exists in the FATA and thus it is not clear how Pakistani law applies in a straightforward way, absent constitutional change.

FATA and Pakistan's Internal Security Crisis

Militancy is a problem throughout Pakistan's provinces, particularly in parts of Khyber Pakhtunkhwa (KPK) and Baluchistan. Yet until November 2013, every American drone strike took place in the FATA (New America

Foundation 2013). In that month, the United States conducted its first and, at the time of this writing, only strike outside of the FATA (Paracha 2012). This nearly exclusive focus on FATA has much to do with the special legal regime that governs the region. FATA is composed of seven political agencies and six frontier regions that cover more than ten thousand square miles along Pakistan's western border and are home to between three and six million Pakistanis (S. W. A. Shah 2012: 3). The special legal status of the tribal areas (particularly the political agencies) predates the founding of Pakistan and has its roots in nineteenth-century British colonial rule. As Joshua White (2008) makes clear, the shape the state should take on the northwest frontier of the British Raj was the focus of much contention throughout the colonial period. Different factions of British administrators argued over whether the frontier should be governed with a modernized state bureaucracy or whether it was better suited for personalized rule in the form of a political agent who would supervise the local tribes. Still other debates erupted over whether the British should seek to rule the native populations directly or via local elites.

The British relied on the political agents' ability to bribe or coerce tribal leaders (known as *maliks*) to maintain order within agencies and refrain from raids into the settled areas. The agents had two primary tools for maintaining the peace: a system of payments based on the maliks' supposed position within a tribal hierarchy determined by the British and the agents' right under colonial law to inflict severe punishments on tribes whose leaders refused to cooperate (S. W. A. Shah 2012: 3). These included not just mass detention and the seizure of property but also "blockading," in which the recalcitrant tribe was forcibly cut off from the rest of the British territories (O. Siddique 2012: 11).

When Pakistan became an independent state its new leaders saw no reason to alter the colonial system. Rule by political agents was viewed as a relatively cheap and efficient way of controlling the "warlike Pashtun" and of maintaining an effective buffer along the contested border with Afghanistan (White 2008: 228). The new state of Pakistan thus retained not just a colonial mind-set regarding the frontier (until 2010, KPK was known as the North-West Frontier Province) but also the legal regime for the tribal areas, including special constitutional provisions exempting FATA from democratic governance by the National Assembly. Articles 246 and 247 of the Pakistani constitution remove FATA from the jurisdiction of the federal judiciary and the Pakistani parliament. Only the federal executive (Pakistan's indirectly elected president) has control over the area, and no law applies there without the president's express stipulation (ICG 2013: 31).

In place of regular Pakistani law, FATA is governed by the Frontier Crimes Regulation (FCR), which has existed in some form since 1872 and has barely been revised or updated since 1901 (O. Siddique 2012: 12). The FCR was, and remains, an atavistic legislation, designed to exert a bare minimum of control over FATA without requiring the Pakistani government to invest in any of the trappings of a modern state, such as police, courts, or public services. In place of courts, trials are conducted by tribal councils, called *jirgas*, the members of which are selected and appointed by the political agent; law enforcement, such as it is, is provided by tribal militias (*khasadars*) (O. Siddique 2012). The political agent can require an inhabitant whom he suspects might soon commit a crime to post a bond ensuring good behavior; if the bond is not forthcoming, the tribesman can be imprisoned for up to three years (ICG 2009).

Most notoriously, until 2011 the FCR provided for the collective punishment of tribes whose members were suspected of committing crimes or simply harboring criminals. These provisions were somewhat altered by recent reforms that protect women, children, and the elderly from collective punishment and allow political parties to operate within FATA (A. Siddique 2011). But as the International Crisis Group reports, "without proper courts to enforce the new measures, they largely exist only on paper. Women and children, for example, are still being detained under the FCR's collective responsibility clause" (ICG 2013: 31). Virtually at the same time he enacted the reforms to the FCR, President Zardari signed legislation giving the army virtually unlimited powers of detention in the tribal areas.

As a result, the inhabitants of FATA have become what Osama Siddique calls "lesser citizens" (2012: 5). The results of the area's neglect by the central government are clear: a study conducted by the Pakistani government in 2009 put the average literacy rate among those over ten years of age at 21 percent (7.5 percent for women)—unsurprising given that only 28 percent of children of primary school age were enrolled in school (and less than one out of five girls) (FATA Secretariat 2009: 25–27). When it comes to security, furthermore, the FCR institutes a draconian legal regime in FATA that at the same time makes the enforcement of law and order almost impossible during periods of upheaval. When the tribes are willing to fully cooperate with the political agent and the federal government, the tribal levies can at least keep the peace, but even under the best of circumstances traditional police work—such as the investigation of crimes and arrest of criminals, not to mention preventive policing—is impossible.

Pakistan, and FATA in particular, has long been home to militant groups sponsored and supported by the Pakistani government. In recent years, however, certain militant elements (many of them former state proxies) have turned on the state and have taken advantage of the government's almost nonexistent presence in FATA to turn the area into a militant stronghold (Fair 2011). In order to consolidate their control, their first target was the local leaders: by one estimate, the Pakistani Taliban and related antistate groups operating within FATA have killed 1,500 maliks (Mahsud 2012: 154).

While a full account of Pakistan's struggles with militancy over the last ten years is far beyond the scope of this chapter (see Tankel and White in this volume for a more comprehensive discussion), it is important to recognize that the past ten years of warfare have destroyed the social order in FATA and rendered traditional methods of keeping the peace irrelevant. A 2011 survey found that only 43 percent of the inhabitants of the tribal areas feel safe; 19 percent of respondents reported having to leave their home due to insecurity. This finding is even more remarkable given that, as the report's authors make clear, the enumerators were only able to conduct the survey in the less than 60 percent of FATA that was accessible at the time and did not interview any of the thousands of inhabitants of camps for internally displaced persons (IDPs) from the tribal areas (Shinwari 2012).

Pakistan's Options in FATA

The Pakistani state's response to the internal security threat has been to launch military operations against the militants, both within FATA and in the Provincially Administered Tribal Areas (PATA) of KPK. A 2011 article offered a noncomprehensive list of eight major (named) operations as well as numerous smaller ones (Khattak 2011). These operations have been heavily criticized by some of the same human rights organizations that oppose the drones. Amnesty International (2012) has documented numerous cases of torture and extrajudicial execution, with the armed forces acting in a general atmosphere of impunity (facilitated by Pakistani laws that grant them wide authority in FATA when acting in aid to the civil power).

While it is difficult to estimate the number of civilian casualties resulting from these operations, they have certainly resulted in the displacement
of hundreds of thousands of persons, stripping the tribal areas of nearly
their entire population: by July 2010 the ranks of the internal refugees
included "about 70% of the population of South Waziristan Agency, 84%
of the Orakzai Agency population, nearly half of the Mohmand Agency
population and 16% of the Bajaur population. . . . More than 100,000 from
Kurram and up to 80,000 from Khyber had also become . . . IDPs" (Taj
2011: 403). The International Crisis Group estimates that the war on terror
as a whole has resulted in the displacement of 4 million people; in mid-
2009, when the army began a major offensive against militants in the Swat
district, 2.8 million inhabitants of the area were forced to leave (ICG 2012).
Many of the IDPs have been forced to return when the fighting is officially
"over," despite their continued concerns about the security situation in
their home agency (ICG 2010). Those who remain are housed in camps
that are notoriously squalid and overcrowded, with few if any social services
and no access to jobs or education.

As far as Pakistan is concerned, drones are technically not "the only game
in town" when it comes to combating militancy in the tribal areas (Shachtman 2009). But the dismal record of military operations in FATA shows that
Pakistan's other options are unattractive, to say the least. Those Pakistanis
who accept that Pakistan has a security crisis, believe that the militants cannot
(and should not) be appeased with temporary peace deals, and recognize that
the military has failed to confront Pakistan's internal security issues in an
effective and humane manner have come to accept the drone strikes as Pakistan's only hope. While far from a majority within Pakistani society, they
present an important and too-often neglected viewpoint.

Pakistani advocates of the drone program begin from the assumption
that militancy poses an existential threat to the state. As Amir Zia (2011), a
pro-drone commentator, asked, "are the drone attacks a bigger challenge
for our sovereignty, or those bands of foreign and local militants who freely
roam around establishing a state within a state, masterminding and planning acts of terror and sabotage across Pakistan?" They properly reject the
(false) claim, popular in the Pakistani media, that militancy is caused by
the drone strikes and that once the strikes stop the militants will lay down
their arms. As Kasif Chaudhry (2011), for instance, points out, militancy in
Pakistan predates the drone program by decades, and deaths in suicide
attacks far outpace those from drone attacks for every year of the program.

Nor do they believe that right-wing Pakistani politicians' proposals for negotiations with the Taliban will ever bear fruit (Haider 2013). As these commenters recognize, every single one of the many previous official peace agreements between the militants and the Pakistani government has collapsed within a few months, having lasted just long enough to allow the militants to regroup and regain their strength (Khattak 2012). The longest-lasting deals have been not these official peace treaties but the unofficial "understandings" between the militants and provincial governments, in which the militants agree not to attack within the province while the provincial government agrees to turn a blind eye to their recruiting and fund-raising activities (Rizvi 2013). At the time of writing, Pakistan had embarked on a seemingly serious attempt at negotiations with the TTP. But the gulf between the two parties is wide, and perhaps unbridgeable; as one of the TTP's appointed representatives put it, "the government wants the talks within the limits of the Constitution but the Taliban believe only in the Holy Quran and Sunnah" (Gishkori 2014). Given the unlikeliness of the two sides arriving at an agreement that the majority of Pakistanis can accept and that the militants will hold to, Pakistan will be forced to continue relying on military solutions to its internal security challenges.

After 2014: Possible Futures for the Pakistani Drone Program

As President Obama made clear in his May 2013 speech, America's primary rationale for conducting drone strikes in Pakistan is based on the threat Pakistan-based militants pose to U.S. forces in Afghanistan: as that threat diminishes, he promised, the drone strikes would come to an end. While it is possible that thousands of American military advisers will remain in Afghanistan following the 2014 drawdown, their changed roles will make them less vulnerable to militant activity, in turn making the United States less likely to deploy drones to defend them (Shanker 2013). The United States is, in a sense, calling Pakistan's bluff after years of public diplomatic protests against drones and claims by government officials that "the ideological space for these terrorists is the supposed American occupation of Afghanistan. Once that excuse is not there, these people will have to face the music" (Walsh 2013b).

It is true that Pakistan's cooperation with the United States in the war in Afghanistan is a major element of militant propaganda, but most Pakistan analysts are far less sanguine that the end of a high-profile American presence in the area means the end of the insurgency. The militants that have profited so handsomely off ephemeral peace deals with the Pakistan government are unlikely to easily relinquish their leverage. The Pakistan military is equally unlikely to end its relationship with those militant proxies—many with bases in the tribal areas—which target the Indian presence in Kashmir and Afghanistan. But as long as the militants (and the Pakistani military) resist the extension of governance to FATA, it will remain welcoming to both Pakistan-focused and international terrorists.

From a narrow American perspective, FATA is primarily important insofar as it continues to provide a refuge to terrorists who seek to attack the United States, especially in Afghanistan. However, this is not the only American security priority in Pakistan. As noted in the introduction, Americans have an enduring interest in Pakistan's stability. The reasons for this are twofold. First and foremost, Americans fear that nonstate actors will acquire nuclear weapons from the Pakistan army by breaching the army's security arrangements (see Clary in this volume). Second, Americans and others believe that the most likely precipitant of a future Indo-Pakistan war is a terrorist attack on Indian soil. As Pakistan's terrorist organizations continue to evolve, it may prove difficult for the Pakistani state to prevent unauthorized attacks on India. Thus the Americans have an intrinsic interest in helping Pakistan eliminate those terrorists it does not control, even if it means that the United States must temporarily turn a blind eye to Pakistan's ongoing support for those terrorists it views as assets.

For Pakistan, the drone program is of more intimate interest. Those members of the Pakistani public who are aware of the program almost universally despise it (see Kaltenthaler and Miller in this volume). Yet given Pakistan's continuing challenges on its western frontiers, and the now almost exclusive use of drones to attack threats to Pakistan rather than threats to American interests, we can assume that the Pakistan army and intelligence agencies recognize the program's utility. Ironically, the Pakistan security agencies may find themselves in the odd position of trying to keep the Americans engaged and willing to do Pakistan's dirty business.

There are some signs that this is the case. The so-called strategic dialogue has resumed: in January 2014, a large delegation of Pakistani defense officials arrived in Washington, D.C., to make the case that U.S.-Pakistan relations should be strategic, not transactional. Pakistan's prime minister Nawaz Sharif has dramatically dialed down his anti-drone rhetoric since his return to office, likely because he garnered a better understanding of the realities confronting Pakistan. The United States has also reduced drone strikes over the last year, mostly by curtailing the highly controversial signature strikes, while continuing to use armed drones to eliminate targets who pose a threat to the Pakistani state rather than solely those who seek to harm American interests.

There may be a sufficiently adequate overlap of American and Pakistani interests for the program to continue, at least in a reduced form. If so, the United States will need bases from which to launch the drones (either in Afghanistan or Pakistan), as well as continued access to the ground intelligence that is crucial to finding and identifying targets. This may well serve Pakistan's financial interests as well: should the United States continue the drone strikes in FATA, the need to maintain this infrastructure will continue to secure Pakistan's relevance to the United States—and the revenues such relevance secures. However, unless Pakistan's role is made clear to Pakistan's public as well as to global audiences, a U.S.-led drone program in which Pakistan's security establishment remains a silent, free-riding partner—in opposition to civilians' stated preferences—will have a negative effects on Pakistan's struggling democracy and recent civilian efforts to exert greater control over Pakistan's foreign and national security policy.

Should the United States end the program altogether, it may create space for a rapprochement between Pakistan's varied anti-drone publics and Washington. This leaves the question of what will happen in the (very likely) event that the current peace talks with the Pakistan Taliban fail. Pakistan's military and intelligence agencies will be forced to accept full responsibility for the nation's security and confront the militancy problem on their own. This has the virtue of being an indigenous and sovereign solution. But doing so will probably involve a return to the indiscriminate artillery fire and aerial attacks the military has employed in the past. The end of the drone program, should it indeed lead to such an outcome, will please Pakistan's right-wing agitators and their militant friends; but it will not be a clear victory for the ordinary Pakistanis in the path of the destruction.

Notes

1. The disparity between Mir's figures and those offered by the New America Foundation (NAF) is likely due to the fact that Mir counted only named Taliban

fighters as militants. Any victim who was not directly named as the target of the strike was thus counted as a civilian. The NAF numbers, by contrast, are based on the assumption that militants are often found in groups with other militants. Thus, while the explicit purpose of the strike may be to kill a particular militant commander, members of his militia who are killed with him are not counted as collateral damage.

2. This time period includes, for instance, the March 2011 strike at Datta Khel in North Waziristan, which killed dozens of men. Opinion, even within the U.S. government, is divided as to whether all of those killed in the strike were miliants (Mazzetti 2013b: 290).

3. Sharif, like every major Pakistani politician, is publicly anti-drone, and he campaigned on a promise to bring the strikes to an end (Yousaf 2013). In the context of Pakistani politics, however, his objections to the program are rather lukewarm. Although Sharif declared that he would not "tolerate" the strikes (Dawn 2013), his position is moderate in comparison with those of the religious parties such as the Jamaat-e-Islami and the center-right Pakistani Tehreek-e-Insaf, whose leader Imran Khan vowed that he would shoot the drones out of the sky (Ilyas and Firdous 2013).

4. For some recent comprehensive treatments of the legality of the drone program and of targeted killings under U.S. and international law, see Barnidge 2012; Blank 2012a; Blank 2012b; Daskal 2013; Radsan and Murphy 2012; Sadat 2012; Sterio 2012; and Vogel 2010/

5. Recent assertions to the contrary, such as the report by Ben Emmerson, the UN special rapporteur for counterterrorism, do not alter this picture. Emmerson, who visited Pakistan at the request of the Pakistani government to conduct a study of the U.S. drone program there, concluded that Pakistan had never consented to the strikes and that they represented a violation of Pakistani sovereignty (Office of the High Commissioner for Human Rights 2013). Emmerson spent only three days in Pakistan, however, did not travel outside of Islamabad, and did not speak with any Pakistani military or intelligence officials—leading skeptics to questions whether he could truly have untangled the Pakistan establishment's complex attitude toward the program (Foust 2013).

6. The South Asia Terrorism Portal offers the most comprehensive database of casualties resulting from Pakistan's war on terror, but it does not distinguish between civilians killed by terrorist attacks and those killed in military operations. The Pak Institute for Peace Studies (PIPS) provides an estimate of those killed by terrorist attacks, but it does not distinguish civilian and military casualties, and it does not provide cumulative figures. For purpose of comparison, PIPS estimates that in 2011 (the latest year for which figures are available publicly), 2,391 Pakistanis were killed in 1,966 terrorist attacks (Pak Institute for Peace Studies 2012

7. Important treatments of the first question include Brooks 2004, Balendra 2008, Sitaraman 2009, Solis 2010, and Blank 2012b; for further discussion of targeted killing under LOAC, see Daskal 2012, Rona 2008, and Blum and Heymann 2010.

8. The AUMF authorizes the president "to use all necessary and appropriate force against those nations, organizations, or persons he determines planned, authorized,

committed, or aided the terrorist attacks that occurred on September 11, 2001, or
harbored such organizations or persons, in order to prevent any future acts of international terrorism against the United States by such nations, organizations or persons."
Authorization for Use of Military Force of 2001, S.J. Res. 23, September 18, 2001. Text
at http://www.gpo.gov/fdsys/pkg/PLAW-107publ40/pdf/PLAW-107publ40.pdf. The
statute's use of the past tense (planned, aided, and so on) makes clear that the use of
force should be limited, at the least, to members of groups that were already part of
the terrorist universe by September 11, 2001.

Works Cited

Agence France-Presse. 2013. "Drone Death a Blow to Pakistani Taliban—and to Peace
    Efforts." GlobalPost.com, May 30. http://www.globalpost.com/dispatch/news/afp/
    130530/drone-death-blow-pakistani-taliban-and-peace-efforts.
Amnesty International. 2012. *"The Hands of Cruelty": Abuses by Armed Forces and the
    Taliban in Pakistan's Tribal Areas.* London: Amnesty International.
Balendra, Natasha. 2008. "Defining Armed Conflict." *Cardozo Law Review* 29 (6):
    2461–2516.
Barnidge, Robert P., Jr. 2012. "A Qualified Defense of American Drone Attacks in
    Northwest Pakistan Under International Humanitarian Law." *Boston University
    International Law Journal* 30 (2): 409–448.
Becker, Jo, and Scott Shane. 2012. "Secret 'Kill List' Proves a Test of Obama's Princi-
    ples and Will." *New York Times*, May 29. http://www.nytimes.com/2012/05/29/
    world/obamas-leadership-in-war-on-al-qaeda.html?pagewanted = all.
Bergen, Peter. 2012. "Drone Is Obama's Weapon of Choice." CNN.com, September
    19. http://edition.cnn.com/2012/09/05/opinion/bergen-obama-drone/index.html.
Blank, Laurie R. 2012a. "After 'Top Gun': How Drone Strikes Impact the Law of War."
    University of Pennsylvania Journal of International Law 33 (3): 675–718.
———. 2012b. "The Consequences of a 'War' Paradigm for Counterterrorism: What
    Impact on Basic Rights and Values?" *Georgia Law Review* 46 (3): 719–742.
Blum, Gabriella, and Philip Heymann. 2010. "Law and Policy of Targeted Killing."
    Harvard National Security Journal 1:145–170.
Braun, Meg. 2012. "Counting Civilian Casualties in CIA's Drone War." *Foreign Policy*,
    November 2. http://afpak.foreignpolicy.com/posts/2012/11/02/counting_civilian_
    casualties_in_cia_s_drone_war.
Brooks, Rosa Ehrenreich. 2004. "War Everywhere: Rights, National Security Law, and
    the Law of Armed Conflict in the Age of Terror." *University of Pennsylvania Law
    Review* 153 (2): 675–761.
Bumiller, Elisabeth, and Jane Perlez. 2011. "Pakistan's Spy Agency Is Tied to Attack
    on U.S. Embassy." *New York Times*, September 22.
Bureau of Investigative Journalism. 2014. "Pakistan 2004–2014 CIA Drone Strikes,"
    n.d. http://www.thebureauinvestigates.com/category/projects/drones/drones-pak
    istan/.

Chaudhry, Kasif. 2011. "Hiding Behind the Drones." *Newsline*, May 20.

Cohen, Michael. 2013. "Give President Obama a Chance: There Is a Role for Drones." *Guardian* (London), May 23. http://www.guardian.co.uk/commentisfree/2013/may/23/obama-drone-speech-use-justified.

Cohen, Stephen P. 2004. *The Idea of Pakistan*. Washington, D.C.: Brookings Institution.

Daskal, Jennifer C. 2013. "The Geography of the Battlefield: A Framework for Detention and Targeting Outside the 'Hot' Conflict Zone." *University of Pennsylvania Law Review* 161 (5): 1165–1234.

Dawn. 2013. "'N' Won't Tolerate Drones If Voted to Power." March 28. http://beta.dawn.com/news/791132/n-wont-tolerate-drones-if-voted-to-power-nawaz.

DeYoung, Karen, and Bob Miller. 2014. "U.S. Said to Curtail Drone Strikes in Pakistan as Officials There Seek Peace Talks with Taliban." *Washington Post*, February 4.

Entous, Adam, Siobhan Gorman, and Saeed Shah. 2014. "U.S. to Curb Pakistan Drone Program: CIA to Target Short List of High-Level Terrorists." *Wall Street Journal*, February 5.

Express Tribune. 2013. "Waliur Rehman:_From Madrassa Teacher to Taliban Commander." May 31.

Fair, C. Christine. 2011. "The Militant Challenge in Pakistan." *Asia Policy* 11 (January): 105–137.

FATA Secretariat (Planning and Development Department). 2009. *Multiple Indicator Cluster Survey: Federally Administered Tribal Area (FATA) Pakistan*. Peshawar: Government of Pakistan.

Fazl-e-Haider, Syed. 2013. "US Drone Injured Sharif's Policy of Talks with Taliban." *National* (Abu Dhabi, UAE), June 14. http://www.thenational.ae/thenationalconversation/comment/us-drone-injured-sharifs-policy-of-talks-with-taliban.

Foust, Joshua. 2013. "Ben Emmerson's ISI Shuffle." Registan.net, March 18. http://registan.net/2013/03/18/ben-emmersons-isi-shuffle/.

Gishkori, Zaid. 2014. "Peace Initiative: Maulana Aziz Strikes a Discordant Note." *Express Tribune*, February 8. http://tribune.com.pk/story/669088/peace-initiative-maulana-aziz-strikes-a-discordant-note/.

Haider, Ejaz. 2013. "Comedy of the Grotesque."*Express Tribune*, June 5.

Haqqani, Husain. 2005. *Pakistan: Between Mosque and Military*. Washington, D.C.: Carnegie Endowment for International Peace.

Hussain, Tom. 2013. "Pakistani Army Makes Key Gains Against Taliban Militants." McClatchyDC.com, June 11. http://www.mcclatchydc.com/2013/06/11/193620/pakistani-army-makes-key-gains.html#.Ucy_0Pmsim4.

Hussain, Tom, and Jonathan S. Landay. 2013. "Drone Strike Kills Pakistani Linked to '09 Blast at CIA Afghan Base." McClatchyDC.com, May 29. http://www.mcclatchydc.com/2013/05/29/192520/drone-strike-kills-pakistani-linked.html#.UcELmvmsim4.

ICG (International Crisis Group). 2009. *Pakistan: Countering Militancy in FATA*. Asia Report No. 178. Brussels: International Crisis Group.

———. 2010. *Pakistan: The Worsening IDP Crisis.* Asia Briefing No. 111. Brussels: International Crisis Group.

———. 2012. *Pakistan: No End to Humanitarian Crises.* Asia Report No. 237. Brussels: International Crisis Group.

———. 2013. *Drones: Myths and Reality in Pakistan.* Asia Report No. 247. Brussels: International Crisis Group.

Ilyas, Ferya and Iftikhar Firdous. 2012. "PTI Will Shoot Drones Down Once in Power: Imran Khan." *Express Tribune*, February 10. http://tribune.com.pk/story/334469/pti-will-shoot-drones-down-once-in-power-imran-khan/.

Khan, Zia. 2012. "Pakistan Not Pushing for End to US Drone Strikes." *Express Tribune*, July 6. http://tribune.com.pk/story/404368/pakistan-not-pushing-for-end-to-us-drone-strikes/.

Khattak, Daud. 2011. "Evaluating Pakistan's Offensives in Swat and FATA." *CTC Sentinel* 4 (10): 9–11.

———. 2012. "Reviewing Pakistan's Peace Deals with the Taliban." *CTC Sentinel* 5 (9): 11–13.

Landay, Jonathan. 2013. "Obama's Drone War Kills 'Others,' Not Just al Qaida Leaders." McClatchyDC.com, April 9. http://www.mcclatchydc.com/2013/04/09/188062/obamas-drone-war-kills-others.html#.UcC18vmsim4.

Mahsud, Saifullah. 2012. "Combating Militancy in Bajaur and North-Waziristan Agency in Federally Administered Tribal Areas (FATA) of Pakistan—A Comparative Analysis." *Tigah* 2 (December): 149–164.

Mazzetti, Mark. 2013a. "A Secret Deal on Drones, Sealed in Blood." *New York Times*, April 6. http://www.nytimes.com/2013/04/07/world/asia/origins-of-cias-not-so-secret-drone-war-in-pakistan.html?pagewanted = all.

———. 2013b. *The Way of the Knife: The CIA, a Secret Army, and a War at the Ends of the Earth.* New York: Penguin Press.

Miller, Greg. 2012. "Brennan Speech Is First Obama Acknowledgment of Use of Armed Drones." *Washington Post*, April 30.

Miller, Greg, and Bob Woodward. 2013. "Secret Memos Reveal Explicit Nature of U.S., Pakistan Agreement on Drones." *Washington Post*, October 23.

National Assembly of Pakistan. 2010. Constitution of the Islamic Republic of Pakistan. Available at http://www.na.gov.pk/publications/constitution.pdf.

New America Foundation. 2008. "Pakistan Drone Strikes: 2008." http://natsec.newamerica.net/drones/pakistan/2008.

———. 2013. "The Drone War in Pakistan." December 25. http://natsec.newamerica.net/drones/pakistan/analysis.

Obama, Barack. 2013. "Remarks by the President at the National Defense University." May 23. http://www.whitehouse.gov/the-press-office/2013/05/23/remarks-president-national-defense-university.

Office of the High Commissioner for Human Rights. 2013. "Statement of the Special Rapporteur Following Meetings in Pakistan." March 14. http://www.ohchr.org/EN/NewsEvents/Pages/DisplayNews.aspx?NewsID = 13146&LangID = E.

Pak Institute for Peace Studies. 2012. *Pakistan Security Report, 2011.* Islamabad: Pak Institute for Peace Studies. san-pips.com/download.php?f = 74.pdf.

Paracha, Abdul Sami. 2013. "US takes drone attack beyond Fata," *The Dawn.* November 22. http://www.dawn.com/news/1057740.

Plaw, Avery. 2013. "Counting the Dead: The Proportionality of Predation in Pakistan." In *Killing by Remote Control: The Ethics of an Unmanned Military,* ed. Bradley Jay Strawser, 126–153. New York: Oxford University Press.

Radsan, Afsheen John, and Richard Murphy. 2012. "The Evolution of Law and Policy for CIA Targeted Killing." *Journal of National Security Law and Policy* 5 (2): 439–463.

Raja, Mudassir. 2013. "Pakistani Victims: War on Terror Toll Put at 49,000." *Express Tribune,* March 27. http://tribune.com.pk/story/527016/pakistani-victims-war-on-terror-toll-put-at-49000/.

Rizvi, Hasan Askari. 2013. "The Search for a New Drone Policy." *Express Tribune,* June 3.

Robertson, Nic, and Greg Botelho. 2013. "Ex-Pakistani President Musharraf Admits Secret Deal with U.S. on Drone Strikes." CNN.com, April 12. http://edition.cnn.com/2013/04/11/world/asia/pakistan-musharraf-drones.

Rona, Gabor. 2008. "A Bull in a China Shop: The War on Terror and International Law in the United States." *California Western International Law Journal* 39 (1): 135–158.

Sadat, Leila Nadya. 2012. "America's Drone Wars." *Case Western Reserve Journal of International Law* 45 (1–2): 215–234.

Shachtman, Noah. 2009. "CIA Chief: Drones 'Only Game in Town' for Stopping Al Qaeda." *Wired.com Danger Room,* May 19. http://www.wired.com/dangerroom/2009/05/cia-chief-drones-only-game-in-town-for-stopping-al-qaeda/.

Shah, Saeed. 2013. "Pakistani Taliban Call Off Peace Talks." *Wall Street Journal,* May 30. http://online.wsj.com/article/SB10001424127887324412604578515554172082078.html.

Shah, Sayed Wiqar Ali. 2012. "Political Reforms in the Federally Administered Tribal Areas of Pakistan (FATA): Will It End the Current Militancy?" Working Paper No. 64. South Asia Institute, Heidelberg University.

Shanker, Thom. 2013. "General Says 20,000 Troops Should Stay in Afghanistan." *New York Times,* March 5. http://www.nytimes.com/2013/03/06/world/middleeast/us-general-says-20000-troops-should-stay-in-afghanistan.html.

Shinwari, Naveed Ahmad. 2012. *Understanding FATA: 2011.* Islamabad: Community Appraisal and Motivation Program.

Siddiqa, Ayesha. 2011. "Pakistan's Counterterrorism Strategy: Separating Friends from Enemies." *Washington Quarterly* 34 (1): 149–162.

Siddique, Abubakar. 2011. "Pakistan's Tribal Area Reforms: Too Little, Too Late." *Radio Free Europe,* August 20.

Siddique, Osama. 2012. "The Other Pakistan: Special Laws, Diminished Citizenship and the Gathering Storm." Working Paper. http://papers.ssrn.com/sol3/papers .cfm?abstract_id = 2185535.

Sitaraman, Ganesh. 2009. "Counterinsurgency, the War on Terror, and the Laws of War." *Virginia Law Review* 95 (7): 1745–1839.

Solis, Gary D. 2010. *The Law of Armed Conflict: International Humanitarian Law in War*. Cambridge: Cambridge University Press.

South Asia Terrorism Portal. 2014. "Fatalities in Terrorist Violence in Pakistan, 2003– 2014." SATP.org, June 1. http://www.satp.org/satporgtp/countries/pakistan/data base/casualties.htm.

Stanford Law School International Human Rights and Conflict Resolution Clinic and New York University School of Law Global Justice Clinic. 2012. *Living Under Drones: Death, Injury, and Trauma to Civilians from US Drone Practices in Pakistan*. http://livingunderdrones.org/.

Stein, Jeff. 2010. "CIA Drones Killed U.S. Citizens in Pakistan, Book Says." SpyTalk (blog). WashingtonPost.com, September 22. http://voices.washingtonpost.com/ spy-talk/2010/09/cia_drones_killed_us_citizens.html.

Sterio, Milena. 2012. "The United States' Use of Drones in the War on Terror: The (Il)Legality of Targeted Killings Under International Law." *Case Western Reserve Journal of International Law* 45 (1–2): 197–214.

Swami, Praveen. 2012. "In Secret Deal, ISI Allows US Drone War to Resume." *Hindu* (Chennai), February 25. http://www.thehindu.com/news/international/in-secret-deal-isi-allows-us-drone-war-to-resume/article2929240.ece.

Taj, Farhat. 2010. "The Year of the Drone Misinformation." *Small Wars & Insurgencies* 21 (3): 529–535.

———. 2011. "A Critical Perspective on a Recent Survey of Opinion in Pakistan's Tribal Zone." *Small Wars & Insurgencies* 22 (2): 402–413.

Vogel, Ryan J. 2010. "Drone Warfare and the Law of Armed Conflict." *Denver Journal of International Law and Policy* 39 (1): 101–138.

Walsh, Declan. 2013a. "U.S. Disavows 2 Drone Strikes over Pakistan." *New York Times*, March 4.

———. 2013b. "U.S. Shift Poses Risk to Pakistan." *New York Times*, May 25. http:// www.nytimes.com/2013/05/26/world/asia/us-shift-poses-risk-to-pakistan.html?pagewanted = all.

Walzer, Michael. 2006. *Just and Unjust Wars: A Moral Argument with Historical Illustrations*. New York: Basic Books.

White, Joshua. 2008. "The Shape of Frontier Rule: Governance and Transition, from the Raj to the Modern Pakistani Frontier." *Asian Security* 4 (3): 219–243.

Yousaf, Kamran. 2013. "Sticking to Its Guns: Islamabad Reiterates Drone Strikes Violate Sovereignty." *Express Tribune*, May 25.

Zia, Amir. 2011. "The Inner Conflict." *Newsline*, June 28.

Chapter 4

The Safety and Security of the Pakistani Nuclear Arsenal

Christopher Clary

Pakistan presents two major threats to the U.S. homeland: as a possible safe haven from which large-scale terrorist attacks against the West could be planned and as a potential source of a nuclear weapon obtained by nonstate actors. These threats persist, despite the considerable energy expended to manage them since 2001. The United States has directed the majority of its effort toward preventing the first threat, waging a thirteen-year counterinsurgency campaign in Afghanistan and a similarly long, pseudo-covert counterterrorism campaign in Pakistan's frontier regions. Nuclear fears linger, however, sometimes surfacing when policy makers, pressed for a rationale for the U.S. presence in Afghanistan, suggest that instability in Afghanistan can spread to Pakistan, endangering the safety and security of Pakistan's nuclear weapons. But while nuclear risks may be more worrisome to U.S. policy makers and analysts than those posed by traditional terrorism, the policy tools to manage those risks are wanting. American attempts to engage Pakistan through the provision of aid and technology are based on the calculation that containing or weakening Pakistan might enhance nuclear risk. With the United States fatigued by persistent counterinsurgency and counterterrorism, nuclear risks will take on a heightened role in arguments for a sustained American "Af-Pak" presence (Sanger and Schmitt 2014). During the 2014 transition, then, it is worthwhile to take stock of what those nuclear risks actually are and how they are likely to develop in the foreseeable future.

This chapter reviews four types of command and control challenges facing Pakistan's arsenal. In practice there are risk spillovers across types, but it is beneficial conceptually to separate them first prior to aggregation. First, this chapter reviews the command and control challenges that stem from Pakistan's complicated relationships with violent nonstate actors. This presents a fundamental challenge to stability on the subcontinent. Second, it discusses the vulnerability of the Pakistani arsenal to insider threats, followed in the third section by a discussion of risks associated with outsider threats. The fourth section discusses briefly how these risks are amplified in the context of crisis and war. The chapter concludes by examining Pakistani efforts to develop battlefield nuclear weapons and focuses on how that development alters risk calculations in all four areas.

Taken together, Pakistan's nuclear dangers are small but real. The absolute possibility of an adverse nuclear event emanating from Pakistan is low, just as it is from any single country globally. But Pakistan's relative risk is high, presenting a danger from nuclear weapons on par with that from turbulent North Korea's tiny arsenal or Russia's sprawling nuclear weapons complex. The source of this relative risk is not a lack of professionalism on the part of Pakistan's nuclear custodians. All outward signs indicate that they take their task seriously. Rather, nuclear risk is a by-product of Pakistan's instability, an outgrowth of its dangerous neighborhood coupled with the complicated relationship between the Pakistani state and violent extremism. The analytic question is whether Pakistan's dedication to protect its arsenal—which is evident—will be sufficient to defend against internal and external dangers. This chapter cannot answer that question definitively, but it can survey the constituent risks. To that task, it now turns.

Command and Control and Nonstate Actors

Optimism about the prospects for nuclear deterrence is grounded in the belief that rational, unitary states will not take actions to achieve comparatively small political gains at the prospect of unbounded political risk. Once multiple players are introduced into the mix, however, incentives vary more widely. Individuals—whatever the goals of their resident states—are not solely concerned with maximizing state security in a dangerous world. They may be willing to take risks that state leaders would find unacceptable.

Pakistan has permitted a set of violent nonstate actors to operate in its territory, many of whom target Pakistan's traditional foe, India (Perkovich 2012). Analysts debate the degree to which the state actively supports these groups and whether this support is driven more by a desire to maintain coercive tools against India or by fear that a crackdown on such groups would generate dangerous domestic instability in Pakistan (see Tankel in this volume). In general, most Indian observers believe Pakistan has strong control over anti-India violent groups, most American observers believe Pakistan has moderate-to-strong control over anti-India violent groups, and most Pakistani observers believe Pakistan has weak-to-moderate control over anti-India violent groups.

This disjuncture in beliefs about Pakistani support is itself deeply problematic. If Indian leaders believe Pakistan is responsible for a terrorist attack, but Pakistani leaders believe it is not, it makes bargaining success to resolve a crisis difficult to achieve. Even within Pakistan, different elements of the state bureaucracy might have different views of an event. Perhaps some individuals in the Pakistani intelligence agency know Pakistan's culpability. Perhaps Pakistan's civilian bureaucrats, diplomats, and political leaders are uninformed. How is a state supposed to act coherently in the absence of information about itself?

In a different context, Scott Sagan observed that these principal-agent challenges, with different incentives and asymmetric information, provide part of the reason for the failure of cultures of safety in complex organizations. "Even if political elites and organizational leaders have consistent objectives of safety, they may be misinformed about the nature or frequency of dangerous operations by lower-level operators, whose interests include keeping their jobs and therefore not getting caught when rules are violated" (Sagan 1993: 38). To borrow Sagan's idea, ties with violent nonstate actors constitute dangerous operations. Those at the top may not fully grasp the provocations of those below, and they may make bargaining mistakes as a result. This possibility does not require that the Inter-Services Intelligence Directorate (ISI) be a rogue organization. When a state authorizes part of itself to have covert ties with violent nonstate actors under certain circumstances, it is in fact generating a broader set of contacts and relationships than it can monitor fully.

George Perkovich argues that this permissive environment for violent nonstate actors should be the focus of analytic attention and external pressure when examining Pakistan's nuclear stewardship. "[T]he general level of violence, insurrection, and political instability in Pakistan poses the greatest long-run threats to the security of Pakistan's nuclear arsenal, either from insiders or outsiders, than do specific nuclear security practices of the Pakistani security establishment. Focusing, as many US officials and commentators do, on the presumed insecurity of Pakistan's nuclear assets distracts attention and effort from the more fundamental objective of redressing militancy and disorder within Pakistan" (Perkovich 2012: 4–5).

Any assessment of nuclear risk in Pakistan must account for the primary source of that risk: the threat environment that surrounds Pakistan's nuclear arsenal. While acknowledging that reality, and despite Perkovich's injunction, it is still useful to assess how such a threat might manifest in nuclear risk. Given that Pakistan does operate in an environment with an abundance of violent nonstate actors, what are the risks to the arsenal? Are they most likely to come from insiders operating within the nuclear establishment or from the outside? Are the dangers present at a low level everyday or are they especially heightened during periods of tension and crisis? If attempts to manage militancy within Pakistan fail, answers to such questions are important for the management of subsidiary dangers.

Command and Control and Insider Threats

In the early years of Pakistan's overt nuclear existence, international attention to the Pakistani arsenal primarily saw it in a hyphenated context with India. The United States pressured Pakistani diplomats and military officials to pursue "strategic restraint" and begin the early stages of confidence building and arms control with India (Khan 2012: 289–301). If the Pakistani bomb must come out of the basement, best that it not come far out of the basement. Could existential or recessed deterrent postures be pursued?

But that changed in 2001, when the focus of international emphasis became the security of the arsenal. The possible danger of insider threats was flagged first as a result of the activities of two retirees, Sultan Bashir-ud-Din Mahmood and Chaudiri Abdul Majeed. Both Mahmood and Majeed had peripheral involvement, at best, with Pakistan's nuclear weapons program. Mahmood, trained as a chemist, and Majeed, an engineer, had careers working in Pakistan's nuclear establishment but focused primarily on the problems of nuclear energy production. In retirement, they had founded an organization, Ummah Tameer-e-Nau (UTN), focused on the reconstruction of war-torn Afghanistan. This led them to contacts with Osama bin Laden. In a now infamous meeting in August 2001, they reportedly discussed the necessary steps for al-Qaeda to acquire weapons of mass destruction. As former director of central intelligence George Tenet recounted in his memoirs, "Mahmood and Majeed met with Usama bin Laden and Ayman al-Zawahiri in Afghanistan. There, around a campfire, they discussed how al-Qa'ida should go about building a nuclear device" (Tenet 2007: 264).

UTN appears to have had wide-ranging interests beyond its reconstruction work and scientific consultancy in Afghanistan. Tenet claims the Pakistani scientists approached Libya with offers to transfer nuclear technology (Tenet 2007: 400), and when UTN offices were searched in Kabul, Western reporters discovered a variety of documents relating to anthrax dissemination (Frantz and Rohde 2001; Albright and Higgins 2003: 49–55). Tenet claims Mahmood and Majeed confirmed their conversation with bin Laden after undergoing interrogation in Pakistan with the help of U.S. polygraphists, though Mahmood has subsequently denied that his conversation with bin Laden was anything but an academic discussion about nuclear energy in general (Khan 2012: 362–363).

The anthrax plans seemed harebrained and unlikely to succeed. And Mahmood and Majeed's nuclear weapons knowledge was likely much more limited than they may have claimed to others, or than Western officials might have claimed in an effort to highlight the dangers of nuclear terrorism. In fact, all available information suggests their knowledge was so limited that Tenet's claim of a Libya offer seems implausible. As one intelligence official anonymously told the *New York Times*, "These two guys were nuclear scientists who didn't know how to build one [a nuclear weapon] themselves. . . . If you had to have guys go bad, these are the guys you'd want—they didn't know much" (Frantz and Rohde 2001).

Even so, the Majeed and Mahmood case understandably alarmed American officials. Late 2001 also saw the case of two other Pakistani scientists, Suleiman Assad and Mohammed Muktar, who reportedly traveled to Burma shortly after September 2001. There were suspicions that Assad and Muktar were sent to Burma so that they could avoid questions from Western intelligence officials. Despite the intervening years, information about Assad and Muktar is still so limited that it is difficult to judge whether they were involved in sharing nuclear secrets with others and, if so, with whom (Frantz, Risen, and Sanger 2001; Press Trust of India 2001; TV Myanmar 2001).

As these reports filtered into Washington, U.S. officials also were peer-ing deeper into a nuclear smuggling network centered on the Pakistani scientist Abdul Qadeer Khan. From 1987 to 2003, Khan was engaged in an increasingly elaborate effort to provide Pakistan's nuclear secrets to foreign buyers for cash or in sensitive technology swaps. He provided centrifuge designs and components, nuclear weapons designs, technical consulting, plans for uranium processing facilities, and uranium hexafluoride gas. Based on publicly available information, Libya appears to have received the most help from the Khan network, followed by North Korea, and finally Iran. Khan appears to have offered his services to Iraq in the mid-1990s, though he was turned down, and he may have attempted to assist other states, with his visits to Syria and Saudi Arabia often being mentioned as destinations of concern.

While quite a bit is known about what Khan provided to his clients, much less is known about the degree of Pakistani state involvement. Tenet reports, "It was extremely difficult to know exactly . . . to what extent his efforts were conducted at the behest and with the support of the Pakistani government" (2007: 282). Nongovernmental analysts also disagree. One American academic has claimed that evidence of state sponsorship is "over-whelming" (Kroenig 2009: 129) and "incontrovertible" (Kroenig 2010: 136), though this likely overstates the solidity of that case. Others, such as journalist Gordon Corera, suggest that some of Khan's nuclear assistance might have been approved by Pakistani leaders while other episodes were not, with Corera concluding that the "precise degree" of official involve-ment "remains unclear" (2006: 120–121). Similarly, while not ruling out collaboration of Pakistani leadership, William Langewiesche concludes that "*policy* is probably too strong a word for what occurred. Pakistan's sale of nuclear-weapons technology abroad did not require a deliberative process, a chain of command, or a formal commitment to proceed. More likely it took the form of opportunities that occasionally arose, and that were acted upon by a small circle of friends" (2008: 156, emphasis in original).

Those convinced that Pakistani senior leaders were involved commonly pursue two lines of argument. First, the Pakistani government must have known and acquiesced at least tacitly to Khan's international travel (cf. Ganguly 2013: 383). Second, the Pakistani government had to be aware of Khan's considerable accumulation of wealth, far in excess of what his offi-cial salary would permit. Those who believe that Khan was operating with-out leadership approval argue that Khan had always been free from interference, first as he set up his illicit procurement network and, later, as he sought to expand into conventional arms development and sales. With regard to Khan's lifestyle and assets, Pakistani officials assumed he had been skimming from Khan Research Laboratories' substantial budget. Former Pakistani military officer Feroz Hassan Khan argues, "KRL never existed on paper as a legitimate government entity, and KRL was essentially unaccountable. . . . With tacit protection from the government, KRL was able to operate with near impunity and without informing authorities of its activities. . . . The Pakistan government overlooked Khan's activities because it believed the benefit he provided outweighed the cost of corruption" (Khan 2012: 370).

The basic conclusion to be drawn from A. Q. Khan's activities remains the same, however, whether or not he was acting with state knowledge: during this period, Pakistan provided at best reckless stewardship of its nuclear weapons. If Khan did in fact act without leadership support, then basically leakage at any scale was possible. Khan inadvertently makes this argument in an effort to refute the claim that his network transferred uranium hexafluoride to Libya: "I did not ask anybody in KRL to send any gas to Libya and it is impossible to get 2 tons of gas out of Kahuta without this discrepancy being found out or caught. Our material balance sheet is foolproof. If one believes in the disappearance of this quantity of gas, one could also accept the possibility of the disappearance of Kg 200 or 300 weapon-grade material, which is also impossible" (FoxNews.com 2011). If, on the other hand, Khan acted with leadership support, perhaps in exchange for budgetary remuneration for the state or bribes to individual leaders, then these leaders acted with a remarkably narrow view of Pakistan's national interest. A rational nuclear weapons state does not offer to transfer nuclear technology to likely adversaries (Iran) or the adversaries of key allies (Iran and Iraq) or to countries of marginal importance (Libya). Such behavior is certain to draw the ire of friend and foe alike.

Despite the decade that has passed since Khan's public apology for his actions, our knowledge of those actions is not substantially richer. As David Sanger notes, making a biting comparison with the aftermath of the 2011 Abbottabad raid, the United States has stopped asking hard questions about the awareness of Pakistani authorities of the activities of the Khan network (Sanger 2012: 113). As a matter of U.S. policy, this is understandable. International politics, after all, is not a morality play. Whether the Pakistani state is "guilty" of past nuclear misconduct is irrelevant as long as future behavior will be different.

In this respect, the Pakistani state has taken numerous, concrete, and public steps to demonstrate insider threats are taken seriously. Pakistan established a screening program for both its military officers and civilian scientists, it enacted a "two-man rule" for individuals accessing nuclear weapons or fissile material (and in some cases a "three-man rule"), it developed the functional equivalent of a "permissive action link" (PAL) to prevent nuclear use without authorization codes, it stores at least some portion of the arsenal partially disassembled or without triggers, it enacted a nuclear material protection, control, and accounting (MPC&A) regime that includes external audits of strategic organizations, it created a security division within the joint Strategic Plans Division (SPD) to protect the arsenal, and it charged a portion of Pakistan's Inter-Services Intelligence to help with the protection mission (Salik and Luongo 2013; Clary 2010; Lavoy 2008; Luongo and Salik 2007). In at least some of these areas, Pakistan has also accepted U.S. assistance (Mullen 2009; Armitage 2007; Sanger and Broad 2007). All of these steps suggest a seriousness of purpose and professionalism by Pakistan's nuclear managers. The problem is that effort alone is insufficient.

Nuclear risk is a function of the number of weapons (more weapons, ceteris paribus, are more dangerous), readiness (readier weapons are more dangerous), security measures (more secure weapons are less dangerous), and the threat environment (more threats present a greater danger to the arsenal). Pakistan's nuclear developments over the last fifteen years have involved an unequivocal and dramatic expansion of the arsenal, some hints of heightened readiness, clear improvements for security, and a worsening threat environment. In other words, if nuclear risk is a function of four variables, three of them have moved in dangerous directions. Even if one believes A. Q. Khan likely acted without state approval and if one believes that Pakistan's Strategic Plans Division is a dedicated professional body, it is difficult to deny the negative trajectory of the other portions of the puzzle (also see Bunn, Harrell, and Malin 2012: 5).

The Size of the Arsenal

Most nongovernmental estimates place the Pakistan arsenal at approximately one hundred nuclear weapons today, though Bruce Riedel, a former

U.S. official, estimates that the Pakistani arsenal could consist of more than two hundred weapons (Kristensen and Norris 2011; Riedel 2013).[1] Depending on assumptions about when the Khushab-III and Khushab-IV reactors come on line and the amount of fissile material required for each warhead, Pakistan's plutonium route is producing fissile material for an additional four to eleven warheads per year. Pakistan's long-standing highly enriched uranium pathway might provide fissile material sufficient for an additional three to seven warheads per year. If Pakistan combined plutonium and highly enriched uranium to create composite cores, it could achieve modest efficiencies in the use of fissile material overall, and the number of additional warheads produced per year would be slightly higher than the above estimates. In sum, it is easy to generate estimates for a Pakistani arsenal of between two and three hundred weapons by 2020, a substantial increase from an arsenal that perhaps numbered only a few tens of weapons in 2001 (Clary 2013; Tertrais 2012; Mian, Nayyar, and Rajaraman 2009).

The Readiness of the Arsenal

Assessing any change in the readiness of the force is murkier than gauging the quantitative expansion of the arsenal. Generically, readiness is the ability of a unit to execute its military missions, though in this context I am using readiness specifically to mean the intermediate steps between the peacetime status of nuclear forces and their ability to be used. In theory, there are many possible steps: assembly of a functional warhead, mating warhead and delivery vehicle, dispersing the warhead and launch vehicle from their peacetime location to their crisis or wartime location, providing a valid arming and/or launch code, and launching the missile or dropping the nuclear bomb. It is not entirely apparent in the Pakistani context if warheads are stored assembled or disassembled, whether warhead components are physically separated, whether warheads are physically separated from delivery vehicles, and whether central authorities alone retain arming codes.

Information suggesting physical separation of warhead components or separation of warheads and delivery vehicles is abundant, but increasingly dated. The passage of time does not necessarily imply change, but it does decrease our confidence amid all of the other changes in the Pakistani arsenal. The most recent official U.S. assessment is a 2001 Department of

Defense report, which states, "Islamabad's nuclear weapons are probably stored in component form," but also states "Pakistan probably could assemble the weapons fairly quickly" (U.S. Department of Defense 2001). In 2003, Pakistan's then president Pervez Musharraf told an Indian journalist, "Missiles and warheads are not permitted together. There is a geographical separation between them" (Reddy 2003). A Pakistani defense spokesmen told Kyodo News in 2006, "The launch mechanism, the device and various other mechanisms, they are kept at different places. To launch them, you have to first put them together" (Kyodo News 2006).

In recent years, the number of assurances of physical separation of components has decreased, while there have been inklings of greater readiness in peacetime storage. A 2008 report of scientists associated with the Landau Network–Centro Volta, an Italian nongovernmental group that in the past has had good access to the Strategic Plans Division, suggested that nuclear warheads might be readier in peacetime than previously believed. Khalid Kidwai, at the time, director-general of the SPD, told the group that "weapons will be ready when required, at the shortest notice; [but] the Pakistani doctrine is not endorsing a US-USSR model with weapons on hair trigger alert." Somewhat cryptically, Kidwai told the group that "separation is more linked to time rather than space." Based on Kidwai's comments, one group member concluded that Pakistan's fissile cores and weapons detonators are not stored apart (Martellini 2008). At a press briefing in early 2008, Kidwai made a set of related, but distinct comments about the physical separation of warheads from delivery vehicles. When discussing the status of mating, he told the journalists, "Whether separated by a yards or miles the weapons will be ready to go in no time" (Moreau 2008).

The Security of the Weapon from Unauthorized Use

Physical separation of components may have initially been used in lieu of technical safeguards (Warrick 2007; Luongo and Salik 2007), but since at least 2004 Pakistani scientists have been assuring interlocutors that Pakistan has permissive action links that prevent unauthorized detonation. By far the most detail on this capability comes from a 2004 interview with Samar Mubarakmand, a Pakistani physicist who led Pakistan's nuclear weapons efforts from 1994 to 2007, who told his interviewer:

It is a very important part of [the Pakistan command and control] system that secret codes must be installed in all our weapons. When a weapon needs to be used, the person who is using it is given the code a few moments prior to the weapon's use, and when he feeds that code via the computer, then that weapon is armed and the weapon can only be used in this way. So we have developed these codes ourselves and when these codes are installed at the time of the manufacture of these weapons and they cannot be installed on them later on. [sic] Our Command Authority knows what are these codes and these are very secure. (Mubarakmand 2004)

When pressed as to whether the codes were tamperproof, Mubarakmand insisted: "put a nuclear weapon on the road, you can keep it there for 10 months and I guarantee you that no one can use it or detonate it or cause any destruction from it" (ibid.).

Jeffrey Lewis and Bruno Tertrais, in separate analyses of the Pakistani program, both question the full extent of these technical safeguards. After reviewing Mubarakmand's statements, Lewis (2010: 4–5) argues, "Pakistan has installed coded control devices that allow the arming of a nuclear weapon from either the cockpit of an aircraft or a missile launcher. . . . Such use-control devices are an important safeguard, but codes (which are typically assigned to large groups or classes of weapons) can be exposed and external devices bypassed. 'Tamper resistance' is a distinguishing feature of the modern Permissive Action Links, which are designed to resist efforts to bypass them and remain secure during maintenance activities such as replacing batteries." Pakistani devices' degree of tamper resistance is by no means clear.

Tertrais raises a similar set of concerns, though he underscores the separate question of which elements of the nuclear chain of command have access to the codes. As he asks, "Are the arming mechanisms buried deep in the warhead design, or can coding be bypassed? Do they include disabling features? Is there a code for each warhead or set of warheads, or just a general nuclear release enabling mechanism? Does arming physically depend on a code transmitted down the chain of command at the last minute, or would the code(s) already present at the base be enough?" (2012: 24). To the extent more individuals have access to the codes, there is greater danger of arming without authorization from the National Command Authority itself.

The United States sought to design embedded PALs that were incredibly difficult to disable. As Dan Caldwell and Peter Zimmerman (1989: 159) recount, "Bypassing a PAL should be, as one weapons designer graphically put it, about as complex as performing a tonsillectomy while entering the patient from the wrong end." Tertrais alludes to the additional fact that the U.S. PALs, if tampered with, would render the warhead nonfunctional, perhaps permanently so (see also Cotter 1987: 50).

Despite these concerns about tamper resistance and the distribution of arming codes within the nuclear command chain, there should be no doubt that the technical and procedural safeguards on a Pakistani warhead are almost certainly stronger than they were in the aftermath of the 1998 tests. Institution of these additional technical barriers to use, however, may have caused Pakistani decision makers to make a modest increase in readiness.

The Nature of the Insider Threat

The previous three elements (size, readiness, security) have dealt with the arsenal and its protections. The last element of an insider threat is the risk that motivated individuals would be able to gain access to a weapon, even if they might have difficulty detonating the weapon or using its fissile material. Insiders, by definition, have greater knowledge of the location of sensitive materials and protections of those materials. A 2012 U.S. State Department fact sheet stresses, "Almost all known cases of theft of nuclear material involved an insider" (U.S. Department of State 2012). As mentioned earlier, Pakistan's arsenal has procedural safeguards—namely, a "two-man rule" and material protection and accounting programs—to prevent an individual, even an insider, from gaining unfettered access to a device or its constituent fissile materials. The coding devices discussed above would make it more difficult even for an insider with access to a complete device to be able to detonate it. Assuming such procedures are followed, the risk comes from an individual, or a conspiracy of individuals, willing to use violence to overcome those procedural barriers. Conspiracies could involve multiple insiders or insiders working with outsiders. Dangerous insiders could be motivated for ideological reasons or pecuniary ones.

Once violence is involved, the distinction between insiders and outsiders for purposes of risk assessment largely disappears. Discussion of violent scenarios occurs in the next section. This section focuses on three interrelated problems: (1) the number of potential insiders; (2) the protections in place to prevent dangerous individuals from becoming insiders; and (3) Pakistan's track record in being able to effectively screen insiders.

The number of potential insiders is reasonably large. Perhaps ironically, the largest single pool of potential insiders is the security force protecting the weapons from outsiders. That force has expanded rapidly and is on track to reach 28,000 personnel, according to Naeem Salik and Kenneth Luongo (2013). Adding new guards increases the amount of force an outsider would have to employ to seize sensitive materials but increases the pool of insiders, an example of what Scott Sagan refers to as "the problem of redundancy problem" (2004: 938–939). It is difficult to compare the size of the security force to that of members of the scientific and technical establishment who have access to nuclear matériel or knowledge. Kidwai told reporters in 2008 that 2,000 scientists working in particularly sensitive areas were subject to screening and scrutiny, which corresponds with what he told an Italian nongovernmental organization that same year (though he also told them the screening program would expand in the future to encompass an additional 8,000 personnel with sensitive knowledge) (Pennington 2008; Martellini 2008: 3). This in turn is roughly consistent with Kidwai's 2009 estimate of 7,000–8,000 scientific personnel in the nuclear establishment, of which 2,000 had "critical knowledge" (Sanger 2009). Bruno Tertrais, for his part, reports that 2,000–4,000 personnel might be subject to screening, acknowledging that "numbers vary" from source to source (2012: 17–18).

Yet at no point has the number of those subject to screening equaled the number of individuals in the SPD security division. Recall again that there are three and a half times as many security personnel as there are scientific and technical staff. This omission of the security force in public statements might be the result of a misunderstanding. Feroz Hassan Khan (2009) reports the existence of a personnel reliability program for military personnel and a human reliability program for civilian personnel. It is at least possible that Kidwai has only been stating numbers for the latter program. It also seems possible that some substantial portion of the military security force is not subject to screening, which would suggest the "guarding the guardians" problem is considerable. Further still, while I am aware of no public estimates of the size of the military's strategic forces (the units responsible for mobilizing and utilizing nuclear weapons in the event of war), such forces could easily number in excess of one thousand personnel, with roughly ten individuals involved in handling each weapon. It is true that military security personnel, unlike nuclear scientists, might not need to be informed whether they are truly guarding a nuclear weapon rather than phony bunkers and dummy warheads, which Pakistan has been alleged to employ (Khan quoted in Ricks 2007). But this mitigates rather than eliminates the problem.

For those subject to screening, the process seems reasonably comprehensive. Candidate individuals submit a seventy-page questionnaire (Martellini 2008: 3) and are scrutinized by Pakistan's three intelligence agencies—the Inter-Services Intelligence Directorate, Military Intelligence, and the civilian Intelligence Bureau (Cotta-Ramusino and Martellini 2002)—in a process that can initially last one year and is followed by an additional probationary period prior to access to sensitive areas (Wonacott 2007). Follow-on reviews take place every two years, with more frequent spot checks as necessary (Luongo and Salik 2007). Individuals with sensitive information might still be subject to screening after retirement, an important measure, as Majeed and Mahmood's conspiracy suggests. Finally, the Strategic Plans Division collaborates with the Inter-Services Intelligence Directorate to identify new potential threats, in addition to ISI's role in the initial and follow-on screening of employees (Lavoy 2008: 152).

Is such a screening program sufficient? Robert Gates pointedly told David Sanger of the New York Times that "there is no human vetting system that is entirely reliable," noting the U.S. intelligence community's failure to identify spies in its ranks using techniques very similar to Pakistan's program (Sanger 2009). The concerns over the Pakistani program, then, are threefold: whether it is sufficiently scoped to cover all individuals with access to dangerous materials, whether it is thoroughly executed in practice, and whether the general threat environment is so severe as to swamp even a well-designed program. Note that expanding the scope to cover more individuals involves opportunity costs: the Pakistani state faces resource constraints, and it seems at least plausible that the screening program would be diluted as the number of individuals it covers increases. This is a challenge if the Pakistani scientific effort expands, but also a cautionary fact to consider when attempting to prevent outsider threats through increased security manpower.

With regard to the severity of the threat—the willingness and capability of individuals to attempt to penetrate the Pakistani nuclear program—there is ground for concern. American officials periodically report of "steadfast efforts of different extremist groups to infiltrate the labs and put sleepers" in them, though almost invariably such fears are expressed anonymously (Sanger 2009). Moreover, there are signs that militants and radicals have occasionally made it into the ranks of the Pakistani security forces, including into sensitive positions. Pakistan military personnel appear to have been involved in two different assassination attempts against Musharraf in 2003 and 2006 (Clary 2010: 24). The Hizb ut-Tahrir, a secretive Islamist organization, has been implicated in three separate episodes of attempting to infiltrate the Pakistan armed forces, including a 2003 episode when it successfully recruited thirteen Special Services Group (SSG) commandos and a 2012 episode that resulted in the court-martial of a serving brigadier general (Asad 2012). Outside of the military, the Punjab police infamously not only employed Mumtaz Qadri, who killed Punjab governor Salman Taseer over Taseer's position on Pakistan's blasphemy laws, but also assigned Qadri to a sensitive position as Taseer's bodyguard. Qadri was able to join the elite force guards despite stated concerns by other police officials that his religious zealotry might make him unfit for such positions, and it is still unclear why these warnings were not heeded within the Punjab police (CNN 2011).

In most of these instances, the individuals in question were not in a unit subject to additional screening (with Qadri and the SSG commandos perhaps being exceptions). But it should certainly indicate that the concern about radicals in the military undertaking violence injurious to Pakistan's interests is not theoretical. Are the screening programs able to prevent such individuals from entering the nuclear program in the future? If they are not, are other protective measures sufficient to minimize the harm they can do?

Command and Control and Outsider Threats

The years after the 1998 nuclear tests saw a dramatic worsening in the threat environment within Pakistan. After experiencing virtually no suicide terrorism in the late 1990s, Pakistan suffered nearly eighty suicide terrorist attacks in 2009, according to the Chicago Project on Security and Terrorism. Using a more expansive metric, the U.S. National Counterterrorism Center World Incident Tracking System recorded approximately 150 incidents in Pakistan in 2004 and over 1,750 incidents in 2009. In both databases, 2009 was the worst year for terrorist violence in Pakistan, which has since improved considerably with regard to suicide terror and less markedly for terrorist attacks overall.

With so many attacks, it should be no surprise that many of them tar-geted military installations and that some of them struck military installa-tions suspected of housing nuclear weapons (Gregory 2009). The exact location of Pakistan's nuclear weapons are a secret, and understandably so: as Jordan Seng (1997: 83) noted, secrecy is helpful against both counter-force strikes and outsider threats to the arsenal, "Just as it is hard to hit what cannot be seen, it is hard to steal what cannot be found." Whether or not nuclear weapons were at a facility attacked by militants, one hopes the Pakistani state would deny that they were ever at risk. In any event, it is possible that Pakistani spokesmen are being truthful when they say that no attack has occurred proximate to Pakistan's nuclear weapons.

Even so, militants' ability to target sensitive installations—even if they do not necessarily house nuclear weapons—should be acutely worrisome, both to Pakistanis and to outsiders. Such attacks provide some indication of the threat environment and of the Pakistani state's ability to defend against it (although Pakistani authorities might assign more resources to defending nuclear weapons than they do other sensitive installations). Since 2009, three attacks stand out for their audacity and success in targeting military facilities.

- On October 10, 2009, ten gunmen, wearing military uniforms, attacked the Pakistan army's general headquarters (GHQ) in Rawal-pindi. They attacked and overran the initial checkpoint. Once inside, the militants were able to take hostages and operate for approximately twenty hours before Pakistani commandos killed or captured all of the known militants (Goodspeed 2011). The attackers killed nine Pakistan military personnel, in addition to two civilians.
- On May 22, 2011, fifteen attackers breached the perimeter of the Meh-ran naval base at a location not covered by security cameras, suggest-ing insider knowledge. They attacked and damaged and destroyed aircraft worth millions of dollars, killed several naval personnel, and engaged in a fierce gun battle with commandos attempting to reclaim the base. The operation was declared complete approximately sixteen hours after the militants entered the base. All the attackers were killed, as were eighteen Pakistan military personnel (Haider 2011).
- On August 16, 2012, nine attackers, again in military uniforms, were detected crossing the perimeter into the Minhas air base at the Kamra air complex. This 5-hour attack was less successful than those before,

only damaging one aircraft, killing two airmen, and resulting in the deaths of all nine attackers (*Dawn* 2012; *News International* 2012). The attack received considerable attention, however, as did bombings against or near the Kamra complex in 2007 and 2009, because some outside analysts associate the Kamra complex with the Pakistani nuclear weapons complex. It is unclear whether the complex houses nuclear weapons or sensitive materials during peacetime (Hodge 2012).

Putting these attacks in perspective, Salik and Luongo (2013) note that British and U.S. forces were unable to protect Camp Bastion, in Afghanistan's Helmand Province, when it was attacked by the Afghan Taliban in September 2012. The intruders breached security, killed two U.S. Marines, destroyed six Harrier II aircraft, and damaged two more Harriers. Salik and Luongo's point is that attacks on air bases should not be an indicator of poor nuclear security, and that is true. Where the comparison ceases to be instructive is that neither the United States nor any other nuclear power to date has based nuclear weapons in active war zones.

What if intruders—with luck or inside knowledge—manage to attack a facility where Pakistan does store nuclear weapons or their components? There are still several more safeguards to overcome that might not be present at a conventional installation like Mehran, Kamra, or the Army GHQ. First, there are reasons to suspect that intruders would confront security personnel that are both quantitatively more numerous and qualitatively better trained than the perimeter security at a Pakistani military installation. Rather than having to defend the vast expanses of an airfield, these forces would have a smaller area to protect.[2]

Salik and Luongo report that SPD's security division, currently manned at 20,000 personnel, is projected to reach 28,000 in coming years (2013: n.p.). While they admit that initially the force "comprised mostly retired military personnel," it has now set up a training academy to provide "specially selected Pakistani recruits with training similar to that given to the special forces. These recruits have become the backbone of the nuclear security force and gradually will replace most of the retired military personnel" (Salik and Luongo 2013: n.p.).[3] They further report that the security division regularly engages in field exercises and war games to test its capabilities. SPD has also created, in Salik and Luongo's words, "an elite response force" to deal with any emergency at a nuclear installation. As of

June 2013, that force had reached 1,000 personnel total (Inter-Services Public Relations 2013).

Additionally, these forces are likely protecting facilities that are themselves hardened (Khan 2012: 344). Breaching the facilities would prove challenging, particularly in the context of simultaneously defeating security personnel. If the intruders managed to reach a Pakistani nuclear device, reasons for comfort diminish rapidly, but are not yet extinguished. Intruders are faced with a choice: destroy the device on-site or attempt to remove it. If they were to attempt to detonate the device on-site, they would face a series of obstacles. If weapons are stored partially disassembled they would have to try to assemble them, something that would likely prove beyond their technical capability. If weapons are stored separately from triggers, then the intruders would be forced to "knock over two buildings to get a complete bomb," in Harvard expert Matthew Bunn's phrase (quoted in Warrick 2007). If weapons are stored intact, they would still have to defeat whatever locks or permissive action links exist.

In such a situation, intruders might attempt to use conventional explosives to generate a partial yield instead of relying on the devices' own triggers and explosives. In all likelihood, this would do little more than distribute the radioactive fissile core of the device. Samar Mubarakmand, in his 2004 interview with Geo TV, made just this claim, saying that a suicide bomber attempting to detonate the weapon along with himself would "only break the nuclear weapon by hitting it but it will not detonate" (Mubarakmand 2004).

But if the device is not "one point safe"—defined in the U.S. system as when when a weapon's high explosive is detonated at any one point, the probability of producing a nuclear yield exceeding four pounds TNT equivalent is less than one in a million (Assistant Secretary of Defense for Nuclear, Chemical, and Biological Defense Programs 2011)—there is a chance it might produce a yield event. The degree of that risk is almost unknowable without knowledge of the precise designs of Pakistani warheads. U.S. weapon designs incorporate a series of technical innovations and design elements that collectively make accidental yield unlikely (ibid.). It is simply impossible to tell whether Pakistani weapons include such measures as strong link/weak link features, "insensitive" high explosive that is less susceptible to detonation from shock or heat, or fire-resistant pits. What is clear is that the United States conducted extensive testing to ensure that its warheads were one point safe. Pakistan has not had this luxury, because of both limits on its fissile material production and the emergent norm against nuclear weapons testing.

It is also true that the Pakistani arsenal is believed still to contain highly enriched uranium (HEU) weapons, which are thought to be easier to detonate than their plutonium or composite core counterparts. Moreover, the highly enriched uranium itself is dangerous in ways that plutonium is not, since sufficient highly enriched uranium can be used to generate an improvised nuclear explosive device without much technical capability. Recall that the "Little Boy" gun barrel design bomb employed on Hiroshima was not tested prior to its use, in part because its designers were so confident that it would work that they believed testing was unnecessary. The Alamogordo "Trinity" test was for the more difficult plutonium implosion design.

Nobel laureate and physicist Luis Alverez wrote in his 1989 memoir, "With modern weapons-grade uranium, the background neutron rate is so low that terrorists, if they have such material, would have a good chance of setting off a high yield explosion simply by dropping one half of the material onto the other half. Most people seem unaware that if separated HEU is at hand it's a trivial job to set off a nuclear explosion . . . even a high school kid could make a bomb in short order" (quoted in Ferguson and Potter 2005: 133). This would require more material than is likely contained in one warhead—Frank von Hippel has estimated on the order of forty-five kilograms of uranium might be necessary—but if militants captured a few warheads, they might obtain sufficient material to generate yields on the order of kilotons (quoted in Wald 2002). This scenario receives too little attention in Pakistani refutations of the risks posed by their arsenal, but is perhaps the most likely path to a dangerous weapon if it is in fact true that Pakistan's permissive action links will not permit unauthorized detonation of an intact warhead. This scenario also suggests why storing warheads intact might not necessarily increase nuclear risk. As Paul Kerr and Mary Beth Nikitin (2013: 15) astutely note, "although separate storage may provide a layer of protection against accidental launch or prevent theft of an assembled weapon, it may be easier for unauthorized people to remove a weapon's fissile material core if it is not assembled."

Whatever the intruders attempted on-site, they would have substantial but not unlimited time. The Army GHQ attack lasted approximately twenty hours, the Mehran attack lasted fifteen, and the Kamra attack lasted five hours. (The Camp Bastion attack lasted four hours [Smith, Smith, and Ripley 2012].) Given the technical obstacles to detonating a device on-site, intruders might decide to remove one or more nuclear devices. The difficulties of removal are also substantial. First, the warheads are likely to be heavy when intact. The design the A. Q. Khan network provided Libya was for a warhead weighing 450 kilograms. Even if Pakistani designers have been able to half that weight in the subsequent decade, the device would easily weigh more than could be carried (Khan 2012: 439 n. 79). They would need to be loaded onto vehicles. The intruders would then have to fight their way off the base in these vehicles. If they were able to remove the fissile cores absent surrounding high explosives and other material, these would be much lighter and might be movable on foot. To date, intruders have not been able to escape en masse following the raids against high profile Pakistani military targets.

If the weapons are removed from the base, the risk escalates. Pakistani forces may still be able to locate and recover the device before it could be detonated or taken outside of Pakistan. Even with substantial time, the militants might not be able to find a way to detonate the device in such a manner that it generates substantial yield. The permissive action links could be design-embedded, essentially rendering the device unusable without a code. In such a circumstance, the fissile material core would still be dangerous. If the intruders were able to separate the material, particularly if the weapon were built around a highly enriched uranium core, they would have the ability to reconstitute a nuclear weapon, even if the warhead they acquired was rendered unusable by safety mechanisms.

Command and Control and Battlefield Nuclear Weapons

The most significant Pakistani technological and doctrinal development in the last decade has been the apparent decision to develop a battlefield nuclear capability. This decision is evident in the development of new launch vehicles, the overall expansion of Pakistani fissile material production, and public statements Pakistani military personnel make about employment of the nuclear force, where they have stopped discussing nuclear weapons as weapons of "last resort" only and began discussing roles for nuclear weapons as part of Pakistani efforts to maintain "full spectrum deterrence" (Clary 2013).

In peacetime, the decision to pursue battlefield nuclear weapons affects safety and security in two ways. First, warheads for battlefield use, capable of being delivered aboard the relatively small diameter and relatively short-range sixty-kilometer Hatf-IX missile, could well be lighter and more compact than warheads designed for the longer-range Ghauri or Shaheen missiles. The warhead design A. Q. Khan allegedly transferred to Libya weighed approximately 450 kilograms and had a diameter slightly under one meter (Khan 2012: 189). Open-source analysis by Indian researchers has concluded a warhead for the Hatf-IX Nasr might have a diameter no larger than 361 milimeters and mass no greater than 150 kilograms (Nagappa, Vishwanathan, and Malhotra 2013). This would make theft of an intact warhead de-mated from its delivery system marginally easier.

The pursuit of a battlefield nuclear capability also implies more fissile material converted into more warheads. Pakistan appears on track to reach two hundred to three hundred warheads by 2014, but given Pakistan's nuclear infrastructure it is conceivable that it could acquire fissile material for three hundred to six hundred warheads in that time frame, if it were able to overcome the bottlenecks and operational friction that would be associated with such a rapid increase in its arsenal (Clary 2013; Patton 2012). As stated at the outset of this chapter, all things being equal, more warheads are more dangerous than fewer warheads, though such risk does not increase in a strictly linear fashion. In peacetime, many warheads are likely stored together and even when dispersed in crisis and war, they are likely dispersed in missile batteries. According to publicly available images, each Nasr transporter-erector-launcher vehicle can hold two to four missiles, and it seems plausible that multiple vehicles would deploy together in wartime. Security personnel would have relatively fewer sites to protect than looking at just warhead numbers alone would indicate.

The security of nuclear weapons in the field is not necessarily worse than nuclear weapons in peacetime. The threat from outsiders might drop. Attacking the Pakistani state might be a lower priority in the midst of a serious external crisis. For instance, Baitullah Mehsud offered a ceasefire in his war against the Pakistani state in November 2008 to allow Pakistan to focus on the eastern front after the Mumbai attacks prompted fears of an India-Pakistan war. Additionally, while fixed sites likely have better static defenses than mobile, deployed nuclear units, precisely because the sites are fixed, outsiders can plan extensively to defeat these defenses. Mobile units in the field, especially for the short time frames associated with Indo-Pakistani wars, might be even more difficult for outsiders to locate than static targets shrouded in secrecy.

Pakistan's recent interest in battlefield nuclear weapons is not necessarily associated with renewed interest in decentralized command and control. Early analysis indicated such decentralization was probable given Pakistan's technological capabilities and deterrence challenges (Hoyt 2001), but the balance of public and private statements by current and recent SPD officials appears to suggest centralization of control throughout the spectrum of conflict, a development enabled by the creation of technology akin to permissive action links (Khan 2012).

Despite their pronouncements to date, it is still possible that in deep crisis or full-scale war, Pakistani leaders might decide to pre-delegate launch decisions to missile battery commanders in the midst of major conventional military setbacks and disruption to command and control networks. Such pre-delegation would necessitate that many more individuals have the capacity to arm and detonate a nuclear warhead. It would still be difficult for these individuals to steal a device. They would be operating in the midst of security personnel and likely part of a missile battery staffed by individuals screened for their reliability. It also seems likely that even with pre-delegation, "two-man rules" for arming and use would apply. Pre-delegation dramatically increases the odds that nuclear weapons would be used against Indian forces in the context of full-scale war. The whole point of such a posture is to make full-scale war very risky for India. It is worth reemphasizing, though, that Pakistan's decision to pursue battlefield nuclear weapons may only marginally increase the risk to the arsenal during peacetime and even crisis. Only during severe crises or wars would pre-delegation increase nuclear risks dramatically.

Nuclear Risk After 2014

This chapter has reviewed the sources of nuclear risk associated with Pakistan's nuclear arsenal. These safety and security risks are small, but non-zero. A violent nonstate actor seeking to acquire or detonate a Pakistani nuclear weapon would have tremendous challenges. Pakistan has taken nearly all of the steps that one would ask a responsible nuclear weapons state to take, in fact having taken perhaps more steps than India next door (Nuclear Threat Initiative 2014). The root of the problem is that Pakistan's internal environment is more dangerous than any other nuclear weapons state, past or present. Additionally, Pakistan's has expanded its arsenal and appears to have increased peacetime nuclear readiness so that it can more credibly generate risk in any potential crisis with India. These steps, taken to deter Indian adventurism, inadvertently generate risks outside of the India-Pakistan dyad. The past fifteen years of nuclear developments in South Asia contain ample reason to fear the coming fifteen years. As policy makers extrapolate from the present, three questions have both uncertain and consequential answers relevant for future nuclear risk.

After 2014, will Pakistan's internal threat environment worsen or improve? For the last thirty years, it has been a safe bet to project that Pakistani society would become more violent and more extreme. Tankel's chapter in this volume provides evidence for worry going forward. The arguments for hope are not inspiring, but center around Pakistan being more able to divert violence from its soil in the years ahead, as the salient violence for assessing nuclear risk is that directed at the Pakistani state. It is at least possible that Pakistan could be home to many violent groups operating in Afghanistan and many violent groups targeting Shia at home, but have less violence directed at the state, and hence less threat to the nuclear arsenal. The U.S. presence in Afghanistan provided an easy recruiting message for extremists while simultaneously pushing some violent actors onto the Pakistani side of the Durand Line where they were at diminished risk from coalition forces. Consistent with some of the arguments made by Paul Staniland in this volume, the reduction of that presence will moderately decrease the salience of the Afghan fight for potential extremists while also permitting them to operate with greater impunity from Afghan soil. As it did in the 1980s and 1990s, Pakistan *might* be successful in directing its most extreme individuals against external targets. This would no doubt be a tragedy for Afghanistan, but might somewhat diminish the threat to the Pakistani nuclear arsenal. Additionally, since the Pakistan government would not be directly helping the United States in the Afghan effort, the justification for attacks against Pakistani soldiers and civilians might also diminish, even though many radicals will not be satisfied until Pakistan is a fully Islamist state. It seems unlikely that Pakistan will directly confront radicals of all stripes, so all the optimists can argue is that Pakistani triage and diversion efforts will be effective. The pessimists, for their part, scowl and argue that such compartmentalization of radicalism will fail and that threats to the Pakistani state will increase alongside threats to Pakistan's neighbors. If they are correct, Pakistan will have to remain extremely good at protecting its most dangerous weapons from growing internal dangers.

Will the Pakistani arsenal continue to expand after 2014? The number of weapons Pakistan has to protect could also vary widely in the coming years. The future size of the arsenal depends on the outcomes of ongoing budgetary and political debates in Islamabad and Rawalpindi. Pakistani political and military leaders will have to ask whether an ever-growing nuclear arsenal is the correct use for scarce national resources. With even one hundred weapons, Pakistan can employ its nuclear forces in a mix of battlefield and strategic roles, and Pakistan could build multiples of that number in the coming decade. But nuclear weapons expansion is not cost free. It means fewer conventional "guns" for the military and less "butter" for the nation. Nuclear infrastructure has had priority so far, and while there is no longer a compelling deterrence argument for the open-ended expansion of the arsenal, nuclear powers have historically been creative in finding compelling bureaucratic and organizational logics for larger arsenals. Pakistan may have difficulty saying "enough is enough."

Politically, an improved relationship with India would diminish the rationale for an expanded arsenal. The last two civilian governments in Islamabad have shown little interest in the rivalry with India, and the salience of Kashmir in the daily lives of Pakistanis has dropped considerably in the past ten years. As C. Christine Fair reviews in Chapter 5, Pakistan's civil-military dynamics are still uncertain, but if civilian ascendance solidifies, Pakistan's relationship with India may come to reflect the flexible views of its recent civilian leaders, rather than the skepticism of Pakistan army leaders. The requirements for nuclear deterrence would relax as India-Pakistan animus fades.

Will Pakistan continue to find patrons? As Aparna Pande details in this volume, Pakistan has depended on the United States, China, and Saudi Arabia for support since independence. These states have directly and indirectly subsidized Pakistan's conventional military and strategic programs. U.S. support has been erratic; when it found Pakistani behavior incompatible with American interests it has withdrawn support, when it believed Pakistani assistance was necessary for U.S. ends, Washington has been profligate. Each patron has brought different resources to its relationship with Pakistan, but if one patron restrained its support the others could imperfectly substitute for the loss through increased aid. The question for the coming decade is whether these patrons will on net decrease their assistance to Pakistan. If so, this would exacerbate the "guns versus butter" debate highlighted above, forcing strategic soul-searching about the best deterrent mix for Pakistan. The most dangerous scenario for Islamabad is the simultaneous loss of U.S. and Chinese support, perhaps brought about by present trends combined with greater extremism from Pakistan to China's restive western provinces.

An isolated Pakistan could well spiral downward. Pakistan as an incubator for instability would provide the rationale for its isolation, and the loss of external support would decrease state capacity to confront that instability. But it is also true that an isolated Pakistan might force Pakistani elites to pay more fully for their strategic choices. Presented the bill for extremism at home and rivalry with India, Pakistani elites might opt for a different path. The last time Pakistan's strategic choices led to disaster—in 1971—Pakistani leaders entered into a twenty-year period where rivalry with India was placed on the back burner.

If the U.S. relationship with Pakistan significantly worsens, one cause might be global U.S. retrenchment. In that context, the Saudi-Pakistani relationship may strengthen as Saudi Arabia looks for security guarantors and Pakistan looks for resources. If Iran nuclearizes *and* Saudi Arabia determines Western defense commitments are insufficient or incredible *and* if Pakistan determines Saudi aid can compensate for international opprobrium, then Saudi Arabia and Pakistan *might* consider a nuclear bargain. This scenario is not likely, but is more likely under the narrow scenario of U.S. abandonment of Riyadh and Islamabad (Urban 2013; Kahl, Dalton, and Irvine 2013; Clary and Karlin 2012). The complicated deterrence calculations and custody arrangements likely to accompany any Saudi-Pakistan nuclear bargain mean such a scenario would enhance nuclear risk globally.

If violence against the state plateaus or diminishes and if the nuclear expansion is arrested, then Pakistan's nuclear risk will remain manageable. If instability worsens at the same time as unending growth in Pakistan's arsenal, then the risks may be difficult to contain—even in the face of determined and professional efforts by Pakistan's nuclear stewards. If Pakistan becomes more internationally isolated, it is difficult to predict whether Islamabad will make more cautious or riskier choices. To date, nuclear fears about Pakistan have been overblown. The optimists have had the stronger case based on the evidence so far. The pessimists, sadly, may not be wrong about the future.

Notes

1. Feroz Hassan Khan speculated that the arsenal might be as large as 80 to 120 warheads in 2007, implying today's arsenal could be as large as Riedel's 2013 estimate (Khan quoted in Ricks 2007).

2. Even in the event of some sort of exercise involving aircraft and nuclear weapons, it is reasonable to assume that Pakistani standard operating procedures might involve cordoning a portion of the base for additional security.

3. It should be stressed that it appears only a portion of the security division receives heightened training. After all, Pakistan's actual Special Services Group likely does not contain more than six thousand personnel.

Works Cited

Albright, David, and Holly Higgins. 2003. "A Bomb for the Ummah." *Bulletin of the Atomic Scientists*, March–April, 49–55.

Armitage, Richard, 2007. Interview by Charlie Rose. *Charlie Rose*, PBS, November 6.

Asad, Malik. 2012. "Hizbut Tahrir Made Three Attempts to Penetrate Army." *Dawn*, October 29.

Assistant Secretary of Defense for Nuclear, Chemical, and Biological Defense Programs. 2011. *The Nuclear Matters Handbook*. Expanded ed. Washington, D.C.: Department of Defense.

Bunn, Matthew, Eben Harrell, and Martin Malin. 2012. *Progress on Securing Nuclear Weapons and Materials: The Four-Year Effort and Beyond*. Cambridge, Mass.: Harvard Project on Managing the Atom.

Caldwell, Dan, and Peter D. Zimmerman. 1989. "Reducing the Risk of Nuclear War with Permissive Action Links." In *Technology and the Limitation of International Conflict*, ed. Barry M. Blechman, 151–175. Baltimore: Johns Hopkins Foreign Policy Institute.

Clary, Christopher. 2010. *Thinking About Pakistan's Nuclear Security in Peacetime, Crisis, and War*. Occasional Paper no. 12. New Delhi: Institute for Defense Studies and Analyses.

———. 2013. "The Future of Pakistan's Nuclear Weapons Program." In *Strategic Asia, 2013–2014: Asia in the Second Nuclear Age*, ed. Ashley J. Tellis, Abraham Denmark, and Travis Tanner, 131–160. Seattle: National Bureau of Asian Research.

Clary, Christopher, and Mara E. Karlin. 2012. "The Pak-Saudi Nuke, and How to Stop It." *American Interest*, July–August, 24–31.

CNN. 2011. "Official: Warning Signs Missed Ahead of Governor's Assassination." January 6. http://www.cnn.com/2011/WORLD/asiapcf/01/05/pakistan.governor.killed/index.html.

Corera, Gordon. 2006. *Shopping for Bombs: Nuclear Proliferation, Global Insecurity, and the Rise and Fall of the A. Q. Khan Network*. New York: Oxford University Press.

Cotta-Ramusino, Paolo, and Maurizio Martellini. 2002. *Nuclear Safety, Nuclear Stability and Nuclear Strategy in Pakistan: A Concise Report of a Visit by the Landau Network–Centro Volta*. Como, Italy: Landau Network–Centro Volta. http://www.centrovolta.it/landau/content/binary/pakistan%20January%202002.pdf.

Cotter, Donald R. 1987. "Peacetime Operations: Safety and Security." In *Managing Nuclear Operations*, ed. Ashton B. Carter, John D. Steinbruner, and Charles A. Zraket, 17–74. Washington, D.C.: Brookings Institution.

Dawn. 2012. "Taliban Claim Attack on Minhas Base; Nine Militants Killed." August 16. http://beta.dawn.com/news/742608/militants-attack-pakistani-airbase-at-kamra.

Ferguson, Charles D., and William C. Potter. 2005. *The Four Faces of Nuclear Terrorism*. New York: Routledge.

FoxNews.com. 2011. "A. Q. Khan's Thirteen-Page Confession." September 15. www.foxnews.com/world/2011/09/15/aq-khans-thirteen-page-confession/print.

Frantz, Douglas, James Risen, and David E. Sanger. 2001. "Nuclear Experts in Pakistan May Have Links to Al Qaeda." *New York Times*, December 9.

Frantz, Douglas, and David Rohde. 2001. "A Nation Challenged: Biological Terror; 2 Pakistanis Linked to Papers on Anthrax Weapons." *New York Times*, November 28.

Ganguly, Sumit. 2013. "Diverging Nuclear Pathways in South Asia." *Nonproliferation Review* 20 (2): 381–387.

Goodspeed, Peter. 2011. "Pakistan's Nuclear Arsenal May Be 'Compromised': Report." *National Post* (Canada), June 14.

Gregory, Shaun. 2009. "The Terrorist Threat to Pakistan's Nuclear Weapons." *Counter Terrorism Center Sentinel* 2 (7).

Haider, Sajjad. 2011. "Timeline of Events—PNS Mehran Siege." Dawn.com, May 23. http://www.dawn.com/2011/05/23/pns-mehran-siege-timeline.html.

Hodge, Amanda. 2012. "Raid Exposes Fresh Security Fears." *Australian*, August 17.

Hoyt, Timothy D. 2001. "Pakistani Nuclear Doctrine and the Dangers of Strategic Myopia." *Asian Survey* 41 (6): 956–977.

Inter-Services Public Relations. 2013. Pakistan Joint Staff Headquarters. Press release no. PR99/2013-ISPR, June 10. http://ispr.gov.pk/front/main.asp?o = t-press_release&id = 2325.

Kahl, Colin H., Melissa G. Dalton, and Matthew Irvine. 2013. *Atomic Kingdom: If Iran Builds the Bomb, Will Saudi Arabia Be Next?* Washington, D.C.: Center for a New American Security.

Kerr, Paul K., and Mary Beth Nikitin. 2013. *Pakistan's Nuclear Weapons: Proliferation and Security Issues*. CRS Report RL34248, March 19. Washington, D.C.: Congressional Research Service. Khan, Feroz Hassan. 2009. "Nuclear Security in Pakistan: Separating Myth from Reality." *Arms Control Today*, July–August.

———. 2012. *Eating Grass: The Making of the Pakistani Bomb*. Stanford, Calif.: Stanford University Press.

Kristensen, Hans M., and Robert S. Norris. 2011. "Pakistan's Nuclear Forces, 2011." *Bulletin of the Atomic Scientists* 67 (4): 91–99.

Kroenig, Matthew. 2009. "Exporting the Bomb: Why States Provide Sensitive Nuclear Assistance." *American Political Science Review* 103 (1): 113–133.

———. 2010. *Exporting the Bomb: Technology Transfer and the Spread of Nuclear Weapons.* Ithaca, N.Y.: Cornell University Press.

Kyodo News. 2006. "Pakistan Sets Up Tri-Command Nuclear Force: Officials." *Yahoo! News Asia*, August 9. http://asia.news.yahoo.com/060809/kyodo/d8jcsvcg0.html.

Langewiesche, William. 2008. *The Atomic Bazaar: Dispatches from the Underground World of Nuclear Trafficking.* New York: Farrar, Straus and Giroux.

Lavoy, Peter R. 2008. "Islamabad's Nuclear Posture: Its Premises and Implementation." In *Pakistan's Nuclear Future: Worries Beyond War*, ed. Henry Sokolski, 129–165. Carlisle, Pa.: Strategic Studies Institute, U.S. Army War College.

Lewis, Jeffrey. 2010. "Managing the Danger from Pakistan's Nuclear Stockpile." *National Security Studies Program Policy Paper.* Washington, D.C.: New America Foundation.

Luongo, Kenneth N., and Naeem Salik. 2007. "Building Confidence in Pakistan's Nuclear Security." *Arms Control Today*, December.

Martellini, Maurizio. 2008. "Security and Safety Issues About the Nuclear Complex: Pakistan's Standpoints." Report of visit to Islamabad by Landau Network–Centro Volta (LNCV) mission, February 9–13.

Mian, Zia, A. H. Nayyar, and R. Rajaraman. 2009. "Exploring Uranium Resource Constraints on Fissile Material Production in Pakistan." *Science and Global Security* 17 (2–3): 77–108.

Moreau, Ron. 2008. "Pakistan's Nukes." *Newsweek*, January 25.

Mubarakmand, Samar. 2004. Interview with Hamid Mir. Geo TV, "Capital Talk Special," March 5. http://www.pakdef.info/forum/showthread.php?9214-Dr.-Samar-Mubarakmand-s-Interview-with-Geo-TV.

Mullen, Michael. 2009. "Defense Department Briefing Transcript." *Federal News Service*, May 4.

Nagappa, Rajaram, Arun Vishwanathan, and Aditi Malhotra. 2013. *Hatf-IX/Nasr—Pakistan's Tactical Nuclear Weapon: Implications for Indo-Pak Deterrence.* Bangalore: National Institute of Advanced Studies.

News International (Pakistan). 2012. "Kamra Assault: Death Toll Rises to 11." August 17. http://www.thenews.com.pk/article-63734-Kamra-assault:-Death-toll-rise-to-11--.

Nuclear Threat Initiative. 2014. *Nuclear Materials Security Index.* 2nd ed. http://ntiindex.org/wp-content/uploads/2014/01/2014-NTI-Index-Report1.pdf.

Patton, Tamara. 2012. "Combining Satellite Imagery and 3D Drawing Tools for Nonproliferation Analysis: A Case Study of Pakistan's Khushab Plutonium Production Reactors." *Science and Global Security* 20 (2–3): 117–140.

Pennington, Matthew. 2008. "Pakistan Says Its Nuclear Assets Are Safe from Militants." Associated Press, January 26.

Perkovich, George. 2012. "The Non-Unitary Model and Deterrence Stability in South Asia." Henry L. Stimson Center, Washington, D.C., November 13. http://www.stimson.org/images/uploads/research-pdfs/George_Perkovich_-_The_Non_Unitary_Model_and_Deterrence_Stability_in_South_Asia.pdf.

Press Trust of India. 2001. "Myanmar Gives Sanctuary to Pak Nuke Scientists." *Indian Express*, November 23.

Reddy, B. Muralidhar. 2003. "'No Chance for Accidental N-War with India.'" *Hindu*, January 11.

Ricks, Thomas. 2007. "Calculating the Risks in Pakistan." *Washington Post*, December 2.

Riedel, Bruce. 2013. "The United States, India, and Pakistan: To the Brink and Back." Presentation at the Brookings Institution, Washington, D.C., February 26. http://www.brookings.edu/~/media/events/2013/2/26%20india%20pakistan/20130226_india_pakistan_armageddon_transcript.pdf.

Sagan, Scott D. 1993. *The Limits of Safety: Organizations, Accidents, and Nuclear Weapons*. Princeton, N.J.: Princeton University Press.

———. 2004. "The Problem of Redundancy Problem: Why More Nuclear Security Forces May Produce Less Nuclear Security." *Risk Analysis* 24 (4): 935–946.

Salik, Naeem, and Kenneth N. Luongo. 2013. "Challenges for Pakistan's Nuclear Security." *Arms Control Today*, March.

Sanger, David E. 2009. "Obama's Worst Pakistan Nightmare." *New York Times*, January 11.

———. 2012. *Confront and Conceal: Obama's Secret Wars and Surprising Use of American Power*. New York: Random House.

Sanger, David E., and William Broad. 2007. "U.S. Secretly Aids Pakistan in Guarding Nuclear Arms." *New York Times*, November 18.

Sanger, David E., and Eric Schmitt. 2014. "Afghanistan Exit Is Seen as Peril to CIA Drone Mission." *New York Times*, January 26.

Seng, Jordan. "Less Is More: Command and Control Advantages of Minor Nuclear States." *Security Studies* 6 (4): 50–92.

Smith, Christina, Nicola Smith, and Tim Ripley. 2012. "Bastion Raid Signals Birth of Taliban SAS." *Sunday Times* (London), September 23.

Tenet, George. 2007. *At the Center of the Storm: My Years at the CIA*. New York: HarperCollins.

Tertrais, Bruno. 2012. *Pakistan's Nuclear Programme: A Net Assessment*. Paris: Fondation pour la Recherche Stratégique.

TV Myanmar. 2001. "Burma Dismisses Report Two Pakistani Nuclear Scientists Given Political Asylum." Telecast December 3. *BBC Monitoring*, December 4.

U.S. Department of Defense. 2001. *Proliferation: Threat and Response*. Washington, D.C.: Government Printing Office.

U.S. Department of State. 2012. "Insider Threat to Nuclear and Radiological Materials." Fact Sheet, Bureau of International Security and Nonproliferation. March 12. http://www.state.gov/t/isn/rls/fs/186682.htm.

Urban, Mark. 2013. "Saudi Nuclear Weapons 'On Order' from Pakistan." *BBC News*, November 6.

Wald, Matthew L. 2002. "A Nation Challenged: Nuclear Security; Suicidal Nuclear Threat Is Seen at Weapons Plants." *New York Times*, January 23.

Warrick, Joby. 2007. "Pakistan Nuclear Security Questioned." *Washington Post*, November 11.

Wonacott, Peter. 2007. "Inside Pakistan's Drive to Guard Its A-Bombs." *Wall Street Journal*, November 29.

PART II

Domestic Political
and Economic Issues

Chapter 5

Democracy on the Leash in Pakistan

C. Christine Fair

With the general elections of May 2013, Pakistan arrived at an unprecedented historical moment. On March 16, 2013, when the outgoing Thirteenth Parliament dissolved, it became the second parliament to complete its term since the restoration of democracy in 1988 and the third to do so in all of Pakistan's history. The Fifth Parliament (1972–1977) was the first to complete its term. The Twelfth Parliament (2002–2007), elected under General and President Pervez Musharraf's military government, became the second to do so. Apart from these three, *all* other parliaments were prorogued either through extraconstitutional means (for example, dissolved by a viceregal governor-general or by a military coup) or through the use of a constitutional amendment that permits the president to dismiss the prime minister.

Analysts feared that the political polarization of the country, massive electoral violence, the quixotic rise of a third party under Imran Khan (the famed former cricketer and lothario turned conservative politician), and voter disillusionment would result in low voter turnout and a hung parliament. Contrary to those dismal expectations, voter turnout was a robust 60 percent (Grare 2013). When the votes were tallied, the party of former prime minister Nawaz Sharif, the Pakistan Muslim League–N (PML-N), came out a clear winner. The PML-N secured 166 seats, a mere 6 seats shy of the 172 needed for a simple majority. Sharif was easily able to cobble together the remainder of needed votes from ally parties to form the government (*News International* 2013).

Sharif has taken the helm of a Pakistan saddled with a shambolic economy, plagued by energy shortages (see Khan in this volume), riven by massive internal insecurity challenges (see Tankel, Watson and Fair, and Clary in this volume), and burdened with the regional fallout of the American drawdown in Afghanistan. At the time of writing, the much-debated Bilateral Security Agreement (BSA) between the Americans and the Afghans has yet to be signed. Without this BSA, it is possible that the Americans will leave no troops in Afghanistan. Whatever happens in Afghanistan will have important impacts upon Pakistan's interests (see Gartenstein-Ross and Vassefi in this volume). Absent unforeseen events, Sharif is likely to be the prime minister of Pakistan when the last American soldier leaves Afghanistan.

Much is at stake in this transition. While Nawaz Sharif campaigned on the promise of sending the military back to its barracks and asserting greater control over foreign and security policies, the army is busily seeking to thwart those same goals. Democracy's gains will be the army's loss. In the past, the army has confidently seized the reins of power following domestic crises that the military itself helped to engineer (with the assistance of venal politicians more interested in regaining power than providing governance). Nawaz Sharif is no stranger to the tumults of civil-military relations. Sharif's first government fell in 1993 after protracted wrangling with the president. In 1999 after Sharif tried to dismiss General Pervez Musharraf from his position as army chief of staff, Musharraf removed Sharif from power in a coup. Sharif had vexed the men in khaki because he had dismissed the army chief Jehangir Karamat in 1998 and had pursued high-stakes diplomatic overtures toward India in 1998. Pakistanis generally prefer democracy to military rule, and while it still has cards to play, the army has lost some of its traditional tools of interference. Its ability to act per its own prerogative has been further constrained by the ongoing legal battles of former dictator Pervez Musharraf, who now faces a raft of treason charges. This essay seeks to evaluate the gains in democratization thus far and, at the same time, examine the scope and means for military intervention.

The remainder of this chapter is organized as follows. In the first section below, I discuss the army's past, present, and future options for controlling the government, whether indirectly or perhaps, in the future, directly. Second, I review the rise of Pakistan's judiciary and what this means for democratization and the rule of law in Pakistan. Third, I evaluate the important gains in democratization since 2008. Fourth, I identify some of the key governance challenges Sharif is likely to face. Fifth, I review the various unprecedented legal cases confronting Musharraf and their import for civilian-military relations in Pakistan. I conclude this chapter with a discussion of the possible futures of Pakistan's civil-military relations and of the consequences for Pakistan and beyond.

The Army's Well-Worn Book of Ruses

While much is at stake for Pakistan's nascent democracy, the army also has a great deal at risk: namely, its ability to run roughshod over a country that it has ruled, directly or indirectly, for most of that country's existence. The army has long promoted itself as the only institution able to protect Pakistan from domestic and foreign foes. In its attempts to prove its own efficacy, it has exploited interparty rivalries to sow discord and maximize political incompetence: the worse the politicians appear, the nobler and more competent the army seems in contrast. The army has used its privileged place in Pakistani society to demand a lion's share of the budget and to pursue risky policies toward Afghanistan and in India. The army has also attracted international opprobrium for its history of sponsoring nuclear proliferation through the "procurement networks" of A. Q. Khan, among others (see Clary in this volume). Analysts suspected that the army's preferred outcome of the election May 11, 2013, was a weak government composed of a fissiparous coalition that would be unable to resist the army's powers of persuasion and coercion (Fair 2013b).

While much public trust in the army has been restored, it has faced numerous challenges to its public standing since Musharraf's 2001 decision to cooperate with the Americans in Afghanistan. Pakistanis were vexed that their prized army appeared little more than an American "rental," engaging in operations against valued allies and even Pakistanis. Pakistanis were particularly disconcerted by the bin Laden raid, in which the Americans entered Pakistani airspace by helicopter, engaged in an hour-long operation at the bin Laden compound, refueled the helicopters on Pakistani territory, and exfiltrated into Afghanistan before Pakistan's air force even understood that the breach had taken place (Sanger 2012). Pakistanis were less agonized by the fact that the world's most notorious terrorist had found sanctuary in their country than they were by the prospect that the United States,

India, or even Israel could conduct such an attack on Pakistan's prized nuclear weapons (Associated Press 2011). Unfortunately, the parliament ultimately rallied around the military, reserving most of its vituperations for the United States and its policies. The subsequent investigation of the "Bin Laden Affair" focused on American attacks upon Pakistan's sovereignty rather than on identifying those persons and organizations within the government that aided and abetted bin Laden (Al Jazeera 2011). The army was able to cultivate support from the parliament and baffled citizenry alike by bemoaning America's technological advantage and painting the military as a victim, while at the same time assuring Pakistanis that India could never carry out such an operation (Perlez 2011).

Parliament's role in examining the bin Laden affair and the broader inquiry into U.S.-Pakistan relations demonstrates that civilians walk a fine line with the military establishment. Parliament asserted itself, but not to the point that it has seriously undermined the governing role of the army in these policies. Nonetheless, the Pakistani electorate has become more accustomed to seeing the army's authority publicly questioned and now expects politicians to be active in crafting security policy. More generally, while the army shoulders most of the blame for the decrepit state of Pakistan's democracy, it is also true that the army has never come to power alone. During periods of direct military rule, the army engages in what Anil Kalhan calls "transformative preservation, by which he means undertaking "legal, political, and institutional transformations with the effect of preserving and extending its dominance into periods of civilian rule" (Kalhan 2013: 15). In doing so, the army has consistently followed a well-established pattern of undertaking sweeping constitutional reforms to strengthen its "viceregal aspects," most notably to preserve "its primacy over defense and foreign policy," among other areas (Kalhan 2013: 15). This army-orchestrated constitutional transformation depends on civilian institutions, including the judiciary as well as mainstream political party representatives and party workers. Over time, this set of practices has allowed the military to entrench itself so deeply in Pakistan's social, economic, and political structure that it has been virtually impossible to pry out.

One of the first steps that the army takes to prepare for a coup is to declare some sort of existential threat to the state that "justifies" suspending the constitution and ousting a democratically elected government. It is a notable—if lamentable—fact that when the generals seize power, they usually do so with the support of the people. To secure that enthusiasm, the army usually drums up a political crisis in advance to make its interventions seem legitimate. The army chief then hoists up a provisional constitution order (PCO) to supplant the constitution and to buttress the army's power. Typically the army chief then anoints himself the head of government, suspends the constitution, and dismisses parliament. (These actions constitute high treason under the constitution [Fair 2013b; Kalhan 2013].)

The PCO then becomes the "extra-constitution" that supplants the actual constitution. To secure legal and institutional blessing for this measure, the military leader requires the justices of the Supreme Court to take an oath to the army chief-cum-chief executive and the PCO. Thus the army simultaneously reconstitutes the judiciary and constrains it (Kalhan 2013). Justices with integrity choose not to swear the oath and retire or are forced out, but the regime easily replaces them. This exercise is repeated on down the ranks of the judiciary (Kalhan 2013; Fair 2013b). The reconstituted, regime-friendly judiciary plays a critical role in validating the takeover under the "doctrine of necessity."[1]

In accordance with the army's view that the civilians are unfit to govern, the military must also manipulate the foundations of the political system. Pakistan's military leaders have rarely done so by banning political parties outright; complete suspension of politics is usually short-lived because the army chief cannot rule alone. Thus, he generally engineers elections to produce a parliament that will be amenable to his rule. He can do so either by holding elections on a nonparty basis or by reestablishing parties provided that the military can regulate who can contest elections and/or hold office. The latter requires the regime to create a "king's party," which is cobbled together by poaching willing politicians from existing parties. Pakistan's intelligence agencies also construct an "opposition of choice," featuring Pakistan's various Islamist parties (Fair 2013b). Eventually, the parliament is reconstituted via flawed elections in which the king's party prevails and the opposition of choice adopts the role of "loyal opposition."

The legislature next adopts the dictator's various extraconstitutional legal orders and renders them into law. Through this process of engaging a compromised legislature, the army preserves its supremacy, despite the ostensible return to civilian rule. Article 58(2)(b), the eighth amendment to Pakistan's 1973 constitution, which was passed in 1985, is the best example of this. This provision, initiated by Muhammad Zia-ul-Haq, permitted the president to unilaterally dismiss the government, and it required the appointment of a caretaker government, with appointments to the same deriving from consultations of the outgoing prime minister and opposition leader. This became codified in Pakistan's constitution when the Seventh National Assembly passed the Eighth Amendment in 1985. Between 1988, when democracy was restored following Zia's death, and 1996, the legislation was used to dismiss all four elected governments (Kalhan 2013). The army also used the mere threat of dissolving the government to manipulate politicians into endorsing its preferred policies.

Eventually, however, even the most beloved dictators wear out their welcome. When the army realizes (usually after a decade or so) that the people have turned against military rule, it finally relinquishes direct control. At this point, democracy will be reestablished but, due to the hiatus, the political parties will be rusty and less than competent. The politicians do not usually censure their colleagues who collaborated with the army. Similarly, the judiciary does not punish those justices who broke their oath to uphold the constitution. And, although treason is a capital crime under Pakistan's constitution, before Musharraf no general had ever been tried for it. Worse, because the politicians fear that their time in power will be short, they tend to focus not on governance but rather on looting what they can before they are forced to flee the country or tossed into jail. What's worse, whichever party lands in the opposition has often retarded the return to democracy by conniving with the army to bring about early elections. In the 1990s, governments were lucky if they lasted three years, with the prime ministership handed back and forth between the inefficacious and corrupt Benazir Bhutto and Nawaz Sharif. The army is pleased to oblige; the chaos gives weight to the idea that it is Pakistan's sole responsible player, trying to save the country while inept civilian dolts run it into the ground.

The last few steps of the civilian-military power cycle played out differently in 2013. Although no one was foolish enough to believe that Pakistan's democracy was strong, the army's space for chicanery did shrink. This was likely due to the simple fact that the public remained deeply opposed to military rule. According to a 16,000-person, nationally representative survey fielded by myself and several colleagues, nearly 50 percent of respondents said that it is "extremely important" to live in a country that is governed by elected representatives of the people while another 32 percent said it was "very important to do so." In that same survey 40 percent said that it was "extremely important" that the civilians exercise control over the military while another 30 percent said that it was "very important" (Fair et al. 2013).

Moreover, the military itself it still reeling from the negative effects of General Pervez Musharraf's nine years as ruler of Pakistan. Musharraf made the controversial decision to cooperate with the United States in the deeply detested war on terror. He also agreed to permit U.S. drones to operate in and from Pakistan, allegedly scaled back Pakistani support for militants in Kashmir, and launched a series of wildly unpopular military operations across Pakistan's border areas (in Baluchistan, the tribal areas, and Swat). In addition, the Supreme Court decried several sales of public enterprises to Musharraf's cronies at below-market prices as evidence of his corruption. All this diminished the public's support for the military, even though it still remains quite popular (Kalhan 2013).

Pakistan's Activist Judiciary: Securing or Undermining Rule of Law?

In recent years, Pakistan's Supreme Court, under the guidance of Chief Justice Iftikhar Muhammad Chaudhry, has garnered accolades for its "judicial independence." Unfortunately, it is far from clear that Pakistan's courts have advanced democracy or deepened a commitment to constitutionalism or even fundamental rights or rule of law (Kalhan 2013). Chaudhry became chief justice in 2005. Along with most other judges of this period, he took an extraconstitutional oath after Musharraf's 1999 coup, and he signed off on the court's judgments validating the coup. However, under his leadership, the court began distancing itself from the military regime by expanding public interest litigation via its expansive *suo moto* powers. The court antagonized the military by overturning the regime's privatization schemes and subjecting it to questioning about persons who were "disappeared" as part of Pakistan's counterterrorism efforts. Musharraf responded in March 2007 by suspending Chaudhry and referring him for disciplinary proceedings. Unfortunately for the regime, the cameras were rolling when the police abused Chaudhry. His plight galvanized the so-called "lawyers' movement," which made his reinstatement its primary goal. In July 2007, the Supreme Court dismissed Musharraf's charges and reinstated Chaudhry.

But this was not the end of the affair. Musharraf declared a state of emergency in November 2007—in many ways a coup against his own coup. He once again suspended the constitution, promulgated a PCO, and forced judges to take an oath to it. Musharraf designated Justice Abdul Hameed

Dogar as the new chief justice, and once again, the newly reconstituted Supreme Court validated the emergency and Musharraf's reelection as president. This was Musharraf's fatal overstep. At this point, the lawyers' movement was joined by civil society actors as well as by the mainstream political parties. While Musharraf was sworn in again as president on November 29, 2007, he promised that the emergency would end by mid-December and elections would be held soon thereafter.

Musharraf was fairly certain that his regime would survive the elections. His confidence stemmed from a deal that he had forged with the former prime minister Benazir Bhutto of the Pakistan Peoples Party (PPP). This deal was brokered by the United Kingdom and the United States and became law when Musharraf's government passed the National Reconciliation Ordinance (NRO) in October 2007. The NRO suspended all corruption charges against PPP politicians, allowing them to contest elections. (It did not extend amnesty to the PPP's main rival, the PML-N.) The logic of the NRO was simple: Bhutto's popularity at the ballot box would restore Musharraf's dwindling legitimacy; she would serve as prime minister and he would remain on as president.

However, Bhutto was assassinated later, in December 2007. Elections were postponed until March 2008. With many Pakistanis blaming Musharraf for her death, it was unlikely that he and his party would fare well in the elections. Instead, the PPP, led by her widower, Asif Ali Zardari, swept the polls. However, the PPP did not have sufficient seats for a simple majority. Initially, in an unprecedented move, it joined hands with the PML-N. Bonds between the two parties had been strengthened when they collaborated on the Charter for Democracy, signed in London in 2006. The Charter for Democracy held significant moral power in the early efforts to jump-start democracy. But the PPP and PML-N alliance was short-lived (Kronstadt 2008). The PML-N, which had joined the lawyers' movement, insisted that Chaudhry be reinstated as chief justice. The PPP, under new party president Asif Ali Zardari, demurred because Zardari feared (correctly, as it turned out) that as chief justice Chaudhry would strike down the NRO, invalidating his government. Zardari's refusal to reinstate Chaudhry prompted the PML-N to pull out of the coalition and launch massive protests against PPP intransigence. The months-long impasse was resolved by General Ashfaq Parvez Kayani, the army chief of staff, in March 2009. Kayani, fearing that the standoff between the two parties would cause the government to collapse, persuaded Zardari to reinstate the chief justice (Nawaz 2009).

Chaudhry, once reinstated, proved true to his word: he voided the NRO and ordered the government to reinstate all pending cases against Zardari and other PPP politicians. The Supreme Court has since used these cases as a cudgel with which to beat the PPP. Former prime minister Yousuf Raza Gilani was one victim (the court pushed him out of office in 2012). Although the court justifies its dogged pursuit of the party as a sign of its commitment to rule of law, its impartiality is suspect: politicians notorious for corruption fill the ranks of every Pakistani political party (Fair 2011; 2013b; 2013c).

Furthermore, judicial activism against the PPP government tended to peak when the army seemed to have a viable alternative to the PPP. After all, why would the army attempt to undermine the government when the only alternative was the PML-N, which, given Sharif's history with the army, had a soured relationship with general headquarters? Sharif had first crossed the military in October 1998, when he dismissed army chief Jehangir Karamat, ostensibly for advocating a stronger military role in policy making. Karamat accepted his dismissal, and Sharif appointed Pervez Musharraf to take over as army chief (Dugger 1998). Following the debacle of the 1999 Kargil crisis, Sharif tried to oust Musharraf in October 1999. Sharif made this decision while Musharraf was in Sri Lanka, and when Musharraf attempted to return Sharif forbade the plane carrying him to land in Pakistan. The army understood this order as an assassination attempt, because the civilian aircraft lacked adequate fuel to land elsewhere. The army rescued its chief by taking over the Karachi airport, beginning the coup of October 1999 (Dugger 1999). After Musharraf seized power, Nawaz Sharif was exiled to Saudi Arabia, where he remained until November 2007 when he was allowed to return to Pakistan as a result of Saudi pressure (Wilkinson 2007). (Saudi Arabia was no doubt unhappy that the United States was promoting the left-of-center Benazir Bhutto and PPP in the looming governance transition.)

During 2011 and 2012, Supreme Court efforts to prosecute PPP figures coincided with Imran Khan's surge in popularity. At its height, Khan drew large crowds that spanned generations and ethnicity. His self-proclaimed "tsunami" reinvigorated the electorate and mobilized them on the themes of corruption, restoring Pakistani sovereignty, opposition to U.S. drone strikes, and scaling back military cooperation with the United States. Yet it was clear that Khan could not seize the government without playing coalition politics, something he declined to do. As Khan's prospects dimmed, the court returned to relative quiescence until the sudden arrival, in January 2013, of Tahir Qadri (Fair 2013b and c).

Although Qadri had ties to two previous military rulers—Zia and Musharraf—few Pakistanis had even heard of the Canadian religious scholar. His protests against corruption were nonetheless able to marshal some of the largest crowds ever gathered in Pakistan. His rapid rise, extensive funding, and access to Pakistan's media caused many to believe that he, too, had the support of the army. Many Pakistanis wondered about the provenance of the "martyrdom-proof container" in which he moved about. The fortified mobile residence offered resistance to high velocity ammunition and even improvised explosive devices. Even Pakistan's police and politicians do not have access to such secure vehicles. The bizarre spectacle of Qadri moving about in his truck—mounted, armored, and possessing a command center—left many wondering how a foreign, private citizen could arrive in Pakistan from Canada and immediately obtain such high-level protection and draw such massive crowds (Fair 2013b and c).

Qadri and his followers camped out in front of the parliament and insisted that the government end its term early and form a caretaker government in consultation with him and the army. Although many of his complaints were reasonable, his methods were outrageous. Many Pakistanis feared that the army planned to use the weeklong confrontation to justify a coup, but such a move was never likely. Instead, the army was biding its time, using an unelected and unelectable Canadian citizen to bring the previous government to its knees. It was no coincidence that the Supreme Court took the opportunity to order the arrest of the prime minister as the Qadri drama unfolded (Fair 2013b and c).

In the end, Pakistanis gave a collective sigh of relief when the standoff ended with the government agreeing to set an election date and appoint a caretaker government in consultation with Qadri and the army. The popular reading of these events is that the politicians were able to sideline Qadri and undercut a coup in the making. That is too generous: Qadri in fact managed a soft coup on behalf of the army. Qadri coerced the government into agreeing to dissolve the parliament before March 16, even though the parliament's term was set to expire on March 18. As a Canadian citizen, Qadri had no standing to demand that a popularly elected government dissolve prematurely. Yet, with the support of his allies in uniform, it seemed as if he would be able to dictate terms. As it turned out, the government ended up on its own schedule rather than Qadri's. Nonetheless, this episode, and the bizarre accord it produced, tainted the legitimacy of the May 2013 electoral transition and demonstrated that the army still has democracy on a leash. It also hurt the popularity of the PPP, which suffered a drubbing at the polls (Fair 2013b and c).

The Supreme Court sought to "act as ultimate arbiter of political integrity and morality" under the PPP-led government (Kalhan 2013: 66). Several of its initiatives illustrate this judicial hubris. First, the court sought to undo elements of the Eighteenth Amendment (discussed below) because the court "contested the notions that Parliament's power to amend the constitution was 'unfettered,' even though the constitution's text expressly states that it is" (Kalhan 2013: 77). Second, the court again hijacked parliament's authority when it indicted Prime Minister Gilani for contempt of court. Gilani had refused to ask Swiss officials to reinstate corruption charges against President Zardari after the court vacated the NRO in December 2009. After two years of wrangling, the court found Gilani in contempt and disqualified him from holding office. The court threatened to also oust Zardari, but ultimately did not. (This likely had as much to do with the army's preferences as the court's judgment: after all there was no alternative to Zardari.) Third, in the fall of 2011, the court inserted itself into what became known as "Memogate." In the days after the bin Laden raid, Pakistan's ambassador to the United States, Husain Haqqani, allegedly warned the United States of a coming coup and requested that it intervene to secure the civilian government. In that instance, the military communicated directly with the court without any agency of the civilian government directing it to investigate the matter. Throughout the drama, the court played its "traditional role of facilitating the subversion of representative institutions—relying in the process, once again, on an underlying discourse that coincides with the military's own" (Kalhan 2013: 86). At the time of writing, it remains unclear to what extent Nawaz Sharif, the judiciary, and the military will enact the traditional dynamics during the PML-N administration.

Assessing Civilian Gains Since 2008

The outgoing PPP government came into power in March 2008 following reasonably free and fair elections. However, the PPP was forced to forge a fragile coalition, including, at first, the PML-N, its principal rival. Never before had the two parties governed together and many observers interpreted this as a sign of electoral maturity after nearly a decade of President and General Musharraf's military rule. Pakistanis optimistically greeted the new government even though the coalition lasted only six months (Press Trust of India 2012). After five years of its administration, the PPP most distinguished itself by its massive corruption, inability to collect taxes (and refusal to expand Pakistan's miniscule tax base by imposing industrial and agricultural taxes on parliamentarians and their patronage networks), incapacity to address the colossal power and gas shortages that have plagued the country, weakness in addressing Pakistan's pervasive security problems, and inability to stem intolerance against religious and ethnic minorities (Fair 2013b and c). But the PPP also had remarkable achievements during its five-year tenure. First, the parliament (Pakistan's thirteenth) passed more legislation than any other in Pakistan's recent history (National Assembly of Pakistan 2014). In fact, only the 1973 parliament, which passed the current constitution of Pakistan, passed more bills than the Thirteenth National Assembly. The Pakistan Institute of Legislative Development and Transparency (PILDAT), an independent organization that monitors legislative affairs in Pakistan, observed that "while the outgoing Government deserves appreciation as it did not bulldoze legislation through the House, the opposition should also be applauded for playing a positive and constructive role in bringing major changes in the 1973 constitution and for positively contributing to key legislation" (PILDAT 2013b; Fair 2013b and c).

The PPP-led government made considerable strides in institutionalizing democracy. Perhaps its most controversial moves were the government's efforts to take greater responsibility for foreign and defense policy making, which have been traditionally the bailiwicks of the powerful army. The parliament set up the Parliamentary Committee on National Security (PCNS) in November 2008 through a joint resolution of the House and the Senate. According to PILDAT (2013b), the PCNS has been "one of the effective Committees during the past five years. The unanimous passage of the 14-point recommendations of the Parliamentary Committee on National Security by the Parliament marked the beginning of an oft-demanded Parliamentary overview and ownership of Pakistan's foreign policy" (see also Fair 2013b and c). The PCNS certainly drew strength from Pakistani public outrage over events such as the unilateral U.S. raid on Osama bin Laden's Abbottabad safe house (Schifrin, Tapper, and Khan

2013); the Raymond Davis affair, in which Davis, a CIA contractor, shot and killed two suspected ISI contractors that he claimed attempted to rob him at gunpoint (Waraich 2011); and the deadly operation in which U.S. and NATO forces attacked a Pakistani military post at Salala, accidentally killing twenty-four Pakistani troops (Masood and Schmitt 2011). Some of the PCNS recommendations irked the United States, such as the closure of the ground lines of supply to the war in Afghanistan between November 2011 and July 2012 (CNN 2012) and the closing of the Shamsi air base to U.S. drone operations (Masood 2011). These actions degraded the U.S. ability to resupply the war in Afghanistan cost-effectively and constrained U.S. drone operations, at least temporarily (see Watson and Fair in this volume for a more complete discussion of the drone program).

But over the longer term, PCNS activism ultimately advanced America's strategic interests in having Pakistan's civilian institutions of governance assume a more prominent role in providing security governance in the country. Ultimately the government did not follow the PCNS's framework for restructuring U.S.-Pakistan relations, which was a key element of the parliamentary resolution that came out of the PCNS review. After all, the military—not the civilian government—is the final arbiter of Pakistan's foreign and security policies. Nonetheless, "the facilitation of this review and the unanimous approval of these recommendations indicated the Government's maturity and due regard to the institution of Parliament" (PILDAT 2013b). Equally important, the PCNS and the review process it began did help to establish some semblance of parliamentary oversight of governmental policies in the realms of defense and foreign policy. Even though the government did not follow the PCNS guidelines and has carefully managed this process to avoid fundamentally challenging the army, the Pakistani people nevertheless became increasingly accustomed to seeing politicians weighing in on these hefty issues prior to the elections of 2013. Attesting to this development, all of the major political parties discussed civil-military relations in their various party manifestos (PILDAT 2013a; Fair 2013b and c).

With the passage of the Eighteenth Amendment in April 2010, President Asif Ali Zardari became the first sitting Pakistani president to have ever voluntarily devolved his extensive presidential powers to the prime minister. In fact, this was the most extensive "deconcentration" of power since the 1973 constitution. This was no small accomplishment in a country where the president has often enjoyed more power than the prime minister or parliament. The Eighteenth Amendment modified some 97 out of a total of 280 articles of the Pakistani constitution. This amendment denuded the president of the powers to circumvent the legislative function of the parliament and decreased the period of time that the president can consider bills that have been passed by the parliament before approving them. It also removed the afore-noted, deeply problematic Article 58(2)(b), first promulgated under the military dictator General Zia and then revived under Musharraf. The Eighteenth Amendment also removed the term limits that precluded prime ministers from serving more than two terms (Fair 2013b and c).

With the Eighteenth Amendment, Pakistan formally returned to a parliamentary democracy in which the prime minister and his ministers compose the "federal government." It reinstated the prime minister, rather than the president, as the chief executive of the nation. But despite this important constitutional change, for all intents and purposes President Zardari retained power over those aspects of the state where there is space for meaningful civilian engagement. Equally important, the international community continued to engage with President Zardari, as well as the army chief. Thus despite the important devolution of power from the presidency to the prime minister, the prime minister remained largely irrelevant. A testament to the irrelevance of this post is the ubiquitous celebratory contention that this current government served out its term, even though the Eighteenth Amendment clearly defines the government as the prime minister. Given Gilani's ouster, the claim that this government has served out its term would be suspect in any country with a more robust tradition of parliamentary democracy (Fair 2013b and c).

An equally important contribution of the Eighteenth Amendment is that it was the first serious effort to devolve power to the provinces. It eliminated the so-called "Concurrent List," which enumerates areas in which federal and provincial governments may both legislate but where federal law governs. As part of devolution of power from the center to the provinces, the amendment also altered the way in which the National Finance Commission establishes the distribution of national revenue to the provinces. Unfortunately, this will likely remain a source of increased friction between the central government and provinces. Ultimately, however, significant devolution of power to the provinces may be an important way of mitigating some of the significant concerns of ethnic groups who feel

dominated by the "Punjabi state." Other amendments ratified by the Thirteenth Parliament are the nineteenth, which changed the way judges are
appointed to the superior judiciary, and the twentieth, which established a
new procedure to handle government transitions through the consensual
appointment of a caretaker government (Fair 2013b and c).

This impressive slate of legislative initiatives represents an important
and unprecedented, if modest, step toward involving civilian institutions
in security governance (Malik 2009). This does not mean, of course, that
Pakistan's democracy is in the clear. There are numerous daunting tasks
ahead for the next government. It must consolidate democratic institutions,
strengthen civilian control over the military, forge consensus among its
restive coalition partners, resist political infighting and military interference, and bravely seek economic reforms, often against the wishes of its
constituents and party members' own economic interests. This may prove
too herculean an agenda. While the government has moved forward by
leaps and bounds in the last few years, progress might be slower in the ones
ahead despite Sharif's electoral mandate (Fair 2013b and c).

Navigating the Preferences of a Vexed, Divided Electorate

Since the 1990s, Pakistani politics has been dominated by the PPP and the
PML-N, the only parties with national standing. In recent years, the Pashtun nationalist party, the Awami National Party (ANP), has taken root in
places well beyond the northwest, like Karachi, where Pashtuns live in large
numbers, but has not expanded its appeal beyond Pashtuns. The Muhajjir
party, the Muttahida Qaumi Movement (MQM), has struggled to establish
itself beyond its traditional stronghold in Sindh.[2] It has been very difficult
for these parties to establish an extra-regional presence, much less a truly
national one. Imran Khan's emergence as a national politician is an important and recent exception. His party, the Pakistan Tehreek-e-Insaf, has been
in existence since 1996, but for years Khan and his party were marginal
players of little or no political consequence (Baxter et al. 2002: 195–225;
Talbot 2009). By 2011, Khan had succeeded in attracting a substantial following that spanned age groups, ethnic groups, and even regions. Khan
referred to his movement and the rallies it attracted as a "tsunami (*Economist* 2011; Yusuf 2011). Khan's unexpected shift into prominence fostered
suspicions that he enjoyed the backing and even the active assistance of the

Pakistan army, which was anxious to find an alternative to the PPP and PML-N.

One of the positive externalities of Imran Khan's rise—irrespective of the identities of his backers—is that he and his party galvanized youth in an almost unprecedented way. In the run-up to election, the Pakistani daily *Express Tribune* published polls that assessed the much-anticipated "2013 youth vote." This voting youth cohort was the largest in Pakistan's history: Pollsters estimated that twenty-five million registered voters were between the ages of eighteen and twenty-nine years of age and that some thirteen million first-time voters would participate in the election (Iqbal 2013). Young voters, however, were the most pessimistic about the Pakistan's future. When surveyed about the most important issues in their lifetimes, they identified the earthquake of 2005, the floods of 2010, and the assassination of Benazir Bhutto. More disturbing is that a quarter of all young people have been directly impacted by violence. Contrary to Western expectations, the "youth vote" need not necessarily support liberalism and democratic values. In fact, in the above-noted survey, 64 percent of male youth describe themselves as conservative/religious, and 75 percent of the women describe themselves in such terms. When asked about their political inclinations, 29 percent believe in democracy as a system, while 29 percent believe in military rule, and another 38 percent believe in sharia (Iqbal 2013). At the time of writing, no statistics were available covering turnout by age, although the Election Commission of Pakistan put overall turnout at 55 percent. This was a record: during the election of 1988, only 43 percent of registered voters cast a ballot; in 1990, 45 percent; 1993, 40 percent; 1997, 35 percent; 2002, 41 percent; and in 2008, 44 percent (*Express Tribune* 2013).

Not only are Pakistan's young voters divided, so is the rest of Pakistan's polity. The *Herald* (a Pakistani monthly magazine), in conjunction with the Sustainable Development Policies Institute (SDPI), fielded a poll in early 2013 that demonstrated that Pakistanis are deeply divided along party lines and are deeply conflicted about which of the issues confronting the state are the most important. Survey respondents were given a list of issues and asked to select the most pressing problems facing Pakistan. While poverty, corruption, power crises, illiteracy, and extremism were the most common choices, no issue garnered more than 17 percent of the responses. Responses differed according to the respondent's socioeconomic status, place of residence (rural or urban), and level of education (SDPI 2014). Pakistanis are even more deeply conflicted when it comes to Pakistan's foreign policy, including relations with the United States, India, Afghanistan, and China. The United States and Pakistan have a long and tortured history together. While both sides have frequently been disappointed in the alliance, the last decade has been particularly challenging. SDPI asked respondents whether or not Pakistan should "have a strong alliance with the US?" Despite the public outrage over drones and other unpopular U.S. policies, respondents were evenly divided, with nearly one-third answering "yes," another third "no," and the remainder "maybe" (SDPI 2014). Pakistanis are similarly divided about their country's relations with India. One of the Sharif government's greatest accomplishments so far has been offering India "most favored nation" (MFN) status. (India offered Pakistan the same status in 1996.) Respondents surveyed by SDPI were not terribly enthusiastic about this important breakthrough. In fact, the plurality of interviewees believed Pakistan should not have done so (43 percent), with 28 percent agreeing with the move and another 29 percent undecided (SDPI 2014).

The previous PPP-led government tried to make overtures to Afghanistan. Pakistani policy makers have emphasized that they would like a cooperative relationship with Pakistan's western neighbor, even though the army backed and continues to back a more interventionist approach. According to the SDPI poll, Pakistanis are equally divided about how best to pursue relations with Kabul. When asked whether Pakistan should "actively promote a government favorable to its own interests in Afghanistan?" roughly equal percentages of persons responded "yes" (33 percent), "no" (35 percent) and "maybe" (32 percent) (SDPI 2014). Should Nawaz Sharif carve out a greater role for himself in directing Pakistan's foreign affairs, there is no clear public mandate dictating the course of policy action he should pursue toward Afghanistan.

Despite all of the anti-American fulmination in Pakistan, Pakistanis do not appear to be ready to oust the Americans. Survey respondents were asked to select the countries they believed were most beneficial to Pakistan from a list that included China, India, Iran, Russia, Saudi Arabia, the United States, as well as countries associated with the South Asian Association for Regional Cooperation (SAARC) and "Muslim countries" in general. China proved most popular, with 15 percent of the respondents identifying it as the "most beneficial." But the other countries and groups of countries, including the United States, polled similarly, at roughly 11 to 13 percent; statistically, this is a dead heat (SDPI 2014).

This discussion of the *Herald*/SDPI survey results suggests that the new PML-N government will have to navigate a fractured electorate whose priorities vary by province and ethnicity. While Nawaz Sharif received a clear mandate to govern Pakistan, it is less clear how this mandate will translate into prioritizing and prosecuting the varied domestic and foreign policies that attract voters and what space the army will provide the government to do so.

Musharraf and the Army on Trial

The Musharraf regime's end was an unusual one, as far as Pakistani military regimes are concerned. During the emergency of fall 2007, Musharraf agreed to step down as army chief. In October 2007, he promoted Lieutenant General Ashfaq Parvez Kayani, then serving as the head of the ISI, to the rank of four-star general and appointed him vice chief of army staff. When Musharraf retired from the army on November 28, 2007, Kayani became the new chief of staff. Musharraf retained his position as president. Had his plans with Benazir Bhutto been realized, he likely would have remained in this position. However, Musharraf ultimately was forced resign amid threats of impeachment. Never before had a military dictator been threatened with such a dramatic repudiation (Kalhan 2013; Fair 2011).

The threat of impeachment, and Musharraf's subsequent resignation, were the result of several developments. First, the lawyers' movement helped mobilize public sentiment against Musharraf's accumulating dictatorial powers. Second, both the PPP and PML-N agreed to begin impeachment proceedings (doing so requires a two-thirds majority in a joint session of the senate and national assembly). Third, the army had to overcame a collective action problem: while no senior leader wants to challenge the writ of his former chief, the army's leadership—including Kayani—feared that should President Musharraf be subjected to impeachment proceedings, the process might have evolved into a referendum on the army and its political role. While the lawyers' movement and political unity were secondary precipitants for Musharraf's resignation, army pressure appears to have been the proximal cause. Musharraf's departure, with or without impeachment, was a victory for civilian control over the military (Fair 2011).

However, Musharraf's troubles did not end there. Living in London in self-imposed exile, Musharraf decided to return to Pakistan to contest the 2013 elections, despite numerous threats to his life. Musharraf, who faced a plethora of legal charges, apparently made his decision to return to Pakistan against the advice of the military. In April of 2013, judges ordered Musharraf's arrest to answer allegations that he had committed treason in 2007. Musharraf literally fled the courtroom on foot. This ignominious retreat motivated considerable ridicule in Pakistan's media (Zahra-Malik 2013). In August 2013, he was formally charged with murder, criminal conspiracy to murder, and facilitation related to the murder of Benazir Bhutto (Crilly 2013). In September 2013, Musharraf was charged with contributing to the death of the radical cleric and well-known terrorist Abdul Rashid Ghazi. Ghazi was killed, along with many others, during a stand-off with the military at the Red Mosque in Islamabad, which Ghazi and his militant associates had turned into their base (*BBC News* 2013). These murder charges represented an important further step in challenging the activities of military dictators: never before had one been forced to answer for his actions while in power.

While these murder-related charges are grave, Musharraf's case took a still more dangerous turn in December 2013, when Nawaz Sharif's government filed a complaint of five counts of high treason against the former dictator. The complaint detailed five major "personal penal acts for the purposes of his personal aggrandizement and a consequential vendetta," which Musharraf allegedly performed on or after November 3, 2007 (Butt 2013). The first charge of high treason stems from Musharraf's promulgation of the Proclamation of Emergency. The second charge is for issuing the Provisional Constitutional Order (PCO) of 2007, another blatant violation of the constitution. In addition, during this period Musharraf suspended fundamental rights enshrined in several constitutional articles. The third charge derives from Musharraf's demand that that judges take a new oath to abide by the PCO of November 2007. The fourth and fifth charges of high treason derive from Musharraf's issuance of two constitutional orders, both in violation of Part XI of the constitution (Butt 2013). The federal court did not pursue treason charges with respect to his first coup in 1999. The reasons for this are unfortunate: the courts and parliament ratified that coup.

At the time of writing, Musharraf has employed numerous delaying tactics to avoid appearing in court. He missed several appearances after suffering an alleged heart attack and being hospitalized at a military hospital. His request to leave the country for treatment was turned down by the courts (Boone 2014). Now Musharraf's legal team is challenging the jurisdiction of the civilian court that issued an arrest warrant for his persistent refusal to appear in court (Symington 2014). This prolonged confrontation has several important implications for the future of civil-military relations. There is no question that the army is uncomfortable with this turn of events. No previous military dictator has ever faced trial for high treason, which carries the death penalty, even though each surely qualified. That the army has been unable to resolve this impasse indicates that the army is not as free to intervene in civilian affairs as it would have been in the past. At the time of writing, it is impossible to say whether Musharraf's parade of delaying tactics will succeed in buying him time for the army to negotiate his exit, or whether Musharraf will stand trial (much less be convicted). No matter how this drama eventually resolves, however, there can be no question that Musharraf's legal woes will make future coups very difficult—which is exactly why Nawaz Sharif is so doggedly pursuing him.

In the Shadow of 2014

Nawaz Sharif has vowed to take control of the defense and foreign policy portfolios. He has virtually no chance of succeeding. His commitments to peace with India provoked former army chief General Kayani to caution him against acting rashly. In an effort to further consolidate some semblance of control over the military, in November 2013, Prime Minister Sharif named a fellow Kashmiri, General Raheel Sharif, as the new army chief. This appointment caused some grumbling because two more senior generals were passed over (Waraich 2013). Yet General Sharif and Nawaz Sharif are already quietly at odds. The latter campaigned on a platform of negotiating with the Pakistan Taliban while the former, representing the equities of the army, seems less willing to negotiate with militants given the enormous losses the army has suffered fighting them since 2004. General Sharif wants to ensure that Nawaz Sharif understands that his remit is restoring civilian law and order rather than putting a bridle on Pakistan's army (de Borchgrave 2014). General Sharif has nonetheless shown considerable forbearance—or exposed the army's institutional weakness—by declining to rescue Musharraf from his legal entanglements.

How do the various developments in civil-military relations in Pakistan affect American interests? First and foremost, the United States, under the guidance of its special representative for Afghanistan and Pakistan James Dobbins, is anxious to find some negotiated settlement with the Taliban in Afghanistan that will permit it some degree of an honorable exit. There are many actors who have a clear stake in this outcome. President Karzai, who is rapidly becoming irrelevant as he faces the end of his final term, is uncomfortable with any process that leaves Pakistan and the Taliban with the initiative. Karzai and his non-Pashtun allies fear that the Taliban will be given power that they could not earn via the ballot box. Pakistan, for its part, is anxious that the Taliban have some role in Afghan governance, particularly in the south and east, where the group can prevent India from gaining influence in the Afghanistan-Pakistan border areas. India, Iran, and many of Afghanistan's neighbors are worried about any initiative that puts power in the hands of the Taliban due to the Taliban's past and present alliance with other Sunni militant Islamists, including al-Qaeda. For the near term, the army's preferences—not those of Nawaz Sharif—are likely to remain the priority for U.S. policy makers.

The army will also likely maintain the upper hand over civilian policy makers in other crucial areas, including the ongoing U.S. drone program (see Watson and Fair in this volume). The degree to which Pakistan's government—or elements therein—continue to participate in the program is open to dispute. At times, strikes carried out with the apparent collusion of the military have clearly vexed the civilian leadership. While Pakistan's military maintains ties with some militants, it has also vigorously maintained its right to pursue those militants who target the Pakistani state, especially the armed forces. The battle for public support has been a losing one, according to yearly data collected by Pew's Global Attitudes survey: in 2013, only 35 percent of polled respondents supported using the army to fight extremists, 29 percent opposed using the army in this way, and the balance declined to even answer the question (Pew 2013). If the ISI and Pakistan's military want the U.S. drone program to continue, it likely will. After all, under the current regime, the ISI and the Pakistan army benefit from the drone program because it eliminates Pakistan's foes without cost to the army. As an added bonus, Pakistani politicians who decry the program while failing to stop it look ever more feeble in the eyes of the electorate. As 2014 nears, the future of the drone program is in question for multiple reasons.

Perhaps the most critical question facing the United States after 2014 is what to do about Pakistan's ongoing support for terrorism under its expanding nuclear umbrella. This is also an area in which the army is unlikely to cede much ground: Pakistan has shown absolutely no willingness to abandon jihad as a tool of foreign policy. Equally disconcerting, Pakistan has publicly pursued an expansion of its nuclear program, including tactical nuclear weapons (Smith 2013; see Clary in this volume). This is likely a deliberate calculation to keep the United States engaged in the region generally and with Pakistan in particular: Pakistan understands that preventing an India-Pakistan war remains a key U.S. policy objective, and Pakistan's development of tactical nuclear weapons coupled with India's limited-war doctrine (Cold Start) threatens to redefine red lines and diminish the timelines of conflict escalation. Thus while the temptation may be for Washington to dramatically redefine its relations with this troublesome country, Pakistan has developed various insurance measures to make such redefinition less likely. It is unlikely that Nawaz Sharif and his newly elected government will have any meaningful role in shaping those Pakistani policies that most deeply concern Washington.

Notes

Parts of this chapter reproduce and expand upon previous work by the author (Fair 2013a, b, and c).

1. Pakistan's Supreme Court first articulated this doctrine in the 1950s amid a conflict between the first Constituent Assembly and the governor-general, who did not agree with the constitution proposed by the Constituent Assembly and the "vision of parliamentary supremacy and federalism animating that document" (Kalhan 2013: 26). In that case, the court upheld the dismissal of the assembly.

2. The Muhajjirs hail from North India, speak Urdu as a mother tongue, and came to Pakistan either during partition of British India in 1947 or shortly thereafter.

Works Cited

Al Jazeera. 2011. "Pakistan Slams US over Bin Laden Raid." May 14. http://www .aljazeera.com/news/asia/2011/05/201151461340733845.html.

Associated Press. 2011. "Bin Laden Raid Sparks Rare Criticism in Pakistan." *USA Today*, May 7. http://usatoday30.usatoday.com/news/world/2011-05-07-pakistan-criticism_n.htm.

Baxter, Craig, Yogendra K. Malik, Charles H. Kennedy, and Robert C. Oberst. 2002. *Government and Politics in South Asia.* 5th ed. Boulder, Colo.: Westview Press.

BBC News. 2013. "New Charges Laid Against Pakistan Ex-Leader Musharraf." September 3. http://www.bbc.co.uk/news/world-asia-23899085.

Boone, Jon. 2014. "Pervez Musharraf Misses Third Court Appearance After Alleged Heart Attack." *Guardian.com*, January 2. http://www.theguardian.com/world/2014/jan/02/pervez-musharraf-misses-third-court-appearance-heart-attack-treason-trial.

Butt, Tariq. 2013. "Five Charges Framed Against Musharraf." *News International* (Pakistan), December 13. http://www.thenews.com.pk/Todays-News-13–27254-Five-charges-framed-against-Musharraf.

CNN. 2012. "Pakistan Reopens NATO Supply Routes to Afghanistan." July 3. http://www.cnn.com/2012/07/03/world/asia/us-pakistan-border-routes.

Crilly, Rob. 2013. "Pervez Musharraf Charged with Murder of Benazir Bhutto." *Telegraph* (London), August 20. http://www.telegraph.co.uk/news/worldnews/asia/pakistan/10253784/Pervez-Musharraf-charged-with-murder-of-Benazir-Bhutto.html.

de Borchgrave, Arnaud. 2014. "Commentary: New Dawn in Pakistan?" UPI, January 28. http://www.upi.com/Top_News/Analysis/de-Borchgrave/2014/01/28/Commentary-New-dawn-in-Pakistan/UPI-76661390909410/.

Dugger, Celia W. 1998. "Pakistani Premier Prevails in Clash with General." *New York Times*, October 20. http://www.nytimes.com/1998/10/20/world/pakistani-premier-prevails-in-clash-with-general.html?pagewanted = all&src = pm.

———. 1999. "Pakistan Calm After Coup; Leading General Gives No Clue About How He Will Rule." *New York Times*, October 14. http://www.nytimes.com/1999/10/14/world/pakistan-calm-after-coup-leading-general-gives-no-clue-about-how-he-will-rule.html.

Economist (London). 2011. "Second Coming." November 12. http://www.economist.com/node/21538200.

Express Tribune (Pakistan). 2013. "Pakistan Elections 2013 Total Voter Turnout: 55%." May 21. http://tribune.com.pk/story/552368/pakistan-elections-2013-total-voter-turnout-55/.

Fair, C. Christine. 2011. "Why the Pakistan Army Is Here to Stay: Prospects for Civilian Governance?" *International Affairs* 87 (3): 571–588.

———. 2013a. "In a World of Our Own." *Herald* (Pakistan), February, 70–80.

———. 2013b. "The Pakistani Military's New Coup Playbook." *Foreign Affairs*, March 14. http://www.foreignaffairs.com/articles/139054/c-christine-fair/the-pakistani-militarys-new-coup-playbook.

————. 2013c. "Pakistan on the Brink of a Democratic Transition?" *Current History* 112 (753): 130–136.

Fair, C. Christine, Rebecca Littman, Neil Malhotra, and Jacob N. Shapiro. 2013. "Relative Poverty, Perceived Violence, and Support for Militant Politics: Evidence from Pakistan," Working paper. July 31. http://www.princeton.edu/~jns/papers/FLMS_2013_Poverty_Violence_Support_for_Militancy.pdf.

Grare, Frederic. 2013. "Pakistan's Foreign and Security Policies After the 2013 General Election: The Judge, the Politician and the Military." *International Affairs* 89 (4): 987–1001.

Iqbal, Amna. 2013. "Election 2013: The Youth Vote." *Express Tribune* (Pakistan), April 3. http://tribune.com.pk/story/530330/election-2013-the-youth-vote/.

Kalhan, Anil. 2013. "'Gray Zone' Constitutionalism and the Dilemma of Judicial Independence in Pakistan." *Vanderbilt Journal of Transnational Law* 46 (1): 1–96.

Kronstadt, K. Alan. 2008. "Pakistan's 2008 Elections: Results and Implications for U.S. Policy." Washington, D.C.: Congressional Research Service. http://fpc.state.gov/documents/organization/104699.pdf?.

Malik, Salma. 2009. "Security Sector Reforms in Pakistan: Challenges, Remedies, and Future Prospects." *South Asian Survey* 16 (2): 273–289.

Masood, Salman. 2011. "C.I.A. Leaves Base in Pakistan Used for Drone Strikes." *New York Times*, December 11. http://www.nytimes.com/2011/12/12/world/asia/cia-leaves-pakistan-base-used-for-drone-strikes.html.

Masood, Salman, and Eric Schmitt. 2011. "Tensions Flare Between U.S. and Pakistan After Strike." *New York Times*, November 26. http://www.nytimes.com/2011/11/27/world/asia/pakistan-says-nato-helicopters-kill-dozens-of-soldiers.html?pagewanted=all&_r=0.

National Assembly of Pakistan. 2014. Acts of Parliament. http://www.na.gov.pk/en/acts-tenure.php?tenure_id=1.

Nawaz, Haq. 2009. "Kayani Steps in to Break Impasse." *Nation* (Pakistan), March 14. http://www.nation.com.pk/pakistan-news-newspaper-daily-english-online/politics/14-Mar-2009/Kayani-steps-in-to-break-impasse.

News International (Pakistan). 2013. "PML-N Gets Simple Majority to Form Govt." May 26. http://www.thenews.com.pk/article-102564-PML-N-gets-simple-majority-to-form-govt-.

Perlez, Jane. 2011. "Denying Links to Militants, Pakistan's Spy Chief Denounces U.S. Before Parliament." *New York Times*, May 13. http://www.nytimes.com/2011/05/14/world/asia/14pakistan.html.

Pew. 2013. "On Eve of Elections, a Dismal Public Mood in Pakistan." Pew Research Global Attitudes Project, May 7. Washington, D.C.: Pew Research Center. http://www.pewglobal.org/2013/05/07/on-eve-of-elections-a-dismal-public-mood-in-pakistan/.

PILDAT (Pakistan Institute of Legislative Development and Transparency). 2013a. "A Comparative Analysis of Election Manifestoes of Major Political Parties." Islamabad: PILDAT. http://www.pildat.org/Publications/publication/elections/Election 2013_ManifestoesComparison.pdf.

———. 2013b. "Five Years of 13th National Assembly of Pakistan: Positive Trends and Areas of Concern." Islamabad: PILDAT. http://www.pildat.org/eventsdel .asp?detid = 614.

Press Trust of India. 2012. "PPP Formed Alliance with PML-N to End Musharraf's Rule: Zardari." 2012. *Hindustan Times*, April 7. http://www.hindustantimes.com/ world-news/Pakistan/PPP-formed-alliance-with-PML-N-to-end-Musharraf-s-rule-Zardari/Article1-836876.aspx.

Sanger, David. 2012. *Confront and Conceal: Obama's Secret Wars and Surprising Use of American Power*. New York: Random House.

Schifrin, Nick, Jake Tapper, and Huma Khan. 2011. "Pakistan Might Allow U.S. Access to Osama Bin Laden's Wives but Not to Compound." ABCNews.com, May 9. http://abcnews.go.com/Politics/osama-bin-laden-raid-bitter-us-split-pakistan/ story?id = 13561191#.UVtY3jf5WS8.

SDPI (Sustainable Development Policy Institute). 2014. *Political Barometer: A Study of Public Opinion—Voters' Preferences and Political Parties' Popularity Across Pakistan (Phase 2)*. Islamabad: Sustainable Development Policy Institute. https://www .sdpi.org/publications/files/Political%20Barometer%20II%20Final-%20(Phase% 202).pdf.

Smith, David O. 2013. "The US Experience with Tactical Nuclear Weapons: Lessons for South Asia." Washington, D.C.: Stimson Center. http://www.stimson.org/sum maries/smith-on-tactical-nuclear-weapons-in-south-asia-/.

Symington, Annabel. 2014. "Pakistan's Musharraf Skips Another Hearing in Controversial Treason Court." *Christian Science Monitor*, February 7.

Talbot, Ian. 2009. *Pakistan: A Modern History*. London: Hurst.

Waraich, Omar. 2011. "U.S. Diplomat Could Bring Down Pakistan Gov't." *Time*, February 9. http://www.time.com/time/world/article/0,8599,2047149,00.html.

———. 2013. "A Very Important Man: Meet Pakistan's New Army Chief." *Time*, November 27. http://world.time.com/2013/11/27/a-very-important-man-meet-pakistans-new-army-chief/#ixzz2smu1SxFS.

Wilkinson, Isambard. 2007. "Nawaz Sharif Returns to Pakistan." *Telegraph* (London), November 26. http://www.telegraph.co.uk/news/worldnews/1570491/Nawaz-Sharif-returns-to-Pakistan.html.

Yusuf, Huma. 2011. "Explaining the Rise of Imran Khan." ForeignPolicy.com, October 31. http://afpak.foreignpolicy.com/posts/2011/10/31/explaining_the_rise_ ofeimran_khan.

Zahra-Malik, Mehreen. 2013. "Pakistan's Musharraf Flees Court After Judges Order His Arrest." Reuters.com, April 18. http://www.reuters.com/article/2013/04/18/us-pakistan-musharraf-idUSBRE93H06M20130418.

Chapter 6

New Media in Naya Pakistan: Technologies of Transformation or Control?

Huma Yusuf

For months before Pakistan's last general elections in May 2013, cricketer-turned-politician Imran Khan avoided engaging with the mainstream media. The waiting list for television talk show hosts and reporters seeking interviews with Khan—who as the head of the increasingly popular Pakistan Tehreek-e-Insaf (PTI) party was aspiring to be prime minister—was two months long. Unlike his political rivals in more established parties, Khan chose not to make nightly appearances on the twenty or so privately owned television news channels that have come to dominate the news media landscape since reforms in 2002. Instead, he built his political momentum online, reaching out to supporters—many of them young, urban, and middle-class—through tweets, Google hangouts, and status updates on Facebook.

By October 2012, Khan's official Facebook page had attracted 487,000 "likes" and had 100,000 more followers than the PTI's official website; he had also become the most followed Pakistani on Twitter (M. Haider 2012). He publicly dismissed the mainstream media as corrupt and "marginal to vested interests" and instead championed the "democratic and incorruptible" forces of social media (W. S. Khan 2012). The PTI mobilized a twenty-five-member social media team comprising volunteers from around the world to keep the party's online platforms buzzing at all hours. Unnerved by PTI's social media frenzy, other parties began launching online campaigns—the Pakistan Muslim League–Nawaz (PML-N), for example, became the second party to establish a dedicated social media wing focused on improving the party's Facebook presence (Manan 2011).

Khan's detractors dismissed him as a virtual politician, warning that Facebook "likes" would not translate into votes in a country where only 16 percent of the population has access to the Internet and there are more rural constituencies than urban. Months before the election, Awab Alvi, a blogger and PTI supporter who became the de facto head of the party's social media wing, clarified that the party was "under no misconception that [PTI] would win the election on Twitter and social media" (Alvi 2012). He was right: PTI won 23 National Assembly seats in the May 2013 elections, compared to the PML-N's 143; most of the PTI's seats were in the northwestern Khyber Pakhtunkhwa Province and Federally Administered Tribal Areas (FATA), regions of Pakistan with the lowest rates of Internet connectivity.

Why, then, did Khan concentrate on social media for the majority his election campaign? Part of the answer is pragmatic: until the last few weeks of the campaign, PTI did not have the financial resources to purchase commercial airtime on television. There were strategic considerations too: according to Alvi, Khan's media advisers suggested he minimize television appearances so that other members of the party could enjoy airtime, thereby preventing PTI from being dismissed as a one-man show. But Khan's rhetoric about the incorruptibility and democratizing tendencies of social media suggests another reason.

In recent years, a growing number of Pakistanis have come to believe in the revolutionary potential of new media technologies, particularly in the political context. By launching his campaign online, Khan was better able to position himself as a political outsider and revolutionary, the much-needed antidote to Pakistan's established politics, which has for decades been dominated by the PML-N and Pakistan Peoples Party (PPP). Khan's call for a *naya* (new) Pakistan—the slogan that defined his campaign—was grounded in the principles of equality and inclusivity as well as the participatory fervor that social and other new media seek to embody.

The faith in new media's capacity to effect change has implications for a post-2014 Pakistan, one that is simultaneously experiencing democratic consolidation and unprecedented internal security challenges (see Fair and Tankel's contributions in this volume). The spread of new media technologies—likely to accelerate following the auction of third generation (3G) mobile spectrum in 2014, which will bring mobile Internet access to millions of Pakistanis—offers the possibility of a greater public role in decision making about contentious security and foreign policies, a domain that has long been the shadowy preserve of the Pakistan military. It also offers a platform for new entrants like Khan, who promise a departure from duplicitous and corrupt politics, the kind that Pakistan has pursued not only vis-à-vis militant groups but also in its relationship with the United States. It is not surprising that, in an effort to differentiate himself from his political counterparts, Khan has used his first few months in office to confront Pakistan's relationship with the United States, challenging the American drone program in FATA and blocking NATO supply routes through Khyber Pakhtunkhwa to protest strikes. These policies have found vocal support among PTI's online community. As other political actors at the provincial and national levels use new media to garner followings, they too are likely to take firmer positions on Pakistan's security and foreign policies, adding new dimensions to Pakistan's strategic calculus. Of course, there is a strong possibility that the new voices that emerge in the political debate to exert pressure on long-standing policies will be radicalized voices seeking to introduce new narratives—not just about Pakistan's external affairs, but also domestic issues such as the rights of religious minorities and the Islamic credentials of the constitution.

This chapter, however, questions the revolutionary potential of new media technologies, including social media platforms, in Pakistan, arguing that social media operate in the context of established power dynamics and social processes, often reinforcing rather than disrupting them. Given social media's close affiliation with the processes of democratization in Pakistan, this chapter also suggests that the use of such media offers valuable insight into Pakistan's democratic transition, and is a litmus test of the resilience of gains in this regard. As such, mapping new media use is central to understanding the "naya" Pakistan that will emerge in the wake of U.S. withdrawal from Afghanistan in 2014 and the subsequent regional recalibration.

Social Media and Political Change

Since 2007, new media technologies have been linked to what has been termed Pakistan's period of democratic transition. That year, then president General Pervez Musharraf fired the chief justice of the Supreme Court, sparking civil society protests in support of an independent judiciary. Although the movement was initiated by lawyers, it rapidly gained support among human rights activists, students, and other middle-class professions, and evolved into a broader pro-democracy agitation after General Musharraf imposed emergency rule in November 2007 and briefly blocked the broadcasts of all privately owned television news channels. Sustained pro-democracy protests and campaigns brought about General Musharraf 's resignation, general elections in 2008, and the reinstatement in 2009 of the chief justice by the newly elected civilian government. The PPP-led coalition government that came to power in 2008 became the first-ever popularly elected civilian government to complete its five-year parliamentary term in a country that has been under military rule for more than half its existence. The 2013 elections were thus a historic milestone, marking the first time that one civilian government transferred power to another via the ballot box.

The 2007–2008 lawyers' movement, as it is popularly known, was driven by new media technologies. During this period, anti-Musharraf activists used SMS networks to organize flash mobs; university students used a combination of blogs, e-mail lists, and SMS messages to organize protests; and protesters used cameras on their mobile phones to document and archive their actions on Flickr and YouTube. A blog named *The Emergency Times* became the backbone of a parallel online movement by publishing emergency-related news, live-streaming protests, live SMS-2-blog updates from rallies and other pro-democracy meetings, and inspirational multimedia messages from lawyers and activists, as well as crowd-sourcing information needed to launch campaigns against particular political figures. Meanwhile, members of the Pakistani diaspora were able to support and amplify these initiatives through Facebook (Yusuf 2009).

In the imagination of a particular urban, middle-class, and largely youthful constituency, this successful use of digital and social media to coordinate a pro-democracy movement has tied new media technologies to notions of resistance, revolution, and political change. By using social media, Khan sought to invoke the promise of political transformation, this time harnessing the online activism for his own campaign. By 2011, when his campaign gained momentum, he could also summon global faith in the revolutionary potential of social media following the Twitter-fueled "Green Movement" in Iran in 2009 and the Arab Spring, particularly in Egypt, where Facebook was described by the international media as a key factor in mobilizing the Tahrir Square protests. (Ironically, General Musharraf also turned to social media to reignite his own political career, remaining active on Facebook following his ouster. During his years of exile in the United Kingdom, he repeatedly told interviewers that his social media following— 825,000 Facebook "likes" in March 2013, far more than Khan's tally— demonstrated his continuing popularity in Pakistan [Waraich 2013b].)

New Media Versus Old Media

The public perception of the transformative potential of new media in Pakistan was initially an extension of overall attitudes toward the opening of Pakistan's media landscape. In 2002, the Pakistani government introduced significant media reforms and liberalized the broadcast media market. Between 2002 and 2010, 89 private Pakistani television channels launched, 26 foreign channels were granted landing rights, and 115 private FM radio stations came on air (PEMRA 2010). This media liberalization—along with urbanization and economic growth—is, in the words of Maleeha Lodhi, one of the "transformative dynamics that can eventually open the way for a reconfiguration in power relations, and eventually the redistribution of power in a more widely enfranchised and empowered polity" (Lodhi 2011: 49). Indeed, the deregulated media, especially television news channels, have played an important role in the process of democratic consolidation, for example, by mobilizing and amplifying the 2007 civil society movement for the restoration of an independent judiciary and, more recently, by launching on-air campaigns to encourage Pakistanis to vote during the 2013 general elections. In the mid-2000s, the emboldened media also exposed corruption among government officials, highlighted poor service delivery and other governance issues in urban centers, and brought attention to human rights violations by militant groups, the army, and the intelligence agencies. The independent news media have also played a vital role in relief efforts during humanitarian crises sparked by natural disasters such as the 2005 earthquake in Pakistan's northern areas as well as extensive flooding in 2010 and 2011.

In recent years, however, the mainstream news media, especially national Urdu-language television channels, have increasingly been publicly perceived as corrupt and co-opted by the government, political parties, and the security establishment (comprising Pakistan's powerful military and intelligence agencies). For example, in June 2012, a behind-the-scenes video was leaked on YouTube showing the Dunya TV news anchors Meher Bokhari and Mubashir Lucman taking instructions from politicians and the channel's managers on how to pose questions during an interview (Popalzai 2012). The leaked video comprised excerpts from an exclusive interview with Malik Riaz, a property tycoon who had accused the son of the Supreme Court chief justice of corruption. The video revealed that during the course of the interview, both the news anchors and Riaz received phone calls from serving politicians, including the then prime minister's son. This evidence of the close and inappropriate ties between media and politics provoked a Supreme Court inquiry into the matter: on June 15, 2012, the chief justice convened a full court meeting, the first ever in Pakistan's history to be aired live on television, and interrogated the head of Pakistan's media regulatory authority about its oversight of the industry (Zaidi 2012). Moreover, the video provoked widespread criticism from the public— expressed through calls to television and radio talk shows, in online chat forums and the comments section of blogs, and via social media—of the mainstream media for being complicit with the venal political elite.

The mainstream media's credibility was also damaged by revelations about a "secret expenditure fund" maintained by the Ministry of Information and Broadcasting under the PPP-led coalition government (2008– 2013), which it claimed was used to ensure the "welfare of journalists" and which was worth up to PKR 120 million (U.S.$1.2 million) in the 2012– 2013 financial year (the fund was worth PKR 153.5 million, or U.S.$1.5 million, in 2011–2012) (*Express Tribune* 2012b). The government initially refused to share details about the fund's purpose with the Supreme Court, raising concerns that it is used to buy off journalists. Following further investigations and hearings, the Supreme Court in April 2013 released a list to the public of all the journalists who had benefited from the fund through perks such as plane tickets and hotel accommodation as well as nonspecific "financial assistance" (the court is still withholding details of 174 payments worth approximately U.S.$1 million) (*Dawn* 2013). Though less scandalous than had been feared, the revelations raised more questions about the extent of the mainstream media's corruption.

Television news channels' reluctance to criticize the military or intelligence agencies has also undermined their reputation. For example, when a YouTube video allegedly showing extrajudicial killings by Pakistani troops went viral in September 2010, local media outlets did not pick up the story or further investigate the army's claims that the clip had been fabricated

(BBC 2010). This is because the Pakistan army closely monitors, and discourages, journalists' activities with regard to media coverage of security issues. In the years following the liberalization of broadcast media, the Inter-Services Public Relations (ISPR), the public relations wing of the Pakistan army, was expanded to comprise separate wings to monitor and engage with print media, FM radio, private television channels, and social media outlets such as Facebook and Twitter (Yusuf 2011). In addition to the military, Pakistani journalists may come under threat from the country's powerful intelligence agencies. For example, on May 29, 2011, Saleem Shahzad, the Pakistani correspondent for *Asia Times Online*, disappeared after writing a two-part article about the terrorist organization al-Qaeda's infiltration of the Pakistan navy. His tortured body was found two days later. Before his abduction, Shahzad had told colleagues that he was receiving death threats from the Inter-Services Intelligence (ISI). In September 2010, Umar Cheema, an investigative reporter with the Pakistani daily *News International* was abducted and assaulted by intelligence officials (Ricchiardi 2012). While the mainstream media's reasons for avoiding criticism of the security establishment may be valid, they have negatively impacted public perception of the industry.

Compared to the mainstream media, social media outlets have emerged as the more reliable and more democratic medium. It is not lost on members of the public that important revelations about media corruption and human rights violations have trickled up through social media platforms such as YouTube, rather than the efforts of investigative journalists. As such, the democratizing and revolutionary credentials of new media technologies have been bolstered in the broader context of a fourth estate that cannot be fully trusted.

The perception of social media technologies as a parallel watchdog is furthered by their repositioning as tools to keep the mainstream media in check. This is in contrast to the earlier use of such platforms: old and new media collaborated during the lawyers' movement, with mainstream media amplifying online voices while social media was used to circulate mainstream media content more widely. One example of the use of new media to provide oversight of the mainstream media occurred in January 2012, when Maya Khan, a morning show host on the privately owned news channel Samaa TV, visited a park in Karachi and chased down couples meeting there, asking if they were married or if their parents had sanctioned their outing. Outraged by this "moral policing" and invasion of privacy, many net-connected Pakistanis, loosely organized under the banner of Citizens for Free and Responsible Media, used blogs, tweets, and Facebook status updates to criticize Khan and Samaa TV. They also uploaded a petition against "media vigilantism" on Change.org, which gathered 4,800 signatures in forty-eight hours. Activists launched an e-mail and SMS campaign that aimed to flood the channel owner's e-mail and phone in-boxes with messages calling for Khan's show to be taken off the air (Sarwar 2012). Samaa TV first attempted to resolve the problem by asking Khan to issue an apology, but was eventually forced to fire her.

Such media regulation has led to greater optimism about new media's potential not only for political but also social transformation. The public's growing perception that it can participate in the national conversation and effect change through online mobilizations has broad implications for Pakistan's policy makers, both military and civilian, going forward. Top-down and often opaque decisions that have long been the hallmark of Pakistani policy making, especially in the arenas of security and foreign policy making, are increasingly likely to be scrutinized and challenged, and new political actors seeking to seem responsive to the public are likely to respond to these challenges, creating a shift toward populist policy making. In a post-2014 scenario, as Pakistan tackles difficult questions about its domestic security situation—particularly in light of the evolving militant nexus Stephen Tankel describes in his chapter in this volume—its relationship with the United States (see Staniland in this volume), and its role in Afghanistan (see Gartenstein-Ross and Vassafi in this volume), growing deference to populist pressures could lead to contradictory and unpredictable policy making.

A Revolutionary Class?

Critiques of social media's potential as transformative technology in the Pakistani context often focus on the class aspect, pointing out that social media use is the preserve of a small community of net-connected, English-speaking elites. As Marta Bolognani has argued, "Pakistani media consumption is highly influenced by class and economic background. . . . The widely held assumption that technology accelerates societal changes seems somehow very simplistic if applied to Pakistan, where we would have to hypothesize at least that media-related societal changes are occurring at two speeds, depending on class" (2010: p.408). Such critiques are valid: only between 9 and 16 percent of Pakistan's 180-million-strong population has access to the Internet—a total of between 20 and 30 million people. The critiques are further validated by past campaigns' use of social media. For example, after running a months-long political campaign concentrated on social media outreach, the PTI embraced the mainstream media in the immediate run-up to the May 2013 elections: two weeks before the election, PTI was the top political advertiser with a 39 percent share of all political advertisements on the privately owned broadcast media as compared to the PML-N's 22 percent (Almeida 2013).

But even these critics argue that more widespread access to new media technologies would lead to "civic education among the uneducated" resulting from their inclusion into the "informal process of learning about 'democracy'" that occurs online (Bolognani 2010: p.409)—in other words, that greater Internet access would lead to further democratization as a greater number of people would use new media in ways akin to how it was deployed during the pro-democracy lawyers' movement. Such readings are supported by the soaring popularity of social media in Pakistan. Facebook is the most-visited site in the country, with just over eight million users, or 4.3 percent of the population (Socialbakers 2013); though low, this number is increasing rapidly—in the six months prior to January 2013 more than one million users joined. The number of bloggers in Pakistan is also growing rapidly, with the BBC reporting that there were 3.4 million bloggers in the country in June 2011 (TechInfo 2011).

But will increased access to social media and other new media technologies spur political and social transformation in Pakistan? This question has become more important as the country stands on the cusp of near-universal Internet access. In June 2011, the Pakistan Telecommunication Authority (PTA), the government body that regulates the Internet and telecommunications, started the process of licensing a 3G network in the country, which would provide high-speed data for mobile users. The greatest potential for widespread Internet access in Pakistan currently rests with mobile phones, since the country's mobile teledensity—the availability of mobile phone connections—is high at 68.8 percent of the total population (PTA 2012). The 3G license auction was repeatedly delayed under the PPP-led coalition government, but on coming to power in June 2013 the new federal minister for information technology and telecommunication announced that the PML-N government would hold the auction and seek to introduce 3G to

Pakistan in 2014. In other words, at a time of intense sociopolitical flux and growing insecurity, Pakistan is also poised to leap into the information age, with millions of Pakistanis able to access and circulate information online, and thus to take a public position on political developments. The implications of this development could be immense, pushing rent-seeking politicians to adopt a culture of issue-based politicking, and opening up for debate those security and foreign policy decisions that have historically been the exclusive preserve of the security establishment. How will Pakistan behave when all its citizens want a say in the high-stakes decisions that lie ahead for the country, particularly in the context of escalating violent extremism and evolving regional bilateral relationships? Unfortunately, at this critical juncture, it is not clear whether greater access to new media technologies will lead to further democratic consolidation; it is equally possible that the social media landscape will emerge as a space where existing political actors reinforce their position and seek to establish greater control.

Pakistan's Net Delusion

Claims of social media's transformative potential are challenged by writers such as Evgeny Morozov. In *The Net Delusion: The Dark Side of Internet Freedom*, Morozov argues that increased dependence on mobile- and Internet-based communication can make marginal political voices more vulnerable, as the state can limit expression and mobilization by shutting down mobile networks and censoring or controlling Internet access. The Internet "empowers the strong and disempowers the weak," writes Morozov. "It is impossible to place the Internet at the heart of the enterprise of democracy promotion without risking the success of that very enterprise" (Morozov 2011: xvii).

Morozov's concerns certainly apply to the Pakistani context. As Internet access has grown and virtual debate becomes increasingly blunt, Pakistani authorities have made greater efforts to control and censor online content. As of July 2012, more than 15,000 websites had been blocked by the government (Saleem 2012). The decision to block websites is taken by the Inter-Ministerial Committee for the Evaluation of Websites (IMCEW), which was created by the Ministry of Information Technology in September 2006 and comprises representatives from the ministry, PTA, the Ministry of the Interior, the federal cabinet, the Pakistan army, and the three branches of the national intelligence agencies (Open Net Initiative 2012). In the absence of specific legal frameworks defining which government body or court is authorized to regulate Internet content, the IMCEW directly orders Internet service providers (ISPs) to block websites. In recent years, local digital rights groups such as Bytes for All and Bolo Bhi have requested that the IMCEW's membership be made public and that the committee provide an up-to-date list of all blocked websites and reasons for their being blocked. However, the committee has not responded to calls for greater transparency.

In February 2012, Pakistan demonstrated its increasingly authoritarian attitude toward Internet censorship when the National ICT Research and Development Fund floated a tender for a URL filtering system capable of blocking fifty million websites as part of an effort to censor "undesirable, blasphemous, objectionable, obscene" content (Shackle 2012). The plan to build a "Pakistani firewall" was ultimately shelved following a successful protest against the filtering system that caught the attention of the international media. However, in December 2012, the then interior minister Rehman Malik announced in an official tweet that the PTA was in negotiations to acquire "powerful firewall software to totally block pornographic and blasphemous material" (*Express Tribune* 2012a). Subsequently, in June 2013, Citizen Lab, a research group at the University of Toronto, released a report stating that the Pakistan government is using Netsweeper technology, which offers automated mechanisms to categorize and bulk filter billions of websites (*Express Tribune* 2013).

New Media, Old Tactics

The authorities' blocking of online content fits an established pattern of media censorship in Pakistan. Since the country's independence in 1947, print and broadcast media have served as the state's mouthpiece, used to perpetuate narratives to serve military interests, present a cohesive national identity centered on Islam, and increase the clout of established political actors.

Media control in Pakistan was fully institutionalized under the country's first military dictator, General Ayub Khan (1958–1973). General Ayub passed the Press and Publication Ordinance in 1960, which enabled the state to dictate and censor content and take over media institutions such as the Associated Press of Pakistan (APP) news agency and Progressive Papers Limited (PPL) (*Dawn* 2010). In 1964, PPL was converted into the National Press Trust media group, which went on to acquire newspapers that supported the actions of successive military regimes (Mezzera and Sial 2010). The government also began to exert greater control on private outlets through the distribution of newsprint quota. The 1960s also saw Pakistan's broadcast media expand with the launch of the state-owned Pakistan Television Network (PTV). Established in 1964, PTV quickly expanded and by 1974 was broadcasting from Karachi, Rawalpindi, Islamabad, Peshawar, and Quetta (Niazi 2010). From the start, broadcast media was used to disseminate propaganda and portray state—and particularly military—viewpoints on domestic and foreign policy issues, particularly ties with India. Strict government control of media outlets also meant that there was little criticism of the military in the public sphere.

Unfortunately, the media did not become more independent during Pakistan's turbulent "decade of democracy" in the 1990s. Under a caretaker government installed in the run-up to the 1988 elections, the interim information minister Illahi Bux Soomro amended the draconian Press and Publication Ordinance, a change that laid the foundations for General Musharraf's far-reaching media reforms. However, the PPP and PML-N civilian-led administrations did not liberalize the media when they came to power, and in fact continued to intimidate and bribe journalists to ensure favorable coverage, a practice that continues. They also largely upheld the unspoken rule that the media remain uncritical of the military.

Online censorship of websites by the state continues to privilege military interests and protect the government. Banned websites often contain politically sensitive, anti-army or, less frequently, antigovernment content. For example, in July 2011, Pakistani web users were denied online access to the American magazine *Rolling Stone* after it published an article criticizing the Pakistan army's expenditures (York 2011). In October 2010, the army ordered the PTA to block a video showing a military officer beating a civilian from popular content-sharing sites (Open Net Initiative 2012). More regularly, PTA blocks hundreds of websites maintained by Baluch and Sindhi activists calling for political autonomy or secession and documenting human rights abuses against fellow activists.

Residents of the western province of Baluchistan have increasingly used digital media to air grievances against the Pakistani state. Since 2005, Baluch groups have been waging a nationalist insurgency to protest against the province's underdeveloped conditions; state security forces have tried to suppress this insurgency through the abduction, torture, and extrajudicial killings of Baluch nationalists and separatists and have successfully censored most mainstream media coverage of the province (Human Rights Watch 2011). To counter the media vacuum, Baluch activists launched online newspapers, blogs, Facebook groups, and video-sharing channels to facilitate communication, document human rights violations, and share photographs of missing persons believed to have been abducted by state security forces (Ahmad and Dad 2011). These are regularly blocked by ISPs acting on the PTA's instructions; for example, the *Baloch Hal,* the first English-language news website focusing on Baluch grievances, has remained banned since a year after its inception in 2009 (*Baloch Hal* 2010). The research group Citizen Lab also found that the Baluch news site *Balochwarna News* has been blocked by Netsweeper filters (Citizen Lab 2013). Thus, rather than facilitate democratization through the inclusion of marginalized voices in the national debate, new media technologies are reinforcing the military's position as well as its narratives and policies. This has far-reaching implications as Pakistan enters the post-2014 world, when the military's long-standing security policies will be subject to renewed debate. The state's need to maintain long-established narratives that help justify its security and foreign policies will be more urgent than ever. As a result, it will likely seek to tighten control over the media sphere in order to dominate public messaging and to undermine developments that could enable the public to have an unprecedented ability to engage, critique, refute, or amplify that messaging.

As part of its effort to control narratives and public discourse, the state relies on deeply entrenched concerns about religiosity and morality in Pakistan. The government justifies its blocking of many politically sensitive websites by claiming that they contain pornographic or blasphemous material. Additionally, the PTA censors websites and social media platforms that do in fact carry material that is deemed offensive (by the state) to religious sensibilities within Pakistan. This too is in keeping with the state's historic basis for controlling and censoring media content. Since independence, the Pakistani state—in both its civilian and military incarnations—has used Islam to create a cohesive national identity distinct from that of India and to suppress the distinct linguistic, ethnic, and cultural identities that compose the population. Given the country's centralized state structure and authoritarian characteristics—the legacies of decades of military rule—

Islam's role in nation building is promoted as "part of a top-down national-ist project" (Z. Haider 2011: 117). State media control has long been a key component of that project.

General Zia-ul-Haq (1977–1988) oversaw the media's most overtly ideological nation-building role under his Islamization policies. By granting the religious political party Jamaat-e-Islami control of the Ministry of Information and Education, General Zia ensured that the media was domi-nated by ideologically sympathetic journalists (Mezzera and Sial 2010). Similar attempts are now under way to Islamize Pakistani cyberspace, largely relying on the country's controversial blasphemy laws. Pakistan has strict blasphemy laws that impose the death penalty for "defiling Prophet Muhammad," life imprisonment for "defiling, damaging, or desecrating" the Quran, and ten years' imprisonment for "insulting another's religious feelings" (U.S. Department of State 2012). Public debate about blasphe-mous content, the blasphemy laws, or the validity of blasphemy accusations is extremely charged and highly contentious, often leading to violence. In January 2010, Salman Taseer, then governor of Pakistan's Punjab province, was assassinated by his bodyguard for criticizing the blasphemy laws and defending a Christian woman accused of blasphemy.

In this context, digital media is routinely censored as "blasphemous" as part of the government's top-down nationalist project, which involves defending Islam in an effort to earn political legitimacy. For example, in February 2006, the PTA directed all ISPs in Pakistan to block websites (with a focus on Google and Blogspot) displaying caricatures of the Prophet Muhammad, originally published in a Danish newspaper (Ahmad 2012). Similarly, in 2010, the Lahore High Court banned Facebook for hosting blasphemous content after the site refused to remove a page titled "Every-body Draw Mohammad Day" (Ahmed 2010b). The ban also resulted in the blocking of 10,548 other websites, including pages on YouTube, Flickr, and Wikipedia, and BlackBerry services. More than 240 URLs, including web pages of international news organizations such as the New York Times and CNN, were blocked in September 2010 as the government tried to control news coverage about an American pastor's campaign to burn copies of the Quran (Open Net Initiative 2012). In September 2012, the government placed an indefinite ban on YouTube after the site refused to remove an anti-Islam film titled Innocence of Muslims, which sparked protest riots across the Muslim world (Tsukayama 2012). On taking office in June 2013, the new minister of information technology and telecommunications threatened to ban Google across Pakistan if YouTube did not block "blasphemous and objectionable" content (Isaacson 2013). Such measures reiterate government control of public debate, thereby undermining the transformative potential of social media and new media technologies. But they also keep religious discourse central to the national debate, an increasingly tricky proposition in a Pakistan where the battle for a dominant Islamist ideology is going to be waged with greater intensity. (For a discussion on the evolving militant nexus, see Tankel in this volume).

To further consolidate Islam's top-down role in fostering cohesion and nation building, and to limit public criticism of the military and government, the authorities have also increasingly censored the websites of religious minorities. In recent years, there has been a spike in targeted violence against religious minorities, especially Shia Muslims and Ahmadis, by violent extremist groups: more than four hundred Shia were killed across Pakistan in 2012, double the number killed in 2011 (Waraich 2013a); there were also forty-four attacks against Ahmadis, with twenty-two incidents resulting in the death of twenty-three individuals between January 2012 and January 2013 (USCIRF 2013). In this context, Shia and Ahmadi communities have launched websites and blogs to document instances of sectarian violence and campaign for their rights. However, in July 2012, the government temporarily blocked two websites—one managed by members of the Shia community and the other by Ahmadis—documenting violent incidents and discrimination against minority communities (Bytes for All 2012). Growing instances of such censorship discount the social media's perceived potential for transformation, and conversely exacerbate the marginalization of religious minorities.

This is especially true since the online presence of violent extremist organizations has not been checked by the government. Violent extremist organizations increasingly use social networks and video-sharing platforms to spread hate-inciting and propaganda messages and recruit new members (Ahmed 2010a). Online video-sharing is particularly common: groups upload amateur videos of suicide bombings, militant attacks against Pakistan army convoys, training sessions in militant camps, and video footage of tribal villages allegedly destroyed by American drone strikes to various extremist websites, YouTube, and other video-sharing sites (Michaelsen 2011). Militant groups also use viral text-messaging campaigns to call for violence against religious minorities or to rouse anti-West sentiments.

Extremist organizations such as the anti-Shia Lashkar-e-Jhangvi and anti-India Lashkar-e-Taiba (LeT), among others, maintain Facebook and Twitter accounts for both incitement and recruitment; Abu Jundal, a member of LeT, the group held responsible for the 2008 terrorist attacks in Mumbai, told his Indian interrogators that the organization maintains a trained web team to manage its web servers, online video sharing, and social media presence (Chauhan 2012). Similarly, Hizb ut-Tahrir, a global Islamist group that is outlawed in Pakistan, uses SMS messages and Facebook to appeal to young, middle-class Pakistanis. The fact that extremist groups' online presence has been allowed to grow in this way raises the question of what happens when these actors emerge as valid, media-savvy participants in the national debate, no longer parroting the narratives and policies of the military, but introducing their own stance on the role of religion in public life as well as security and foreign policies (including Pakistan's future relationships with the United States and India, and the need for continued jihad in Afghanistan)?

Already, the state's attempt to use religious justifications to control the public sphere is creating greater space for extremist groups to peddle their own viewpoints and engage Pakistanis—particularly young, urban, middle-class, and net-connected Pakistanis who should be at the forefront of anti-radical thinking. In June 2013, the chief justice of the Supreme Court took *suo moto* notice of blasphemous content circulating online and directed the PTA to submit a report on the extent of the problem. The chief justice acted on the basis of a petition filed by a British Pakistani lawyer against the "ever-increasing blasphemous material circulating in the internet domain having . . . implications on the minds, the lives and liberties of mainstream Muslim population" (A. Khan 2012). Subsequently, the Peshawar High Court, which in May 2013 had blocked two Facebook pages for containing blasphemous content, called for Pakistan's federal government to meet with U.S. government officials and demand that Google and other search engines and social networks operate under Pakistani law to ease the blocking of blasphemous materials (*News International* 2013). These events suggest that charges of blasphemy are likely to be increasingly invoked to censor online debate, particularly the views of marginalized political groups or persecuted minorities who challenge the state's Islam-based, cohesive national identity, the military's security policies, or, increasingly, the extremist positions of jihadi groups. Given this selective censorship of social media platforms, it remains to be seen what kind of revolution new media technologies might precipitate following the drawdown of U.S. troops from Afghanistan in December 2014, particularly as the state struggles to retain control of the public sphere and violent extremist groups are further emboldened in their rhetorical stance.

What Kind of Transformation?

Of course, top-down control of social media cannot be absolute. Already, Pakistanis use proxy servers, peer-to-peer networking technologies, and secure services such as BlackBerry Messenger to circumvent government controls: indeed, nine months after the government banned YouTube, it remained the tenth-most visited website in Pakistan, down from third before the ban (Alexa 2013). As access to the Internet and new media technologies spread, so will knowledge about how to circumvent top-down government control of cyberspace. This chapter has until now argued that optimism about social media's potential for bringing about political or social transformation is unfounded given the state authorities' increasing attempts to control and censor Pakistani cyberspace. This optimism may be less misplaced, however, if new media literacies are seen as key to ensuring that the transformative potential of social media is not quelled by government control.

However, recent use of new media technologies within Pakistan suggests that their use will not exclusively be democratic. For example, in May 2010, the Lahore High Court banned Facebook in Pakistan for ten days on charges that it was circulating blasphemous content following the launch of the controversial "Everybody Draw Mohammed Day" page. Rather than mobilize against the ban and champion principles of free speech and open discourse, some Pakistanis called for its indefinite extension. A group also launched Millat Facebook, Pakistan's first indigenous social network, which sought to appeal to devout Muslim users and support online censorship in the name of Islam (Tanveer 2010).

Indeed, cyberspace increasingly reflects the polarization and intolerance that plagues Pakistani society. This was most apparent following the assassination of former Punjab governor Salman Taseer, who was killed by his bodyguard, Mumtaz Qadri, on account of his support for amending Pakistan's controversial blasphemy laws. Immediately after Taseer's death, Facebook groups in support of Qadri proliferated and received thousands of fans and "likes." When Facebook shut down these groups, Qadri's champions continued to venerate him by replacing their profile picture with his image. Videos depicting a uniformed Qadri reciting a *naat* (devotional song) were circulated via YouTube and social networking sites, and generated dozens of comments in praise of Qadri and expressing hatred toward Taseer. Millat Facebook also sanctioned hate speech against Taseer on its pages and even launched an officially administered pro-Qadri page (W. S. Khan 2011). The many social media platforms that sprang up in support of Qadri were largely indistinguishable from the proliferating websites and Twitter feeds of violent extremist organizations described above, and point to a future where new media in Pakistan could be a divisive tool defined by radical discourse, rather than a platform for democratic consolidation.

Conclusion

Going forward, social media mobilizations will offer insight into Pakistan's democratic transition and serve as a litmus test of the resilience of its gains. Rather than automatically signaling the country's democratization, new media technologies will instead provide insight into what kind of political and social transformation lies ahead. Among the many difficult choices that Pakistan faces is one regarding the role of new media: at the time of writing, the Pakistan government was simultaneously readying to license 3G spectrum—and with it the promise of universal Internet access—and investing in Internet blocking systems capable of censoring vast online content on political, religious, or moral grounds. In a rapidly evolving regional scenario, it remains to be seen how the Pakistani state will manage this balancing act, and what the impact of greater connectivity will be on Pakistani democracy and policy making and on regional dynamics. New media technologies could enable the rise of new political actors and the empowerment of public voices seeking a comprehensive revision of Pakistan's domestic, security, and foreign policies in ways that further estrange Islamabad and Washington as well as recast other bilateral relationships. Or they could serve as tools for the state to reiterate well-established narratives in justification of flawed policies at a time of regional flux. More problematically for Pakistan's near-term future, new media technologies could amplify the reach of radicalized and destabilizing forces that will seek to take advantage of shifting regional dynamics following the U.S. troop drawdown from

Afghanistan in 2014 and the security and foreign policy recalculations that are sure to follow.

Note

This chapter is based on research funded by Open Society Foundations as part of their *Mapping Digital Media* project. For more information, see Yusuf 2013.

Works Cited

Ahmad, Shahzad. 2012. "Internet and Human Rights in Pakistan: Universal Periodic Review, 14th Session, Pakistan." Association for Progressive Communication, Bytes for All, Freedom House, Islamabad.

Ahmad, Shahzad, and Nighat Dad. 2011. "Pakistan: Fighting for Human Rights in Balochistan Online." *Global Information Society Watch 2011: Internet Rights and Democratisation.* Association for Progressive Communications (APC) and Humanist Institute for Cooperation with Developing Countries (Hivos): printed in Goa, India, by Dog Ears Books & Printing.

Ahmed, Issam. 2010a. "Newest Friends on Facebook? Pakistan Militants." *Christian Science Monitor*, July 8. http://www.csmonitor.com/World/Asia-South-Central/2010/0708/Newest-friends-on-Facebook-Pakistan-militants.

———. 2010b. "Pakistan Bans Facebook, Youtube over 'Draw Mohammad Day.'" *Christian Science Monitor*, May 20. http://www.csmonitor.com/World/Asia-South-Central/2010/0520/Pakistan-bans-Facebook-Youtube-over-Draw-Mohammad-Day.

Alexa. 2013. "Top Sites in Pakistan." Accessed July 2. http://www.alexa.com/topsites/countries/PK.

Almeida, Cyril. 2013. "Nawaz Warns Against Split Mandate." *Dawn* (Pakistan), May 10. http://x.dawn.com/2013/05/10/nawaz-warns-against-split-mandate/.

Alvi, Awab. 2012. Author interview, Karachi, December 7.

Baloch Hal. 2010. "The Baloch Hal Banned." November 9. http://www.thebalochhal.com/2010/11/the-baloch-hal-banned.

BBC. 2010. "Pakistan Army Says 'Extra-Judicial Killing' Video Faked." BBC.co.uk, October 2. http://www.bbc.co.uk/news/world-south-asia-11455858.

Bolognani, Marta. 2010. "Virtual Protest with Tangible Effects? Some Observations on the Media Strategies of the 2007 Pakistani Anti-Emergency Movement." *Contemporary South Asia* 18 (4): 401–412.

Bytes for All. 2012. "Locking up Cyberspace for Minorities in Pakistan." July 5. http://content.bytesforall.pk/node/58.

Chauhan, Neeraj. 2012. "Lashkar-e-Taiba Has Dedicated Internet Team: Abu Jundal." *Economic Times*, July 2. http://economictimes.indiatimes.com/news/politics/

nation/lashkar-e-taiba-has-dedicated-internet-team-abu-jundal/articleshow/145 73585.cms.

Citizen Lab. 2013. *O Pakistan, We Stand on Guard for Thee: An Analysis of Canada-Based Netsweeper's Role in Pakistan's Censorship Regime.* June 20. https://citizenlab .org/2013/06/o-pakistan/.

Dawn (Pakistan). 2010. "Excerpt: Freedom of Expression." *Books & Authors*, November 7. http://dawn.com/2010/11/07/excerpt-freedom-of-expression/.

———. 2013. "SC Releases List of Journalists Paid 'Secretly.'" April 22. http://dawn .com/2013/04/22/explosive-list-of-bribed-journalists-to-be-made-public-today.

Express Tribune (Pakistan). 2012a. "Christmas Cheer? YouTube to Be Unblocked in '24 Hours,' Tweets Rehman Malik." December 28. http://tribune.com.pk/story/ 485918/christmas-cheer-youtube-to-be-unblocked-in-24-hours-tweets-rehman-malik/.

———. 2012b. "Secret Fund: Govt Refuses to Share Details with SC." September 13. http://tribune.com.pk/story/435871/secret-fund-govt-refuses-to-share-details-with-sc.

———. 2013. "Pakistan Government Using Netsweeper for Internet Filtering: Report." June 20. http://tribune.com.pk/story/565879/pakistan-government-using-netsweeper-for-internet-filtering-report.

Haider, Murtaza. 2012. "Tweeting from Pakistan." *Dawn* (Pakistan), September 5. http://dawn.com/2012/09/05/tweeting-from-pakistan.

Haider, Ziad. 2011. "Ideologically Adrift." In *Pakistan: Beyond the "Crisis State,"* ed. Maleeha Lodhi, 113–130. London: Hurst p.113–130).

Human Rights Watch. 2011. *"We Can Torture, Kill or Keep You for Years": Enforced Disappearances by Pakistan Security Forces in Balochistan.* July. http://www.hrw .org/reports/2011/07/28/we-can-torture-kill-or-keep-you-years.

Isaacson, Betsy. 2013. "Pakistan Threatens to Ban Google over Controversial YouTube Content." *Huffington Post*, June 12. http://www.huffingtonpost.com/2013/06/12/ pakistan-google-youtube_n_3422595.html.

Khan, Azam. 2013. "Chief Justice Takes Suo Motu Notice of Blasphemous Content on the Internet." *Express Tribune* (Pakistan), June 10. http://tribune.com.pk/story/ 561362/chief-justice-takes-suo-motu-notice-of-blasphemous-content-on-the-internet/.

Khan, Wajahat S. 2011. *A Generally Bellicose Society's Antisocial Media.* Joan Shorenstein Center on the Press, Politics and Public Policy, Discussion Paper Series D-66. http://shorensteincenter.org/wp-content/uploads/2012/03/d66_khan.pdf.

———. 2012. "Can Social Media Propel 'Rock Star' Politician Imran Khan to Power in Pakistan?" NBC News, October 17. http://worldnews.nbcnews.com/_news/ 2012/10/17/14321961-can-social-media-propel-rock-star-politician-imran-khan-to-power-in-pakistan?lite.

Lodhi, Maleeha. 2011. "Beyond the Crisis State." In *Pakistan: Beyond the "Crisis State,"* ed. Maleeha Lodhi, 45–78. London: Hurst.

Manan, Abdul. 2011. "Discovering Facebook: PML-N Prepares New Plan to Win Youth Vote." *Express Tribune* (Pakistan), November 2. http://tribune.com.pk/story/286288/discovering-facebook-pml-n-prepares-new-plan-to-win-youth-vote.

Mezzera, Marco, and Safdar Sial. 2010. *Media and Governance in Pakistan: A Controversial Yet Essential Relationship.* (Brussels: Initiative for Peacebuilding; and The Hague: Clingendael Institute (Netherlands Institute of International Relations). http://www.clingendael.org/publications/2010/20101109_CRU_publicatie_mmezzera.pdf

Michaelsen, Marcus. 2011. *New Media vs. Old Politics: The Internet, Social Media, and Democratisation in Pakistan.* FES Media Asia Series. Berlin: Friedrich-Ebert-Stiftung.

Morozov, Evgeny. 2011. *The Net Delusion: The Dark Side of Internet Freedom.* New York: PublicAffairs.

Niazi, Zamir. 2010. *The Press in Chains.* Ed. Zubeida Mustafa. Karachi: Oxford University Press.

News International (Pakistan). 2013. "PHC Suggests Way for Blocking Blasphemous Materials." June 26. http://www.thenews.com.pk/Todays-News-7–186065-PHC-suggests-way-for-blocking-blasphemous-materials.

Open Net Initiative. 2012. "Pakistan." August 6. http://opennet.net/research/profiles/pakistan.

PEMRA (Pakistan Electronic Media Regulatory Authority). 2010. "Annual Report 2010: To Facilitate Growth of Free and Fair Media." Islamabad, June 30. http://pemra.gov.pk/pemra/images/docs/pub-rep/annual_report_2010.pdf.

Popalzai, S. 2012. "Video Leak: Lucman, Bokhari Run 'Planted Show' with Malik Riaz." *Express Tribune* (Pakistan), June 14. http://tribune.com.pk/story/393636/video-leak-lucman-bukhari-run-planted-show-with-malik-riaz.

PTA (Pakistan Telecommunication Authority). 2012. "Telecom Indicators." November. http://www.pta.gov.pk/index.php?option = com_content&task = view&id = 269 &Itemid = 658.

Ricchiardi, Sherry. 2012. *Challenges for Independent News Media in Pakistan.* Washington, D.C.: Center for International Media Assistance.

Saleem, Sana. 2012. "Blocked, Denied, Censored: 15,756." BoloBhi.org, July 18. http://bolobhi.org/press-release-public-statements/press-releases/blocked-denied-censored-15756/.

Sarwar, Beena. 2012. "No to Vigil-aunties: Thousands Protest Media's Moral Policing in Pakistan." January 25. http://beenasarwar.wordpress.com/2012/01/25/no-to-vigil-auntyism-thousands-protest-medias-moral-policing-in-pakistan/.

Shackle, Samira. 2012. "Excessive Internet Bans Worrisome for Pakistan." *Dawn* (Pakistan), November 5. http://dawn.com/2012/11/05/excessive-internet-bans-worrisome-for-pakistan/.

Socialbakers. 2013. "Pakistan Facebook Statistics." Accessed February 6. http://www.socialbakers.com/facebook-statistics/pakistan.

Tanveer, Rana. 2010. "Missing Facebook?" *Express Tribune* (Pakistan), May 26. http://tribune.com.pk/story/16222/missing-facebook/.

TechInfo. 2011. "Pakistani Bloggers Surging to 3.4 Million: BBC." June 20. http://www.techinfo.pk/pakistani-bloggers-surging-to-3-4-million-bbc.html.

Tsukayama, Hayley. 2012. "YouTube Blocked in Pakistan." *Washington Post*, September 17. http://www.washingtonpost.com/business/economy/youtube-blocked-in-pakistan/2012/09/17/30081fa2-00ea-11e2-b257-e1c2b3548a4a_story.html.

USCIRF (U.S. Commission on International Religious Freedom). 2013. *Annual Report of the USCIRF*. http://www.uscirf.gov/images/2013%20USCIRF%20Annual%20Report%20(2).pdf.

U.S. Department of State. 2012. *International Religious Freedom Report for 2011*. Washington, D.C.: U.S. Department of State. http://www.state.gov/j/drl/rls/irf/2011/sca/192933.htm

Waraich, Omar. 2013a. "Pakistan's Newest Martyrs: Why Anti-Shiite Violence May Be Pakistan's Biggest Problem." *Time*, January 15. http://world.time.com/2013/01/15/pakistans-newest-martyrs-why-anti-shiite-violence-may-be-the-countrys-biggest-problem/#ixzz2OJGExuio.

———. 2013b. "The Return of the General: Why Is Musharraf Running for Office in Pakistan?" *Time*, March 29. http://world.time.com/2013/03/29/the-return-of-the-general-why-is-musharraf-running-for-office-in-pakistan/.

York, Jillian C. 2011. "Pakistan Escalates Its Internet Censorship." *Al Jazeera*, July 26. http://www.aljazeera.com/indepth/opinion/2011/07/2011725111310589912.html.

Yusuf, Huma. 2009. "Old and New Media: Converging During the Pakistan Emergency (March 2007–February 2008)." *MIT Center for Civic Media Blog*, January 12. http://civic.mit.edu/blog/humayusuf/old-and-new-media-converging-during-the-pakistan-emergency-march-2007-februaly-2008.

———. 2011. "Conspiracy Fever: The US, Pakistan and Its Media." *Survival: Global Politics and Strategy* 53 (4): 95–118.

———. 2013. *Mapping Digital Media: Pakistan*. Open Society Foundation. http://www.opensocietyfoundations.org/reports/mapping-digital-media-pakistan.

Zaidi, M. 2012. "Thou Shalt Not Judge." *Herald* (Pakistan), July 10. http://herald.dawn.com/2012/07/10/thou-shalt-not-judge.html.

Chapter 7

Pakistan's Self-Inflicted Economic Crises

Feisal Khan

A national crisis, of one sort or another, seems a permanent theme in Pakistan. Herbert Feldman (1972) titled his masterful study of the decline and fall of Ayub Khan, Pakistan's first military ruler, *From Crisis to Crisis: Pakistan, 1962–1969*. Having successfully undergone its first transition from one democratically elected government to another in June 2013, Pakistan faces no immediate political crisis; but it is currently undergoing an economic crisis that will only be exacerbated by the post-2014 U.S. drawdown from Afghanistan.

In 2001, following the 1998 nuclear tests (ordered by the civilian government of Prime Minister Nawaz Sharif but with the concurrence of the Pakistani military) and General Pervez Musharraf's 1999 military coup that deposed Nawaz Sharif, Pakistan was a near-pariah state subject to severe sanctions by the United States. Pakistan's status changed virtually overnight after the 9/11 attacks; as a reward for supporting the U.S. Global War on Terror in Afghanistan, sanctions were lifted, arms and military spare-parts sales resumed, and the foreign aid tap was once more turned on full strength.

In 2004 the George W. Bush administration designated Pakistan an "official non-NATO ally" of the United States, theoretically putting it on par with, say, Australia or Japan, and allowing it access to all but the most sensitive U.S. military hardware. The United States was also instrumental in convincing the Pakistan Development Forum (that is, bi- and multilateral aid donors) to restructure most of Pakistan's external debt on extremely favorable terms. But Pakistan got neither the debt write-off or open access to U.S. markets that (it argued) it really needed.

From late 2001 onward (as detailed later in this chapter), the U.S. "alliance" with Pakistan, while extremely problematic for both sides, meant that the International Monetary Fund (IMF) and the World Bank were deeply engaged with Pakistan. Pakistan received both massive direct budgetary assistance and Coalition Support Funds from the United States; what's more, the United States did not impose major sanctions on Pakistan's nuclear program. After the U.S. drawdown from Afghanistan in 2014, the United States is highly unlikely to continue this level of support (whether direct financial assistance or "good wishes" in international forums). At the same time, given its status as a nuclear weapons state, it is equally unlikely that Pakistan will again be either ignored or heavily sanctioned by the United States, as it was during the 1990s after the United States' post-Soviet withdrawal disengagement from Afghanistan. Simply put, Pakistan is too important—too dangerous, if you will—to be neglected and allowed to fail.

Unfortunately Pervez Musharraf's administration did not use the fiscal opportunity offered by the post-9/11 environment to carry out desperately needed essential structural reforms of the Pakistani economy. While his administration did initiate some reforms at first, its overall economic policy rapidly degenerated into cheerleading a massive foreign aid- and remittance-fueled consumption boom. In a post-2014 environment that is unlikely to see the same level of external fiscal resources made available to Pakistan, this squandered opportunity is likely to have serious negative consequences.

In this chapter, I provide a brief overview of the structural issues facing the Pakistani economy, followed by a more detailed analysis of the country's two current economic crises (massive electricity blackouts and an inability to raise sufficient tax revenue). I then discuss the likelihood of meaningful economic reforms under the Nawaz Sharif administration, and, in the final section, conclude the chapter with a brief discussion of Pakistan's prospects after the U.S. withdrawal.

The Overall Economic Picture; or, Is There Any Good News?

There are many major long-term problems confronting Pakistan, and to focus on even the economic ones would be an unenviable task for any government. The issues confronting Pakistan include poor and rapidly deteriorating physical infrastructure, relatively high population growth rates and a crumbling state education system, severe water scarcity (periodic floods notwithstanding), abysmally low—and by some estimates declining—labor productivity, an inability to diversify into and expand higher value added exports, a cumbersome and highly corrupt administrative bureaucracy, and overall inadequate and insufficiently developed markets.[1] Consequently, Pakistan has been unable to sustain a high enough economic growth rate that would propel it once and for all out of its "economic crisis state" status and onto a self-sustaining economic growth trajectory. However, these are all long-standing structural issues that predate the U.S. involvement in Afghanistan. In the post-2014 environment of reduced U.S. interest and financial assistance to Pakistan, the immediate economic crises that the Nawaz Sharif government will have to address are the country's abysmally low ratio of tax to gross domestic product (GDP) and the massive electricity blackouts that plague it.

The Pakistani state's inability to raise sufficient government tax revenue has meant that the country runs a perpetual budget deficit and faces severe financial constraints that preclude the formation and implementation of an effective economic development strategy, while the massive electricity blackouts (the results of decades of mismanagement, neglect, corruption, outright power theft, and massive unpaid bills) have the concomitant knock-on effects of retarding GDP growth and thus tax revenue and so feed back into the Pakistan government's financing constraint.

The Electricity Debacle; or, Why Have the Lights Been Turned Off When Everyone Is Still Here?

The electricity blackouts, termed "load shedding" in Pakistan, began in the summer months of the late 1970s when, usually for an hour or two daily, electric supply would be turned off sequentially to different parts of Pakistani cities and rural areas when peak electricity demand exceeded installed power-generating capacity or when water levels in the reservoirs of the two great hydroelectric dams, Tarbela and Mangla, were too low to generate their installed capacity.[2] From a temporary expedient, load shedding rapidly became standard operating procedure for both the Water and Power Development Agency (WAPDA) and the Karachi Electric Supply Corporation

(KESC), then the two state-owned main electricity providers for the country. WAPDA was decentralized and restructured in 1992, and the Pakistani government established eight regional independent power distribution companies (roughly corresponding to major urban areas and still government-owned but no longer controlled by WAPDA). In 1998 the National Transmission and Dispatch Company (NTDC) was spun off from WAPDA to control the national electricity transmission grid (Pervez 2011: 10), and KESC was privatized in 2005 (KESC 2013). However, none of these "reforms" made any permanent improvement in load shedding except for an extremely brief period in the beginning of this century when Pakistan actually had surplus available electricity-generating capacity. On the contrary, by 2008 large-scale load shedding was the norm again, and getting worse.

By 2008 rolling blackouts of one hour on and one hour off were common in many urban areas and reaching eighteen to twenty hours daily in some rural ones (Munir and Khalid 2012: 73). By 2012–2013, it was no longer remote rural areas that saw the worst load shedding. In May 2013 all urban areas were allocated up to eighteen hours of load shedding daily as "at any given moment, 70 percent of Pakistan is without electricity" and authorities feared a repeat of the load-shedding riots that had hit parts of Pakistan earlier (A. F. Khan 2013).

Unsurprisingly, given its extent, load shedding has had a serious effect on GDP growth. The *Economic Survey of Pakistan, 2012–2013* estimates that in fiscal year 2011–2012 and fiscal year 2012–2013, power shortages had shaved two percentage points off Pakistan's already anemic economic growth prospects to give about 3.5 percent annual GDP growth (Ministry of Finance 2013: i).[3] Overall, Pakistan's GDP growth rate "has been stuck at a level [about] half" of Pakistan's long-term potential output growth of 6.5 percent, or an average of 2.9 percent annually for the period 2008–2012 (Ministry of Finance 2013: 1). That is, due to the structural problems mentioned earlier, the Pakistani economy, which could potentially grow at about 6.5 percent annually, has struggled to reach even half this rate for the past five years. Other official, and probably much more realistic, estimates put Pakistan's long-term potential annual GDP growth rate at being about 5 percent, with the possibility of perhaps raising it to 7 percent if the economy's structural obstacles can be overcome (Planning Commission 2011: 3).

To put the Pakistani data into perspective, the Organization for Economic Cooperation and Development (OECD) estimate of India's potential

GDP growth rate was 7.4 percent for 2001–2007 and projected at 7.2 percent for 2012–2017; while that of China was 10.2 percent for 2001–2007
and projected at 8.9 percent for 2012–2017 (OECD 2012: 200).[4] Two percentage points of lost GDP growth is a conservative estimate, in fact an
improvement of sorts: in 2011 the Pakistani minister for water and power
informed a visiting U.S. State Department delegation that actual GDP
growth losses were in the range of three to four percentage points (Mustafa
2011). According to World Bank estimates, load shedding had cost the
Pakistani economy roughly 400,000 industrial jobs, jobs that are relatively
desirable by Pakistani standards (World Bank 2011: 24) and so exacerbated
an already dismal un- and underemployment situation.

Pakistan's Electricity Production Mix

The total installed nominal electricity-generating capacity in Pakistan as
of the end of June 2012 was 23,538 megawatts (MW), of which 16,035 MW
(68.12 percent) was thermal (that is, generated by coal, fuel oil/diesel, or
natural gas powered generating plants), 6,716 MW (28.53 percent) was
hydroelectric, and 787 MW (3.34 percent) was nuclear (NEPRA 2012: 43).
This is a substantial change from the late 1980s when roughly 52 percent
of Pakistan's electricity generation was from much cheaper hydroelectric
sources and the remaining was from the comparatively more expensive
thermal power generation (Trimble et al. 2011: 5).

Since the estimated peak electricity demand in 2012 in Pakistan was
only 22,622 MW, there should—theoretically—have been a 916 MW surplus generating capacity in the country. Even allowing for capacity off-
line due to maintenance or other reasons, there ought to have been only
intermittent load shedding. However, nominal generating capacity is very
different from actual available capacity; the best sources estimate available
generating capacity as at most 14,000 MW. This immense differential
between installed versus available capacity is due to massive unpaid bills
(the "circular debt" issue; see later in this chapter for details) that prevent
power generators from purchasing expensive imported fuel oil; insufficient/
shoddy maintenance that resulted in between 1,500 to 2,000 MW of generating capacity remaining permanently off-line; low water levels in dams,
which reduced generating capacity by 1,500 to 2,000 MW on average; and
Pakistan's chronic "transmission and distribution" losses due to an aging

and ill-maintained power distribution net (NEPRA 2012: 4–5).[5] For example, the load-shedding situation was particularly dire in 2013 partly because the water level in the hydroelectric dam reservoirs was so low that they were generating only 2,800 MW versus an installed capacity of 6,500 MW, that is, a shortfall of 3,700 MW in hydroelectric power alone (*Nation* 2013).

The change in electricity-generation source from cheap hydroelectric to much more expensive thermal was not due to a lack of hydroelectric potential in Pakistan but due to a government policy that favored private thermal over public hydroelectric power. An Asian Development Bank study had estimated that Pakistan's potential hydroelectric power generation capacity was approximately 54,000 MW, far in excess of even future peak electricity demand (Asian Development Bank 2010: 4). WAPDA's own estimate for Pakistan's hydroelectric potential is 59,208 MW (WAPDA 2013: 4). Even if technical or political factors make these assessments overoptimistic, it is clear that Pakistan's hydroelectric potential is far in excess of current generation capacity.[6]

The cost differential between hydroelectric and thermal is huge, with the latter an order of magnitude more expensive. The average hydroelectric cost in April 2013 was 1.59 Pakistani rupees (PKR) per kilowatt-hour (KWH) while thermal (furnace oil) was PKR 18/KWH (*Nation* 2013); that is, roughly US$ 0.0162/KWH and US$ 0.184/KWH respectively. If hydroelectric power is so much cheaper to generate on a per-kilowatt-hour basis, why has Pakistan followed a thermal-based power-generating strategy?

In 1994 Benazir Bhutto's second administration decided to allow an independent (that is, privately owned) power producer (IPP), the Hub Power Company, to build a privately owned electricity-generating operation (HUBCO) in order to help alleviate the chronic load-shedding problem. This was an attempt to utilize the principle of public-private partnerships to improve both societal welfare and Pakistan's economic prospects. The proposed 1,292-megawatt project would have increased Pakistan's then generating capacity by approximately 12 percent but the financial structure of the plan was flawed from the outset. HUBCO and the fifteen other IPPs that followed in its footsteps were guaranteed two types of payments by the Pakistani government: a fixed capacity charge and an electricity purchase fee. The fixed capacity charge covered the firm's entire fixed costs (debt servicing, 15–18 percent return on investment, and so on) while the electricity purchase fee was the guaranteed payment per kilowatt-hour supplied, calculated on a "cost plus" basis but capped at US$ 0.065/

KWH.[7] The IPPs were also given massive tax exemptions, provided foreign exchange risk insurance by the Pakistani central bank, and had their loans guaranteed by the Government of Pakistan. Finally, the government's payments to the IPPs were denominated in US dollars, so that whenever the rupee depreciated against the dollar, the Pakistani government's financial obligations to the IPPs automatically increased.[8]

Kamal Munir and Salman Khalid (2012: 76) argue that the terms of the 1994 IPP agreement make no economic sense whatsoever. Using as their case study a hypothetical 100-megawatt thermal plant costing US$ 100 million and financed by a 25:75 equity-to-loan ratio (the common ratio in actual IPPs), they show that, for the amount that the Pakistani government ended up paying HUBCO and the other IPPs, the state could have built the power plants itself. WAPDA borrowed from Pakistani banks at 12 percent versus blue-chip private firms at 14–15 percent on a ten-year loan, and the Pakistani government had guaranteed the IPP investors an annual equity return of 15 percent on their investment over the (projected) twenty-five-year lifespan of the plant (Munir and Khalid 2012: 76–77). Munir and Khalid's analysis even assumes no depreciation of the Pakistani rupee against the U.S. dollar; in fact, the Pakistani rupee has depreciated from 30.9372 to the dollar in January 1995 to 98.3943 in April 2013 (State Bank of Pakistan 2013a), causing the Pakistani government's financial obligations to the IPPs to skyrocket.[9]

The second major problem with the IPP policy was that not only were most of the IPPs relatively small thermal electricity plants, they used almost exclusively imported and very expensive fuel (mainly furnace oil).[10] In 2010, WAPDA generated electricity at PKR 1.03/KWH (US$ 0.012/KWH), public sector thermal generating plants (GENCOs) at PKR 8.5/KWH (US$ 0.10/KWH), and IPPs at PKR 9.58/KWH (US$ 0.112/KWH). Thus the average cost of electricity generation was PKR 6.6/KWH (US$ 0.077/KWH), which, after accounting for transmission and delivery losses, grew to PKR 9.81/KWH (US$ 0.115/KWH) (Munir and Khalid 2012: 78).

Munir and Khalid carefully refrain from stating outright that the sole purpose of the IPP program was to provide "sweetheart deals" to politically well-connected parties, presumably with concomitant kickbacks to the politicians who approved the contracts. With the dismissal of the Bhutto government in 1996 on the grounds of corruption and misadministration, and the return of her archrival Nawaz Sharif's Pakistan Muslim League to power, the IPP policy ran into serious difficulties.[11] The Sharif government filed suit on corruption grounds against the IPPs—thereby evading the mandatory arbitration clause in the original contracts—and the Pakistani Supreme Court found in favor of the government and ordered the agreements renegotiated after canceling eleven contracts. Negotiations resulted in the guaranteed returns and the tariff cap per kilowatt-hour being reduced.[12]

The general charges alleged by the Sharif government were at least partly upheld by a World Bank report which concluded that because the IPPs were not selected through competitive bidding but by an internal procedure that "was not transparent and subject to political influence" the perception of widespread corruption in the process existed and "the public and political perception was that the cost of private power is too expensive" (Fraser 2005: 7). The World Bank, an enthusiastic supporter of HUBCO and other projects, argued in its defense that it had recommended the installation of only 2,000 megawatts of IPP capacity (instead of the actual 4,312 megawatts) by 2005 and that private power should have been used as, in effect, an expensive insurance policy against insufficient capacity at peak times rather than for normal electricity-generation purposes (Fraser 2005: 7).

A major contributor to the current load-shedding crisis is the massive "circular debt" problem. A full discussion of the Government of Pakistan's extremely complex system of electricity tariff regulation and subsidy is not possible here. At the risk of some oversimplification, however, the issue can be described thus: the National Transmission and Dispatch Company (NTDC), which is both the Central Power Purchasing Agency for the national grid for IPPs and GENCOs and the transmission grid owner and operator, cannot pay the IPPs and GENCOs because it, in turn, has not been paid by its customers or reimbursed by the Pakistani government for subsidized electricity provision.[13] The IPPs and GENCOs, in turn, then cannot pay their fuel oil and other suppliers or carry out needed maintenance, upgrades, or repairs. Thus online thermal generating capacity is substantially below potential and the national grid is also very badly maintained—which contributes, again, to Pakistan's notoriously high transmission and distribution losses.

At the end of fiscal year 2012–2013, total circular debt was an estimated PKR 872 billion (roughly US$ 9.3 billion, or a staggering 4 percent of GDP), up from PKR 537 billion (around US$ 6.2 billion) in fiscal year 2011–2012 and a mere PKR 84 billion (US$ 1.6 billion) in fiscal year 2005–2006

(USAID/PCoP 2013: 1, 25). The three largest components of the PKR 234 billion (US$ 2.4 billion) increase in circular debt in fiscal year 2012–2013 were subsidy payment arrears (PKR 106 billion), tariff rate increase delays (PKR 72 billion), and nonpayment by private customers (PKR 55 billion) (USAID/PCoP 2013: 8).[14] Of the total circular debt of PKR 872 billion in fiscal year 2012–2013, the three largest components were non-collection from consumers (PKR 330 billion, with PKR 197 billion unpaid bills in the private sector and PKR 133 billion in unpaid bills from government entities), the unreimbursed subsidy to low-income consumers (PKR 293 billion), and tariff rate increase delays (PKR 72 billion) (USAID/PCoP 2013: 6). It is thus clear that two of the three largest circular debt components, subsidies and rate reevaluation delays (together totaling some 42 percent of the debt), are the direct result of policy choices made by the Bhutto administration in the early 1990s and reaffirmed by every subsequent Pakistani government, civilian or military. The use of relatively small and inefficient fuel-oil plants means that the per-kilowatt-hour cost of electricity is far higher than it would be if hydroelectric or even gas-fired plants were used.[15]

To much public fanfare and loud proclamations that load shedding was now over, the new Nawaz Sharif government cleared PKR 480 billion (roughly US$ 4.5 billion) of the circular debt by July 2013. This was essentially the amount due the IPPs and GENCOs from the Pakistani government.[16] The government also announced the conversion of four fuel-oil-fired plants, including that of HUBCO, the largest Pakistani IPP, to coal by 2015 (Kundi 2013).[17] However, since the Sharif government did not review, much less reverse, the flawed policy that created the circular debt in the first place, three months later the government's portion of the circular debt was back up to PKR 157 billion (US$ 1.5 billion) (Ghumman 2013).[18]

Despite the "settlement" of the circular debt, there has been no appreciable decrease in load shedding in much of the country, and it seems clear that the Sharif government had no effective solution for the load-shedding crisis and the massive financial cost of "subsidizing" electricity. The new administration's continued adherence to a deeply flawed energy policy that has cost Pakistan massively in both budgetary outlay and lost GDP growth becomes more understandable if one realizes that some key Sharif advisers on energy issues own several IPPs each and so would obviously benefit from continuing the current policy and clearing arrears (Kiani 2013). Sharif is unlikely to radically overhaul the existing policy since doing so would alienate important sectors of his own political support.

The Tax Debacle; or, What Happens When Only the Little People Pay Taxes

The Pakistani state's inability to raise sufficient government tax revenue has meant that the country runs a perpetual budget deficit—estimated at 8.7 percent of GDP in 2012–2013—and faces severe financing constraints that preclude the formation and implementation of an effective economic growth and development strategy. This necessitates Pakistan's continual rounds with the beggar's bowl among the IMF and other multi- and bilateral donors. The growth slowdown caused by load shedding helps feed the vicious cycle by reducing tax revenue, but this is not the major cause of Pakistan's fiscal woes.

The most recent such IMF bailout for Pakistan was in September 2013 when the IMF announced the approval of a three-year Extended Fund Facility (EFF) of US$ 6.64 billion, with an initial disbursement of US$ 545 million and equal quarterly disbursements afterward if the Pakistani government meets strict budgetary and fiscal criteria: budget deficit reduction to 5.8 percent of GDP by fiscal year 2013–2014 and to 3.5 percent by fiscal year 2016–2017 (IMF 2013).[19] In addition, the Pakistani government (again) pledged to widen the tax base and improve the tax administration and collection process, as well as to reform/restructure state-operated enterprises and increase central bank autonomy.[20] The government proposed to achieve its immediate deficit reduction goal through higher gas and electricity tariffs totaling PKR 180 billion (US$ 1.7 billion) and spending cuts totaling PKR 130 billion (US$ 1.1 billion) (Rana 2013). Since the vast majority of the spending cuts (PKR 115 billion, or US$ 1 billion) are from the development budget, this means that work on both new and upgrading/repairing of existing hydroelectric capacity will be adversely impacted (Rana 2013).[21] The consequences for Pakistan's load-shedding situation and thus GDP growth and tax collection can be easily deduced.

The 2013 EFF was Pakistan's twentieth trip to the IMF well since 1958; the penultimate EFF for US$ 7.6 billion (later increased to US$ 11.3 billion), agreed to in 2008, was suspended in 2010 and finally canceled outright in late 2011 when the Pakistan Peoples Party government failed to live up to virtually all of its major commitments to the IMF regarding improvements in tax-revenue administration and collection, namely a comprehensive value-added tax (VAT). Tax reform faced both "the opposition of two major political parties in coalition with the government and . . .

the vehement opposition of the business community who were determined to resist the imposition of the newly proposed sales tax regime" (Hyder 2012: 18).

In addition to the IMF, Pakistan has also received massive financial assistance from the United States. During fiscal year 2002–2013, the U.S. Congress authorized US$ 25.9 billion in financial assistance (US$ 17.2 billion in military aid and US$ 8.7 billion in economic assistance) to Pakistan, but actual disbursements were only US$ 18.9 billion (U.S. $13.9 billion in military aid, including US$ 10.7 billion in Coalition Support Funds, and US$ 5 billion in economic aid).[22] Furthermore, while U.S. assistance to Pakistan will continue at least through 2014 under the 2009 Enhanced Partnership with Pakistan Act (a.k.a. Kerry-Lugar-Berman), which mandates US$ 1.5 billion annually in U.S. economic assistance to Pakistan, actual disbursements have varied. Thus Pakistan has consistently been the third-largest recipient of U.S. foreign assistance (after Israel and Afghanistan but ahead of Iraq and Egypt) for the last several years (Sharp 2013: 22). In addition, annual remittances from expatriate Pakistanis in the United States, Saudi Arabia, and the Persian Gulf have hovered in the US$ 10–13 billion range (almost 6 percent of GDP in 2013) annually for the past several years and are climbing steadily (State Bank of Pakistan 2013b).

External debt servicing was at a tolerable 1 percent of GDP in 2011–2012 and actually decreased to below 1 percent in 2012–2013, averaging only 5 percent of foreign exchange earnings for 2011–2013. This was a substantial improvement over 2003–2004, when external debt service reached 3.3 percent of GDP and 15 percent of export earnings.[23] Pakistan should not have been in such dire straits economically that it had to ask for another IMF bailout.

The reason for its economic desperation was Pakistan's inability and/or unwillingness to raise sufficient tax revenue. Pakistan's tax-revenue-to-GDP ratio declined from a recent high of 13.81 percent in 1996 to 10.1 percent in 2012, an improvement over 2006's all-time low of 8.7 percent (World Bank 2013). In comparison, the South Asian average during the first decade of this century ranged from 11.5 percent to 13.1 percent (World Bank 2009: ii). The 2012 Pakistani tax-to-GDP ratio was also low compared to that of other large, poor, non-oil-exporting countries such as Ghana (14.9 percent), Egypt (14 percent), the Philippines (12.4 percent), and the lower middle-income country average of 10.8 percent (World Bank 2013).[24]

Furthermore, the composition of the tax revenue collected is skewed toward more regressive indirect taxes (about 70 percent of tax revenue) while direct (progressive) income taxes accounted for barely 10 percent of total revenues throughout the first decade of this century (World Bank 2009: viii–xi). A recent study found that, in 2007–2008, the top (richest) decile of the Pakistani population paid 5.9 percent of all indirect taxes while the bottom (poorest) decile paid 9.3 percent (*Express Tribune* 2013b). This is in sharp contrast to the United States where income taxes provided 46 percent of tax receipts in 2012 and excise taxes barely 9 percent (CBPP 2013).[25]

Why Can't the Government Raise Revenue?

The relative unimportance of personal income tax revenue for Pakistan is not surprising when one realizes that there are barely any income-tax payers in a population of some 180 million: "The tax authorities can identify a mere 768,000 individuals who paid income tax last year. Even fewer—just 270,000—have paid something in each of the past three years" (*Economist* 2012).

This is true also of the Pakistani legislature. Sixty-seven percent of federal legislators have paid no income taxes or have not bothered to register for a national income tax number (NITN), needed to file an income tax return with the Federal Board of Revenue (FBR), Pakistan's internal revenue service (Cheema 2011: 17–18). The most prominent nonpayer was President Asif Ali Zardari, who did not file a tax return in 2011; neither did thirty-five of the fifty-five members of the federal cabinet (Cheema 2011:17–18). Then prime minister Yousaf Raza Gilani did file a tax return for 2011, but he had only obtained his NITN in 2010; there are no income tax records for him before then although he had been in politics since 1985 (Cheema 2011: 19). Such a state of affairs can only exist if there is no penalty for tax evasion: as per the FBR's own admission, there have been no prosecutions for income tax evasion or fraud for over twenty-five years (Tran 2013).

Unsurprisingly, Pakistan's general sales tax (GST), its version of the value-added tax (VAT), is as inefficient at raising revenue as is the income tax and it is probably among the least efficient tax systems in the world. Its tax collection efficiency (C-efficiency)[26] is only 22.3 percent (Hassan and

Sarker 2012: 420) versus 45 percent for Sri Lanka (Tran 2013) and a 2011 OECD average of 58 percent (Owens 2011: 9). While never actually efficient, the Pakistani tax system was much less inefficient in the past, with a C-efficiency of 32.3 percent in 2002 (Hassan and Sarkar 2012: 420) and a much more respectable 39 percent in the 1990s (Ahmad 2010: 13).

The reasons for this appalling tax inefficiency are twofold. First, the Pakistani taxation system is extremely corrupt, and tax evasion and fraud is rampant. While, by definition, it is impossible to calculate the extent of corruption in any tax system, the fact that Pakistan's score of twenty-seven on Transparency International's Corruption Perception Index (on a scale of zero to one hundred, with zero being the most corrupt) put it as 139th out of 174 countries in terms of perceived honesty means that it is unlikely that the FBR is more honest than the rest of Pakistan's administration.[27] Quite on the contrary, in 2009 the (unsurprisingly short-tenured) finance minister claimed that corruption in the FBR alone cost the government at least PKR 500 billion (then US$ 6 billion) annually in lost tax revenue and this exceeded the combined losses of the entire state-operated-enterprise sector (PKR 300 billion, or US$ 3.7 billion) (Abbasi 2011). In his previous term Prime Minister Sharif launched a much-ballyhooed "anticorruption drive" in 1997 but quietly exempted officials of the Ministry of Finance, Customs, and the FBR from scrutiny when word was apparently passed on to him that any attempt to take them to task would result in budget making and revenue collection grinding to a halt (F. Khan 2007: 232).

Second, important sectors of the Pakistani economy are untaxed. For example, agricultural income is tax-exempt, and thus it is common to declare one's income source as "agricultural" and claim tax-exemption.[28] The lack of tax audits ensures no penalty for evasion.

Furthermore, the FBR has the statutory authority to reduce the GST (or even "zero rate" it) on any item or sector of the economy that it wishes to. Not only is the item in question not subject to the 17 percent GST,[29] the firm can apply for a refund of the tax paid on inputs purchased to manufacture the product.[30] Thus the FBR "zero rated" the entire "textiles, sports goods, leather products, surgical instruments, carpets and rugs" sectors of the economy, that is, Pakistan's largest export items, for all sales (both domestic and export) and suspended all auditing in favor of a "no questions asked self-assessment scheme" (Ahmad 2010: 12).

At times, the Pakistani government's dealings with international lending agencies slip into outright farce. On April Fool's Day 2011, as the Pakistani government was apparently desperately negotiating with the IMF for an extension on implementing the reforms it had agreed to in 2008, the FBR issued Statutory Regulatory Order (SRO) 283(1)/2011, which reduced the GST levied on 184 categories of imports and manufactures from 16 percent to 6, 4, or 0 percent (FBR 2011).[31]

While there may be several legitimate reasons for reducing GST on some sectors of the economy—de facto export subsidies, temporary relief to natural-disaster-hit industries, and so on—the practice can (and in Pakistan does) rapidly degenerate into political favoritism, crony capitalism, and outright corruption. Regulations such as SRO283(1)/2011 explain why GST refunds rose from 5.3 percent of total GST revenue in 2009–2010 to 7.4 percent in 2010/11—and this was before the full impact of SRO283(1)/2011 on tax revenue. An internal FBR study in 2002–2003 concluded that at least one-fourth of all GST refunds were fraudulent and that, in the absence of any meaningful enforcement effort, no improvement in this was likely (Hoti 2003). Given the massive level of over-invoicing and outright business fraud rampant in Pakistan, the "leakages" out of the system are not leaks but gushers and the level of fraud in GST refunds has increased substantially since 2002–2003.

The Likelihood of Meaningful Reforms Under Nawaz Sharif

Pakistan has a long history of unsuccessful attempts to reform its tax administration. In 1985 the National Tax Reforms Commission concluded that "the three basic maladies from which Pakistan is suffering at present are tax evasion, smuggling and corruption. These are interrelated and one feeds on the other" (quoted in Ahmad 2011: 3). Ironically, the impetus for the formation of the commission was the decline of the tax-to-GDP ratio from 14 percent in 1981 to 11.3 percent in 1985.

In the 1990s the World Bank funded a US$ 120 million overhaul of the tax administration that produced no tangible results. Hope springs eternal, however, and in 2007 the World Bank, with the supposed full cooperation of the Pakistani government and the FBR, began the extremely ambitious US$ 149 million Taxation Administration Reform Program (TARP). The goal was to raise the tax-to-GDP ratio from 10.4 percent in 2007–2008 to 13.9 percent by 2012–2013 (World Bank 2009: ii), that is, to raise the state's ability to generate revenue to levels last seen in 1981.

Box 7.1. The Wholesale and Retail Trade Sector
of the Pakistani Economy

A look at the wholesale and retail trade (W&RT) sector highlights many of the problems plaguing the Pakistani tax system. W&RT accounted for 16.6 percent of gross domestic product (GDP) in 2006–2007 but contributed only 0.7 percent of total tax revenue collected. By 2011–2012 the sector made up 17.3 percent of GDP while its tax revenue share had declined to 0.5 percent. An internal Federal Board of Revenue (FBR) study estimated that there were 1.47 million W&RT firms in 2006–2007, about 12 percent of which were registered with the FBR. But only about half of those registered actually filed returns.

W&RT firms are subject to two forms of taxes: sales and income (actually, turnover) tax. Firms with turnover under PKR 5 million (US$ 50,000) have no tax liability; firms with between PKR 5 and 10 million in sales are taxed at 0.5 percent; and firms with revenues greater than PKR 10 million are taxed at 0.75 percent. In 2006–2007, only an estimated 46.7 percent (40.7 percent in 2011–2012) of firms that met the tax thresholds filed sales tax returns and only 42.7 percent (62.4 percent in 2011–2012) of firms that met the income tax threshold filed tax returns.

However, this seeming improvement in income tax compliance is actually quite misleading. Between 2006–2007 and 2011–2012, small and large-scale retailers essentially stopped paying taxes, as their share of total tax revenue collection declined from 58.1 and 7.1 percent, respectively, to 18.5 and 2.7 percent, while the tax share of wholesale firms rose from 34.8 to 78.8 percent. That is, under the self-assessment scheme where the tax authorities accept all tax returns at face value, most retail establishments understated their turnover and so evaded taxes, while wholesalers (being larger targets and so harder to hide from the FBR) took up some of the slack. Total tax revenue for this period actually declined, from PKR 4.56 billion to 4.05 billion, despite the substantial increase in the number of firms filing income tax returns. Small retailer tax payments declined precipitously from PKR 2.65 billion to 0.75 billion, large from PKR 0.33 billion to 0.11 billion, while wholesalers rose from PKR 1.59 billion to 3.2 billion.

Thus government policy, massive corruption, and an almost complete absence of tax code enforcement ensures that a very large portion of the economy pays virtually no taxes.

(Data source: Naeem Ahmed 2013)

The governing assumption of TARP, which was crafted with major Pakistani input,[32] was that this time the Pakistani government was absolutely serious about implementing real reforms: as the World Bank stated, "The Pakistan government has now taken on board the challenge of stepping up revenue mobilization" (2009: i). While appreciative of the difficulties involved, the World Bank was quite hopeful in what the project could achieve: "The rise in tax revenues, in addition to a decline in interest payments, will allow the government to reduce the fiscal deficit from 7.4 percent of GDP in 2007–08 to 2.4 percent of GDP in 2012–13" (World Bank 2009: ii). Considering that the actual budget deficit in 2012–2013 was 8.7 percent of GDP, the entire project may be classified as a complete failure.

By 2010 it had become apparent that the Pakistani government was both unwilling and unable to deliver on any of its commitments and the project was "restructured." An official "implementation, completion and results report" (World Bank 2012: 6–17) concluded that the project suffered from "a challenging political environment" and a "failure in risk assessment by overestimating GoP's [Government of Pakistan's] political will and institutional buy-in" and that at the "root of these problems was a lack of consistent political commitment to the major reorganization of tax administration initially envisioned in the GoP's own strategy." The report concluded, in typically circumspect Bank-speak, that "Borrower Performance [was] Unsatisfactory."

The long list of failed attempts to reduce leakages in Pakistani tax administration and widen the tax net must lead us to conclude that new attempts, despite the Sharif administration's 2013 commitment to the IMF, will also end in failure. The Pakistani elite and the Pakistani industrial, agricultural, and service sectors (dominated by firms/families who are an integral part of the elite) have systematically refused to pay anything even remotely approaching their "fair" share of taxes.

If Pakistan could increase its tax-to-GDP ratio to the 14 percent that it had once achieved, it would "solve" most of its current fiscal crisis and make a start at tackling its long list of structural problems. Pakistan's immediate economic crises are self-inflicted wounds that are, in large part, the result of the creation of a rentier mentality in its elite. Just as substantial mineral wealth avoids the need to develop a modern economy and/or build an efficient tax administration, since the 1980s Pakistan's geopolitical position has made it among the world's largest aid recipients and obviated the need for its government to carry out any meaningful reform. Pakistan's near-pariah status in the 1990s, after the United States had washed its hands of Afghanistan and suddenly realized that Pakistan's nuclear program was weapons-oriented, should have spurred internal reform but did not. Remittances from expatriate Pakistanis and some donor assistance allowed the country to limp along without any real structural reforms. Barring some truly revolutionary developments in Pakistani politics, anything more than incremental change is highly unlikely. Pakistan will continue to remain an unstable, economic crisis state.

Conclusion: Pakistan After the Withdrawal

Every sign so far indicates that the Nawaz Sharif administration will not be able to cope effectively with either Pakistan's serious load-shedding problem or its inability to raise enough tax revenues to actually fund government operations. Since Nawaz Sharif has been in power less than a year at the time of this writing, it might seem both premature and unduly pessimistic to deem his administration a "failure" already. It should be kept in mind, however, that this is actually Sharif's third go-round as prime minister of Pakistan. Neither of his past two administrations showed him to be fiscally competent or to have the will to carry out difficult and unpopular economic reforms.

On the contrary, Sharif's administrations have been notorious for gross fiscal mismanagement and profligacy. Shortly after his deposal in 1999, the Pakistani government officially informed the IMF that there had been "misreporting" of official budget deficit data for 1997–1998 and 1998–1999—the deficit was actually 1.4 to 2 percent of GDP higher than the figure reported by the Sharif administration. Furthermore, "discrepancies" and "erroneous recording" of data resulted in serious understatements of the amount of government borrowing during those same years (IMF 2000). Senator Ishaq Dar, Sharif's finance minister during this period and the man who authorized the "misreporting," is now finance minister again. While "misreporting" of budgetary data by Third World governments to the IMF to secure the next tranche of loans is an open secret known to all knowledgeable observers, it is unheard of for governments to officially confirm this to the IMF.

Despite this track record of serious fiscal mismanagement by all Pakistani governments, a failing Pakistan is clearly not in anyone else's interest. Therefore, some level of U.S. fiscal assistance will likely continue in the near future, even if it will be nowhere close to past levels. Similarly, the United States will likely continue to exert pressure on the IMF and the Pakistan Development Forum to continue assisting Pakistan, even if only at a reduced level, precisely because it is in no one's interest for Pakistan to fail more than it already has: a Pakistan limping along is infinitely preferable to a failed Pakistan.

Finally, Saudi Arabian assistance to Pakistan is another factor that would allow Pakistan to limp along. When the United States last imposed sanctions on Pakistan (after its successful nuclear weapons tests in 1998), Saudi Arabia agreed to provide Pakistan 80,000 barrels of oil a day on a "deferred payment facility" basis. Pakistan did not make any payments until 2000 (when the facility was reduced to 40,000 barrels a day) and apparently some two billion dollars of this deferred debt was quietly written off by the Saudis before the facility was phased out in 2003.[33] Given the ongoing Saudi-Iranian (that is, Sunni versus Shia) struggle for influence in the broader Persian Gulf, and the de facto Saudi-Pakistani military alliance, there is little doubt that Saudi Arabia would offer another such facility to Pakistan if circumstances became sufficiently dire.

Thus the real danger lies in the chance that Pakistan will get just enough fiscal assistance to allow it to continue on its current course for several more years, without being forced to carry out any substantial reforms. This would mean that the already shambolic Pakistani state could well become so decrepit that no reform could resuscitate or revitalize it. This would indeed ensure that Pakistan becomes a failed state.

Notes

1. The 2011 policy paper *Pakistan: Framework for Economic Growth* from the Planning Commission, Pakistan's official economic planning body, prepared in consultation with considerable external donor input, has an excellent analysis of the structural constraints facing the Pakistani economy; it also discusses possible reform strategies (Planning Commission 2011). However, given that it was a product of the Peoples Party government, Prime Minister Nawaz Sharif's Muslim League administration is unlikely to follow up on any of its policy recommendations.

2. For example, due to inadequate rainfall, late snowmelt, or, quite often, the release of water for irrigation.

3. The Pakistani fiscal year runs from July 1 to June 30 of the following year.

4. Official Indian government estimates are higher at about 8 percent for the post-2012 period (Jha 2013); other, more optimistic, estimates put it at 9 percent.

5. The actual transmission and distribution losses are probably much less than the stated figures, varying from 20 percent to 40 percent, as the remaining losses are a euphemism for outright electricity theft.

6. For example, the Kalabagh Dam on the Indus River, with a potential electricity-generating capacity of between 3,000 and 3,800 MW, will probably never be built as it is strongly opposed by the lower riparian province of Sindh (Pakistan).

7. HUBCO was initially guaranteed an 18 percent return on investment; under the 2002 revision to the IPP policy, this was lowered to about 15 percent for other IPPs. Some of the earlier generous concessions granted to HUBCO were also modified (Munir and Khalid 2012).

8. Above data, unless otherwise noted, is from Ali and Beg 2007: 3–6.

9. Munir and Khalid (2012) do not explore a scenario in which the plant was financed by the Government of Pakistan issuing a Eurobond with, say, an 8 percent coupon (common in the pre-financial-crisis years before 2008). The post-2008 Pakistani economic crisis pushed the yield on Pakistani Eurobonds to over 25 percent. The Pakistani government (or anyone else for that matter) could have purchased the US$ 25 million in Eurobonds on the secondary market for roughly thirty-two cents on the dollar—assuming of course that it had the necessary financial resources or acumen. An extreme example of this strategic behavior occurred in March 1988, when Bolivia repurchased US$ 308 million (face value) of its then US$ 670 million outstanding commercial debt for US$ 34 million; Bolivia had attempted to repurchase the entire amount but was unable to do so since news of the repurchase caused the price of Bolivian commercial debt to immediately jump to 0.11 cents on the dollar from 0.06 (Bulow and Rogoff 1990: 34).

10. Ten of the fifteen plants were below 200 megawatts (MW) in generating capacity and two were under 20 MW; these low-capacity plants were inefficient and thus very expensive electricity generators compared to the three IPPs that were above 400 MW capacity. Only three of the fifteen were (more efficient) natural gas-fired plants (Fraser 2005: 17). The cost differential between furnace oil and gas-fired combined cycle plants is substantial: about US$ 450–600 per kilowatt generated versus US$ 1,000 per kilowatt generated (Fraser 2005: 7).

11. While undoubtedly politically motivated and opportunistic, the charges were also substantively accurate.

12. The exact nature and validity of the charges against the IPPs and the mechanism by which they were negotiated are too complicated to go into detail here, but see Fraser 2005 for an excellent summary of the issues involved. A recent anonymous letter, clearly written by someone with insider knowledge of the issues, was sent to Pakistani media sites alleging that due to over-invoicing, falsifying generation efficiency data, and various other technical measures, the IPPs had been systematically defrauding the government of billions of rupees in overpayments; it concluded that the IPPs' actual return on investment is 35–40 percent. "Inclusive of original project cost—a payback period of two years. Not bad" (*Spokesman* 2013).

13. The subsidies are for electricity provided to low-income consumers at below generating cost or reimbursement to high-cost generating plants for providing electricity at the lower government-set rate (the tariff differential subsidy—TDS) as Pakistan has a uniform electricity rate for each category of consumer across the entire country.

14. In theory the National Electric Power Regulatory Authority (NEPRA) is supposed to evaluate electricity rates ("tariffs") on a monthly basis to take into account rapidly changing world fuel oil prices. In practice, tariff revaluation can take up to six months to process. The IPPs and GENCOs can then claim retroactive reimbursement from the Pakistani government for losses incurred due to the delay.

15. In formal testimony before the Pakistan Supreme Court, the managing director of NEPRA stated that the cost of electricity production in Pakistan could be reduced by 40 percent if the existing gas-fired plants could be supplied with sufficient natural gas to operate at capacity (Iqbal 2013). Pakistan has a severe natural gas shortage; gas is reserved for domestic and industrial use and not for power generation.

16. PKR 342 billion (US\$ 3.4 billion) was in actual monetary payment, partly financed through a large government bond issue, to IPPs and GENCOs, while PKR 138 billion (US\$ 1.4 billion) was in "noncash transactions," essentially offsetting debts owed to various corporate and government entities against debts owed by them; see *Express Tribune* 2013a for a detailed breakdown.

17. Pakistan has significant coal reserves; unfortunately most Pakistani coal is of fairly poor quality (low BTU and high sulfur content) and in difficult-to-mine areas. The government also announced a plan to double power-generating capacity in five years, an extension from thirty to sixty days for payment credit (i.e., the government would now have sixty days to make payments to IPPs before interest and penalties accrued), and a pledge to look into altering "the present skewed energy [generation] mix, which was at the core of the present energy crisis" (Kundi 2013). WAPDA is also more aggressively pursuing hydroelectric power generation, a process initiated by the previous administration.

18. This amount includes PKR 81 billion in earlier charges, mainly involving liquidated damages, penalties, interest charges, and so on, disputed by the government and not settled in June–July 2013.

19. The government's initial proposal of a 2013–2014 budget deficit of 6.3 percent of GDP was rejected.

20. See the IMF Country Report on Pakistan (IMF 2013) for details on the impressive laundry list of economic and fiscal reforms agreed to by the Pakistani government.

21. The proportion of GDP allocated to the development budget (i.e., "Public Sector Development Expenditure" in the official terminology) has been steadily declining over time: from 9 percent of GDP in the 1970s to about 3.5 percent now (*Express Tribune* 2013b).

22. See Epstein and Kronstadt 2013 for a detailed breakdown of U.S. assistance to Pakistan. Pakistanis disagree with this assessment of total "aid," since, of the military

assistance, US$ 10.7 billion was in Coalition Support Fund (CSF) payments, that is, ostensibly reimbursements for actions carried out by the Pakistani military in support of the U.S. intervention in Afghanistan. However, some CSF funds in the past have been claimed for such items as naval patrol boats that have minimal possible use in Afghanistan, a landlocked country with no navigable rivers, so "reimbursements" is probably a generous description of these payments. CSF payments are now coming under much greater scrutiny in the United States.

23. See Ministry of Finance 2013 for more details; data is from "Table 8.9: Workers' Remittances" and "Table 9.3: Annual Commitments, Disbursements, Service Payments and External Debt Outstanding" of the Statistical Appendix to the *Pakistan Economic Survey, 2012–2013*.

24. This is the World Bank category that Pakistan falls into: countries with 2012 Gross National Income per capita between US$ 1,036 and US$ 4,085.

25. The United States has its own source of tax regressivity, the payroll tax, which has grown from about 10 percent of GDP in the 1950s to 35 percent in 2012 (CBPP 2013: 1).

26. The actual tax revenue collected as a percentage of the amount of revenue theoretically collectable for a given tax rate.

27. See the Transparency International website, http://www.transparency.org/, for more on rankings, corruption levels, and methodology.

28. Other than essentially nominal water-use fees and land-revenue taxes. Since most farmers are small/subsistence cultivators, they would not be liable to pay taxes even if the income tax was extended to them, but the larger landowners who dominate rural Pakistan would be.

29. Up from 16 percent in 2012. The Pakistani Supreme Court declared the one percentage point increase to be illegal, but the government has vowed to fight this ruling.

30. For firms, the amount of VAT actually payable is on the difference between VAT levied on their sales minus the VAT paid on their inputs, that is, only the value added by the firm is VAT liable. This prevents tax cascading as VAT would be levied on inputs otherwise. If an item is "zero rated," the sales are taxed at "zero percent" but the inputs would have been taxed at the normal rate. Thus the firm is automatically due a substantial refund from the FBR since, as it has zero VAT payable, all VAT paid on inputs becomes a refund. The same holds true if the firm's sales are taxed at, say, 4 percent but its inputs are taxed at 17. If an item is tax exempt, no tax is levied on the sales but no rebate is allowed for taxed inputs. Thus it is of vital importance for firms if they are "zero rated" for GST/VAT or merely tax-exempt.

31. It is not clear if the choice of the date was simply a coincidence or done on purpose by someone with a sense of humor.

32. A common criticism of World Bank and IMF programs is that they are designed by "foreigners" who have minimal specialized knowledge of the country's

history, sociopolitical realities, and internal government issues. This project had Pakistani involvement in all aspects of its formulation and implementation.

33. For obvious reasons the exact details of such programs are difficult to determine. Pakistan has received such "deferred oil facilities" from Iran and Abu Dhabi as well, although only the Saudi one was turned into an outright grant. See Husain 2008 for more details on the Saudi facility.

Works Cited

Abbasi, Ansar. 2011. "Transparency Says Corruption Touching Rs3 Trillion in Pakistan." *News International* (Pakistan), July 13. http://www.thenews.com.pk/Todays-News-13-7383-Transparency-says-corruption-touching-Rs3-trillion-in-Pakistan.

Ahmad, Ehtisham. 2010. *The Political-Economy of Tax Reforms in Pakistan: The Ongoing Saga of the GST.* London School of Economics, Asia Research Centre Working Paper No. 33. http://www.lse.ac.uk/asiaResearchCentre/_files/ARCWP33-Ahmad.pdf.

———. 2011. *Why Is It So Difficult to Implement a GST in Pakistan?* International Growth Centre Working Paper No. 10/0876. London: International Growth Centre.

Ahmed, Naeem. 2013. "Industry Profile: Wholesale and Retail Trade Sector in Pakistan." *FBR Quarterly Review* 12 (2): 14–33. http://www.fbr.gov.pk/ShowDocument.aspx?Actionid=3505.

Ali, Fahd, and Fatima Beg. 2007. *The History of Private Power in Pakistan.* SDPI Working Paper No. 106, April. Islamabad, Pakistan: Sustainable Development Policy Institute. http://www.sdpi.org/publications/files/A106-A.pdf.

Asian Development Bank. 2010. *Integrated Energy Sector Recovery Report and Plan.* Manila, Philippines: Asian Development Bank. http://www.adb.org/sites/default/files/pub/2010/energy-recovery-report-plan.pdf.

Bulow, Jeremy, and Kenneth Rogoff. 1990. "Cleaning Up Third World Debt Without Getting Taken to the Cleaners." *Journal of Economic Perspectives* 4 (1): 31–42.

CBPP (Center for Budget and Policy Priorities). 2013. *Policy Basics: Where Do Federal Tax Revenues Come From?* April 12. http://www.cbpp.org/files/PolicyBasics_WhereDoFederalTaxRevsComeFrom_08-20-12.pdf.

Cheema, Umar. 2012. *Representation Without Taxation! An Analysis of MPs' Income Tax Returns for 2011.* Islamabad, Pakistan: Centre for Peace and Development Initiatives and Center for Investigative Reporting in Pakistan.

Economist. 2012. "Pakistan's Economy: Plugging Leaks, Poking Holes." December 8. http://www.economist.com/news/asia/21567999-who-will-pay-pakistans-state-plugging-leaks-poking-holes.

Epstein, Susan B., and K. Alan Kronstadt. 2013. *Pakistan: U.S. Foreign Assistance.* Washington, D.C.: Congressional Research Service. https://www.fas.org/sgp/crs/row/R41856.pdf?.

Express Tribune (Pakistan). 2013a. "Not Out of the Woods: Details of Rs480.1b Circular Debt Pay-off Released." July 24. http://tribune.com.pk/story/581219/not-out-of-the-woods-details-of-rs480-1b-circular-debt-pay-off-released/.

———. 2013b. "Out of Pocket: Suffering from the Perpetual Shortage of Revenues." September 15. http://tribune.com.pk/story/604635/out-of-pocket-suffering-from-the-perpetual-shortage-of-revenues/.

FBR (Federal Board of Revenue). 2011. "Revamping of Sales Tax Zero-Rating Scheme for Exports." SRO283(1)/2011, April 1. Islamabad: Government of Pakistan, Ministry of Finance. http://www.fbr.gov.pk/#.

Feldman, Herbert. 1972. *From Crisis to Crisis: Pakistan, 1962–1969*. London: Oxford University Press.

Fraser, Julia M. 2005. *Lessons from the Independent Private Power Experience in Pakistan*. Energy and Mining Sector Board Discussion Paper No. 14. Washington, D.C.: World Bank. http://info.worldbank.org/etools/docs/library/240338/Lessons%20from%20the%20Independent%20Private%20Power%20Experience%20in%20Pakistan.pdf.

Ghumman, Mushtaq. 2013. "Energy Sector: Circular Debt Again Peaks to Rs 157 Billion." *Business Recorder* (Pakistan), October 11. http://www.brecorder.com/market-data/stocks-a-bonds/0/1240038/.

Hassan, Bilal, and Tapan Sarker. 2012. "Reformed General Sales Tax in Pakistan." *International VAT Monitor*, November–December, 419–421. http://www.academia.edu/3258519/Reformed_General_Sales_Tax_in_Pakistan.

Hoti, Ikram. 2003. "Only 33pc Businessmen Paid GST in 2002–03." *Dawn* (Pakistan), December 13. http://forum.pakistanidefence.com/index.php?showtopic=23184.

Husain, Syed Rashid. 2008. "Saudi Oil Facility or Grant?" *Dawn* (Pakistan), July 28. http://www.dawn.com/news/313698/saudi-oil-facility-or-grant.

Hyder, Syed Nazre. 2012. *IMF Standby Arrangement for Pakistan and Its Inconclusive End: What Went Wrong?* Research Monograph No. 23. Islamabad, Pakistan: Sustainable Development Policy Institute. http://www.sdpi.org/publications/files/IMF%20Stand%20by%20Arrangement%20for%20Pakistan%20and%20its%20Inconclusive%20end%20What%20Went%20Wrong.pdf.

IMF (International Monetary Fund). 2000. "IMF Executive Board Reviews Pakistan Misreporting, Remedial Steps." *News Brief* 00/23, April 28. http://www.imf.org/external/np/sec/nb/2000/nb0023.htm.

———. 2013. *Pakistan*. IMF Country Report No. 13/287. Washington, D.C.: International Monetary Fund. http://www.imf.org/external/pubs/ft/scr/2013/cr13287.pdf.

IMF Survey. 2013. "Pakistan Gets $6.6 Billion Loan from IMF." September 4. http://www.imf.org/external/pubs/ft/survey/so/2013/car090413a.htm.

Iqbal, Nasir. 2013. "SC Hints at Order Against Tariff Hike." *Dawn* (Pakistan), October 2. http://dawn.com/news/1046895/sc-hints-at-order-against-tariff-hike.

Jha, Somesh. 2013. "India's GDP Growing Below Potential: Moody's Analytics Says Govt's Belief of 8% Growth Rate Unlikely, Sees Potential Growth Rate at 7%." *Business Standard* (India), May 23. http://www.business-standard.com/article/economy-policy/india-s-gdp-growing-below-potential-moody-s-analytics-113052 300181_1.html,.

KESC. 2013. *Karachi Electric Supply Corporation.* http://www.kesc.com.pk.

Khan, Ahmad F. 2013. "Violence as Shortfall Rises to 7,000MW." *Dawn* (Pakistan), May 28. http://beta.dawn.com/news/1014407/violence-as-shortfall-rises-to-7000 mw.

Khan, Feisal. 2007. "Corruption and the Decline of the State in Pakistan." *Asian Journal of Political Science* 15 (2): 219–247.

Kiani, Khaleeq. 2013. "Govt Orders Third Party Audit of Rs480bn Paid as Circular Debt." *Dawn* (Pakistan), September 27. http://dawn.com/news/1045752/govt-orders-third-party-audit-of-rs480bn-paid-as-circular-debt.

Kundi, Imran Ali. 2013. "Rs. 480b Circular Debt Cleared." *Nation* (Pakistan), July 23. http://www.nation.com.pk/pakistan-news-newspaper-daily-english-online/business/23-Jul-2013/rs-480b-circular-debt-cleared.

Ministry of Finance. 2013. *Economic Survey of Pakistan, 2012–2013.* Islamabad: Government of Pakistan. http://www.finance.gov.pk/survey_1213.html.

Munir, Kamal A., and Salman Khalid. 2012. "Pakistan's Power Crisis: How Did We Get Here?" *Lahore Journal of Economics* 17 (September): 73–82.

Mustafa, Khalid. 2011. "Annual Loss of 3–4% GDP Due to Power Shortages." *News International* (Pakistan), September 15. http://www.thenews.com.pk/TodaysPrint Detail.aspx?ID = 8816&Cat = 13.

Nation (Pakistan). 2013. "Hydel Power Generation Cut to 2,800 MW." April 16. http://www.nation.com.pk/pakistan-news-newspaper-daily-english-online/lahore/16-Apr-2013/-hydel-power-generation-cut-to-2-800mw.

NEPRA (National Electric Power Regulatory Authority). 2012. *State of Industry Report, 2012.* Islamabad, Pakistan: National Electric Power Regulatory Authority.

OECD (Organization for Economic Cooperation and Development). 2012. *OECD Economic Outlook, Ch.4: Medium and Long Term Scenarios for Global Growth and Imbalances,* vol. 2012/1. http://www.oecd.org/berlin/50405107.pdf.

Owens, Jeffrey. 2011. "Improving Performance of VAT Systems." *World Commerce Review* 5 (3): 8–10. http://www.oecd.org/ctp/consumption/48826272.pdf.

Pervez, Aslam. 2011. *Pakistan Power Sector.* Karachi, Pakistan: Consulate General of Switzerland.

Planning Commission. 2011. *Pakistan: Framework for Economic Growth.* Islamabad: Government of Pakistan. http://www.pc.gov.pk/hot%20links/growth_document_english_version.pdf.

Rana, Shahbaz. 2013. "IMF's Condition: Pakistan Agrees to Slice Budget Deficit Target." *Express Tribune* (Pakistan), September 10. http://tribune.com.pk/story/602206/imfs-condition-pakistan-agrees-to-slice-budget-deficit-target/.

Sharp, Jeremy M. 2013. *Egypt: Background and U.S. Relations*. Washington, D.C.: Congressional Research Service. http://fpc.state.gov/documents/organization/124082.pdf.

Spokesman (Pakistan). 2013. "Energy Scam? Anonymous Letter Raises Important Questions." June 21. http://thespokesman.pk/index.php/template/item/6268-energy-scam-anonymous-letter-raises-important-questions.

State Bank of Pakistan. 2013a. "Historical Exchange Rates: US Dollar." www.sbp.org.pk/ecodata/HER-USDollar.xls.

———. 2013b. *Home Remittances*. Karachi, Pakistan: State Bank of Pakistan. http://www.sbp.org.pk/ecodata/index2.asp.

Tran, Mark. 2013. "Pakistan Needs to Recoup More in Taxes Before Any Aid Boost, Say MPs." *Guardian* (London), April 3. http://www.theguardian.com/global-development/2013/apr/04/pakistan-recoup-taxes-aid-mps.

Trimble, Chris, Nobuo Yoshida and Mohammad Saqib. 2011 *Rethinking Electricity Tariffs in Pakistan*. World Bank Report Number 62971-PK. Washington, D.C.: World Bank. http://www-wds.worldbank.org/external/default/WDSContentServer/WDSP/IB/2011/08/31/000386194_20110831050158/Rendered/PDF/6297 10ESW0whit0020110Final00PUBLIC 0.pdf

USAID/PCoP (United States Agency for International Development and Planning Commission of Pakistan). 2013. *The Causes and Impacts of Power Sector Circular Debt in Pakistan: March 2013*. Islamabad: Government of Pakistan. http://www.pc.gov.pk/hot%20links/2013/Final_USAID-Pakistan%20Circular%20Debt%20Report-Printed%20Mar%2025,%202013.pdf.

WAPDA (Water and Power Development Agency). 2013. *Hydro Potential in Pakistan*. Islamabad, Pakistan: Water and Power Development Agency.World Bank. 2009. *Pakistan: Tax Policy Report: Tapping Tax Bases for Development*. Vol. 1. Washington, D.C.: World Bank. https://openknowledge.worldbank.org/bitstream/handle/10986/3099/500780v10ESW0P11official0use0only10.pdf?sequence = 1.

———. 2011. *More and Better Jobs in South Asia*. Washington, D.C.: World Bank.

———. 2012. *Implementation Completion and Results Report (IBRD-72640 IDA-40070 TF-54392)*. Washington, D.C.: World Bank. http://www-wds.worldbank.org/external/default/WDSContentServer/WDSP/IB/2012/07/11/000356161_201207 11004432/Rendered/PDF/ICR21470P077300LIC0dislosed07090120.pdf.

———. 2013. "World Development Indicators." http://databank.worldbank.org/data/views/variableSelection/selectvariables.aspx?source = world-development-indicators.

PART III

Foreign Relations

Chapter 8

America and Pakistan After 2014: Toward Strategic Breathing Space

Paul Staniland

The drawdown of American forces from Afghanistan will substantially change the relationship between Pakistan and the United States. The United States is likely to have much more limited needs as regards Pakistan. American interests in counterterrorism and general regional stability will replace its deep reliance on Pakistan for logistical support related to the U.S. war in Afghanistan. America's security establishment will instead devote far more attention to the rise of China and the enduring instability in the Middle East. Within South Asia, India will be the key strategic player because of its relevance to the rise of China and its sustained, if variable, economic growth. Pakistan, in turn, will be consumed by domestic politics, economic crisis, and constrained attempts at broadening its influence in Afghanistan.

As a result, America and Pakistan are likely to drift even further apart after 2014. A relationship under severe strain will become more distant and focused on fewer issues. This American separation from the region will surely create serious dislocation and may exacerbate Afghanistan's already-intense civil war. Yet it may also create valuable strategic breathing space between Pakistan and the United States that will be healthier and even, over the long run, more "normal." The strained codependency of the two countries is a major liability in America's strategic posture and has done little to create a more stable Pakistan. This chapter makes the case that less may be more. The United States has limited interests and weak leverage in South Asia. It will benefit from a restrained strategy that seeks to avoid ambitious commitments and entanglements. In turn, Pakistan may very well benefit from escaping America's shadow. A less engaged United States can open space for bolder Pakistani domestic and international initiatives by reducing politicians' vulnerability to accusations that they are selling out to American interests.

The chapter first outlines the basic thrust of American strategy toward Pakistan since 9/11. This strategy has been characterized by efforts to balance a number of deep trade-offs, often without much success. It has also changed over time, as growing anti-American sentiment in Pakistan and corresponding suspicion of Pakistan within the U.S. government undermined bilateral relations. The Bush administration focused heavily on security aid and military cooperation with Pervez Musharraf. Aid and arms sales surged to new heights as previous concerns about Pakistan's proliferation record were swept away. As the Musharraf regime faltered and then fell, greater emphasis was put on nonmilitary aid. Development and civil society engagement became—at least rhetorically—coequal to military efforts. An influx of aid into Pakistan was intended to complement the military surge in Afghanistan to stabilize the region. Yet there is little evidence that these efforts had much of an effect. The 2011 killing of Osama bin Laden, along with other incidents during 2011–2012, shattered the already-unrealistic goal of a sustained, respectful partnership. The Obama administration's decision to substantially draw down the U.S. force presence from Afghanistan by 2014 signals a new American distance, though not disappearance, from the region.

The chapter then considers the broader implication of America's changing posture. There will be undeniable downsides to the U.S. shift, but I argue that it may actually benefit both countries. A reduced American presence will likely leave Pakistan relatively more powerful in the region, especially in Afghanistan, but this will not buy it much in terms of actual security. The facts on the ground suggest that Pakistan will not be able to cleanly impose its will on Afghanistan. Instead, a tenuous and complex set of political orders will emerge on the Afghanistan-Pakistan borderlands with unclear, at best, benefits to Pakistan. As long as the Kabul government continues to receive international support from India, Russia, and the United States, Pakistan is unlikely to be a kingmaker. India will continue to be the strategic key to South Asia, and a more valuable long-run partner for the United States than Pakistan. The underlying balance of power in the region will limit Pakistan's ability to project influence.

Domestically, a reduced American presence will provide room to maneuver for Pakistani politicians, who will become less vulnerable to claims of being American puppets. This is no panacea for Pakistan's myriad domestic problems, but it nevertheless might allow more conciliatory policies toward India and the Afghan government. It may also facilitate aggressive targeting of militant groups with anti-Islamabad war aims. The post-2014 posture will not help the United States put pressure on the government or army to crack down on the Afghan Taliban or Lashkar-e-Taiba, but neither has the more ambitious policy since 2001. The less the United States is perceived to be a key player in Pakistan, the better for both countries.

Ultimately, a smaller American footprint may allow the United States and Pakistan to deal with one another in a more forthright way. The two countries have had exceptionally unpleasant dealings in recent years, and less involvement, rather than grandiose public diplomacy goals and huge aid inflows, can lead to a more normal relationship. This is not a perfect outcome, since it will add to a narrative of American volatility and lack of commitment while allowing Pakistan to continue dangerous strategies in the region. Nevertheless, it is one that both sides should be able to live with compared to the unpalatable alternative of stringing along a broken alliance.

American Strategy Since 9/11

This section outlines the basic contours of American Pakistan strategy since 9/11, building on Fair and Watson's introduction. It highlights the deep tensions, even contradictions, in U.S.-Pakistan relations during this period. The United States tried to maintain good relations with both India and Pakistan, tried to reassure Pakistani leaders of American commitment while also trying to threaten conditionality, bolstered a military dictatorship while rhetorically upholding democracy, and facilitated a political economy of predation and rent seeking while decrying such behavior. Some of these tensions were inevitable given the circumstances, but others were avoidable and ultimately counterproductive. The interaction of American and Pakistani strategies bred an acrimonious codependency that achieved some short-term goals without laying the basis for longer-term partnership.

This chapter focuses on the post-2001 period, but it is worth noting that the current mixture of ambivalence and alliance is not new: the 1950s and 1960s, for instance, also saw the United States trying to maintain good terms with both India and Pakistan while pursuing broader aims at odds with the core interests of Pakistani leaders (Kux 2001). The dysfunctions of the relationship have taken on a new form, but U.S.-Pakistan ties have often been driven by expediency and short-term thinking. There is a deeper structure of conflict between American and Pakistani interests that is only papered over in periods when America needs something in the region and Pakistan's military elite can extract organizational and political benefits from the United States. The 2001–2014 period is thus another iteration of a much longer pattern, rather than a radical break from the past.

The Initial Strategy: Musharraf and the Military

After 9/11, Pakistan became a crucial frontline state in the war on terror. Its geographic and political proximity to Afghanistan immediately made it a central player in U.S. efforts to find Osama bin Laden and overthrow the Taliban. Yet on September 10, 2001, the United States and Pakistan were not on good terms. America had imposed numerous military and economic sanctions on Pakistan since 1990, first in response to Pakistan's nuclear program and then following the 1999 coup by Pervez Musharraf. Increasing American concern, from 1994 onward Pakistan supported the Afghan Taliban as they tried to consolidate their rule over Afghanistan. Domestic political instability and continual civil-military tensions wracked the country. Moreover, India was slowly but surely rising, leading to growing American interest in the late Clinton administration (Cohen 2001; Talbott 2006). The alignments of the late Cold War were breaking down, and India became a greater prize than Pakistan for American policy makers. America and Pakistan were not natural allies; instead, Pakistan was a marginal player in broader U.S. grand strategy.

Then 9/11 changed all of this, at least temporarily, as Fair and Watson's introduction to this volume makes clear. America needed information, logistical and basing support, and cooperation in targeting al-Qaeda members; it also hoped for Pakistani support in coercing the Taliban to turn over Osama bin Laden and assistance in regime change should coercion fail. The United States put great effort into convincing Pakistan's military dictator Pervez Musharraf to support American aims in the region. Pakistan was now back on America's agenda.

From the very beginning, there were strains in the U.S.-Pakistan relationship: Musharraf and his military supporters were not wildly enthusiastic about a robust American presence in Afghanistan. The seeds of current tensions have roots in the foundations of the reinvigorated alliance in late 2001. It was a linkage of convenience rather than of deep and long-term shared interests. The United States combined coercion and bribery to "flip" the weaker Pakistanis. Many Pakistanis—and members of the Pakistan army—were skeptical of, or actively hostile to, the proclaimed war on terror. Musharraf had to navigate this complex political landscape, relying heavily on the military and political elites who had decided to collaborate with the regime rather than hold out in opposition to it. As I discuss later, this limited political base became a major liability later in Musharraf's rule, undermining America's (and Musharraf's) aspirations for him as a reliable and "enlightened" strongman.

Despite these domestic challenges, the payoffs to Pakistan's military elites were substantial (Fair 2011). American sanctions in place were swept away in exchange for Pakistani cooperation in going after al-Qaeda leaders and facilitating the intelligence gathering and logistics of the American war effort. Pakistan regained access to international funding and favor after a long period in the wilderness. In 2004 it was named a major non-NATO ally of the United States. American and international support helped to bolster Musharraf's power base and Pakistan's economy, at least superficially. Musharraf framed his military dictatorship as a bulwark against extremism and radical Islam, arguing that Pakistan needed a strong leader who could instill moderate values (Musharraf 2006). His ability to deliver several al-Qaeda operatives showed that U.S. support for him offered tangible counterterrorism benefits.

Musharraf's political strategy had two key components. He relied heavily on the support of the military, especially the army, which, as I discuss below, initially benefited from dramatically increased aid, sales, and cooperation. It would later, however, became more estranged from the United States. He also tried to build up a civilian political infrastructure to institutionalize his rule. He pursued the latter option by manipulating electoral politics to put allies in power, breaking the back of Pakistan's major national parties, and putting together the Pakistan Muslim League (Quaid-e-Azam) as his civilian front. This strategy was not successful in building a powerful set of civilian allies: they had weak party structures, little ideological independence, and few autonomous sources of political strength. When mobilization against Musharraf escalated in 2007, he found himself without an institutionalized party able to close ranks and protect the regime.

Musharraf's primary power base was the military, which gained in the early years of the U.S.-Pakistan rapprochement. Arms sales and aid to the Pakistan army and air force surged and military-to-military cooperation increased after a long period of sanctions. The army in particular expanded its already historically entrenched power (Nawaz 2008). Military assistance and reimbursements reached heights not seen even during the Cold War, and the International Military Education and Training program grew. The Congressional Research Service notes that American aid has been primarily focused on security issues: "About two-thirds of US aid from FY2002 to FY2012, some $15.8 billion (including Coalition Support Fund reimbursements), has supported security assistance in Pakistan" (Epstein and Kronstadt 2013: 10).

Pakistan received several forms of military aid. The bulk came through the Coalition Support Fund (CSF), which essentially paid the Pakistani military for operational and logistical support for the U.S. campaign in Afghanistan. Some CSF payments were for direct Pakistani military offensives and general operations, while others reimbursed Pakistan for U.S. use of Pakistani facilities. The CSF also provided equipment to Pakistan intended for use in counterinsurgency and counterterrorism operations. The other key area of military aid came in Foreign Military Financing (FMF) and Excess Defense Articles (EDA), which were avenues for Pakistan to acquire arms. Pakistan was able to upgrade several weapons systems through these sources.

The actual use of these various funds became quite controversial, especially among Indians (*Hindu* 2011). CSF oversight was fairly lax for years after 9/11, and the arms that Pakistan procured under the program seemed better suited for conventional warfare with India than for counterterrorism and counterinsurgency operations. Indian and skeptical American observers feared that the Pakistani military was taking advantage of highly fungible resources to build up a modern war machine in the context of a South Asian arms race. There is clearly some truth to this assessment (GAO 2008).

Nevertheless, the Pakistan army also did take some serious losses in operations against militants. The major crisis of militancy did not come until after Musharraf's fall, but the trends in violence clearly were moving in the wrong direction in 2006–2008. Insurgent mobilization in the Federally Administered Tribal Areas (FATA), reinvigorated sectarian militancy, and rogue splinters of previously sponsored anti-India groups threatened the state, even as it tried to maintain good relations with friendly armed groups (Hussain 2007). Pakistan's security forces were not well trained or equipped for ambitious counterinsurgency operations. Local Frontier Corps forces were particularly inadequate for the task at hand, while army units were better trained for aerial bombardments and armor movements than for carefully targeting insurgents (Lalwani 2009). Pakistan's military thus was building up its conventional capabilities while also dealing—sometimes well, often poorly—with a growing militant threat.

The United States also provided some aid for development during this period, though the major emphasis came later after Musharraf's fall. Economic aid, especially through Economic Support Funds (ESF), increased substantially, helping to fuel artificially inflated Pakistani growth rates. The United States was the primary, but not sole, donor, reflecting its key position in the region. The goal of this aid was to shore up an economy that was faltering badly under Musharraf (especially to alleviate debt) and to lay the basis for sustainable growth that could blunt extremism and create political stability. Aid effectiveness is difficult to assess in the best of circumstances, but there is little reason to believe that the aid provided to Pakistan made a substantial difference in long-run governance or development. Debt relief was helpful but key economic fundamentals did not dramatically change under Musharraf, despite ostensibly high economic growth. One key exception was a burgeoning media market appealing to urban middle classes.

After Musharraf: Development and Democracy?

In 2007, Musharraf's clash with Pakistan's Supreme Court escalated into street protests against his rule. Against the backdrop of growing militancy—most dramatically the Lal Masjid debacle during the summer of 2007—Musharraf's rule was becoming increasingly unstable. His inability to build a reliable, institutionalized civilian mechanism of rule became clear. Unlike single-party authoritarian regimes elsewhere, Musharraf had few loyal allies able to mobilize the masses in his defense. Neither Musharraf nor his American backers had been able to embed his rule into durable political institutions. Instead, Musharraf relied on the military, and his command of the military weakened after he relinquished his army position in November 2007. His position became untenable as 2007 went on. Despite the assassination of Benazir Bhutto, elections were held in February 2008, and Musharraf resigned as president in August 2008. He later went into exile, eventually launching an ill-fated comeback before the 2013 elections.

This shift in domestic political conditions undermined the previous American strategy (Coll 2009). No longer was Musharraf available as a friendly military face who could get things done—or at least claim to. American policy makers aimed to spur development, support democracy, and create greater accountability in the use of American funding. Starting in 2008, vast sums of money were poured into Pakistan, with various forms of economic aid now receiving a major increase. The Enhanced Partnership with Pakistan Act in 2009, also known as the Kerry-Lugar-Berman (KLB) bill, advanced an ambitious set of goals: fostering economic growth, supporting expanded counterinsurgency, and imposing greater oversight and accountability on American flows toward Pakistan. The FATA continued to receive particular attention as the hub of security threats facing both the United States and Pakistan (GAO 2010).

This strategy was put in place as the United States also launched a surge of forces in Afghanistan. In both Afghanistan and Pakistan, American policy makers were making a bet on huge resource investments as tools of stabilization and state building. Kerry-Lugar-Berman authorized up to $1.5 billion a year for economic aid, which combined with the military aid being provided to make Pakistan one of the primary recipients of American aid. Support was also provided for governance and civil society initiatives that could improve the working of Pakistan's political system. The underlying theory guiding American policy makers seemed to be that militancy was a product of economic underdevelopment and poor governance. By targeting these underlying conditions, the structural roots of violence could be eliminated.

Military aid continued at high levels, though with some new features (Entous and Barnes 2010). KLB included fairly loose conditions for Pakistani military aid, which triggered discontent among pro-military opinion in Pakistan. This was an effort to rein in the American blank check to the army, but was limited in actually changing the military's behavior. The backlash against KLB showed how American efforts were viewed by many in Pakistan, even when they involved huge amounts of U.S. money flowing into the country.

A dedicated Pakistan Counterinsurgency Fund (PCF) was created in 2009 to help antimilitant operations while trying to limit the use of American resources for conventional warfare preparations (Schmitt and Shanker 2009). Pakistan forces' lack of preparation for counterinsurgency became a major issue in 2008 and 2009 as various factions of the Tehreek-e-Taliban-e-Pakistan (TTP) increased their reach. Arms and training were high priorities to help Pakistani forces hold back the militant tide, which is discussed in more detail in Tankel's chapter in this volume. The key to changing policy, however, was political: no amount of American money alone was sufficient to impel the military and political leadership to launch aggressive counterinsurgency efforts. Only once this leadership actually felt seriously threatened was there sufficient will to crack down against clearly anti-regime factions. The American focus on training and equipment is reasonable, but capacity is not the core issue driving Pakistan's counterinsurgency policies. This is shown by the attempts of the Pakistan military—as well as some civilian politicians—to cut deals with militants and to aggressively target some armed groups while containing or colluding with others (Staniland 2012).

In sum, the new-look Obama strategy aimed to move past the Bush administration's focus on security to build a full-spectrum relationship across economic, political, and military issues. On paper, this seemed like an attractive approach, one that could uphold American ideals like democratic government while also advancing key security interests. Yet the scale of the ambition was unrealistic and the plausible leverage that the United States could summon remained very limited. Even on technocratic issues, the ability to translate money into outcomes was dubious: development, for instance, is not easily triggered by aid inflows and governance reform requires much more than training sessions, funding, and moral support. The American government does not know how to accomplish many of the tasks that were set before it, nor is there a straightforward, easily implemented set of best practices on how to achieve outcomes like thoroughgoing sustainable development. The Obama administration's rhetorical goals were so broad and encompassing that it is not clear how external actors could realistically hope to accomplish them.

Unraveling: Raymond Davis and Osama bin Laden

The grand hopes that drove the massive resource expenditures that began in 2008–2009 largely never materialized. Between 2009 and 2013, the U.S. strategy ran into a series of huge political obstacles that have badly strained, even broken, America-Pakistan ties. By 2013, the United States and Pakistan were locked in an uneasy, distrustful relationship in which neither country's political leadership or military establishment has faith in the other.

Not everything has gone wrong. Pakistan has maintained a democratic form of government, which is a major success. The government and military become somewhat more aggressive in counterinsurgency after major TTP advances in 2009, and now seem to have established a kind of (leaky) cordon sanitaire in Khyber Pakhtunkhwa Province (KPK) and the Federally Administered Tribal Areas (FATA). It is not clear to what extent either outcome is due to American involvement, however. The Pakistan army retains huge power and civilian politicians continue to tread carefully in foreign and security policy. Counterinsurgency offensives seem more driven by the political interests of leaders than U.S. pressure, which was already high well before major changes occurred in counterinsurgency policy. The domestic mobilization of the lawyers' movement, judiciary, and political parties is impressive, though not always unambiguously good for the United States—the sympathy for sectarian militants held by many lawyers, for instance, is deeply disturbing. Pakistan has made some progress since 2007, but this progress is tenuous and driven primarily by domestic politics.

In the areas of governance and development, the two key planks of KLB and of Obama's strategy, U.S. pressure has had no effect. Pakistan is facing a set of deep economic challenges, ranging from the collapse of reliable electricity to extremely low tax collection (Khan's chapter in this volume makes clear the depth of Pakistan's economic challenges). The 7 percent growth rate seen at the height of Musharraf's tenure is a distant memory. Infrastructure and rule of law remain disastrous. As suggested above, the ability of American aid programs and development assistance to change the fundamentals of Pakistan's politics and political economy is extremely limited. Patronage, politicized bureaucracies, and elite predation are difficult to change, especially in a limited time frame. Moreover, anti-American sentiment has not diminished; in fact, it is higher than in 2007. The Obama administration's hope that development and governance investments would lead to change in mass public opinion has not been borne out (Pew 2012). This hope reflects a flawed notion of what drives radicalism (Blair et al. 2013). The causes of Pakistani sentiment are much more complex, and perhaps even less susceptible to American manipulation, than are economic growth and bad governance.

On the security front, Pakistan still faces an intense insurgency while at the same time turning a blind eye to armed groups on its Afghan frontier and in core areas of the country like Punjab and Karachi (Bergen and Tiedemann 2013). The situation has stabilized, but violence remains high, driven by TTP attacks, sectarian militancy, and, in Karachi, armed political competition. The Pakistani security establishment continues to take American money but is deeply distrustful of the United States, a distrust reciprocated in public by a number of senior serving and retired American military officers. The carrots offered by the United States have not led to major policy shifts, while the threatened sticks have not been credible.

This set of outcomes has been driven by a number of causes, many of them with structural roots in Pakistani history (Jalal 1990; Tudor 2013), its low levels of human capital, and crumbling infrastructure, as well as the global recession. It would be unreasonable to expect American aid to straightforwardly surmount these obstacles. Nevertheless, a key contributor to the failure of this strategy was the underlying clash of interests between Pakistan and the United States, and the highly public, controversial events that have flowed from this tension. Such clashes of interest were certainly predictable at the time of the Obama administration's strategy formation and implementation, and wishful thinking may have dominated over a realistic appraisal of the situation.

Two events were particularly salient in showing the divide between America and Pakistan, massive aid flows and hopeful rhetoric notwithstanding. The first was the Raymond Davis affair, in which a covert American operative killed two Pakistani men in Lahore (the American rescue team sent to his aid then killed a Pakistani motorcyclist). Davis was part of a substantial American covert presence in Pakistan that was spying on Pakistani militant groups and the Pakistani security establishment. Pakistan's security elite and mass public were both deeply offended by Davis's actions and by the broader significance of his presence (Mazzetti 2013). Various American efforts to deny his intelligence role—instead insisting that he was engaged in diplomatic activities—further undermined U.S. credibility in the country. While a face-saving compromise was eventually arranged, Davis's presence in country was a striking demonstration of U.S. suspicions of Pakistan.

The other event of 2011 that undermined the Obama strategy was the killing of Osama bin Laden in Abbottabad. The military expressed a strong negative reaction, and much of the commentary in Pakistan focused on the violation of Pakistani sovereignty. This response was met with disbelief by Americans happy at bin Laden's killing and dubious that the Pakistani security establishment could have been completely unaware of bin Laden's presence (Wright 2011). On a deeper level, bin Laden's death and the continued drone strikes in the northwest frontier seemed to have badly degraded al-Qaeda, weakening the case for a continued close engagement with Pakistan and opening the door to a much-reduced American presence in the region.

Further events accelerated this distancing between the United States and Pakistan. In November 2011, twenty-four Pakistani soldiers were accidentally killed by NATO forces along the Afghanistan-Pakistan border, leading to a shutdown of logistics flows into Afghanistan from Pakistan amid outrage at NATO actions. Fair and Watson's introduction highlights this incident as a key tipping point in U.S.-Pakistan relations, even though it did not receive much attention in the United States. In May 2012, the sentencing of Dr. Shakil Afridi, who had helped America gather intelligence about bin Laden, produced further tension. Afridi's imprisonment led to a (small) reduction in American aid and increased criticism of Pakistan by American elected officials. To Americans, helping to find bin Laden was laudable; to many Pakistanis, Afridi was a traitor for facilitating American espionage. America's campaign of regular drone strikes also contributed to tensions, with many Pakistanis opposed to these strikes as violations of sovereignty (even as others supported them as a powerful counterterrorism tool). The complex politics of drones have posed a major challenge to both U.S. and Pakistani policy makers, since drone strikes serve some Pakistani interests but also make Pakistani leaders vulnerable to domestic criticisms of being American lackeys (ICG 2013; see also Watson and Fair's chapter on drones in this volume for a more detailed study of the drone policy). Furthermore, American aid has been disbursed in fits and starts, often delayed or held up by a mixture of politics and bureaucracy.

Against this background, prominent Pakistanis and Americans have called for a fundamental rethinking of the relationship; the former ambassador to the United States Husain Haqqani, for instance, argued that the time had come for a "divorce" between the two countries. In Pakistan's May 2013 elections, Nawaz Sharif's victory and the rise of Imran Khan signaled that skepticism—though not aggressive hostility—toward America was an electoral asset (although the bilateral relationship was a marginal issue compared to the economy). India-Pakistan relations have the potential to improve under Sharif, but largely because of Pakistan's economic crisis rather than American mediation.

The American strategy of pairing development with military aid has run into hard political realities. Extraordinary amounts of money appear to have been wasted, both in Afghanistan and Pakistan, with little to show for the effort. Despite some areas of cooperation, and extensive military aid, the Pakistani security establishment has not been won over; far from it. The blame for these results is widely shared, but the fact remains that Pakistan and the United States have different interests (Fair 2012). This divergence cannot be papered over and it will not go away as a function of aid or public diplomacy.

After 2014: The Contours of U.S.-Pakistan Relations

This is the context heading into the U.S. drawdown from Afghanistan. It seems clear that the United States and Pakistan are not primed for harmonious ties as America reduces its footprint in Afghanistan. Some accounts of the post-2014 security environment point to an aggressive Pakistan taking advantage of generalized chaos and breakdown (Bergen 2013). This is possible, but the more likely outcomes are less dramatic: continued proxy warfare in Afghanistan, Pakistani influence in the region that is nevertheless limited by domestic economic and political constraints, and a more distant, but not necessarily less healthy, U.S.-Pakistan relationship. Such a set of outcomes is compatible with core American goals and is preferable to simultaneously throwing money at Pakistan while being frustrated by it. Being bogged down in Afghanistan and Pakistan is not strategically smart for the United States; while it has important interests in the region, they are limited and do not require ambitious and costly involvement. It can find valuable strategic breathing space from its long decade of deep engagement in South and Central Asia. Both the United States and Pakistan can engage in more honest, forthright policies toward one another without an unpersuasive veneer of close partnership.

Implications for the Region

The U.S. drawdown will open space for Pakistan to pursue a sphere of influence in Afghanistan. With fewer American troops on the ground, the Afghan Taliban will be more militarily effective against the Kabul regime and will have greater bargaining power in any negotiations over a political settlement. There is certainly a chance that this will open the door to full-scale Taliban victory, in a replay of the 1990s. In this case, the U.S. drawdown would radically alter the regional balance of power and achieve Pakistani aims of controlling Afghanistan.

This outcome is possible but unlikely. Pakistan's room to maneuver in Afghanistan will certainly grow, but there are serious limits on its ability to dominate the country. First, the Afghan Taliban are not simple pawns of the Pakistani state. They have shown an ability to defy and manipulate Pakistani governments in pursuit of their own interests (Rashid 2010). Second, the continuing low-level presence of American support will provide a valuable backstop for Kabul's forces, one which can prevent total collapse. (At the time of writing, however, the impasse over the terms of the Bilateral Security Agreement raises the question of whether the United States will maintain even a low-level presence in Afghanistan.) Involvement by other powers, like India and Russia, can also help to keep the regime at least minimally functional, though there should be no illusions about its competence or coherence.

This combination leads to a strong likelihood that instead of clear victory, Pakistan, the Taliban, and the Kabul government, plus various other actors, will be forced into a set of compromises. Different parts of Afghanistan will exist under different levels of state control, and negotiations and bargains are likely to lead to heterogeneous forms of order across Afghanistan (Staniland 2012). This is a messy solution compared to the ideal of an effective and consensually accepted Afghan state, but it may be able to provide basic stability by satisfying local power holders.

A reduced U.S. presence can actually facilitate some of these deals, allowing Afghans—possibly including the Taliban leadership—to make political arrangements that would not be acceptable to international state builders. The model of counterinsurgency and state strengthening guiding the Obama's administration's "surge" has not had much success, and unorthodox alternatives may be worthwhile. This is especially true given that America's core interests in Afghanistan are limited. Preventing a full-scale return of al-Qaeda is the key goal, and anything beyond that may not be worth investing material and political resources. America can live with a fairly broad range of outcomes as long as that core condition is met, reducing the need for enduring involvement and resource investments.

Pakistan will also face domestic constraints on its exercise of influence in Afghanistan. Politicians are more likely to be occupied with economic crises and political infighting than on bids for regional hegemony. The Pakistan army will certainly take great interest in Afghanistan, but it has its hands full with extensive militancy in the northwest frontier area that limits power projection. The point here is simply that Pakistan is not in a good position to seamlessly achieve ambitious interests in Afghanistan even after a U.S. drawdown. Instead, while Pakistani influence will undoubtedly increase after 2014, there will also be powerful countervailing forces that constrain Pakistan. The United States can adopt a mix of containment and bargaining with Pakistan over the new Afghan order, less concerned about its logistics tail and Pakistani leverage over the NATO war effort.

A U.S. drawdown will also not radically transform India-Pakistan relations. There is a good chance that Pakistan will increase jihadi infiltration into Kashmir and urban India as a way of trying to deflect militant attention from its western borders. In the long run, however, India's size and economic growth make it far stronger than Pakistan; terrorist attacks are horrific but do not change the underlying relative power structure. The current American posture does not seem to have delivered clear benefits for India, given Pakistan's expanding nuclear arsenal and continued patronage of Lashkar-e-Taiba, so a reduced American presence may only make a marginal difference to Indo-Pak relations.

One striking aspect of the last decade is just how limited American influence has been on the subcontinent. The United States has managed to find itself intertwined in India-Pakistan tensions without having much control over either actor. This is not new: as Howard Schaffer and Dennis Kux have pointed out, America has been regularly flummoxed by the complexities of South Asia's international relations (Kux 2001; Schaffer 2009). Belief in the U.S. ability to swoop in with money and self-proclaimed goodwill to fix major problems is naive, even counterproductive. True change requires major policy initiatives by Indian and Pakistani domestic players willing to take risks and redefine their core interests and perceptions. This process can be facilitated, but not triggered or sustained, by the United States. Less involvement in this area seems unproblematic from an American perspective.

Finally, India and America have closer long-run interests than the United States and Pakistan, and over time it is likely that America will favor India for strategic reasons. American foreign policy in the foreseeable future will be centered on the implication of China's rise. (Although, as Pande points out in this volume, its long-standing relationship with Pakistan may mean that China's rise has important implications for the balance of power in South Asia.) Though not a peer competitor to China, India will be a valuable partner—though not close ally—of the United States as part of America's mix of cooperation and containment toward China (Mohan 2004; Ganguly 2006). India will also be an attractive source of economic growth as the economies of the developed world struggle. Pakistan has none of these assets: it cannot affect the broader balance of power in Asia and its growth prospects are uninspiring. Pakistan's power will largely come from its ability to keep India off balance, to influence Afghanistan, and to affect global terrorism. In the grand scheme of things, these are not particularly important strategic assets. The leverage that Pakistan can bring to bear is not sufficient to make the United States beholden to it. Over the long run, India is the key power on the subcontinent.

Alarm about the U.S. drawdown therefore overstates American influence in South Asia's security environment and exaggerates U.S. interests in the region. The underlying structural trends point toward enduringly limited, if still substantial, Pakistani influence, both because of domestic weaknesses and the regional balance of power. There will be violent dislocations and conflicts that result from American disengagement, especially in Afghanistan, but there are no strong strategic reasons to maintain a massive force presence in Afghanistan or an awkward codependence with Pakistan. America can remain engaged with the region without being entrenched in it.

Implications for Pakistani Politics

More limited American engagement with Pakistan may have some benefits for Pakistani politicians. Deep anti-American sentiment in Pakistan limits the options available to leaders: they risk being accused of selling out to the United States when cracking down on militants, opposing sectarianism, opening up to India, or being conciliatory toward Afghanistan's government. The parties that did the best in Pakistan's 2013 general election either kept a low profile on these issues (Nawaz Sharif's PML-N) or trumpeted defiance to the United States (Imran Khan's Pakistan Tehreek-e-Insaf). There is little to be gained in Pakistani domestic politics from advancing American interests, and much to be lost in the face of opposition politicians, the security establishment, and a variety of political and social figures who can mobilize protests and launch rhetorical attacks on the government. The street power of Islamists—despite their weak electoral position—and manipulations of the military establishment are formidable obstacles to dramatic policy change, and they are fueled by a narrative of American meddling.

Despite various protestations by American diplomats and politicians that the United States is not involved in conspiratorial activities in Pakistan, within Pakistan there is a widespread perception to the contrary. The U.S. strategy for Pakistan, especially under Obama, has in fact sought to make major changes in Pakistan's economy, society, and politics. Raymond Davis and drone strikes suggest that the United States is indeed involved in a wide range of intelligence and military activities in the country that are not under the firm control of any part of the Pakistani state. From the American perspective the United States is simply trying to advance its interests, and Pakistan's true interests, in the face of a recalcitrant or inept Pakistani state, but in the eyes of many Pakistanis the United States is an aggressively interventionist power with nefarious designs on Pakistan. This creates profound domestic vulnerabilities for politicians who might be otherwise inclined toward broadly pro-American policies.

A reduced American presence may at least partially mitigate these vulnerabilities. I absolutely do not want to suggest that a change in American policy would end conspiratorial thinking or anti-American sentiment in Pakistan. This is extremely unlikely. But changes on the margins could be worthwhile. It may be better for the United States to be seen as an unreliable partner who has once again abandoned the region than as a hegemonic conspirator attempting to undermine Pakistan's sovereignty and security. Irrelevance can be preferable to malevolence. Politicians may be able to refocus political life toward issues that impact the daily quality of life of

Pakistanis, ranging from electricity to center-province relations. India-Pakistan relations are an area in which leaders like Nawaz Sharif may be able to make some helpful moves, and the less the United States is involved (at least publicly) in such initiatives, the better (*Economic Times* 2013).

The Pakistan army will also be affected by a shift in American posture. It will gain more influence in Afghanistan, but lose much of the leverage it has held over the United States. It is likely to continue meddling in Afghanistan and targeting India. There are some signs that other domestic actors are growing in power relative to the military, but the reality is that the military is deeply embedded in Pakistan's political system. A reduced American presence could facilitate further mobilization against certain militant groups, making the Pakistan army more credibly able to persuade its soldiers and the public that it is truly fighting Pakistan's war, rather than doing America's bidding.

That said, the military will only target some armed groups, those with clear anti-regime goals. Others are seen as either strategic assets or as not worth the potential backlash of targeting. The United States probably cannot do much to change the military's behavior on this issue, but without being tied down in Afghanistan it can engage in much more direct containment of and/or bargaining with the army. America will need to pursue a limited liability strategy toward Pakistan's military establishment, one that does not fully cut off cooperation but that does reduce dependence (Staniland 2011). The only way to engage in real conditionality is to make American threats credible, which is only possible if the United States is not reliant on the military for logistics and counterterrorism. Previous American efforts at coercion have failed miserably, while cooperation has been of a grudging and often unpleasant form. The military will be more vulnerable to U.S. pressure after 2014 because it will have fewer benefits to offer America. A cold-eyed appraisal of this relationship is long overdue, and the U.S. drawdown will force it to the surface.

Long-Term U.S.-Pakistan Ties

It is conceivable that the United States will get dragged into continued involvement in Pakistan's politics as a result of another major terrorist attack or regional crisis. In this case, most of this analysis is irrelevant, and the dysfunctional U.S.-Pakistan relationship of 2013 will continue as the status quo. Barring these contingencies, from 2014 onward, the United

States and Pakistan have the potential to reshape their respective policies. This may be ultimately beneficial for both states, especially in comparison to the setbacks and frustrations of the last decade.

America can continue to pursue a few areas of cooperation with Pakistan's civilian government and military without being sucked into a broader, more expensive project. Light footprints and limited aims should guide U.S. policy in the region. Afghanistan may continue to be a site of proxy warfare, or even of a peace deal with the Taliban. As long as there is not a full-scale Taliban victory that leads to a major al-Qaeda resurgence, American interests will be satisfied. Counterterrorism cooperation is the only area in which the United States would continue to need support from Pakistan. Even here, the record in recent years suggests that the United States faces a reduced threat and has developed independent capabilities for pursuing its goals without extensive Pakistani cooperation. Cooperation in counterterrorism would be ideal, and the United States should be prepared to offer something in return, but it should not bind America to Pakistan too tightly. India's growth trajectory makes it more important, especially as U.S. interests are quickly swinging toward a rising China (Gilboy and Heginbotham 2012). This lessens the need to cater to Pakistani goals when they diverge from America's.

South Asia will never return to the strategic periphery, but it neither requires nor is amenable to deep American involvement. The United States risks being manipulated by Pakistan, as well as India, whenever it tries to take on an ambitious leadership role. Instead, South Asia should be primarily managed by South Asians, with America entering the scene only to secure truly vital interests. This outcome is not the same as abandonment. The United States and Pakistan can agree on certain issues, and pursue these mutual benefits, while openly clashing or ignoring one another in other areas. Such a "transactional" relationship has been decried as unacceptable, but this is where the United States and Pakistan already are. America and Pakistan have simply been unable to credibly commit to one another, regardless of rhetoric or resource expenditures. When countries have different interests, they will want different things. It is better to acknowledge this reality and act accordingly. This will be healthier and more straightforward than the current mix of empty platitudes and simmering resentment. The 2014 drawdown provides a welcome opportunity for America to escape a strategic entanglement that has little long-run justification.

These policies can benefit Pakistanis as well. Huge amounts of American aid have had little effect beyond enriching wealthy elites and consolidating military power. American intelligence and military operations in Pakistan have been unpopular. An active, embedded American presence is not what most Pakistanis want. American euphemisms to the contrary, the United States does indeed pursue its own interests rather than being an altruistic actor on the world stage. America can continue to engage in the kinds of development and governance aid it provides around the world, offer a fairly standard set of diplomatic and social relations that neither completely abandon Pakistan nor try to affect major changes, and generally support democratic rule in Pakistan. Having a smaller footprint will reduce—though not eliminate—the ability of demagogues to blame America for all ills. This relationship can become more normal over time, sometimes involving conflict, sometimes involves cooperation. It is time to the end a situation of "mutual dependence rather than mutual respect" (Shaikh 2009: 190). Strategic breathing space is in the best interests of both countries.

Works Cited

Bergen, Peter. 2013 "Abandon Afghanistan? A Dumb Idea." CNN, January 10. http://www.cnn.com/2013/01/10/opinion/bergen-afghanistan-troop-levels.

Bergen, Peter, and Katherine Tiedemann, eds. 2013. *Talibanistan: Negotiating the Borders Between Terror, Politics, and Religion.* Oxford: Oxford University Press.

Blair, Graeme, C. Christine Fair, Neil Malhotra, and Jacob N. Shapiro. 2013. "Poverty and Support for Militant Politics: Evidence from Pakistan." *American Journal of Political Science* 57 (1): 30–48.

Cohen, Stephen P. 2001. *India: Emerging Power.* Washington, D.C.: Brookings Institution Press.

Coll, Steve. 2009. "The Back Channel: India and Pakistan's Secret Kashmir Talks." *New Yorker*, March 2.

Economic Times (India). 2013. "Nawaz Sharif Govt Has Given 'Good Signals': India." June 21. http://articles.economictimes.indiatimes.com/2013-06-21/news/401196 54_1_indian-ocean-economic-growth-pakistan.

Entous, Adam, and Julian E. Barnes. 2010. "U.S. Plans Increased Military Aid for Pakistan." *Wall Street Journal*, October 20. http://online.wsj.com/article/SB10 0014240527023035509045755624928789514822.html.

Epstein, Susan B., and K. Alan Kronstadt. 2013. *Pakistan: U.S. Foreign Assistance.* Washington, D.C.: Congressional Research Service. https://www.fas.org/sgp/crs/row/R41856.pdf?.Fair, C. Christine. 2011. "Why the Pakistan Army Is Here to Stay: Prospects for Civilian Governance." *International Affairs* 87 (3): 571–588.

———. 2012. "Pakistan in 2011: Ten Years of the 'War on Terror.'" *Asian Survey* 52 (1): 100–113.

Ganguly, Sumit. 2006. "Will Kashmir Stop India's Rise?" *Foreign Affairs* 85 (4): 45–56.

GAO (U.S. General Accountability Office). 2008. *Combating Terrorism: Increased Oversight and Accountability Needed over Pakistan Reimbursement Claims for Coalition Support Funds*. Washington, D.C.: GAO. http://www.gao.gov/new.items/d08806.pdf.

———. 2010. *Combating Terrorism: Planning and Documentation of U.S. Development Assistance in Pakistan's Federally Administered Tribal Areas Need to Be Improved*. Washington, D.C.: GAO. http://www.gao.gov/new.items/d10289.pdf.

Gilboy, George J., and Eric Heginbotham. 2012. *Chinese and Indian Strategic Behavior: Growing Power and Alarm*. New York: Cambridge University Press.

Hindu. 2011. "U.S. Worried Pakistan Was Misusing War Funds." May 26. http://www.thehindu.com/news/us-worried-pakistan-was-misusing-war-funds/article2048906.ece

Hussain, Zahid. 2007. *Frontline Pakistan: The Struggle with Militant Islam*. New York: Columbia University Press.

ICG (International Crisis Group). 2013. *Drones: Myths and Reality in Pakistan*. Asia Report No. 247. Brussels: International Crisis Group.

Jalal, Ayesha. 1990. *The State of Martial Rule: The Origins of Pakistan's Political Economy of Defence*. Cambridge South Asian Studies. Cambridge: Cambridge University Press.

Kux, Dennis. 2001. *The United States and Pakistan, 1947–2000: Disenchanted Allies*. Washington, D.C.: Woodrow Wilson Center Press.

Lalwani, Sameer. 2009. *Pakistani Capabilities for a Counterinsurgency Campaign: A Net Assessment*. Washington, D.C.: New America Foundation. http://newamerica.net/sites/newamerica.net/files/policydocs/NAFPakistanSept09.pdf.

Mazzetti, Mark. 2013. "How a Single Spy Helped Turn Pakistan Against the United States." *New York Times Magazine*, April 9. http://www.nytimes.com/2013/04/14/magazine/raymond-davis-pakistan.html?pagewanted=all.

Mohan, C. Raja. 2004. *Crossing the Rubicon: The Shaping of India's New Foreign Policy*. New York: Palgrave Macmillan.

Musharraf, Pervez. 2006. *In the Line of Fire: A Memoir*. New York: Free Press.

Nawaz, Shuja. 2008. *Crossed Swords: Pakistan, Its Army, and the Wars Within*. Oxford: Oxford University Press.

Pew. 2012. "Pakistani Public Opinion Ever More Critical of the U.S." Pew Research Global Attitudes Project, June 27. Washington, D.C.: Pew Research Center. http://www.pewglobal.org/2012/06/27/pakistani-public-opinion-ever-more-critical-of-u-s/.

Rashid, Ahmed. 2010. *Taliban: Militant Islam, Oil, and Fundamentalism in Central Asia*. 2nd ed. New Haven, Conn.: Yale University Press.

Schaffer, Howard B. 2009. *The Limits of Influence: America's Role in Kashmir.* Washington, D.C.: Brookings Institution Press.

Schmitt, Eric, and Thom Shanker. 2009. "Pentagon Seeks $3 Billion for Pakistani Military." *New York Times,* April 2. http://www.nytimes.com/2009/04/03/washington/03military.html.

Shaikh, Farzana. 2009. *Making Sense of Pakistan.* New York: Columbia University Press.

Staniland, Paul. 2011. "Caught in the Muddle: America's Pakistan Strategy." *Washington Quarterly* 34 (1): 133–148.

———. 2012. "States, Insurgents, and Wartime Political Orders." *Perspectives on Politics* 10 (2): 243–264.

Talbott, Strobe. 2006. *Engaging India: Diplomacy, Democracy, and the Bomb.* Washington, D.C.: Brookings Institution Press.

Tudor, Maya Jessica. 2013. *The Promise of Power: The Origins of Democracy in India and Autocracy in Pakistan.* Cambridge: Cambridge University Press.

Wright, Lawrence. 2011. "The Double Game." *New Yorker,* May 16. http://www.newyorker.com/reporting/2011/05/16/110516fa_fact_wright?currentPage=all.

Chapter 9

Partner or Enemy? The Sources of Attitudes Toward the United States in Pakistan

Karl Kaltenthaler and William J. Miller

Pakistan's public has been polled several times since the terrorist attacks of September 11, 2001, and the subsequent start of the "Global War on Terror" (GWOT). All of these polls show a clear trend of increasing negativity toward the United States, and the large majority of Pakistanis now express unfavorable opinions of the United States. The United States is suffering from a very profound image problem in Pakistan. We seek to understand the drivers of this image problem and of Pakistani anger toward the United States.

Why does anti-Americanism in Pakistan matter beyond 2014? As noted in the introduction to this book, the relationship between the United States and Pakistan has long been wracked by frictions, distrust, and competing interests. The tense and often difficult relationship between Pakistan and the United States has driven many Pakistanis to view the United States with deep antipathy. While anti-Americanism has existed in Pakistan for decades, it deepened during the GWOT. Pakistanis believe that their country has lost more than it has gained in the bargain with the United States. It lost an ally in Afghanistan, the Taliban, which could keep the Indians in check. Worse, militant groups based in Pakistan began turning their guns against the Pakistani state to protest the latter's facilitation of U.S. operations in Afghanistan. In recent years, America's use of armed drones in Pakistan's tribal areas has fueled this resentment further. Many Pakistanis in the government and beyond believe that Pakistanis were dying by the thousands because of American policy priorities. Pakistanis fear that American actions will continue to create a lasting legacy of violence in the region that will jeopardize Pakistan's future.

Yet as much as Pakistanis and even the American public would like the United States to pick up and leave Pakistan, neither country will have the luxury of escaping this deadly embrace. Pakistan has few dependable allies willing to provide the economic and even military assistance that Washington has offered (see Pande in this volume). There is no evidence that China or Saudi Arabia will be willing to take over the management of the Pakistan problem from the United States. American policy makers will resist the urge to write off Pakistan because the internal threats to Pakistan are real and enduring (see Clary in this volume; for an alternative take, see Staniland in this volume). The Americans fear Pakistan's nuclear weapons will fall into the hands of militants, either through theft or with the connivance of the military. Pakistan will remain a source of jihadist manpower for the indefinite future and jihadi actions in India remain the most likely precipitant of a future Indo-Pakistan conflict that can escalate to nuclear use (see White, Tankel, and Clary in this volume). Moreover, even after military operations are long done in Afghanistan, Pakistan will be a major player in Afghanistan (see Gaartenstein-Ross and Vassefi in this volume). What Pakistan does in Afghanistan post-2014 will shape Afghanistan's future security.

Whether Pakistan likes it or not, it will require American bilateral assistance and support at multilateral organizations such as the International Monetary Fund (IMF). And whether the United States likes it or not, it will have to find a way to manage the persistent anti-Americanism in Pakistan if it wants to secure significant American security interests in South Asia. Understanding and attenuating anti-Americanism is and will remain a key objective of American public diplomacy in Washington and in the mission in Pakistan. This analysis should inform this important discussion.

We argue that anti-Americanism in Pakistan is driven by two primary ways of thinking about the United States. The first type of anti-Americanism, which we refer to as nationalist anti-Americanism, is driven by a view of the United States as a powerful, global bully that abuses Pakistan and its sovereignty. The second major way of thinking about anti-Americanism in Pakistan is as religion-based, that is, based on an ideological aversion to the United States constructed along religious lines. Religion-based anti-Americanism is more likely to drive Pakistanis to become militantly anti-American and support violence against Americans.

The chapter begins by outlining the shape of Pakistani attitudes toward the United States in recent years. It then lays out the arguments to be explored in the chapter. The next section provides an empirical basis for the arguments, and we conclude with a discussion of the implications of this research.

Common Explanations of Anti-Americanism

Several studies have sought to identify the sources of anti-Americanism in the world (e.g., Ceaser 2003; Chiozza 2004, 2007, and 2009; Haseler 1985; Hertsgaard 2002; Hollander 2004; Judt and Lacorne 2005; Katzenstein and Keohane 2007; Revel 2003; Ross and Ross 2004; Rubin and Rubin 2004; Rubinstein and Smith 1985 and 1988; Tai, Peterson, and Gurr 1973). In one of the first studies on the subject, Chong-Soo Tai, Erick Peterson, and Ted Robert Gurr (1973) examined external and internal sources of anti-Americanism. External anti-Americanism indicates anti-American feelings generated by a U.S. presence in the country. Internal anti-Americanism involves negative feelings toward the United States that are the result of domestic stresses. The authors found that both sources of anti-Americanism are important generators of the phenomenon. Alvin Rubenstein and Donald Smith (1988) created a typology of anti-Americanism, frequently used in subsequent studies, which includes issue-oriented anti-Americanism (dispositions based on American policies); ideological anti-Americanism (based on the ideology of the person in question, whether political or religious in nature); instrumental anti-Americanism (serving a political purpose); and revolutionary anti-Americanism (anti-American views driven by antipathy for a pro-American regime).

A more recent study by Peter Katzenstein and Robert Keohane (2007) develops a typology of anti-Americanism along two dimensions. The first deals with the intensity of anti-American beliefs, classifying three levels of feelings toward the United States: moderate distrust, strong distrust, or bias. Bias is the strongest of the anti-American dispositions and means that the individual will always profoundly distrust the intentions of the United States and the person's feelings are unlikely to change. Individuals whose views correspond to the other two types can be persuaded to view the United States favorably. The other dimension of anti-Americanism in the Katzenstein and Keohane typology deals with the sources of anti-Americanism. They identify social anti-Americanism, which is based on a disdain for the nature of America's society and polity; sovereign-nationalist anti-Americanism, which is a dislike of the United States based on its encroachment on the affairs of the individual's country; and radical anti-Americanism, the belief that the United States is an existential threat to what is good in the world. Those who subscribe to the latter view support radical measures against the United States. We refer to this type of anti-Americanism as militant anti-Americanism. In our schema, holders of such anti-American views would support violence against Americans.

Recently, in response to the events of September 11, 2001, scholars have focused a great deal on anti-American sentiment in the Muslim world (see Chiozza 2004). Anti-Americanism among Muslims is a major security concern for the United States, but there is no consensus in this new and growing literature on Muslim disaffection with the United States on the primary drivers of this phenomenon. Some have argued that the source of rising anti-Americanism in the Muslim world is primarily religious in nature (Lewis 1990; Paz 2003). Others contend that the phenomenon is the consequence of past or present American policy toward Muslim countries (Tessler 2003; Vedrine 2004). Moises Naim (2002), among others, believes that both religion and policy are driving negative views of the United States. A fourth view of anti-Americanism in the Muslim world sees its roots as domestic: either the fault of governments in Muslim countries that blame their citizens' problems on the United States in order to avoid the blame themselves (Rubin 2002).

We create two general categories of explanation to assess in this study. We refer to the first category as nationalist anti-Americanism, which refers to an antipathy toward U.S. policy and has much in common with arguments made by Sigrid Faath (2006), Mark Tessler (2003), Ussama Makdisi (2002), and Moises Naim (2002). The second category is what we call religious anti-Americanism, which has an ideological basis. Anti-Americanism of this type is driven by perceived social/religious differences between Pakistanis and Americans. Many Pakistanis' anti-Americanism is both nationalist and religion-based, but these are fairly distinct sources of the phenomenon. We will explain each category and its forms of operationalization in the sections below.

The Sources of Anti-Americanism: The Narratives of Sovereignty and Religion in Pakistan

We argue that most Pakistanis are socialized to distrust and dislike the United States. This socialization is then bolstered by two dominant, current, running elite narratives of anti-Americanism; the nationalist narrative and a religious, ideological narrative. These narratives are not in competition but are mutually reinforcing.

We posit that there are two broad currents of anti-Americanism that are part of the youth socialization process and are then reinforced through elite narratives in Pakistan. The first type of anti-Americanism in Pakistan has a *nationalist* basis and is primarily issue and policy based. Those who fall into this category of anti-Americanism are convinced that the United States is violating Pakistani sovereignty and harming their country. U.S. political, military, and economic interference are all important for this group: drone strikes, Osama bin Laden's killing, and stringent IMF agreements would be considered meddlesome behavior by the United States.

Pakistanis' predisposition to distrust and antipathy toward the United States stems first from a troubled history of bilateral relations. In Pakistan's case, the negative public attitudes toward the United States are based on the belief that Pakistan has been wronged by the United States for almost its entire existence. Pakistan felt abandoned when the United States lost interest in the region after the Soviets left Afghanistan and Pakistan was left to deal with the aftermath. When Pakistan tested its nuclear weapons in response to Indian tests, the United States responded with severe sanctions. Finally, the United States has historically supported friendly military dictators in Pakistan over civilian, elected politicians, damaging Pakistan's political development.

Second, evidence shows that citizens of a country that has a history of aggression and conflict are likely to have a dimmer view of other countries in general than those who have not had to face conflict or threats (Holsti 2009), and Pakistan is a prime example: it has been involved in conflicts since its creation in 1947, primarily with India. It lost its eastern half in 1971 as a result of conflict (Khattak 1996; Malik 1990; Rubin and Rashid 2008; Sisson and Rose 1990). It was a frontline state in the fight against the Soviets in Afghanistan and was threatened by the disintegration of Afghanistan after the Soviet withdrawal in the late 1980s and early 1990s. A sense of threat arising from its history of conflict is likely to contribute to Pakistan's anti-Americanism and can be reinforced and exacerbated by the narratives of educational, policy, and security elites.

The second type of anti-Americanism in Pakistan is ideological and has religious roots. Many Pakistanis sees themselves as fundamentally different from Americans, primarily because of religious differences, and their sense of negativity toward the United States derives from these differences. Studies have shown that some individuals have worldviews that are shaped mainly by their religious views (Fox 2001; Jelen 1994; Telhami 1993; Tessler and Nachtwey 1998; Toft 2007). Typically, more conservative strains of religion that focus on the negative aspects of humanity and the need for punishment of sin are more likely to have adherents who view the world as inhabited by threatening countries (Uslaner 2000), and as a battleground between virtue and evil. These kinds of people form the core of the religious anti-American group identified above. Mix this religious ideological foundation with the experience of conflict with people from another religion and the sense of religious threat is further heightened.

Religious identity is of paramount importance in Pakistan: it was created as a state for Muslims (not an Islamic state) from the Indian subcontinent in 1947, and state and security elites have consciously bolstered the sense of Pakistani Islamic identity to unite an ethnically fractious state and to establish their authority (Chengappa 2001; Cohen 2004; Fazal 2000; Haqqani 2005; Syed 1982; Hussain 2007; Jaffrelot 2002; Nasr 1994 and 2004; Schmidt 2011; Zia 2003). Pakistanis follow a spectrum of Islamic traditions, from relatively liberal Sufis to conservative Deobandis and militant Salafis. Pakistanis also take great pride in their culture and history. The Pakistanis who subscribe to a religious anti-Americanism see their religion, society, and culture as fundamentally different from that of the United States, and these ideological differences drive negative attitudes toward America. This is not a homogeneous group, as it represents the broad spectrum of Muslims in Pakistan.

Elites play a crucial role in defining the narratives of nationalist and religious anti-American sentiment in Pakistan. John Zaller (1992), in a seminal book on the origins of public opinion, argues that elites play a central role in framing complex issues and shaping their presentation in mass media and public discourse. While this is true in an advanced industrialized democracy, the role of elites is even greater in a developing country with relatively low literacy rates, where governing and media elites can exercise great control over information. Members of the mass public most often assume that the elites have better information on issues than they themselves do, and they take their cues on complex issues from those whom they consider knowledgeable. As Arthur Lupia and Matthew McCubbins (1998) argue, the more expert the elite is assumed to be on an issue, the more likely it is that citizens will follow his or her cues on that issue.

In Pakistan, nationalist anti-American sentiments are pushed by, among others, the security establishment, which views the United States as a quasi-ally and threat to various core Pakistani security interests (Cohen 2004; Johnson and Mason 2008; Khattak 1996; Kronstadt 2009; Misra 2001; Rashid 2008). Politicians of various stripes stress supposed American domination of Pakistan as a way of creating an external enemy on which to focus anger and to blame for Pakistan's misfortunes. Religious, ideological anti-American sentiments are pushed primarily by many in the religious establishment, including religious political parties and prominent religious scholars (Cohen 2004: Haqqani 2005; Nasr 1994). These elites have various motivations for fostering an anti-American narrative: they often truly believe that the United States is an enemy of Muslims, but demonizing the United States is also a way of mobilizing and motivating their followers to vote for them, donate money, and attack their opponents (Blaydes and Linzer 2012).

Are there any countercurrents to the dominating anti-American narratives in Pakistan? Pro-American narratives in Pakistan are very rare, even among those who are deemed friends of the United States. The rhetoric of Pakistani political parties, even though they have maintained a certain level of cooperation with the United States on issues of foreign and security policy, has been largely negative toward the United States: publicly decrying the U.S. drone campaign in the Federally Administered Tribal Areas (FATA), castigating U.S. policies in Afghanistan, sharply rebuking U.S. criticisms of the lack of Pakistani cooperation in fighting the Afghan Taliban, and condemning the U.S. raid on Osama bin Laden's compound in Abbottabad. There is no *significant* pro-American narrative in Pakistan to counter the various strands of anti-American narratives.

The Landscape of Anti-Americanism in Pakistan

We operationalize anti-Americanism as unfavorable attitudes toward the United States and Americans expressed in survey data. We employ data from two survey sources to explore Pakistani views toward the United States and Americans. We use the 2011 Pew Research Global Attitudes Project (GAP) survey as well the 2007 World Public Opinion.org (WPO)/ START survey of Pakistan.

Table 9.1. Pakistanis' Attitude Toward the United States

	Very favorable	Somewhat favorable	Somewhat unfavorable	Very unfavorable	Don't know/ Refused
Percentage who answered	1	10	10	65	14

Source: Pew Global Attitudes Project, Pakistan, 2011.

Table 9.2. Pakistanis' Attitudes Toward Americans

	Very favorable	Somewhat favorable	Somewhat unfavorable	Very unfavorable	Don't know/ Refused
Percentage who answered	2	11	17	50	21

Source: Pew Research Global Attitudes Project, 2011.

Two questions in the 2011 Pew GAP survey measure levels of anti-Americanism. One measures basic views of the United States, asking the respondent: "Please tell me if you have a very favorable, somewhat favorable, somewhat unfavorable, or very unfavorable opinion of the United States?" The second question asks: "Overall, do you think of the United States as more of a partner of Pakistan, more of an enemy of Pakistan, or neither?" This second question is both more specific and more pointed than the first. We believe this question will identify those Pakistanis who have the most deeply held anti-American views by determining those who view the United States as Pakistan's "enemy." Table 9.1 shows the breakdown of Pakistani respondents to the first question.

There has been a distinct trend toward more unfavorable views of the United States since 2004. In particular, favorable views toward the United States, which averaged 21 percent in 2004, were at 11 percent in 2011. Unfavorable views were at 60 percent in 2004 and had gone up to 75 percent in 2011. On the other hand, the distribution of responses is less unfavorable toward Americans (as opposed to the United States), as seen in Table 9.2.

We can see a clear and startling pattern in the responses to the question of whether the United States is more of an enemy or a partner. Table 9.3 shows the distribution of the responses.

Table 9.3. Pakistanis' View of the United States as Enemy or Partner

Do you think of the United States as more of a partner or more of an enemy?

	More of a partner	More of an enemy	Neither	Don't know/ Refused
Percentage who answered	9	68	10	13

Source: Pew Research Global Attitudes Project, 2011.

Table 9.4. Pakistani Attitudes Toward the Current U.S. Government, 2007

	Very favorable	Somewhat favorable	Somewhat unfavorable	Very unfavorable	Don't know/ Refused
Percentage who answered	3.5	10.0	14.8	44.4	27.3

Source: WPO Survey of Pakistani Opinion, 2007.

It is apparent that many more Pakistanis view the United States as an enemy than as a partner. In 2011, 68 percent of Pakistanis viewed the United States as an enemy and only 9 percent considered the United States a partner; 23 percent answered that the United States was neither, or that they were not sure.

Table 9.4 (using the results of the 2007 WPO survey) shows that most Pakistanis have an unfavorable view of the U.S. government, with about 60 percent expressing an unfavorable view, as opposed to only 13.5 percent who had some sort of favorable view of the U.S. government.

What do Pakistanis think about American leadership? Table 9.5 shows the responses to a question asking about confidence in President Obama, Osama bin Laden, and President Ahmadinejad of Iran. The question asks specifically: "Now I'm going to read a list of political leaders. For each, tell me how much confidence you have in each leader to do the right thing regarding world affairs—a lot of confidence, some confidence, not too much confidence, or no confidence at all? U.S. President Barack Obama, Osama bin Laden, Iranian President Mahmoud Ahmadinejad."

Table 9.5 shows that there is a clear lack of confidence among Pakistanis in the American president Barack Obama. In 2011, only 10 percent of Pakistani respondents expressed confidence that Obama would do the right

Table 9.5. Pakistanis' Confidence in Leaders to "Do the Right Thing"

Percentage of respondents who have	Osama bin Laden	Barack Obama	Mahmoud Ahmadinejad
Confidence in:	21	10	44
No confidence in:	42	65	15
Don't know/Refused	38	25	41

Source: Pew Research Global Attitudes Project, 2011.

thing in world affairs. In contrast, 65 percent said that they have *no* confidence in the American president to do the right thing in world affairs. It is particularly noteworthy to compare Obama's confidence ratings with two people who are generally judged harshly in the international community, Osama bin Laden and then Iranian president Mahmoud Ahmadinejad. Despite al-Qaeda attacks in Pakistan, including attempts on the president's life, in 2011 (shortly before his death), 21 percent of Pakistani respondents expressed confidence in Osama bin Laden. That is double the confidence expressed in Barack Obama. Ahmadinejad enjoys confidence from 44 percent of Pakistani respondents, with only 15 percent saying that they do not have confidence in him. While there are historical reasons why bin Laden would enjoy sympathies among some Pakistanis, such as his role in the anti-Soviet jihad in Afghanistan, the Pakistani government has declared al-Qaeda to be an enemy of the state. Ahmadinejad's popularity in Pakistan may be due to the perception that he is a Muslim leader who stands up the United States. But the antipathy toward Barack Obama, who has made efforts to reach out to Muslims globally, indicates that the American president and his policies are viewed in a very negative light in Pakistan. One may surmise that a great deal of this antipathy toward Obama is a result of the drone strike campaign in FATA, which accelerated markedly during his presidency.

Nationalist Views of the United States

As we argue above, we believe many Pakistanis' antipathy toward the United States is based in their belief that U.S. policies are contrary to Pakistani wishes and interests and generally violate Pakistani sovereignty. Several questions in the Pew GAP surveys carried out in Pakistan over the years give us insight into this sovereign-nationalist mix of views in Pakistan.

Table 9.6. Pakistanis' Opinion of Drone Attacks

	Do you think these drone attacks are a very good thing, good thing, bad thing, or very bad thing?				
	Very good	*Good*	*Bad*	*Very bad*	*Don't know/ Refused*
Percentage who answered	2	3	23	72	0

Source: Pew Research Global Attitudes Project, 2011.

Two American policies that have attracted particular attention in Pakistan in recent years are American drone strikes against militants in FATA and the killing of Osama bin Laden. Questions in the Pew surveys address Pakistani views of these policy issues.

Drone strikes are a particularly contentious issue in Pakistan. A Pew GAP question asks: "How much, if anything, have you heard about the drone attacks that target leaders of extremist groups—a lot, little, or nothing at all?" If respondents answer "a lot" or "a little," they are then asked: "Do you think these drone attacks are a very good thing, good thing, bad thing, or very bad thing?" Table 9.6 shows the distribution of responses to the second question.

The table shows that American drone strikes are deeply unpopular in Pakistan. In 2011, 95 percent of Pakistani respondents who knew about drone strikes thought they were a bad thing. Only 5 percent of those respondents thought they were a good thing. Thus, as the drones become better known and become a larger part of the public discourse in Pakistan, they are driving more anger toward the United States. A large part of the anger generated over the drones is that the Pakistani government and many other Pakistani elites argue that the strikes are a violation of Pakistani sovereignty and are killing innocent Pakistanis. On the other hand, the U.S. government does not comment on the drone strikes, so there is no counter-narrative to the very negative one produced by many Pakistani elites. Thus, the drone campaign seems to be stoking the Pakistani notion that the United States is a domineering bully that is doing harm to Pakistanis.

The U.S. raid to kill Osama bin Laden, who was hiding in the Pakistani city of Abbottabad, caused great controversy in Pakistan because the U.S. government did not notify the Pakistani government of its knowledge of

Table 9.7. Pakistanis' Opinion of the Raid That Killed Osama bin Laden

Do you approve or disapprove of the U.S. military operation that killed Osama bin Laden?

	Approve	Disapprove	Don't know/Refused
Percentage who answered	10	63	27

Source: Pew Research Global Attitudes Project, 2011.

bin Laden's whereabouts or its intention to carry out the raid, or give any notice as the raid transpired. The Pakistani public discourse after the raid was largely about how the raid could have taken place under the nose of the Pakistani military and about the army's ability to protect Pakistani airspace and territory. In late spring 2011 Pakistanis were asked (in a follow up to the survey conducted earlier that year) about the raid, with the question: "Do you approve or disapprove of the U.S. military operation that killed Osama bin Laden?" Table 9.7 shows the distribution of the responses to this question.

As can be seen in Table 9.7, the majority of Pakistanis, 63 percent, disapproved of the raid. Only 10 percent approved of the raid. This was not because of a great admiration for Osama bin Laden among most Pakistanis, but because most Pakistanis saw the raid as an infringement of Pakistani sovereignty.[1] This fits with the general belief in Pakistan that the United States ignores Pakistani interests when it makes policy.

Several waves of the Pew surveys have asked if respondents believe that the United States takes their country's interests into account. This gets directly at the notion of the United States as a domineering as opposed to a partner country. The question asks: "In making international policy decisions, to what extent do you think the United States takes into account the interests of countries like Pakistan—a great deal, a fair amount, not too much, or not at all?" Table 9.8 shows the distribution of these responses from 2011.

As we can see in the Table 9.8, Pakistanis have consistently tended to believe that the United States does not take their country's interests into account. This fits with the popular Pakistani perception of the United States as an arrogant bully that does not care about Pakistan. In fact, if we ask Pakistanis about their perception of Westerners' arrogance, they respond

Table 9.8. Pakistanis' Opinion of How Much the United States Takes
into Account the Interests of Their Country

	Great deal	Fair amount	Not too much	Not at all	Don't know/ Refused
Percentage who answered	6	12	13	47	22

Source: Pew Research Global Attitudes Project, 2011.

Table 9.9. Proportion of Pakistanis Who View Westerners as "Arrogant"

Do you associate the word "arrogant" with people in Western countries such as the United States and in Europe?		
	Yes	No	Don't know/Refused
Percentage who answered	60	17	23

Source: Pew Research Global Attitudes Project, 2011.

Table 9.10. Pakistanis' Attitudes Toward Pakistan-U.S. Cooperation

Does our government cooperate too much with the U.S. government?			
	Too much	Not enough	About right	Don't know/ No answer
Percentage who answered	54	13	10	23

Source: Pew Research Global Attitudes Project, 2011.

that they find them, by and large, to be arrogant. Table 9.9 shows the distribution of responses to the question: "Do you associate 'Arrogant' with people in Western countries such as the United States and Europe?"

Many Pakistanis also believe that their government is too compliant with the wishes of the United States. Considering how negatively most Pakistanis tend to view the United States, it would not be surprising that they would be loath to cooperate with the United States. Table 9.10 shows the distribution of responses to the question: "Does our government cooperate too much with the United States government?"

Table 9.11. Pakistanis' Concern About U.S. Military Threat

	Worried	Not worried	Don't know/Refused
Percentage who answered	66	21	13

Source: Pew Research Global Attitudes Project, 2011.

The results in Table 9.10 show that the majority of Pakistani respondents, 54 percent, believe that their government cooperates too much with the United States. Only 13 percent believe that their government does not cooperate enough with the United States. This is a good indication of the sense that many Pakistanis have that the United States is dominating their country. There seems to be a deep concern in Pakistan about sovereignty and the freedom to have independent policies.

Another question in the survey that gets at sovereign-nationalist sentiments asks: "How worried are you that the United States could become a military threat to Pakistan: very worried, somewhat worried, not too worried, or not at all worried?" Table 9.11 shows the distribution of responses to this question.

Pakistanis are, on average, fairly worried that the United States could become a military threat to their country. This is in line with them thinking that the United States is an enemy more than a partner. The percentage of those worried about the United States as a military threat to Pakistan has actually dropped slightly, from 72 percent in 2003 to 67 percent in the 2011 survey. There has been a fair amount of fluctuation among those who do not see the United States as a military threat over the years, with the percentages ranging between 11 and 23 percent. But overall, most Pakistanis are concerned about the United States as a potential military threat. So, Pakistanis do not just worry about the United States as a domineering force in world affairs, they tend to believe that the United States is a *threat* to Pakistan.

Given the very negative view that most Pakistanis have of the United States as a hostile nation, how much do Pakistanis believe the United States dominates the world at large? This question was asked in the 2007 World Public Opinion/START Pakistan survey in the following form: "How much of what happens in the world today would you say is controlled by the United States?" Table 9.12 shows the distribution of responses to this question.

Table 9.12. Pakistanis' View of U.S. Dominance

	Very little	Some	Most	Nearly All	Don't know/ Refused
Percentage who answered	6.7	12.1	27.6	26.6	27

Source: World Public Opinion/START Pakistan Survey, 2007.

Table 9.13. Pakistani Cultural Identity

Our people are not perfect, but our culture is superior to others.		
	Agree	Disagree	Don't know/Refused
Percentage who answered	84	6	10

Source: Pew Research Global Attitudes Project, 2011.

The responses shown in Table 9.12 show that in 2007, 54.2 percent of Pakistani respondents believed that most or nearly all of what happens in the world is controlled by the United States. Thus, most Pakistanis view the United States as an immensely powerful country that is also a threat to their country. Given these views, it is no wonder that the majority of Pakistanis express negative views of the United States and its government.

Religious Anti-Americanism

Several Pew GAP questions capture the religious anti-American perspective. First of all, it is important to establish how important cultural and religious identity is to Pakistanis. One question in the Pew survey asks: "Please tell me whether you completely agree, mostly agree, mostly disagree, or completely disagree with the following statements. Our people are not perfect, but our culture is superior to others." Table 9.13 shows the distribution of responses to this question.

The responses in Table 9.13 clearly show that Pakistanis have a deep sense of pride in their culture. In 2011, 84 percent of respondents believed that their culture is superior to others, with only 6 percent disagreeing with that sentiment.

Conversely, most Pakistanis are negative about American culture. Table 9.14 displays the distribution of responses to a question about favorability to American culture.

Table 9.14. Pakistani Opinion of American Culture

	Very favorable	Somewhat favorable	Somewhat unfavorable	Very unfavorable	Don't know/ Refused
Percentage who answered	2.8	8.0	16.1	45.5	27.6

Source: World Public Opinion/START Pakistan Survey, 2007.

Table 9.15. Pakistanis' Response to the Question of Identity

Do you think of yourself first as Pakistani or first as a Muslim?				
	Pakistani	Muslim	Both equally (volunteered)	Other (volunteered)	Don't know/ Refused
Percentage who answered	9	89	1	0	0

Source: Pew Research Global Attitudes Project, 2011.

It is apparent that the majority of Pakistanis have a very dim view of American culture. More than 60 percent have an unfavorable view of American culture and only about 11 percent have a favorable view of American culture. Thus, while Pakistanis express a great deal of pride in their own culture, they take a very critical view of American culture.

It is also important to know what Pakistanis' cultural identity means to them. Islam is a central part of Pakistani national identity and part of the founding principles for the state of Pakistan. Pakistan was established as a state for Muslims. So how central is Islam to the identity of Pakistanis? A Pew GAP question gets at this by asking: "Do you think of yourself first as a Pakistani or first as a Muslim?" The respondent can answer "Pakistani," "Muslim, "both equally," or "don't know/refuse." Table 9.15 shows the distribution of responses to this question.

The responses in the Table 9.15 show that Pakistanis overwhelmingly view themselves as Muslims first and foremost. In 2011, 89 percent thought of themselves first as Muslims and 9 percent thought of themselves first as Pakistanis.

Next, we examine a Pew GAP survey question that asks: "In your opinion, how many Americans do you think are hostile toward Muslims—

Table 9.16. Pakistani Views of American Hostility to Muslims

			How many Americans do you think are hostile toward Muslims?		
	Most	Many	Just some	Very few	Don't know/ Refused
Percentage who answered	47	23	8	3	20

Source: Pew Research Global Attitudes Project, 2011.

would you say most, many, just some or very few?" Table 9.16 shows the results of the question.

The 2011 Pew results show that 70 percent of Pakistanis thought that most or many Americans were hostile to Muslims. In 2011, just 11 percent of respondents said that just some or few Americans were hostile to Muslims. There is clearly a widespread perception among Pakistanis that Americans are hostile toward Muslims.

The Pew GAP questions related to religious anti-Americanism outline a clear portrait of the United States as hostile to Pakistan because it is a Muslim country. This is likely a deep and fairly intractable source of anti-Americanism, as Pakistani Muslim identity is not likely to fade. Thus, both sovereignty and religious sentiments are driving anti-Americanism in Pakistan. In fact, many Pakistanis likely hold both sentiments simultaneously.

Militant Anti-Americanism: Anti-Americanism at the Extremes

Thus far, we have surveyed views among Pakistanis toward the United States that touch on some of the general themes that motivate Pakistanis to dislike the United States. We know that most Pakistanis want their government to cooperate less with the United States, which is logical given the deep distrust of the United States among Pakistanis. But we have not yet explored the most extreme form of anti-Americanism, *militant anti-Americanism*. Militant anti-Americanism is anti-Americanism that extends to supporting violence against Americans.

Militant anti-Americanism is particularly important to understand in the case of Pakistan due to the connection between Pakistan and violence toward Americans, specifically American troops in Afghanistan. At the time

Table 9.17. Pakistani Views on Attacks on U.S. Military

Please tell me if you approve, disapprove, or have mixed feelings about
[attacks on U.S. military troops in Afghanistan]?

	Approve	Disapprove	Mixed Feelings	Don't know/ Refused
Percentage who answered	28.7	32.5	12.3	25.5

Source: World Public Opinion/START Pakistan Survey, 2007.

or writing, a number of Pakistani militant groups have members fighting in Afghanistan against the United States and its NATO allies, the Pakistani security establishment supports the Afghan Taliban and other groups fighting U.S. troops in Afghanistan, and the tribal areas of Pakistan serve as havens for those fighting against U.S. troops in Afghanistan. Thus, it is very important to understand to what extent the Pakistani public goes beyond simply distrusting and disliking the United States and actually supports fighting Americans in Afghanistan.

Table 9.17 shows the distribution of responses to a question about attacks on U.S. military troops in Afghanistan. The questions asks: "Please tell me, if you approve, disapprove, or have mixed feelings about 'attacks on U.S, military troops in Afghanistan?'"

The results in Table 9.17 show that a slim plurality, 32.5 percent, of Pakistanis disapprove of attacks against U.S. troops in Afghanistan. Among the respondents, 28.7 percent approved attacks against U.S. troops in Afghanistan, and 12.3 percent had mixed feelings. It is important to note that nearly a third of Pakistanis support violence against American troops in Afghanistan. Thus, if the Pakistani security establishment were to admit that they are aiding the Afghan Taliban and allied militant groups, they would find support for this policy among many Pakistanis.

So which Pakistanis are likely to be the most militantly anti-American and support violence against U.S. troops in Afghanistan? The next section is devoted to finding answers to this question.

The Sources of Militant Anti-Americanism in Pakistan

We posit that the primary source of inspiration for militant anti-Americanism in Pakistan is a radical religious narrative that goes beyond that of the more mainstream narrative that the United States is hostile to Muslims. This narrative espouses jihad against infidel occupiers in Muslim lands. According to this narrative, the United States and its NATO allies are the infidel occupiers in Afghanistan and thus violence against them is sanctioned and even necessary. This narrative would be most attractive to Pakistanis who are adherents of or lean toward more Salafi strains of Islam. Salafism is a movement within Sunni Islam that stresses the perfection of Islam during the time of the Prophet Muhammad and the earliest caliphs. Salafis argue that Islam must go back to that earlier model of life as the one true and correct form of Islam. All religious innovations since then are viewed as heretical deviations from correct Islam and are contrary to God's will. Salafism is a conservative strain of Islam that focuses on very strict adherence to Islamic law and practices (following an extremely conservative interpretation of Islamic law) and calls for relatively severe punishments for those who do not adhere to such rules. Salafism tends to be intolerant of other strains of Islam and of non-Muslims. While not all Salafis are militant, militant Islam is most heavily populated by Salafis.

Thus, we argue that adherents of Salafism and those who accept some of its precepts in Pakistan are those most likely to be militant anti-Americans. This is because of the important underlying Salafist narrative that true Islam is in conflict with infidels and because there is a very prominent narrative among many Salafis that the United States is the enemy of Islam and thus warrants violent resistance. This narrative can be found among Salafis and people who lean toward Salafism in Pakistan. Thus, we hypothesize that Pakistanis who share Salafi beliefs are more likely to support violence against Americans than Pakistanis who do not share such religious beliefs.

We test this hypothesis in an regression analysis that includes measures of Salafi beliefs and alternative explanations of militant anti-Americanism. Our categories of explanation are common Salafi views, general religiosity, nationalist views, and controls.

To determine if Pakistanis lean toward Salafi beliefs, we employ four questions from the 2007 WPO/START survey in Pakistan. The first asks participants to respond to this statement: "In Pakistan, people of any religion should be free to try to convert members of other religions to join theirs." Respondents are able to state whether they agree strongly, agree somewhat, disagree somewhat, or disagree strongly with the statement. In Salafi beliefs, conversion from Sunni Islam to another faith is considered a grave sin, often viewed as punishable by death. We posit that Pakistanis opposed to free conversion are more likely to favor attacks on U.S. troops in Afghanistan. The second question utilized asks respondents: "What do you personally feel about [the goal] to unify all Islamic countries into a single Islamic state or caliphate?" Those surveyed can state that they agree strongly, agree somewhat, disagree somewhat, or disagree strongly. The caliphate is considered the correct and God-willed form of Islamic governance to Salafis and its reestablishment is a central goal. Pakistanis who believe in forming a caliphate are hypothesized to be more in favor of attacks on American troops in Afghanistan. A third measure used asks respondents if they think "an attack in which a Muslim blows himself up while attacking an enemy" is justified. Salafis, more than other adherents of Islam, are more likely to support the notion of violence to protect Islam and martyrdom operations/suicide attacks as a way to do that. The provided answer choices include "often justified," "sometimes justified," "rarely justified," and "never justified." Individuals who believe such attacks are justified are believed to be more aligned with militant anti-Americanism. The final question in this category asks Pakistanis, "Overall, would you say your feelings toward Osama bin Laden are: very positive, somewhat positive, mixed, somewhat negative, or very negative?" Osama bin Laden was a hard-core Salafi who openly espoused violence against the United States in order to achieve Salafi goals. Those who are favorable toward bin Laden are also predicted to support attacking the American military in Afghanistan.

While the "Salafi views" category of explanation includes many religious references, there are more mainstream religious views that may be relevant to understanding militant anti-Americanism. In other words, we seek to determine if it is Salafi-type views or simply a strong religious faith in Islam that motivates support for attacks against U.S. troops. We believe that mainstream Islamic views and practices will not likely predispose Pakistanis to support violence against Americans as compared to Salafi-leaning views. We opt to use two separate mainstream religious measures in the current analysis. The first variable is based on a question that asks Pakistanis "How often do you perform prayer?" Respondents can state that they pray more than once a day, at least once a week, at least once a month, only during certain holidays or events, or almost never. The more one prays, it could be hypothesized, the more likely one is to support attacking U.S. troops in Afghanistan. The second mainstream religious measure asked respondents: "How important is God in your life?" Responses range on a ten-point scale from "not at all" to "very." We test our belief that the more important God is to the respondent, the more likely the respondent is to hold militant anti-American views.

Recognizing that something other than religion may drive militant anti-Americanism, we include a measure of nationalistic views. This regression is based on a survey question that asks respondents: "How much of what happens in the world today would you say is controlled by the United States? Very little, some, most, or nearly all?" It could be argued that those who hold nationalist anti-American views may be more supportive of militant attacks against U.S. troops. We test this with responses to the above question: respondents who argue that the United States controls most of what happens in the world would be more supportive of militant anti-Americanism in Pakistan.

We also include controls for four variables in our modeling: education (low, medium, or high), income (low, medium, or high), age range (18–24, 25–34, 35–44, 45–54, 55–59, 60 plus), and gender.

Results of the Analysis

Due to the preponderance of respondents who either responded to a question with "Don't know" or simply opted to not answer particular questions, the analysis was conducted two ways. In the first, missing values led to the deletion of the respondent from the model. In the second, central tendency data was imputed in place of any missing responses. Both statistical and substantive significance were identical in both methods. Table 9.18 shows the results of the analysis utilizing imputed central tendency data.

Several variables clearly emerge as significant predictors of support for attacks against U.S. troops in Afghanistan. Looking at our first category of explanation—Salafi-leaning views—we find all four indicators to be significant predictors at the .01 level of analysis in the hypothesized direction. Pakistanis who opposed religious conversion in their country, felt suicide attacks were justified, believe in creating a caliphate, and supported Osama bin Laden were all significantly more likely to appear as being more militant anti-American by supporting attacks against American troops in Afghanistan.

Looking at our second category of analysis—general religious attitudes—we see that the amount of prayer is statistically significant at the .1 level in

Table 9.18. Ordered Probit Model Estimates

Dependent Variable: Approval of Attacks Against U.S. Troops in Afghanistan			
Independent variable	Coef.	S.E.	First difference
Religious conversion punishable	−.181***	.029	−.171
Believes suicide attacks justified	.144***	.039	.148
Supports caliphate	.174***	.042	.135
Supports bin Laden	.250***	.035	.275
Amount of prayer	.071*	.032	.074
Importance of God	−.010	.036	
Believes U.S. controls world	.059	.038	
Education	.013	.045	
Income	−.068	.061	
Age	−.005	.029	
Gender	.406***	.063	.100
Cut 1	.218		
N	1243		
LR chi2(11)	214.87		
Prob > chi2	.0000		

Notes: Figures are unstandardized coefficients shown alongside standard errors. Cut 1 refers to a "cut point" on a standardized normal distribution. Cut points are used to calculate the predicted probabilities for each category of the dependent variable. The constant of the model would be interpreted as the inverse of Cut 1 (−.218).
*$p < .1$
**$p < .05$
***$p < .01$ (two-tailed)

our hypothesized direction. Thus, the more one prays in Pakistan, the more likely he or she is to support attacks against American troops. The variable assessing the importance of God to a respondent is not significant, however. Likewise, our lone variable used to assess the nationalistic category also is found to be statistically insignificant. Of our control variables, only one is found to have statistically significant predictive power in determining whether a respondent is more or less likely to support attacks on U.S. troops in Afghanistan; men are significantly more likely to offer such support than women.

While these results suggest that Salafi-leaning views are the most important in determining militant anti-Americanism in Pakistan, we can go one step further and examine the substantive results of the analysis by looking at the relative predictive values of each of the significant variables using their first difference. By doing so, we can see what impact different explanatory factors have on shaping militant anti-Americanism in Pakistan when all other variables are held constant. The results of this analysis show that Salafi-leaning views are clearly the most substantively important and powerful factors in the model. Approval of Osama bin Laden is the substantively most powerful variable we use with a first difference of .275. This means that when we take a respondent and move him or her from strongly disapproving of bin Laden to strongly approving, the respondent becomes over 27 percent more likely to support attacks on American troops in Afghanistan. Opposing religious conversion (.171), viewing suicide bombings as justified (.148), and supporting the creation of a caliphate (.135) are the next three most powerful predictors. Thus, the four Salafi-leaning-view variables are the four most useful in terms of substantive interpretation. Frequency of prayer follows at .074, and gender (if considered substantively important as a control) has a first difference that increases the odds of a respondent harboring militant anti-American views in Pakistan by over 10 percent.

Conclusion

This study is an effort to understand the landscape of anti-Americanism in Pakistan. We sought to identify Pakistani attitudes toward the United States. We also sought to understand why so many Pakistanis view the United States as an enemy and why a large number of them are supportive of violence against American troops.

We argued that current Pakistani anti-Americanism is of two major types: nationalist and religious. We contend that both of these strands of anti-Americanism are important contributors to explaining the majority of Pakistanis' negative views toward the United States. Current elite narratives centering on the United States as a dominant bully and the United States at war with Muslims are clearly resonating with many Pakistanis.

More troubling still is the support for violence against U.S. troops in Afghanistan among Pakistanis. While more disapprove of the violence than approve of it, almost a third of the Pakistani population supports such violence. We argue that Salafi-leaning religious narratives are driving this militant form of anti-Americanism and our analysis supports this view. Thus, as this more radical interpretation of Islam finds more adherents in Pakistan, there is ample reason to be concerned about the growth of militant anti-Americanism in the country.

What do the lessons of this study portend for American-Pakistani relations? First, the United States has a mountain of mistrust in Pakistan to surmount before it can convince Pakistanis that the United States is not out to harm Pakistan. This mistrust is not just about drone strikes or the killing of bin Laden. Pakistani anti-Americanism has deep and long-established roots that go back decades and not just years. As noted in the introduction to this volume, the Global War on Terror has led to several sources of friction between Pakistan and the United States. Even though the GWOT seems to be winding down, or at least has entered a new phase with a much smaller profile of forward-deployed U.S. forces, there is still much for which the Pakistani public can blame the United States. The conflict in the tribal areas, which has spilled over into settled Pakistan, is seen by many as a direct result of the U.S. GWOT. That conflict is not likely to be settled soon.

Afghan politics will also continue to be a source of anger among many in Pakistan, even as the United States and its International Security Assistance Force (ISAF) allies depart. The United States will continue to support the present political system, which Pakistani security elites view as pro-India, and Pakistan will continue to support its proxies, which want this anti-Pakistani regime replaced. As the United States continues to support the government in Kabul, many in Pakistan will view this as the United States helping to perpetuate a strategic threat to Pakistan. There is no easy way for American and Pakistani interests to be aligned on Afghanistan, and it will remain a source of friction for years to come, continuing to antagonize the Pakistani public.

The fact that so many Pakistanis' mistrust of the United States has a religious basis is particularly worrying, because religion is a core component of Pakistani identity. It is also worrying because the view of Americans as hostile to Muslims may further inflame Islamic radicalism in Pakistan.

Policies such as seemingly unconditional American support for Israel and the deepening relationship between the United States and India will only further convince those Pakistanis who believe the United States is prone to ally with countries that are viewed as oppressors of Muslims.

What does this deep and broad swath of anti-American opinion in Pakistan portend for U.S.-Pakistani relations? While it is unrealistic to assume that Pakistani public opinion will drive Pakistani state action in Afghanistan, it will play an important constraining role in what options are available to the Pakistani government. The Pakistani public is weary of war and terrorism in its country, intensely distrustful of the United States, and looking to the Pakistani government to bring peace and security to Pakistan, as noted in several chapters in this volume. That sense of threat and wariness has led the Pakistani public to back peace deals with the Pakistani Taliban, despite their bloody record. At the time of writing, most Pakistanis would like the war in Afghanistan to end and see the Americans go home, as they believe the "American" war on terrorism has left Pakistan much worse off. Persistent or worsening anti-Americanism will lead to even more Pakistanis mobilizing to try to get the Americans to leave Afghanistan and leave Pakistan to deal with Islamist militancy in its own way. American officials are correct to worry that anti-Americanism in Pakistan could significantly hamper American efforts to battle Salafi jihadi militancy in the Afghanistan-Pakistan theater of operations.

Is all hope lost for American diplomacy in Pakistan? The short answer is no. Better understanding the sources of Pakistani anti-Americanism is an important first step. Obviously, the next step is to try to improve Pakistani perceptions of Americans and the United States. First, the United States must take steps to impress on Pakistanis, Muslims worldwide for that matter, that it is not hostile to Muslims and Islam. It is telling that the one part of the world where the level of anti-Americanism did not drop after the end of the Bush administration was in the Muslim world. There is a trust gap in Pakistan and in other Muslim countries born of frustrations with American wars in Muslim countries, the U.S. relationship with Israel, and a host of perceived and real slights against Muslims that have caused many frustrated and sensitive Muslims to have a hardened attitude toward the United States. Overcoming this trust gap will take policy change and not just diplomatic initiatives to convince Pakistanis that the United States is more of a partner than an enemy.

Second, the perception that the United States does not take Pakistani interests into account also matters a great deal for anti-American sentiments. The United States can correct this perception by showing through actions, and not just words, that the United States truly cares about Pakistani interests. U.S. support for Pakistan's civilian democracy and nonmilitary aid are both important and positive policies in this regard. American drone strikes and civilian deaths caused by these strikes can easily fit into the narrative that the United States does not care about Pakistani interests, and the United States should take a proactive approach toward limiting policies that may kill a few lower-level militants but end up making U.S.-Pakistani cooperation so much harder to achieve.

Note

1. Pakistanis were not particularly pleased that Osama bin Laden was dead. When asked about this in the late spring 2011 survey, 14 percent said it was a good thing that he was dead and 54 percent said it was a bad thing that he was dead; 32 percent did not know if it was a good or a bad thing.

Works Cited

Blaydes, Lisa and Drew Linzer.2012. "Elite Competition, Religiosity, and anti-Americanism in the Islamic World." *American Political Science Review* 106 (2): 225–243.

Ceaser, James W. 2003. "A Genealogy of Anti-Americanism." *Public Interest* 152 (Summer): 3–18.

Chengappa, B. 2001. "Pakistan: The Role of Religion in Political Evoultion." *Strategic Analysis* 24 (12): 22–43.

Chiozza, Giacomo. 2004. "Love and Hate: Anti-Americanism in the Islamic World." Paper prepared for presentation at the Department of Politics, New York University, November 22.

———. 2007. "Disaggregating Anti-Americanism: An Analysis of Individual Attitudes Toward the United States." In *Anti-Americanisms in World Politics*, ed. Peter J. Katzenstein and Robert O. Keohane, 93–126. Ithaca, N.Y.: Cornell University Press.

———. 2009. *Anti-Americanism and the American World Order*. Baltimore: Johns Hopkins University Press.

Cohen, Stephen. 2004. *The Idea of Pakistan*. Washington, D.C.: Brookings Institution Press.

Faath, Sigrid, ed. 2006. *Anti-Americanism in the Islamic World*. Princeton, N.J.: Markus Wiener.

Fazal, Tanveer. 2000. "Religion and Language in the Formation of Nationhood in Pakistan and Bangladesh." In *Nation and National Identity in South Asia*, ed. S. L. Sharma and T. K. Oommen, 175–200. New Delhi: Orient Longman.

Fox, J. 2001. "Religion as an Overlooked Element of International Relations." *International Studies Review* 3 (3): 53–73.

Haqqani, Hussain. 2005. *Pakistan: Between Mosque and Military*. Washington, D.C.: Carnegie Endowment for International Peace.

Haseler, Stephen. 1985. *The Varieties of Anti-Americanism: Reflex and Response*. Washington, D.C.: Ethics and Public Policy Center.

Hertsgaard, Mark. 2002. *The Eagle's Shadow: Why America Fascinates and Infuriates the World*. New York: Farrar, Straus and Giroux.

Hollander, Paul, ed. 2004. *Understanding Anti-Americanism: Its Origins and Impact at Home and Abroad*. Chicago: Ivan R. Dee.

Holsti, Ole. 2009. *Public Opinion and American Foreign Policy*. Rev. ed. Ann Arbor: University of Michigan Press.

Hussain, Zahid. 2007. *Frontline Pakistan: The Struggle with Militant Islam*. New York: Columbia University Press.

Jaffrelot, Christophe, ed. 2002. *Pakistan: Nationalism Without a Nation*. London: Zed Books.

Jelen, T. G. 1994. "Religion and Foreign Policy Attitudes: Exploring the Effects of Denomination and Doctrine." *American Politics Research* 22 (3): 382–410.

Johnson, Thomas, and M. Chris Mason. 2008. "No Sign Until the Burst of Fire: Understanding the Pakistan-Afghanistan Border." *International Security* 32 (4): 41–77.

Judt, Tony, and Denis Lacorne. 2005. *With Us or Against Us: Studies in Global Anti-Americanism*. New York: Palgrave Macmillan.

Katzenstein, Peter J., and Robert O. Keohane, eds. 2007. *Anti-Americanisms in World Politics*. Ithaca, N.Y.: Cornell University Press.

Khattak, Saba Gul. 1996. "Security Discourses and the State in Pakistan." *Alternatives: Global, Local, Political* 21 (3): 341–362.

Kronstadt, K. Alan. 2009. "Pakistan-U.S. Relations." *CRS Report for Congress*, February 6.

Lewis, Bernard. 1990. "The Roots of Muslim Rage." *Atlantic Monthly*, September 1–10.

Lupia, Arthur, and Matthew McCubbins. 1998. *The Democratic Dilemma: Can Citizens Learn What They Need to Know?* Cambridge: Cambridge University Press.

Makdisi, Ussama. 2002. "Anti-Americanism in the Arab World: An Interpretation of a Brief History." *Journal of American History* 89 (2): 538–557.

Malik, Iftikhar. 1990. "The Pakistan-US Security Relationship: Testing Bilateralism." *Asian Survey* 30 (3): 284–299.

Misra, Amalendu. 2001. "The Centrality of Kashmir in India-Pakistan Security Dynamics." *International Politics* 38 (1): 103–119.

Naim, Moises. 2002. "Anti-Americanisms: A Guide to Hating Uncle Sam." *Foreign Policy*, January–February, 103–104.

Nasr, Vali. 1994. *The Vanguard of the Islamic Revolution: The Jama'at-i-Islami of Pakistan*. Berkeley: University of California Press.

———. 2004. "Military Rule, Islamism, and Democracy in Pakistan." *Middle East Journal* 58 (2): 195–209.

Paz, Reuven. 2003. "Islamists and Anti-Americanism." *Middle East Review of International Affairs* 7 (4): 1–9.

Pew Research. 2011. Global Attitudes Project Survey.

Rashid, Ahmed. 2008. *Descent into Chaos: The United States and the Failure of Nation Building in Pakistan, Afghanistan, and Central Asia*. London: Viking.

Revel, Jean-François. 2003. *Anti-Americanism*. San Francisco: Encounter Books.

Ross, Andrew, and Kristin Ross, eds. 2004. *Anti-Americanism*. New York: New York University Press.

Rubin, Barnett, and Ahmed Rashid. 2008. "From Great Game to Grand Bargain: Ending Chaos in Afghanistan and Pakistan." *Foreign Affairs*, November–December, 1–9.

Rubin, Barry. 2002. "The Real Roots of Arab Anti-Americanism." *Foreign Affairs*, November–December, 73–78.

Rubin, Barry, and Judith Colp Rubin. 2004. *Hating America: A History*. New York: Oxford University Press.

Rubinstein, Alvin Z., and Donald E. Smith, eds. 1985. *Anti-Americanism in the Third World: Implications for U.S. Foreign Policy*. New York: Praeger.

———. 1988. "Anti-Americanism in the Third World." *Annals of the American Academy of Social and Political Science* 497 (1): 35–45.

Schmidt, John. 2011. *The Unraveling: Pakistan in an Age of Jihad*. New York: Macmillan.

Sisson, Richard, and Leo Rose. 1990. *War and Secession: Pakistan, India, and the Creation of Bangladesh*. Berkeley: University of California Press.

Syed, Anwar Hussain. 1982. *Pakistan: Islam, Politics, and National Solidarity*. New York: Praeger.

Tai, Chong-Soo, Erick J. Peterson, and Ted Robert Gurr. 1973. "Internal Versus External Sources of Anti-Americanism: Two Comparative Studies." *Journal of Conflict Resolution* 17 (3): 455–488.

Telhami, Shibley. 1993. "Arab Public Opinion and the Gulf War." *Political Science Quarterly* 108 (3): 437–452.

Tessler, Mark. 2003. "Arab and Muslim Political Attitudes: Stereotypes and Evidence from Survey Research." *International Studies Perspectives* 4 (2): 175–181.

Tessler, M., and Nachtwey, J. 1998. "Islam and Attitudes toward International Conflict." *Journal of Conflict Resolution* 42 (5): 619–636.

Toft, Mark D. 2007. "Getting Religion? The Puzzling Case of Islam and Civil War." *International Security* 31 (4): 97–131.

Uslaner, Eric. 2000. "Producing and Consuming Trust." *Political Science Quarterly*. 115: 569–590.

World Public Opinion.org/START. 2007. *Muslim Public Opinion on U.S. Policy, Attacks on Civilians, and al Qaeda.* World Public Opinion, April 24.

Vedrine, Hubert. 2004. "On Anti-Americanism." *Brown Journal of World Affairs* 10 (2): 117–121.

Zaller, John. 1992. *The Nature and Origins of Mass Opinion.* Cambridge: Cambridge University Press.

Zia, Rukhsana. 2003. "Religion and Education in Pakistan: An Overview." *Prospects* 33 (2): 165–178.

Chapter 10

Friends of Last Resort: Pakistan's Relations with China and Saudi Arabia

Aparna Pande

Pakistan's foreign policy has perennially sought that elusive alliance that would solve its key problems: building its economic and military potential and supporting it in its intractable conflict with India. Pakistan's relationship with the United States has been premised on the former's hope that American aid—both military and economic—will bolster Pakistan's ability to counter Indian economic and military might. However, Pakistan has never been certain of American support and consequently has sought other countries with which Pakistan's leaders feel an affinity—be it ideological or strategic—to diversify its avenues of support. China has been a source of military assistance, while Saudi Arabia is an ideological and economic collaborator. Between them, the two countries are seen as Pakistan's friends of last resort.

When the Americans complete their withdrawal from Afghanistan in 2014, Pakistan may hold less importance for the United States (see Staniland in this volume). To compensate for this lack of American interest, Pakistan's leadership may attempt to make Pakistan pertinent to other countries that may afford Pakistan with the economic and military support that the Americans had provided since 2001. In the event of an American retrenchment, Pakistan is likely to turn ever more to Saudi Arabia and China, even if this means providing military guarantees to Saudi Arabia and acting as China's surrogate against India.

With this post-2014 future in mind, in this chapter I briefly recount the history of Pakistan's ties with Saudi Arabia and China from the 1950s to the present. Next, I examine how Pakistan's relationships with both are likely to evolve in the policy-relevant future.

Roots of the Relationships: India, Identity, and Insecurity

Pakistan gained its independence in 1947, with a weak military and few military supplies and severely limited economic resources. To contend with its myriad weaknesses, Pakistan sought extensive help from the United States. The United States saw Pakistan's overtures in the context of America's expanding role in post–World War II Asia. By the mid-1950s, the United States warmed to Pakistan's entreaties, especially since India under Premier Jawaharlal Nehru was a nonaligned nation. The two countries signed a mutual defense assistance agreement in 1954 and a bilateral executive agreement in 1959. Pakistan also entered into the U.S.-led military alliances known as Southeast Asia Treaty Organization (SEATO), in 1954 and the U.K.-led alliance known as the Central Treaty Organization (CENTO), in 1955. By 1959 the United States was providing $227.7 million per year in economic aid and $61.1 million per year in military aid to Pakistan. Yet while Pakistan viewed the relationship with the United States as a way to counter India, the United States was not interested in being involved in any India-Pakistan conflict.[1]

In the subsequent decades, Pakistan repeatedly sought and obtained American economic and military aid but Pakistan was never been fully satisfied. For the vast majority of their bilateral history, Pakistan and the United States have differed on the nature of the threat that motivated their partnership: for Pakistan it was always India, for the United States it was initially Communism and later global terrorism. Despite American generosity, Pakistanis have long opined that the United States is an "ungrateful and fair weather" ally. To augment the support it received from the United States, Pakistan's leaders have consistently turned to two countries that have in contrast been portrayed as Pakistan's dependable allies: Saudi Arabia and China.

Over the decades Saudi Arabia has been presented to the Pakistani public as the ideal ideological ally of Pakistan, a fellow Muslim country that would stand by Pakistan in any conflict with India. Having constructed an

Islamic identity, both domestically and in foreign affairs, Pakistan's leaders believed close ties with Saudi Arabia—the guardian of the Muslim holy lands—would burnish Pakistan's pan-Islamic credentials.

Pakistani officials and even media accounts portray China as the ideal strategic ally: a country that is strong enough to provide Pakistan economic and military support whenever the Americans stopped or reduced aid but also one that has an antagonistic relationship with India. In Pakistan's eyes this hostility would ensure Chinese support in the event of Pakistan's conflict with India.[2] As an isolated and embargoed regime, the Chinese communist government saw immense benefits in trade and diplomatic contacts with countries—like Pakistan—willing to pursue these ties. Pakistan was China's bridge to the Muslim world in more ways than one. China has a large Muslim minority in its western region and having a friendly Muslim neighbor next door was seen as strategically and diplomatically useful. Friendship with Pakistan helped China build trade and diplomatic ties with the Muslim Middle East and Southeast Asia. Pakistan was the *via media* for China's ties with Saudi Arabia and the Persian Gulf countries, with economic (energy) and defense (military and nuclear) components. In recent years, however, China's window to the Muslim world has become the epicenter of radical Islam and has proven unwilling—and unable—to prevent the spread of radical Islamism into the Xinjiang region of China.

Tested by War and Breakup

Events of the 1960s and 1970s deeply influenced Pakistan's perceptions of its allies. The American reaction to the 1962 Sino-Indian war and the 1965 India-Pakistan war was seen by Pakistan as a betrayal by a close ally. President Ayub Khan's aide-mémoire requested American assistance on the grounds that "Pakistan ha[d] become a victim of naked aggression by armed attack on the part of India" (Kux 2001: 161). In contrast Pakistan believed that the actions of Saudi Arabia and China demonstrated a true commitment to Pakistan. Both countries offered Pakistan aid and loans: China and Pakistan signed an air agreement in 1963 and China offered Pakistan a loan of $60 million.

The American decision to stop military supplies to both India and Pakistan during the 1965 war played a key role in the building of a Sino-Pakistan defense relationship. Right from the start, Chinese investment in the military arena focused on ensuring a captive market for selling its equipment, gaining access to Western technology and equipment from Pakistan, and in later years sharing nuclear and missile technology with Pakistan.[3]

China also developed a durable pattern for its investment in Pakistan: it focused on trade and commercial links, investment in infrastructure, and access to other markets. The investment was not designed to build Pakistan's economy for its own sake but to benefit Chinese companies, and expand access to markets (Central Asia) and energy resources (Middle East).[4] At periodic intervals China has also provided a limited amount of funding either during natural disasters or to help tide Pakistan over its immediate economic problems.[5]

However, Pakistan has generally ignored the nuances of Chinese economic investment and preferred instead to focus on the belief that the Chinese, unlike the Americans, are a trustworthy and dependable ally who has always supported Pakistan's economic development. Over the years, while Chinese aid has been much less than that provided by countries like the United States, it has always received more media coverage and government praise. Even during the 1971 war that led to the loss of East Pakistan, Pakistan ignored the Nixon administration's "tilt" toward Pakistan and ascribed China's inaction to Sino-Soviet tensions. Pakistani policy makers are hesitant to contemplate the possibility that China did not perceive it to be in its interests to enter the India-Pakistan conflict. While neither Saudi Arabia nor China was able to prevent Pakistan's breakup in 1971, the almost mythical faith in their friendship remains intact and will play a key role in framing Pakistan's policies in the future (Pande 2011).

An Islamic Bloc

Pakistan's founders championed pan-Islamism, believing that the unification of Indian Muslims under one entity would help the cause of Muslims around the world. However, in an era of decolonization and nationalism, pan-Islamism was not a popular concept, especially in the Arab world. Pakistan's attempts at trying to build pan-Islamic institutions (and to assume a leadership role in the Muslim world) were resented by other, older Muslim states. It was only in the 1970s that the alliance with Saudi Arabia conferred tangible benefits to Pakistan, especially in the economic and military arenas. Saudi Arabia's assistance to Pakistan has never quite matched the Pakistani expectations despite the effusive rhetoric that Pakistan has long conferred to the kingdom.

Like China, Saudi Arabia has periodically provided Pakistan with loans and short-term emergency aid.[6] On some occasions, the Saudis have been more generous than the United States and Western countries in offering disaster assistance to Pakistan. In the aftermath of a massive earthquake in Pakistan in January 1975, King Faisal of Saudi Arabia offered $10 million for disaster relief. Although the United States and its allies offered aid earlier than the Saudis, their contributions (United States, $ 25,000; Canadian Red Cross, $10,000; Britain, $23,000; and Australia, $32,000) paled in comparison to Saudi generosity (Reuters 1975). More recently, in 2005, when Pakistan was hit by an earthquake, and again in 2010, when massive floods engulfed central Pakistan, the United States was again the first to come in with aid but the Saudis gave far more. Pakistan's leaders have always shied away from praising American support in the form of multilateral inputs, choosing instead to highlight only the bilateral assistance of the so-called dependable allies: Saudi Arabia and China.

Pakistan imports most of its oil from the Gulf and in periods when Pakistan has not been able to pay for this oil the Saudi Arabian government has given them oil at concessional rates or even waived the payment for a few years. For three years after the 1998 nuclear tests Pakistan did not have to pay for the oil that it was provided by Saudi Arabia (Kamal 2008). Pakistan's economic dependence on the Gulf, especially Saudi Arabia, continued through the 1980s and into the twenty-first century. By 1983, there were 500,000 Pakistanis working in Saudi Arabia, and remittances from Pakistanis working in the Gulf amounted to around $3 billion (Addleton 1984). Pakistan also received funding for general purposes, as well as specific projects and relief grants, from Saudi Arabia and the Organization of Petroleum Exporting Countries (OPEC) special fund (Burke and Ziring 1990: 422–423).

The 1970s also saw the start of a worrying trend in Saudi-Pakistani relations: Saudi Arabia's growing role in Pakistan's domestic politics. Saudi Arabia and its fellow Gulf state the United Arab Emirates have often supported one or another political party in Pakistan, provided economic aid, or deferred loan payments or oil payments when their preferred party was in power and offered asylum to political leaders. Prime Minister Nawaz Sharif was hosted in Jeddah, Saudi Arabia, after being toppled in a military coup in 1999, and the Saudis have made it known that they would offer former military dictator General Pervez Musharraf similar sanctuary now that Sharif, at the time of writing, is back in power and Musharraf is on trial.

Saudi Arabia's role in Pakistan's domestic politics started during the political agitation soon after the 1977 elections during Zulfikar Ali Bhutto's rule (Simmons 1977). From the state's inception, Pakistani leaders, policy makers, and even the media have lamented the strong American influence on their domestic politics and sought to label those who are pro-American as "traitors" or "agents"; however, Pakistan has yet to see similar labels applied to those who are close to Saudi Arabia or China. Instead an unspoken rule dictates that Pakistani politicians and journalists avoid criticism of these two ideological and strategic allies of Pakistan.

Although neither country talks about it publicly, Pakistan and Saudi Arabia maintain close military ties. Being short of cash, Pakistan has often looked to Saudi Arabia to finance its purchases of weaponry on the international market. Since the 1970s, Pakistan has sporadically offered military manpower to Saudi Arabia and its Gulf Arab allies in return for financing Pakistani purchases of military equipment. The most recent instance is the induction of Pakistani volunteers into the military and police in Bahrain, where Saudi Arabia has sought to prop up the Sunni regime against Shia protesters since 2011. Such deployments confer to Pakistan the mantle of protector of the Muslim holy lands.[7] Such accolades accord with Pakistan's self-styled role as the Muslim world's protector.

The Saudi-Pakistan defense cooperation originated with a 1976 bilateral agreement that provided for an exchange of defense technical knowledge. By the mid-1980s, approximately 50,000 Pakistani military personnel were serving abroad, with the largest commitment (about 20,000 persons) to Saudi Arabia. Pakistani pilots routinely participated in air defense operations in Saudi Arabia. The Gulf Arab countries prefer foreign fighters from non-Arab countries as it ensures that the foreigners will not be involved in domestic politics. During the Iran-Iraq conflict, in return for $1 billion in aid, Pakistan stationed around 10,000 Pakistani troops in Saudi Arabia.

In return Saudi Arabia assisted by helping Pakistan purchase sophisticated weaponry from the West. To help bolster Pakistan's military, Saudi Arabia provided concessional loans to Pakistan. In many cases Saudi Arabia agreed to be the guarantor whenever Pakistan purchased military hardware from the United States. It helped that both Saudi Arabia and Pakistan were

American allies.[8] This practice continued over the decades and in early 2014 there was a discussion between the two governments about Pakistan providing trained military personnel to man Saudi Arabia's security forces and also talks about creating a Gulf Cooperation Council (GCC) military force to counter Iran (*World Tribune* 2014).

Pakistan's military defeat in 1971 and the realization that India was stronger in conventional military technology led Pakistan to turn to nuclear deterrence. Pakistan has pursued a nuclear weapons program since 1972, conducted nuclear tests in 1998, and is believed to be developing tactical battlefield nuclear weapons. The nuclear arena is another field where Pakistan perceived the United States as unsympathetic to Pakistan's concerns. Nuclear weapons are seen as the only way to maintain Pakistan's military parity with India, which has permanent conventional military superiority, and refusing to support Pakistan's right to nuclear armaments is seen in Pakistan as effective partiality to India. Saudi Arabia and China are seen as sympathetic and supportive of Pakistan's nuclear quest. (For further discussion of Pakistan's nuclear program, see Clary in this volume.)

There are persistent reports of an understanding between Pakistan and Saudi Arabia whereby Islamabad would provide nuclear weapons or a nuclear umbrella to Riyadh if the Saudis feel threatened by a third party with nuclear weapons such as Iran or Israel. Both Pakistan and Saudi Arabia, however, deny any secret deal, most recently in November 2013 when the BBC spoke of it in a documentary (Urban 2013). The rumors can be traced to a much-publicized visit by then Saudi defense minister, and later crown prince, Sultan bin Abdul Aziz, to Pakistan's top-secret nuclear laboratories run by Dr. A. Q. Khan in May 1999.[9] Given Pakistan's lack of funds and the opacity of the financing arrangements for its nuclear program, it is widely believed that Saudi Arabia provided some of the funding that enabled Pakistan to become the world's first Muslim country to build and test nuclear weapons.

Pakistan and Saudi Arabia remain active partners in pan-Islamist organizations sponsored by the Saudis since the 1970s. Pakistan plays a key role in the Organization of the Islamic Conference (OIC), Rabita al-Alam al-Islami (World Muslim League), and Motamar al-Alam al-Islami (World Muslim Congress) and has provided personnel for Saudi Arabia's pan-Islamist projects. These ties have helped Pakistan champion the causes of Kashmir and Palestine as well as obtain Arab aid.

Pakistan has also welcomed donations from wealthy individuals and charities from Saudi Arabia to found and support Wahabbi madrassas and universities in Pakistan. Such institutions have proliferated since the mid-1970s and became major recruiting centers for jihadis in the 1980s. Muslim students from Europe, Africa, the Middle East, and Southeast Asia come to study in Pakistan and many have ended up as foot soldiers in jihadist organizations across the globe.[10]

All-Weather Ally

If Saudi Arabia is the financier of last resort for Pakistan's military, China is the major source of military equipment. The Pakistani military prefers more sophisticated American weapons, preferably provided on concessional terms. But the American habit of rationing spare parts in case Pakistan enters wars that the United States does not like, as well as the imposition of periodic American sanctions, have caused Pakistan to seek a more reliable source of armaments. Since the 1960s, China has been that source. By 1982 Chinese weapons systems formed the backbone of the Pakistani military arsenal, composing 75 percent of the tank force and 65 percent of the air force (Vertzberger 1983). Between 2008 and 2012, Pakistan was the main purchaser of Chinese weapons, buying 55 percent of Chinese weapons exports (Lipin 2013).

China's economic support for Pakistan has been consistent and focuses on high-profile infrastructure projects and small intermittent loans. This differs greatly from the pattern of American assistance, which is far greater ($40 billion between 1949 and 2013) but has been inconsistent and divided across a large number of economic and social projects, making it less visible. Between 1956 and 1979 Pakistan received $620 million in economic aid from China, about one-third of China's total aid to Asia and the Middle East. In June 1978, China and Pakistan opened the all-weather Karakoram Highway, the highest paved road in the world at an elevation of 15,000 feet. Attitudes toward the highway demonstrate how each side viewed the relationship: for Pakistan, the road demonstrated China's commitment and friendship. For China, the highway was a land route through which it could gain access to Central Asia as well as to the oil-rich Persian Gulf. Pakistan viewed itself as being indispensable for China; China viewed Pakistan as a part (but only a part) of securing its energy sources and markets (Krondstadt and Epstein 2013; Vertzberger 1983).

Sino-Pakistani cooperation in the nuclear field can be traced back to the 1980s. As early as 1983, American intelligence agencies reported that the Chinese transferred a complete nuclear weapon design to Pakistan, along with enough weapons-grade uranium for two potential nuclear weapons. In 1986, China and Pakistan concluded a comprehensive nuclear cooperation agreement. Later that year, Chinese scientists began "assisting" their Pakistani counterparts with the enrichment of weapons-grade uranium. Analysts believe that, since 1986, "China has supplied Pakistan with a wide variety of nuclear products and services, ranging from uranium enrichment technology to reactors." There are also reports that China "involved" Pakistani scientists in a nuclear test at its Lop Nur (Xinjiang) test site in 1989.[11]

For Pakistan, the key indicator of true friendship is a country's view of India and of the Kashmir conflict. China used anti-India rhetoric during Pakistan's wars with India in 1965 and 1971. But now it is less willing to encourage Pakistan's anti-India stance. An indication of the change in China's foreign policy was the speech delivered to the Pakistani National Assembly in December 1996 by President Jiang Zemin of the People's Republic of China. The Chinese president started by reiterating the closeness of Sino-Pakistani relations and referred to Chinese and Pakistanis "as friends in need and brothers bound by common fate." Subsequently, Jiang asserted that while it was natural for neighbors to have "differences or disputes," keeping the "larger picture" in mind, "if certain issues cannot be resolved for the time being, they may be shelved temporarily so that they will not affect the normal state-to-state relations" (Jiang 1996). Jiang wanted to convey the message that, just as China had developed economic and cultural ties with India and "temporarily shelved" Sino-Indian border issues because such disagreements could not "be resolved for the time being," it was time for Pakistan to do the same. Pakistan, however, chose not to receive the message.

Three years later, during the 1999 Kargil conflict, China once again demonstrated that it had no intention of entering into an India-Pakistan conflict. Pakistan's prime minister Nawaz Sharif had flown to the United States to seek American support but President Bill Clinton had asked him to "respect the sanctity of the Line of Control" and withdraw his troops. Hoping for Chinese support, Sharif flew to Beijing, where he received a similar message. These messages delivered by the Chinese, however, have not had the intended impact: Pakistan's leaders still have faith that China will stand by them in any conflict with India.

One of the reasons that Pakistan's view of China as an "all-weather friend" persists is that despite these political shifts, economic ties between China and Pakistan grew steadily during the 1990s and 2000s. In 2006 the two countries signed a Free Trade Agreement (FTA) and by 2009 their bilateral trade stood at $6.8 billion.[12] As part of Chinese investment in Pakistani infrastructure projects, in 2002 China promised to help in the construction of the Gwadar seaport. For Pakistan, Gwadar was important for both strategic and economic reasons: the port's development would make Pakistan the gateway to shipping routes for both western China and the Central Asian republics. Pakistan also sought "strategic depth" in Gwadar: Karachi, Pakistan's other main port and naval headquarters, was located too close to the Indian coast.

Gwadar has both strategic and economic benefits for China as well. Gwadar is closer to western China than the ports on China's eastern coast and is located nearer the Persian Gulf, through which most of China's oil tankers travel. From the strategic point of view, the Chinese navy's desire for "blue-water navy" status demands a presence in the Indian Ocean and Persian Gulf.

Pakistan has always sought to leverage its geopolitical location to demonstrate its indispensability (as when it offered bases and assistance to the United States). Pakistan hopes that China will view the Gwadar port as a critical strategic and economic resource. Since China imports most of its oil from the Middle East, overland access to the Persian Gulf would help China avoid concerns over the length of its sea lines of communication (SLOCs) and the fact that the United States still acts as the protector of global shipping. Furthermore, if China decides to station part of its navy at Gwadar, it would send a signal to India. China is not yet sold on using Gwadar, but Pakistan hopes it will do so sooner rather than later.

Chinese support of and aid to Pakistan's nuclear program has also continued unabated. The Chinese government insists that its nuclear cooperation with Pakistan is purely for peaceful purposes. But in December 1992, China transferred to Pakistan technology related to the M-11 missile. Analysts believe this was Beijing's response to the U.S. government's decision to sell F-16 fighter jets to Taiwan. In August 1993, when the Clinton administration threatened sanctions, China insisted that it had not breached arms-control guidelines.[13]

In 1995, American intelligence agencies claimed that "5,000 specially designed ring magnets" from the China Nuclear Energy Industry Corporation

(CNEIC) had been "exported" to an "unsafeguarded Pakistani nuclear laboratory," which was "allegedly" involved in nuclear weapons activity. In April 1996 the Clinton administration threatened but then decided against imposing sanctions on China in return for a Chinese pledge "not to provide nuclear assistance to unsafeguarded facilities" (Smith and Devroy 1996; Lippman and Blustein 1996). However, as per the 1997 report of the U.S. director of central intelligence, China "was the primary source of nuclear-related equipment and technology to Pakistan" during the second half of 1996 (DCI 1997).

Despite being a signatory to the Missile Technology Control Regime (MTCR), China provided weapons technology to Pakistan, a nonsignatory. On May 1, 2001, an American satellite captured an image of a Chinese shipment of parts for Pakistan's Shaheen-1 and Shaheen-2 missiles—both of which can travel up to 1,240 miles and carry nuclear warheads—crossing the Sino-Pakistani border (*Wall Street Journal* 2001).

Evidence of Sino-Pakistani nuclear cooperation during the 1980s and 1990s surfaced in 2004 when the Libyans turned over bomb designs and other papers to the Americans. The packet of documents obtained included material in Chinese with "step-by-step instructions for assembling an implosion-type nuclear bomb that could fit atop a large ballistic missile" (Warrick and Slevin 2004). When the Bush administration offered India a civil nuclear deal in March 2006, Pakistan requested the same from the United States. The Bush administration, however, stated that the United States had started to "de-hyphenate" India and Pakistan policies and each country would be treated differently. Pakistan then turned to China to ask for a similar deal.

Many American analysts believe that during a trip to China in October 2008 then Pakistani president Zardari participated in private discussions on a "step-by-step" approach to fulfilling Pakistan's aspiration for an expanded nuclear energy program. Instead of a deal along the lines of the India-U.S. civilian nuclear agreement, China agreed to "consider further nuclear power reactors" to fulfill Pakistan's needs. In May 2010, one of China's state nuclear agencies agreed to build two new reactors in Pakistan.

Pakistan's post-2008 transition to democracy and its recent economic crisis have complicated Pakistan's ties with its various allies, especially the United States, China, and Saudi Arabia. Facing a balance of payments crisis in April 2008, and not wanting to approach the International Monetary Fund (IMF) for financial assistance, the country's leaders initially turned to

China and Saudi Arabia for loans (Reuters 2008). While China offered an immediate loan of $500 million, the message sent by both Beijing and Riyadh was that if Pakistan wanted further help from either country it needed to go to the IMF and follow its stringent conditions.

In November 2008, when Pakistan approached the IMF for an initial loan of $7.6 billion to avoid massive crises, its request was initially turned down. The IMF cited a history of broken promises by a series of Pakistani governments. According to Pakistan's former representative to the IMF, Dr. Ehtisham Ahmad, the IMF changed its decision and provided an $11.3 billion package only after an intervention from the White House (Rana 2011). Neither Saudi Arabia nor China played a role in this decision, but the people of Pakistan were never told of America's support in securing IMF funding. The Pakistani government maintained the illusion that China and Saudi Arabia were Pakistan's true friends.

Saudi Arabia was also a reluctant participant and contributor to the Friends of Democratic Pakistan (FoDP) grouping. Saudi Arabia did not attend the first meeting of FoDP in September 2008 (Rosenberg and Hussain 2008). While the Saudis attended the next FoDP summit, in April 2009, they remained ambivalent about the amount of aid they would provide Pakistan. In contrast, the United States and its allies provided the bulk of the $4–5 billion pledged, with the United States and Japan pledging $1 billion each and the European Union, United Kingdom, and United Arab Emirates another $500 million each (Solomon 2009).

Once again the largest amount of aid provided to Pakistan came from the United States, its allies, or international institutions over which the United States had influence. Saudi Arabia and China provided only a small amount of aid. Some analysts have argued that the Saudi reluctance to contribute was due to the fact that Saudi Arabia has a better relationship with the Pakistan Muslim League–Nawaz (PML-N) than it does with the Pakistan Peoples Party (PPP), which was in power during the conference. But there could be another reason, something the Pakistanis are loath to consider: Saudi and Chinese reluctance to contribute could be the result of both countries over a period of time becoming tired of repeatedly assisting Pakistan when they see little signs of Pakistan changing its policies.

While China has continued its policy of investing in infrastructure, seeking markets for Chinese goods, and providing periodic, limited economic assistance, there has actually been a decline in private foreign investment from China to Pakistan. This stood at $0.3 million in 2001, rose to

$14 million in 2004, but decreased drastically to $0.4 million in 2005 (State Bank of Pakistan 2014). This decline in Chinese investment resulted from the insecurity throughout Pakistan (e.g., the 2007 takeover of the Red Mosque, the kidnappings and killings of Chinese engineers and business-men, and unrest in Baluchistan). Currently there are some 14,000 Chinese engineers, technicians, and workers in Pakistan, employed by some sixty Chinese-government-run companies engaged mainly in infrastructure, energy, and dam construction (Rashid Ahmed Khan 2013; Associated Press of Pakistan 2009). Future infrastructure projects include a railroad linking the Karakoram Highway to Gwadar, a fiber-optic line and an oil and gas pipeline (*Daily Times* 2008). In June 2009 Pakistan signed a memorandum of understanding (MoU) with EXIM Bank of China for $700 million to generate electricity through twelve small and medium-sized dams and water reservoirs (*Dawn* 2009).

China has also maintained its policy of preserving Pakistan as a captive market for defense matériel. As part of a $700 million military aid package signed in 2005, China delivered four naval frigates to the Pakistani navy. China also equipped the frigates with six helicopters (*Daily Times* 2007; Agence France-Presse 2009). The two countries are also jointly producing the JF-17 Thunder fighter jet. According to analysts, the "very low price" of the JF-17, one-third of the price of a "comparable aircraft" produced by the Europeans or Americans, also makes it "a very lucrative commercial venture" (Bokhari 2008). Sino-Pakistani defense cooperation is Pakistan's answer to the perceived Russian-Indian military-strategic nexus and grow-ing India-U.S.-Israel ties.

The disaster caused by massive flooding in 2010 saw a repeat of earlier years: The U.S. government was the first to offer aid, providing $150 mil-lion, while its ally the European Union donated $135 million more. Saudi Arabia pledged $105 million, but only $5 million of this was in cash, the rest being in-kind contributions. China pledged $247 million worth of aid, of which only $10 million was in cash (Shah et al. 2010). As before, the Pakistani media praised the Chinese and Saudi contributions but glossed over the aid from the United States.

Over the past decade the China-Pakistan relationship has come under some strain due to the rise in jihadi militancy in Pakistan. When China signed the 1963 border agreement with Pakistan, its strategists had hoped that agreement would keep the Sino-Pakistani border secure. Furthermore, Chinese policy makers hoped that friendly relations with Pakistan would prevent their neighbor from providing aid and assistance to insurgents among its Muslim population. (The violent Uighur insurgency has been a domestic security problem for China ever since the 1990s.)

These hopes were partially fulfilled: Pakistan has cooperated with China on the Uighur issue. Despite its self-anointed status as a champion of the rights of Muslim minorities, Pakistan has never taken up the issue of the rights of the Uighurs in China. Pakistan has consistently dissuaded fellow Muslim countries from tabling a resolution on the Uighur issue at the periodic OIC summits of Muslim-majority countries (Malik 2009). In contrast, Pakistan has consistently used these meetings to bring up Kashmir and the status of Indian Muslims.

But despite Pakistani assurances, Chinese civilian and military policy makers remain worried about the large number of Uighurs fighting in Pakistan and Afghanistan, where they receive succor from local and global jihadi groups. They are troubled by the Pakistani government's increasing inability or unwillingness to dismantle and destroy militant groups, which are seen as "assets" vis-à-vis India and Afghanistan. China has always preferred to convey its concerns to Pakistan privately, but in the face of the growing insurgency in Xinjiang and Pakistan's fecklessness, China has slowly started changing its earlier policy (Swami 2008). On June 24, 2013, ten foreign tourists, three of Chinese origin, were killed in an attack by the Pakistan-based jihadi group Tehreek-e-Taliban-e-Pakistan (TTP), reinforcing the Chinese concerns about security problems in Pakistan (Agence France-Presse 2013).

Pakistan's prized alliances with China and Saudi Arabia are also complicated by both countries' improved relations with India. Beginning in the 1990s China improved its ties with India on many levels, as seen in its decision to settle the Sino-Indian border dispute. Similarly, Saudi Arabia's ties with India have deepened on the economic and even the defense/counterterrorism fronts. (In 2012, for instance, Saudi Arabia extradited a Lashkar-e-Taiba operative to India instead of sending him to Pakistan (Press Trust of India 2012).) In January 2006, King Abdullah became the first Saudi monarch to visit India. King Abdullah asserted that the Saudi-India relationship was "historic" and referred to India as "my second homeland" (BBC 2006). By 2013 Saudi oil exports to India stood at 27 million metric tons of crude oil annually, or 700,000 barrels per day, making India one of the top buyers of Saudi crude (Mehdudia 2014). It would be unrealistic for Pakistan to expect that the Saudis would be able to ignore growing economic interests in India in favor of an ideological affinity for Pakistan.

After U.S. Withdrawal?

Pakistan's key objectives are regional and include: parity with India, a pro-Pakistan (read "anti-India") Afghanistan, a China that views Pakistan as a deterrent against India, and countries like Saudi Arabia and the Gulf states that need Pakistan on their side in the Middle East. In other words, Pakistan wants to bring Afghanistan into its sphere of influence, to shrink (or at least maintain) the existing strategic imbalance between itself and India, and to enlist China as a sturdy anti-India ally. Pakistan's vision of the future, however, is not shared by any other actor, in the region or beyond. For decades Pakistan sought to be America's anchor in the Middle East, in the hopes that making itself indispensable to the United States would help Pakistan achieve its goals. Pakistan failed to achieve this goal, however, and with the American military withdrawal from Afghanistan in 2014 it is becoming even more unlikely.

As I've argued in this chapter, Pakistan's leaders' distrust of the United States motivates their pursuit of more enduring alliances with China and Saudi Arabia. Yet these preferred partners have themselves proved unwilling to meet Pakistan's expectations. Pakistan's needs, given its fragile economic base and the persistent political instability that keeps potential investors wary, may be too great for the Chinese or Saudis to continue to meet. China and increasingly Saudi Arabia seem unwilling to match Pakistan's hostility toward India. And as Pakistan struggles to control its militant proxies and to combat the antistate militant groups that have sprung up on its own soil, it becomes less useful to China, either as a security partner or as a conduit for trade.

Both allies have their own objectives in the region, goals that may not be in line with Pakistani interests. Pakistan, for instance, has been on the front lines of the decades-long proxy war between Saudi Arabia and Iran, which has contributed to intense sectarian violence within Pakistan. Saudi Arabia also makes frequent attempts to manipulate Pakistani politics by supporting one or the other political parties or groups in Pakistan. And while the Saudi government turns a blind eye to funding flowing from the Gulf into militant groups in Pakistan and Syria, Saudi Arabia has its own problems with domestic radical Islam and has learned the lessons of its support for the Taliban government in Afghanistan. Looking at the future, Pakistan is in many ways Saudi Arabia's ace in the hole; it provides Saudi Arabia strategic depth in the sense of trained manpower (economic but primarily military), defense capability (conventional but also nuclear), and territory to continue its proxy war with Iran.

In this context, Saudi Arabia will continue to provide limited economic aid primarily during natural disasters and may at intervals also allow disbursed oil payments if the Pakistani economy is in dire straits. However, Saudi Arabia doesn't have weight in international financial institutions like the IMF, World Bank, or Asian Development Bank, where the United States aided Pakistan. With the withdrawal of American interest in the region, these institutions may not look as kindly at Pakistan, unless its other ally, China decides to play a role, which it has not yet done.

Pakistan's defense ties with Saudi Arabia are likely to deepen in the future. In January 2014 both Saudi Arabia's foreign minister Prince Saud Al-Faisal and deputy defense minister Prince Salman bin Sultan bin Abdul Aziz visited Pakistan within a few days of each other to discuss the two countries' strategic ties. At the heart of the discussions was Pakistan's provision of a trained military force in Saudi Arabia and also the setting up of a Riyadh-based Gulf Cooperation Council military force (Al-Rasheed 2014; Syed 2014). A force composed of Pakistanis is attractive to Saudi Arabia for two reasons: there would be no fear that the force would become politicized, and the Saudi regime would be able to post the (Muslim) troops at sensitive religious sites. Growing Sino-Saudi ties may draw the three states even closer: Saudi Arabia may also look to China as a potential superpower ally with vast economic resources and no interest in interfering in other states' domestic issues (read "human rights").

China's policies in the immediate future look like they too will continue along already established lines. China will continue investment in infrastructure and provide relief during natural disasters. However, its aid and investment will be more careful than before. Signs of this future trajectory include the lessened Chinese investment in Pakistan, more limited investment in government-run firms, China's decision to back out of projects like the Iran-Pakistan pipeline, and its reluctance to use the Gwadar port.

Yet Pakistan will remain part of China's efforts to manage India's ascent, and thus China will continue its military and nuclear assistance. Chinese concerns about radical Islam within China—Xinjiang—and also in the central Asian countries bordering China and in Afghanistan will become an increasingly problematic issue in its ties with Pakistan. China may seek the help of Saudi Arabia in its efforts to put pressure on Pakistan and groups within Pakistan but also to try to reduce the funding and support for Uighurs in the greater Muslim world. How far China will be successful on this front is yet to be seen.

Conclusion

Pakistan's leaders and general public have embraced Saudi Arabia and China as ideal and dependable allies. Lacking friendly countries in its immediate neighborhood, and unsure of its distant allies, Pakistan's policy makers have sought to cultivate China as a neighbor and ally. China has given economic and military aid and much needed support in the nuclear arena. Pakistanis often contrast China's "no-strings attached" "generous assistance at moments of our greatest need" with America's "conditionalities." But Pakistan's narrative about the dependability of China does not comport with a more empirical evaluation of the Sino-Pakistan relationship. China's economic aid has been limited (and often given in loans) and its investment has been trade and infrastructure oriented, which services China's objectives first (although these activities certainly benefit Pakistan as well). China will be able to extract maximum values from its investments in highways and ports only when Pakistan's internal security situation improves. Continued insecurity in northwest Pakistan and in Baluchistan will dampen even Chinese interests in such investments, as demonstrated by the sharp decline in Chinese investment in the last few years.

China's defense relationship with Pakistan was geared to ensure a secure market and dependable ally along an unstable border. While China has used the bogeyman of "Indian hegemonism" (U.S. Embassy Beijing 2004) to strengthen ties with India's neighbors over the years, it is now increasingly wary of the growing strategic ties between the United States, India, and China's neighbors in East and Southeast Asia. It would prefer to maintain sufficiently good relations with India so that India does not ally itself with the United States as part of an attempt to contain China. A true Sino-Indian rapprochement would be met with dismay in Pakistan, where the India-centric strategic paradigm remains paramount.

Saudi Arabia has furnished economic assistance, energy aid, and episodic financing of defense purchases. But it has also offered Pakistan substantial ideological and symbolic support. Pakistan's founders and subsequent rulers have always envisioned Pakistan as the leader of the Muslim world—a goal that it has the ambition, but not the resources, to accomplish. Ties with Saudi Arabia, the home of Islam's holy places, helps to prop up this self-image and also helps Pakistan to win the support of the entire Muslim *ummah (nation)* in its fight against "Hindu" India. In recent years, however, Saudi Arabia's economic and political compulsions have drawn it closer to India. Pakistan's leaders and strategists have failed to grasp a fundamental reality of global power politics: in the words of former Malaysian premier Tunku Abdul Rahman, while Muslim countries are willing to build "brotherly ties" with Pakistan, they frame foreign policy "regardless of religious status" (bin Sayeed 1968: 238).

Pakistan's relations with Saudi Arabia and China have been strong over the last six decades, but they still fall short of Pakistan's objectives. In trying to build permanent partnerships that transcend Saudi and Chinese interests, Pakistan may be seeking something that is almost impossible to attain.

Notes

1. As early as 1954, the U.S. secretary of state John Foster Dulles wrote a reservation into the SEATO treaty that America's obligation would only extend to cases of Communist aggression. Under the 1954 Mutual Defense Assistance Agreement Pakistan agreed to use the aid "exclusively" for "internal security" and "legitimate self-defense." Hence, while American military aid bolstered Pakistan's capabilities, there were restrictions on what Pakistan could do with U.S. weapons.

2. Pakistan's hopes of Chinese support and help were fulfilled early in their relationship. In September 1949 differences on currency devaluation led India to halt trade with Pakistan. At a time when it seemed that India was determined to destroy the nascent Pakistani economy, China's offer of a barter agreement whereby China supplied Pakistan with coal in exchange for jute and cotton was viewed as lifesaving. As early as January 1963, the two countries granted "most-favored nation" status to each other. By 1963 China was the largest importer of Pakistani cotton.

3. According to a May 1967 report by the Institute for Strategic Studies, Pakistan struck a $120 million arms deal with China for the delivery of one hundred T-59 tanks, eighty MiG-19s, and ten III-28s aircraft (*Asian Recorder* 1967: 7960).

4. In 1968 the ancient Silk Road was reopened with the first all-weather road linking Pakistani Gilgit and Chinese Xinjiang boosting Sino-Pakistani trade and communications. China helped in the construction of Pakistan's first heavy mechanical

complex at Taxila, near Rawalpindi and helped build East Pakistan's first ordnance factory. In 1967, China and Pakistan signed a maritime agreement to provide port facilities to each other's ships. In 1970, a Sino-Pakistan agreement on Chinese assistance in industry, mining, transport, and communications was signed.

5. In 1967, China offered ten million yuan to support Pakistan's economic development. In 1970, China further offered Pakistan a loan of $200 million for its fourth five-year plan.

6. In 1974 Saudi Arabia provided Pakistan with an interest-free loan of $100 million. In 1975 the Saudi government made a grant of $30 million in addition to the Saudi Development Fund's pledged soft loan of $30 million to help meet Pakistan's balance of payments deficit. In 1976 Pakistan received $500 million in assistance from the Arab Middle East, the bulk of which came from Saudi Arabia itself.

7. Arab-Pakistan ties in the military arena are not only limited to Saudi Arabia. Between 1972 and 1977, Pakistan concluded a series of military protocols with Saudi Arabia, Libya, Jordan, Iraq, Oman, the U.A.E., and Kuwait. Under these agreements, training facilities were provided in Pakistani defense institutions for members of the armed forces of these countries. By the late 1970s there were 893 Pakistani advisers and 914 Middle East military trainers. By the 1980s Pakistan had military missions in twenty-two countries, making it the largest exporter of military manpower in the Third World (Roedad Khan 1999: 937–943; Rashid 1986).

8. In 1976 Saudi Arabia offered to fund Pakistan's purchase of 110 American A-7 fighter bombers. The U.S. government was, however, only willing to allow the purchase if Pakistan agreed not to buy a $150 million nuclear waste reprocessing plant from France. A few years later in 1981 Saudi Arabia financed the $800 million purchase of 40 F-16s from the United States for the Pakistan Air Force. In return, Pakistan agreed to station troops and technicians in Saudi Arabia.

9. According to intelligence tracking by Robert Galluci at the U.S. State Department and Rick Barlow at the CIA, there was evidence that Pakistan supplied Saudi Arabia with nuclear capable missiles and Saudi Arabia considered the Pakistani bomb as its own (Levy and Scott-Clark 2007: 173–174, 225–226, 494; Mir 2005).

10. The International Islamic University in Islamabad was funded by a $10 million grant from the Saudis. The university is located close to the Faisal Mosque, the largest mosque in South Asia, named after King Khalid's successor, King Faisal of Saudi Arabia, who provided the funding for the project. In 1977, Lyallpur, the third largest city in Pakistani Punjab, was renamed Faisalabad in honor of King Faisal.

11. For detailed information on Sino-Pakistani nuclear ties, see the publications of the Center for Nonproliferation Studies, Monterey Institute of International Studies, Monterey, California. Accessible at http://cns.miis.edu/pubs/sasia.htm.

12. Annual trade was $963.7 million in 1996 and $1.8 billion in 2002 (Masood 2010). Details on Sino-Pakistani trade and investment are available on the website of China's Ministry of Foreign Affairs at http://www.fmprc.gov.cn/eng/wjb/zzjg/yzs/gjlb/2757/2758/.

13. In 1993, China and the International Atomic Energy Agency (IAEA) signed an agreement to apply IAEA safeguards to a Chinese nuclear power station sold to Pakistan. Chinese "assistance" was also provided in the construction of a forty-megawatt reactor at Khushab that could be used to provide Pakistan with plutonium for its weapons program (Sun 1993).

Works Cited

Addleton, Jonathan. 1984. "The Impact of International Migration on Economic Development in Pakistan." *Asian Survey* 24 (5): 574–596.

Agence France-Presse. 2009. "China Delivers Warship to Pakistan, Navy." July 30.

———. 2013. "Ten Foreign Victims Identified After Nanga Parbat Attack." *Express Tribune*, June 24. http://tribune.com.pk/story/567637/10-foreign-victims-identified-after-pakistan-attack/.

Al-Rasheed, Madwai. 2014. "Saudi Strategy Includes Alliance with Pakistan." *Al-Monitor*, January 8.

Associated Press of Pakistan. 2009. "China Wants to Cooperate in Hydro Electricity Projects." May 7.

BBC. 2006. "Saudi King on a Rare Visit to India." *BBC News*, January 25.

Bokhari, Farhan. 2008. "China Is Pakistan's Most Steadfast Partner." *Gulf News*, April 13.

Burke, S. M., and Lawrence Ziring. 1990. *Pakistan's Foreign Policy: An Historical Analysis*. London: Oxford University Press.

Daily Times (Pakistan). 2007. "Pakistan to Get F-22 P Frigate from China in 2009: Memon." April 13. http://archives.dailytimes.com.pk/national/13-Apr-2007/pakistan-to-get-f-22-p-frigate-from-china-in-2009-memon

———. 2008. "Pakistan China to Bolster Defense, Energy, Trade Ties." April 22.

Dawn. 2009. "Pakistan Signs $700 Million MoU with China." June 20. http://www.dawn.com/news/830783/pakistan-signs-700m-mou-with-china.

DCI (U.S. Director of Central Intelligence). 1997. *The Acquisition of Technology Relating to Weapons of Mass Destruction and Advanced Conventional Munitions, July–December 1996*. Langley, Va.: Central Intelligence Agency. https://www.fas.org/irp/cia/product/wmd.htm.

Jiang Zemin. 1996. "Carrying Forward Generations of Friendly and Good-Neighborly Relations and Endeavoring Towards a Better Tomorrow for All." Speech by the president of the People's Republic of China at Islamabad, Pakistan, December 2.

Khan, Rashid Ahmed. 2013. "Premier Li's Visit Will Cement Pakistan-China Ties." China.org.cn, May 25.

Khan, Roedad. 1999. *The American Papers: Secret and Confidential India-Pakistan-Bangladesh Documents, 1965–1973*. Karachi: Oxford University Press.

Krondstadt, Alan, and Susan Epstein. 2013. *Pakistan: U.S. Foreign Assistance*. Washington, D.C.: Congressional Research Service.

Kux, Dennis. 2001. *The United States and Pakistan, 1947–2000: Disenchanted Allies.* Washington, D.C.: Woodrow Wilson Center Press.

Levy, Adrian, and Catherine Scott-Clark. 2007. *Deception: Pakistan, the United States, and the Secret Trade in Nuclear Weapons.* New York: Walker.

Lipin, Michael. 2013. "Pakistani Buying of Chinese Arms Makes Beijing 5th Biggest Exporter." *Voice of America*, March 18. http://www.voanews.com/content/china-arms-exporter-5th-largest/1623754.html.

Lippman, Thomas W., and Paul Blustein. 1996. "U.S. Clears Pakistan, China Deals." *Washington Post*, April 17.

Malik, Sajjad. 2009. "Pakistan Saved China from Embarrassment on Xinjiang Violence." *Daily Times*, September 4.

Masood, Salman. 2010. "China Praises Pakistan's Fight Against Terrorism and Vows to Bolster Partnership." *New York Times*, December 20.

Mehdudia, Sujay. 2014. "India to Enhance Crude Oil, LPG Supplies from Saudi Arabia." *Hindu*, January 17. http://www.thehindu.com/business/Economy/india-to-seek-enhanced-crude-oil-lpg-supplies-from-saudi-arabia/article5586575.ece.

Mir, Amir. 2005. "Terror and the Bomb: Dangerous Cocktail." *South Asia Intelligence Review* 3 (51). http://www.ict.org.il/Articles/tabid/66/Articlsid/187/currentpage/23/Default.aspx.

Press Trust of India. 2012. "Saudi Arabia Deports Alleged Terrorist Wanted by Kerala." NDTV.com, October 22. http://www.ndtv.com/article/india/saudi-arabia-deports-alleged-terrorist-wanted-by-kerala-283105.

Rana, Shahbaz. 2011. "IMF Considers Pakistan Economic Managers Deceitful." *Express Tribune*, April 26. http://tribune.com.pk/story/156871/imf-considers-pakistan-economic-managers-deceitful/.

Rashid, Jamal. 1986. "Pakistan and the Central Command." *MERIP Middle East Report* 141 (July–August): 28–34.

Reuters. 1975. "Saudi King Giving Pakistan Vast Aid." *Los Angeles Times*, January 2.

———. 2008. "China to Help Pakistan Out of Economic Crisis—Envoy." October 17.

Rosenberg, Matthew, and Zahid Hussain. 2008. "Pakistan Launches Bid for Saudi Help." *Wall Street Journal*, November 5.

Shah, Saeed, et al. 2010. "Pakistan Floods: US Announces Extra $60m in Aid." *Guardian*, August 19. http://www.theguardian.com/world/2010/aug/19/pakistan-floods-obama-aid-increase.

Simmons, Lewis. 1977. "Arabs Back Pakistan Accord." *Washington Post*, April 30.

Smith, R. Jeffrey, and Ann Devroy. 1996. "U.S. Asks China to End Shipments; Nuclear Exchange with Pakistan at Issue." *Washington Post*, February 28.

Solomon, Jay. 2009. "Pakistan Aid Effort Hits Saudi Hurdle." *Wall Street Journal*, April 15.

State Bank of Pakistan. 2014. *Statistical Bulletins*, 2001–2005. http://www.sbp.org.pk/reports/stat_reviews/Bulletin/.

Sun, Lena. 1993. "China: Sino-U.S. Ties 'in Serious Jeopardy." *Washington Post*, August 28.

Swami, Praveen. 2008. "China's Mid-Air Terror Trail Leads to Pakistan." *Hindu*, March 22.

Syed, Baqqir Sajjed. 2014. "S. Arabia, Pakistan Pledge Regional Cooperation." *Dawn*, January 8.

U.S. Embassy Beijing. 2004. "Proliferation Issues: The View from Beijing Looks Grim." Cable dated April 16, 1991. Released by the National Security Archives at http://www2.gwu.edu/~nsarchiv/NSAEBB/NSAEBB114/index.htm?utm_content = buffer21b77&utm_source = buffer&utm_medium = twitter&utm_campaign = Buffer.

Urban, Mark. 2013. "Saudi Nuclear Weapons on Order from Pakistan." *BBC Newsnight*, November 6.

Vertzberger, Yaacov. 1983. "The Political Economy of Sino-Pakistani Relations: Trade and Aid 1963–82." *Asian Survey* 23 (5): 637–652.

Wall Street Journal. 2001. "Beijing's Broken Promises." August 20.

Warrick, Joby, and Peter Slevin. 2004. "Libyan Arms Designs Traced Back to China; Pakistanis Resold Chinese-Provided Plans." *Washington Post*, February 15.

World Tribune. 2014. "Saudi Arabia Hires Cash-Strapped Pakistan to Bolster Security." January 8.

Chapter 11

Violent Nonstate Actors in the Afghanistan-Pakistan Relationship: Historical Context and Future Prospects

Daveed Gartenstein-Ross and Tara Vassefi

As the United States draws down its troops from Afghanistan, two overarching issues most concern strategic planners. One is the future prospects of violent nonstate actors (VNSAs), including the possibility that both the Taliban and al-Qaeda may experience a resurgence as the number of American forces declines. The other significant issue is the role that neighboring countries will play in Afghanistan's future. Afghanistan's neighbors have for years been positioning themselves to better assert their interests post-withdrawal, and to the extent that the United States maintains strategic interests in Afghanistan, it will have to navigate an increasingly complex landscape of state and nonstate actors.

The twin issues of VNSAs in Afghanistan and interference by that country's neighbors are deeply connected historically, and they will continue to be tied for the foreseeable future. Pakistan has been a particularly important sponsor of insurgent and militant factions operating in Afghanistan in recent years, including the Taliban and the Haqqani Network (Dressler 2012; Waldman 2010). But strong—and, frequently, complex—relationships between the states of the region and VNSAs have far deeper roots than the U.S. war in Afghanistan, or even the Afghan-Soviet war. From the time of Pakistan's creation, in fact, VNSAs played a defining role in the relationship between Afghanistan and Pakistan. In those early years the situation was the inverse of where it stands today: Afghanistan sponsored VNSAs in Pakistan that fought the government and threatened the integrity of the Pakistani state. Afghanistan pursued this set of policies in support of its demand for an independent "Pashtunistan," an ethnic state that Afghan leaders argued should be carved out of Pakistani territory.

Afghanistan's early aggression against Pakistan, which involved such unconventional means as the use of VNSA proxies and irregular forces dressed as tribesmen, looks strikingly similar to Pakistan's later support for VNSAs in Afghanistan. This is no coincidence: Afghanistan's Pashtunistan policies were critical in prompting Pakistan's decisions to support violent Islamist groups in Afghanistan. After Pakistan took the initial step toward supporting violent Islamists, the relationship between Pakistan, Afghanistan, and a variety of VNSAs became increasingly complex. The December 1979 Soviet invasion of Afghanistan prompted the United States and Saudi Arabia to channel enormous sums of money to Pakistan's Inter-Services Intelligence agency (ISI) to support Afghanistan's seven major mujahideen factions, both magnifying the presence and power of VNSAs in Afghanistan and intensifying their ties to the ISI. Pakistan in turn developed strategic doctrines that perceived Islamist VNSAs as a strategic asset. Lasting relationships between ISI officers and religious militants were forged on the bloody battlefields of the Afghan-Soviet war.

Further complicating the role of VNSAs in the region, Arab militants—including Osama bin Laden and the original core of what would become al-Qaeda—were also drawn to the Afghan-Soviet conflict. Bin Laden returned to Afghanistan after that war ended, in 1996, employing it as a safe haven for fighters affiliated with his organization and a host of other jihadist groups. Consistent with the strategic doctrines Pakistani planners had developed, Pakistan took advantage of the jihadist presence in Afghanistan during this period, leveraging these VNSAs to attack Indian interests. After the 9/11 attacks and the American occupation of Afghanistan, however, Pakistan increasingly lost control of its Frankenstein monster. The Tehreek-e-Taliban-e-Pakistan is engaging in insurgent warfare against the Pakistani state, and several military campaigns over the past decade and a half show the limits of Pakistan's ability to contain VNSAs in its own territory.

Pakistan will continue to support a variety of unsavory VNSAs in Afghanistan when the American drawdown is complete. But although Pakistan will momentarily become one of the stronger actors in Afghanistan, the very source of its strength—its long-standing sponsorship of VNSAs—is also the cause of its underlying weakness. Pakistan's initial course as the United States draws down appears predictable, but its weaknesses could ultimately cause Pakistan to dramatically shift its policies, or even collapse.

Pakistan's Creation and Pashtunistan

Afghanistan's eastern border was settled in 1893. Known as the Durand Line, the border was named after its architect, Sir Henry Mortimer Durand. At the time the Durand Line was drawn, Britain had considerable strategic interests in the region, with British India the jewel in the colonial crown. Afghanistan's amir, Abdur Rahman, vehemently opposed Britain's proposal for the Afghan-Indian border, which would force him to relinquish "his nominal sovereignty over the Pashtun tribes" outside the border (Barfield 2010: 154). Historically, the idea of being "Afghan" was tied to being from the Pashtun ethnic group. As James Spain, a former cultural affairs officer at the American embassy in Karachi, has written, the Durand Line thus left "half of a people intimately related by culture, history, and blood on either side" (1954: 30). In addition to dividing the Pashtuns, the Durand Line deprived Afghanistan of access to the Arabian Sea, thus rendering it landlocked. Britain used the threat of economic embargo to force Abdur Rahman to agree to the border: Abdur Rahman depended on British subsidies and was in particular need of them at the time to fuel his internal war against the Hazaras. (He was in the process of expanding the power of Afghanistan's central government by conquering the country's non-Sunni areas.)

Afghanistan has never accepted the Durand Line's legitimacy, but it had little ability to challenge a global superpower like Britain. From Afghanistan's perspective, then, regional dynamics changed significantly after British India was partitioned into the independent states of India and Pakistan—particularly because the disputed Pashtun regions were in Pakistan, the weaker of the two new states. Afghanistan had long been an independent state by the time Pakistan was created in 1947, and there was no particular reason to think Pakistan—an agglomeration of ethnic groups with little uniting them besides the Islamic faith—would last. Further, Pakistan was born of an extraordinarily bloody partition with India, producing an enduring archrivalry. Thus, just as many Indian leaders thought the newly forged state of Pakistan wouldn't survive (Haqqani 2005: 10), so did many Afghan politicians. This perception of Pakistan's weakness spurred Afghanistan to forge an aggressive strategy to recover its lost Pashtun territory.

Afghanistan immediately made its hostility to the new state clear. It was the only country to vote against Pakistan's admission into the United Nations, arguing that Pakistan's northwest frontier "should not be recognized as a part of Pakistan until the Pashtuns of that area had been given the opportunity to opt out for independence" (Hasan 1962: 16). This was a reference to a continuing Afghan demand that its neighbor should allow Pashtuns in the northwestern part of the country to vote on whether they wanted to secede and become an independent state.

The demand was framed in legal and ethical terms. Afghan advocates called the proposed independent state "Pashtunistan," meaning "land of the Pashtuns." Though Afghanistan's Pashtunistan demands were framed as supportive of Pashtun national independence, they were in fact irredentist. If Pashtunistan came to exist, it would be fragile and essentially defenseless and could not remain independent for long. The historical linkage between the Pashtuns and Afghanistan would likely dictate a merger of Pashtunistan into Afghanistan. And even if Pakistan never agreed to the creation of Pashtunistan, Afghanistan had staked its claim to that area in case the Pakistani state failed.

Though the proposed "Pashtunistan" fluctuated in size over time, it frequently encompassed about half of West Pakistan, including areas inhabited by the Baluch ethnic group. (At Pakistan's founding, it was divided geographically into West Pakistan and East Pakistan; the latter is known today as Bangladesh.) Making the Baluch a part of this proposal ensured that, if Pashtunistan became part of Afghanistan, Afghanistan's newly constituted borders would again provide access to the Arabian Sea.

From a legal perspective, Afghanistan's protestations regarding the illegitimacy of its border with Pakistan were rather weak. Though Afghanistan claimed the border had been drawn under duress, the country's representatives had confirmed the demarcation multiple times, including in agreements signed in 1905, 1919 (at the conclusion of the Third Anglo-Afghan War), 1921, and 1930 (Hasan 1962: 15). Yet the weakness of Afghanistan's legal case was largely beside the point, given Afghan elites' feelings of connection to the Pashtun areas and the strategic benefits Afghan planners saw in expanding the country's territory.

Pashtunistan in the Afghanistan-Pakistan Relationship

Less than a decade after Pakistan's birth, James Spain noted that "relations between Pakistan and Afghanistan have come to be centered on one issue," Pashtunistan (1954: 35). Afghanistan's decision to make this border dispute central to the two states' relations would prove fateful. During this period, Kabul launched a series of low-level attacks against Pakistan, maintaining some degree of deniability throughout, just as Pakistan would later do when it sponsored VNSAs that struck Indian, Afghan, and U.S. targets. On September 30, 1950, Pakistan's northern border was attacked by Afghan tribesmen, as well as regular Afghan troops, who crossed into Pakistan thirty miles northeast of Chaman in Baluchistan (Associated Press 1950b). It didn't take long for Pakistan to repel this rather crude invasion, as its government announced that it had "driven invaders from Afghanistan back across the border" after just six days of fighting (Associated Press 1950a). Afghanistan claimed that it had been uninvolved, that the attackers were just tribesmen spontaneously agitating for an independent Pashtunistan. However, its denials lacked credibility.

Tensions between Afghanistan and Pakistan rose again in 1955, when Pakistan announced that it was consolidating its control over its tribal areas. Afghan prime minister Muhammad Daoud Khan criticized Pakistan's actions over the airwaves of Radio Kabul on March 29, 1955. At the time, although Muhammad Zahir Shah was Afghanistan's nominal monarch, Daoud held the real power in the country. Peter Tomsen, a scholar of the region and former special envoy to the Afghan mujahideen, describes Daoud, a career military man who was single-mindedly devoted to the Pashtunistan cause, as characterized by "an autocratic style" and "supreme self-confidence" (Tomsen 2011: 89). Following Daoud's denunciations of Pakistan, government-inspired demonstrations flared up in Kabul, Kandahar, and Jalalabad. S. M. M. Qureshi of the University of Alberta noted that "Pakistan flags were pulled down and insulted and the [Pashtunistan] flag was hoisted on the chancery of the Pakistan Embassy in Kabul" (Qureshi 1966: 105). The two countries withdrew their ambassadors, and relations weren't fully restored until 1957.

The next crisis in Afghanistan-Pakistan relations came in 1960–1961. In late September 1960, an Afghan *lashkar* (irregular militia) dispatched by Muhammad Daoud Khan crossed into Pakistan's Bajaur area. Pakistan announced that the *lashkar* "clashed with loyal tribesmen and fled after suffering heavy casualties" (Reuters 1960b). Conventional Afghan military resources, including tanks, massed on the Afghan side of the border (*Guardian* 1960). Eventually "a major battle" broke out between the two sides, with Pakistan bombarding Afghan forces with its airpower (Reuters 1960a). Rather than escalating the conflict, this quelled hostilities, at least for the moment. But in May of the following year, forces from both sides clashed in the Khyber Pass area. Pakistan announced that regular Afghan forces had attacked Pakistani border posts, and Pakistan's air force strafed Afghan positions (Associated Press 1961). Pakistan also stepped up police patrols and roadblocks. The *New York Times* noted that "relations between Pakistan and Afghanistan appear to have reached a new low, and no relief is in sight" (Grimes 1961).

After a new set of skirmishes broke out in the fall of 1961, Afghanistan and Pakistan formally severed diplomatic relations (Reuters 1961). Pakistan blocked trade routes into Afghanistan, damaging the landlocked state. This temporarily pushed Muhammad Daoud Khan from power. Even while his country suffered economically, Daoud inexplicably demanded that the monarch, Zahir Shah, expand Daoud's powers. Daoud angrily resigned after Zahir Shah said no (Tomsen 2011: 96). With Daoud out of power, the shah of Iran helped mediate a détente between the two neighbors in 1963. The resulting peace lasted about a decade, until Daoud deposed his cousin, King Muhammad Zahir Shah, on July 17, 1973.

Upon assuming power, Daoud immediately set out to reignite the border dispute by fomenting unrest in Pakistan's tribal areas. His regime provided sanctuary, arms, and ammunition to Pashtun and Baluch nationalist groups. Pakistan saw this as a significant challenge, as its Baluch regions were already in "virtual revolt" (R. Hussain 2005: 78). Even as Daoud fomented ethnic insurgency in Pakistan, his regime simultaneously condemned Pakistan before the United Nations as "genocidal" in its treatment of ethnic minorities. This escalation came at a time when Pakistan had already lost nearly a third of its territory with the secession of East Pakistan in 1971. Rizwan Hussain writes that Afghanistan's support for ethnic insurgents "posed the greatest threat to Pakistan's integrity since the secession of East Pakistan" (2005: 78). Such provocation demanded a response.

Pakistani president Zulfikar Ali Bhutto, a secular reformist who often unwittingly empowered the country's Islamists, fashioned a two-prong strategy to confront Afghanistan. The first prong was to suppress nationalist uprisings in Pakistan, and the second was a "forward policy" that supported Islamist VNSAs in Afghanistan (a policy that mirrored the way Afghanistan had supported nationalist VNSAs in Pakistan). Bhutto likely didn't envision Pakistani support for militants as more than a short-term measure. Peter Tomsen argues that even though the young Islamists that Pakistan sponsored were assured that attacking Afghanistan could "spark a general uprising," Bhutto actually "knew the scattered, small-scale military operations would fail" (Tomsen 2011: 107). However, Bhutto thought they could nonetheless serve their purpose by producing a crisis that would cause Afghanistan's government to reach out to him for assistance in clamping down on the perpetrators. By solving the crisis that he had covertly produced, Bhutto planned to improve relations between Pakistan and Afghanistan.

Though Bhutto seemingly had no more than a short-term vision for this Machiavellian scheme, his decision had lasting consequences. Bhutto's policies resulted in personal relationships between Pakistani military intelligence officers and Islamic militants that would last for decades. Afghan Islamists who received covert Pakistani aid during this early period of support included Gulbuddin Hekmatyar and Burhanuddin Rabbani, both of whom were destined to become important figures during the Afghan-Soviet war and beyond (Emadi 1990).

The Enduring Impact of the Afghan-Soviet War

On December 27, 1979, the Soviet invasion of Afghanistan began with Operation Storm-333, in which Soviet special forces attacked the Taj-Bek palace and killed Afghan leader Hafizullah Amin (Feifer 2009). Throughout the Muslim world, Soviet actions engendered an immediate backlash. In January 1980, Egypt's prime minister declared the Soviet invasion "a flagrant aggression against an Islamic state," and said it showed the Soviet Union was "but an extension of the colonialist Tsarist regime" (BBC 1980). By the end of the month, foreign ministers of thirty-five Muslim countries, as well as the Palestine Liberation Organization, passed a resolution through the Organization of the Islamic Conference (OIC) declaring the invasion of Afghanistan a "flagrant violation of all international covenants and norms, as well as a serious threat to peace and security in the region and throughout the world." Afghanistan's Soviet-installed regime was expelled from the OIC, the delegates of which urged all Muslim countries to similarly withhold recognition from that government and sever their relations with it. At the time, the *Christian Science Monitor* described this condemnation of Soviet actions as "some of the strongest terms ever used by a third-world parley" (Dorsey 1980).

Several states channeled aid to the Afghan mujahideen fighting the Soviets. They became the beneficiaries of the largest U.S. covert aid program since the Vietnam War, with American support (totaling around $3 billion) matched dollar for dollar by Saudi Arabia. The United States also provided supplies and weaponry, including Stinger missiles that helped negate the Soviet airpower advantage. This aid was channeled to the mujahideen through Pakistan's ISI. Though there were advantages to this arrangement—it helped obscure America's role in the conflict—one consequence is that it bolstered connections between Pakistani intelligence and Islamist VNSAs.

In addition to drawing states into the conflict in support of the Afghan mujahideen, the Soviet invasion also prompted thousands of Arabs to flock to South Asia to aid the Afghan cause. Many Arabs who traveled to the region provided humanitarian aid, but there was also a contingent of Arab foreign fighters (Hafez 2008). Osama bin Laden transitioned from being part of the former group, a humanitarian worker and financier of mujahideen, to proving himself on the battlefield. He traveled to Pakistan in the early 1980s, where he initially occupied himself by "providing cash to the relatives of wounded or martyred fighters, building hospitals, and helping the millions of Afghan refugees fleeing to the border region of Pakistan" (Riedel 2008: 42). After his first trip to the front lines in 1984, bin Laden developed a thirst for more action, and established a base for Arab fighters near Khost in eastern Afghanistan, where the Soviets had a garrison. Although the exploits of fighters affiliated with bin Laden were irrelevant to the broader war, his involvement launched him to prominence in the Arab media as a war hero (Coll 2004: 163).

Al-Qaeda was founded in August 1988, in the waning days of the Afghan-Soviet war. At the time, bin Laden and his mentor Abdullah Azzam agreed that the organization they had built during the conflict shouldn't simply dissolve when the war ended (National Commission on Terrorist Attacks 2004: 56). Rather, they wanted the structure they had created to serve as "the base" (*al qaeda*) for future efforts. Both the deepening relationship between Pakistan and Islamist groups and the enduring presence of Arab militants would greatly complicate the role of VNSAs in the Afghanistan-Pakistan relationship.

Two points are worth making about Pakistan's evolving relationship with Islamist VNSAs. The first is that the Afghan-Soviet war occurred at a time when the Pakistani military was undergoing significant changes, both from the very top and also among the rank and file. General Muhammad Zia-ul-Haq deposed Zulfikar Ali Bhutto as Pakistan's leader in a July 1977 coup. In addition to being a religious man, Zia was "closely connected to several Islamists by virtue of his social and family origins" (Haqqani 2005: 112). During his period of rule, Zia changed Pakistan's military culture in several ways. He incorporated Islamic teachings (such as S. K. Malik's *The Quranic Concept of War*) into military training, added religious criteria to officers' promotion requirements and exams, and required formal obedience to Islamic rules within the military (Z. Hussain 2007). These top-level changes came at a time when the demographics of the officer corps were shifting. The first generation of Pakistan's officers came from the country's largely secular social elites, while many new junior officers hailed from the poorer northern districts. Pakistani journalist Zahid Hussain notes that "the spirit of liberalism, common in the 'old' army, was practically unknown to them. They were products of a social class that, by its very nature, was conservative and easily influenced by Islamic fundamentalism" (2007: 20).

The second point is that, as Pakistan's support for Islamist VNSAs grew during the course of the Afghan-Soviet war, its strategic doctrine came to embrace such support as a crucial means of advancing the country's interests. Ever since Pakistan's creation, its rivalry with India has been one of its key strategic priorities, and Pakistani planners came to believe that supporting Islamist groups in Afghanistan would give them "strategic depth" against India. Another benefit of supporting Islamist groups was their potential to defuse the Pashtunistan issue: groups whose primary identification was religious were less likely to support ethno-nationalist causes.

The Civil War and the Taliban's Rise

Though observers universally expected Afghan leader Mohammad Najibullah's government to fall shortly after the Soviet Union withdrew its troops in 1989, the regime outperformed expectations for several years. One reason for its success was a major blunder in March 1989, as 15,000 mujahideen fighters—egged on by ISI chief Hamid Gul—attacked the city of

Jalalabad. They were decisively crushed by the Afghan army, aided by the more than four hundred Scud missiles fired by Soviet advisers. The scope of mujahideen losses—around 3,000 dead—without an inch of territory to show for it swung momentum toward Najibullah, who was previously viewed as a dead man walking.

A second reason for Najibullah's success was his soft-power strategy, in which he rebranded himself as a devout Muslim and ardent nationalist, and used a traditional tool of influence in Afghanistan—patronage networks—to neutralize foes (Barfield 2010). The combination of the Soviet departure and Najibullah's patronage caused many former mujahideen to defect to join the government, while still others agreed to ceasefires (Barfield 2010). Though it is impossible to state the number of "irreconcilables" with precision, outside observers considered them a relatively small portion of fighters.

But though Najibullah's regime remained more stable than expected for several years, his strategy depended on continuing Russian support—and after the Soviet Union dissolved in December 1991, that support dried up. Najibullah's regime quickly collapsed, and the country descended into civil war. The Taliban emerged from this chaotic milieu. The group grew rapidly after its founding in 1994, not only because it boasted effective fighters, but also due to the backing of Pakistan's ISI, which helped "uneducated Taliban leaders with everything from fighting the opposition Northern Alliance to more mundane tasks like translating international documents" (Schaffer 2001). By 1996 the Taliban had captured both Kabul and Kandahar.

Bin Laden ended up returning to Afghanistan around this time. After the end of the Afghan-Soviet war, he had lived briefly in Saudi Arabia before relocating to Sudan in 1991, where he began sponsoring terrorist attacks against U.S. targets. As a result of pressure from American and Saudi intelligence services, bin Laden was expelled from Sudan (Riedel 2008: 56). At the invitation of mujahideen leader Yunus Khalis, bin Laden returned to Afghanistan, the country where he had first made his reputation (Stenersen 2013: 72). The Taliban agreed to protect bin Laden from his many enemies, explaining in one statement: "If an animal sought refuge with us we would have had no choice but to protect it. How, then, about a man who has given himself and his wealth in the cause of Allah and in the cause of jihad in Afghanistan" (Atwan 2006: 54). Al-Qaeda established a network of training camps used not only by its own soldiers but also a variety of other transnational jihadist groups.

Some of the groups that trained and found refuge in Afghanistan received Pakistani sponsorship and concentrated their militant activities on an issue of great interest to Pakistan, opposing the Indian presence in the disputed Kashmir region. Pakistan saw pre-9/11 Afghanistan as advantageous to it in other ways, too. As this chapter has explained, the government in Kabul had been hostile to Pakistan ever since its founding, and the period of Taliban rule is the only one since Pakistan's creation that Afghanistan had a strong relationship with Pakistan and an adversarial one with India.

Conclusion: The Post-9/11 Era and the Future of Afghanistan-Pakistan Relations

After al-Qaeda executed the devastating 9/11 attacks, U.S. deputy secretary of state Richard Armitage gave Pakistan an ultimatum: in then-President Pervez Musharraf's words, "we had to decide whether we were with America or with the terrorists . . . [and] if we chose the terrorists, then we should be prepared to be bombed back to the Stone Age" (Musharraf 2006: 201). Armitage's threat, along with material incentives, prompted Musharraf to announce a dramatic about-face on the issue of VNSAs, declaring on January 12, 2002, that "no Pakistan-based organization would be allowed to indulge in terrorism in the name of religion" (Z. Hussain 2007: 51). He announced the ban of five jihadist groups that day, including Lashkar-e-Taiba and Jaish-e-Mohammed.

Pakistan's Continuing Support for Jihadist Groups

However, this striking reversal didn't last. The various factors driving Pakistan's support for violent Islamist groups in Afghanistan were simply too tangled a web. In addition to the strategic calculations behind Pakistan's support for these groups, strong personal relationships had developed between Pakistani officers and the VNSAs they supported. Furthermore, the government of Pakistan does not operate as a unified actor. One schism is between the civilian government and the military: Musharraf is only one of several Pakistani military leaders who executed a coup against a civilian government. But there are also divisions within the military. The most notable is the distinct role of the ISI, which is often described as a "state within a state." The ISI has been the lead Pakistani actor in supporting jihadist groups, and its policies in this regard are well documented (Gartenstein-Ross 2009). But there are divisions even within the ISI. The most obvious internal split is between the S wing, which liaises with militant Islamist groups, and the C wing, which interfaces with foreign intelligence services. The two wings are reportedly often at odds because their missions are almost diametrically opposed.

So when one says that Pakistan supports jihadist groups, what does this mean? There are multiple possibilities. One possibility is that both Pakistan's civilian government and ISI support a particular jihadist group. A second possibility is that Pakistan's support is official government policy, but the civilian government provides only an implicit green light, with no oversight—similar to a black budget. A third possibility is that Pakistan's support is an ISI policy that flouts the civilian government's wishes: the civilian government doesn't want the ISI to adopt a set of pro-jihadist policies, but it does so anyway, pursuant to orders from ISI leadership. A fourth possibility is that the policy is carried out by "rogue elements" within ISI who are supported by neither the civilian government nor ISI at an official level (though ISI's leadership may give the so-called rogue elements an implicit green light while trying to maintain its own deniability).[1] And a fifth culprit is an outer ring of supporters for jihadist militancy who are no longer part of ISI, yet maintain influence within it. Retired ISI officers from the S wing with connections to militancy who have remained influential following their retirement include former ISI head Hamid Gul, who in 2003 declared that "God will destroy the United States in Iraq and Afghanistan and wherever it will try to go from there." In late 2008, the United States sent a secret document to Pakistan's government linking Gul to the Taliban and al-Qaeda, and India has demanded his arrest in connection with the Mumbai attacks (Abbasi 2008; Wax and Lakshmi 2008).

One data point that illustrates the nonunified nature of Pakistan's government is a May 2011 incident in which Pakistani president Asif Ali Zardari covertly sent a letter to the chairman of the Joint Chiefs of Staff, Admiral Mike Mullen, asking for U.S. help in disbanding the ISI's S wing (Nelson 2011; Shah 2011). The fact that Zardari reached out to the United States for assistance in changing ISI's internal dynamics, rather than simply taking action on his own, shows that the civilian government isn't in a position of uncontested authority. The disunity within Pakistan's government often made it difficult for American policy makers to determine which level of

Pakistan's government sanctioned support for jihadism. This in turn impeded an effective U.S. response when it became obvious that, contrary to Musharraf's assurances, jihadist groups continued to both operate inside Pakistan and also receive state support.

The factors outlined in this chapter will continue to drive Pakistan's support for militant Islamist groups in Afghanistan after the U.S. drawdown. Even if the civilian government wanted to reduce or end the country's sponsorship of Islamist VNSAs, the ISI's investment in this set of policies ensures that they will continue absent dramatic changes.

VNSAs in the Afghanistan-Pakistan Relationship

The role of VNSAs in the Afghanistan-Pakistan relationship has grown increasingly complex, and they have become increasingly difficult for any state to sponsor without significant risk. While Pakistan seemingly viewed the proliferation of jihadist groups in South Asia as an unalloyed advantage prior to the 9/11 attacks, today these VNSAs pose a clear threat to the Pakistani state, even as its sponsorship of jihadist groups has continued.

The dangers for Pakistan are clear in its relationship with the Tehreek-e-Taliban-e-Pakistan (TTP). Established in 2007, TTP is "an umbrella organization for Pakistani militant groups" in the Federally Administered Tribal Areas (FATA) and Khyber Pakhtunkhwa, which was formerly known as the North-West Frontier Province (Stenersen 2013: 78). About thirteen militant groups were part of TTP at the time of its founding (Laub 2013). Although Pakistan was still supporting Islamist militant groups focused on Afghanistan at the time, it had also engaged in periodic military offensives against these groups in its own territory. These included a campaign in 2004 against Nek Muhammad Wazir's forces and several hundred foreign fighters west and north of Wana that culminated in the Shakai agreement ending the hostilities; and an early 2005 campaign against fighters commanded by the South Waziristan-based Baitullah Mehsud and Abdullah Mehsud (Mahsud 2013: 190).

Since TTP's formation (announced by Baitullah Mehsud, the antagonist in Pakistan's 2005 campaign), it has had an adversarial relationship with the Pakistani state, one that has only grown worse. TTP's rise to prominence was followed by a massive escalation in violence, as various networked militant groups grew into a full-blown insurgency against the

Pakistani government. In early 2014, TTP sparked concerns about worsening violence in several areas of the country. In Karachi, for example, where TTP "was largely responsible for a 90 percent spike in terrorist attacks" in 2013, insurgents began to take control of neighborhoods, giving rise to "concerns that one of the world's most populous cities is teetering on the brink of lawlessness" (Craig 2014).

In contrast, the Pakistani state's relationship with the Haqqani Network (HQN)—a militant group led by Jalaluddin Haqqani and his son Sirajuddin— is more similar to its traditional support of jihadist VNSAs through which it extended its reach into Afghanistan. Pakistan, however, is increasingly aware of how this support intersects with its domestic vulnerabilities. During the 1980s HQN, which was part of the anti-Soviet insurgency, benefited from the various actors working to oppose the Soviet presence in Afghanistan, establishing a relationship with the ISI and receiving support from American and Saudi intelligence (Dressler 2010). As the Taliban made gains in Afghanistan in the mid-1990s, Jalaluddin Haqqani decided to throw his military might behind them, and he led his forces into several battles with Ahmad Shah Massoud's men.

Since the U.S. occupation of Afghanistan, HQN has been a powerful contributor to the insurgency. Though it has a cooperative relationship with several jihadist groups that have turned against the Pakistani state, Pakistan views HQN as more of a strategic asset—and, as will be discussed momentarily—has even sought to leverage HQN's relationships with some of the anti-Pakistan jihadist groups. The U.S. Department of State believes that HQN has "several hundred core members," but is able to draw on a much larger pool of fighters, described as "upwards of 10,000" (U.S. Department of State 2013).

Jeffrey Dressler observes that Pakistan sees sponsorship of HQN as offering it several strategic benefits:

> The Haqqani Network's territorial control of the southeast could provide the Pakistanis with much needed "strategic depth" in case of a full-scale breakout of hostilities across Pakistan's eastern border with India. Additionally, given Pakistan's concerns of increased Indian involvement in Afghanistan, the Haqqani Network is a tool to target strategically Indian political, diplomatic and economic interests in Kabul and elsewhere around the country. Furthermore, by helping to dissuade anti-Pakistan insurgents, such as Tehrik-e

Taliban Pakistan (TTP), from launching attacks on Pakistani security services and instead reorienting some of their focus on Afghanistan, the Haqqanis are assisting in the campaign to quiet military tensions in Pakistan's tribal frontier, though they have not been successful in doing so. (Dressler 2012: 12)

Thus, even in the case of HQN—which serves to advance traditional Pakistani interests in Afghanistan, such as strategic depth and undermining India—Pakistan has a great deal of domestic concerns, hoping that its relationship with other jihadist factions can quell their anti-Pakistan activities. This illustrates a basic fact about the complex role that VNSAs now play in the Afghanistan-Pakistan relationship: Even though Pakistan's relationship with these actors puts it in a very strong position in Afghanistan as the United States draws down, Pakistan is also vulnerable. There are reasons to think the country might simply implode, as in addition to its domestic insurgency, Pakistan suffers also from rising food prices, rising energy prices, and a growing public realization of the state's incapacity (Perlez 2011).

Pashtunistan no longer plays the central role in Afghanistan-Pakistan relations that it once did: Pashtuns from the FATA and settled areas of Khyber Pakhtunkhwa have no desire to join Afghanistan. Indeed, a recent survey of FATA residents that inquired how the area should be governed found that "becoming part of Afghanistan was the most unpopular choice" (Ballen, Bergen, and Doherty 2013: 251). However, Afghanistan's use of VNSAs to advance its Pashtunistan agenda set in motion a strategic course for both countries that has had a tremendous impact—not only on their relationship, but with unexpected ripples that can be said, with no exaggeration, to reach all corners of the globe. Similarly, Pakistan's support for jihadist VNSAs, which was prompted by Afghanistan's Pashtunistan policy, initially could be said to advance Pakistani interests in a rather Machiavellian yet straightforward way. Now, however, one of Pakistan's major concerns as it continues to support jihadist VNSAs is its hope that the VNSAs it continues to sponsor will dissuade other VNSAs that it helped to empower from attacking the Pakistani state.

There is a powerful lesson here about unintended second-order consequences. At this point, Afghanistan, Pakistan, and their neighbors will have to live with the consequences of the succession of VNSAs that have been spawned over the course of four decades. Jihadist VNSAs will not be decisively defeated anytime soon, and it's a virtual certainty that some variety of VNSAs—not necessarily transnational jihadists, but at least warlords, smugglers, and ethnically aligned militias—will remain a permanent facet of the landscape for the foreseeable future.

Notes

The views expressed here should not be attributed to the Leadership and Development Education for Sustained Peace (LDESP), Naval Postgraduate School (NPS), or the U.S. Department of Defense.

1. The United States responded to a couple of incidents in which the ISI was implicated—the November 2008 Mumbai "urban warfare" attacks and the July 2008 bombing of India's embassy in Kabul—as though rogue elements of ISI were to blame, though many commentators believe this approach let Pakistan off too easy.

Works Cited

Abbasi, Ansar. 2008. "Secret Document Confirms Hameed Gul Wanted by the US." *News International* (Pakistan), December 7.

Associated Press. 1950a. "Invaders Out, Pakistan Says." October 5.

———. 1950b. "Pakistan Says Afghans Launch War." October 4.

———. 1961. "Regular Afghan Army Battles Pakistanis in Khyber Pass Area." May 21.

Atwan, Abdel Bari. 2006. *The Secret History of al-Qaeda*. Berkeley: University of California Press.

Ballen, Ken, Peter Bergen, and Patrick Doherty. 2013. "Public Opinion in Pakistan's Tribal Regions." In *Talibanistan: Negotiating the Borders Between Terror, Politics, and Religion*, ed. Peter Bergen and Katherine Tiedemann, 248–261. Oxford: Oxford University Press.

Barfield, Thomas. 2010. *Afghanistan: A Cultural and Political History*. Princeton, N.J.: Princeton University Press.

BBC. 1980. "Egyptian Prime Minister on Middle East and Afghanistan." *BBC Summary of World Broadcasts*, January 5.

Coll, Steve. 2004. *Ghost Wars: The Secret History of the CIA, Afghanistan, and bin Laden, from the Soviet Invasion to September 10, 2001*. New York: Penguin Books.

Craig, Tim. 2014. "Karachi Residents Live in Fear as Pakistan Taliban Gains Strength." *Washington Post*, February 3.

Dorsey, James. 1980. "Islamic Nations Fire Broadsides at Soviet Military Interventions." *Christian Science Monitor*, January 30.

Dressler, Jeffrey. 2010. *The Haqqani Network: From Pakistan to Afghanistan*. Washington, D.C.: Institute for the Study of War.

————. 2012. *The Haqqani Network: A Strategic Threat.* Washington, D.C.: Institute for the Study of War.

Emadi, Hafizullah. 1990. "Durand Line and Afghan-Pak Relations." *Economic and Political Weekly*, July 14.

Feifer, Gregory. 2009. *The Great Gamble: The Soviet War in Afghanistan.* New York: Harper.

Gartenstein-Ross, Daveed. 2009. "Fixing Our Pakistan Problem." *Journal of International Security Affairs*, Spring.

Grimes, Paul. 1961. "Afghan-Pakistan Border Tense as Dispute on Tribe Worsens." *New York Times*, May 29.

Guardian (London). 1960. "Incursion by Afghans 'Beaten Back,' Says Pakistan." September 29.

Hafez, Mohammed M. 2008. "Jihad After Iraq: Lessons from the Arab Afghans Phenomenon." *CTC Sentinel* (Combating Terrorism Center at West Point), March.

Haqqani, Husain. 2005. *Pakistan: Between Mosque and Military.* Washington, D.C.: Carnegie Endowment for International Peace.

Hasan, Khurshid. 1962. "Pakistan-Afghanistan Relations." *Asian Survey* 2 (7): 14–24.

Hussain, Rizwan. 2005. *Pakistan and the Emergence of Islamic Militancy in Afghanistan.* Hampshire, U.K.: Ashgate.

Hussain, Zahid. 2007. *Frontline Pakistan: The Struggle with Militant Islam.* New York: Columbia University Press.

Laub, Zachary. 2013. "Pakistan's New Generation of Terrorists." *Council on Foreign Relations*, November 18.

Mahsud, Mansur Khan. 2013. "The Taliban in South Waziristan." In *Talibanistan: Negotiating the Borders Between Terror, Politics, and Religion*, ed. Peter Bergen and Katherine Tiedemann, 164–200. Oxford: Oxford University Press.

Musharraf, Pervez. *In the Line of Fire: A Memoir.* New York: Free Press, 2006.

National Commission on Terrorist Attacks Upon the United States. 2004. *9/11 Commission Report: Final Report of the National Commission on Terrorist Attacks Upon the United States.* New York: W. W. Norton.

Nelson, Dean. 2011. "Admiral Mike Mullen Confirms Pakistan Army Plot Letter." *Telegraph* (U.K.), November 18.

Office of the Coordinator of Counterterrorism. 2013. "Foreign Terrorist Organizations." In *Country Reports on Terrorism, 2012*, chap. 6. Washington, D.C.: U.S. Department of State.

Perlez, Jane. 2011. "Many in Pakistan Fear Unrest at Home." *New York Times*, February 3.

Qureshi, S. M. M. 1966. "Pakhtunistan: The Frontier Dispute Between Afghanistan and Pakistan." *Pacific Affairs* 39 (1–2): 99–114.

Reuters. 1960a. "Afghans Report Pakistani Clash." October 8.

————. 1960b. "Pakistan Fears Afghan Invasion." September 23.

————. 1961. "Afghanistan Breaks with Pakistan." September 6.

Riedel, Bruce. 2008. *The Search for al Qaeda: Its Leadership, Ideology, and Future.* Washington, D.C.: Brookings Institution Press.

Schaffer, Michael. 2001. "The Unseen Power." *U.S. News & World Report*, November 4.

Shah, Saeed. 2011. "Husain Haqqani, Pakistan's US Ambassador, Offers to Resign." *Guardian* (London), November 17.

Spain, James W. 1954. "Pakistan's North West Frontier." *Middle East Journal* 8 (1): 27–40.

Stenersen, Anne. 2013. "The Relationship Between al-Qaeda and the Taliban." In *Talibanistan: Negotiating the Borders Between Terror, Politics, and Religion*, ed. Peter Bergen and Katherine Tiedemann, 69–92. Oxford: Oxford University Press.

Tomsen, Peter. 2011. *The Wars of Afghanistan: Messianic Terrorism, Tribal Conflicts, and the Failures of Great Powers.* Kindle ed. New York: PublicAffairs.

Waldman, Matt. 2010. *The Sun in the Sky: The Relationship Between Pakistan's ISI and Afghan Insurgents.* London: Crisis States Discussion Papers.

Wax, Emily, and Rama Lakshmi. 2008. "Indian Official Points to Pakistan." *Washington Post*, December 6.

Christopher Clary is a Ph.D. candidate in the Department of Political Science at the Massachusetts Institute of Technology and a Stanton Nuclear Security Predoctoral Fellow at the RAND Corporation in Washington, D.C. He was a Council on Foreign Relations International Affairs Fellow in India (2009), a country director for South Asian affairs in the Office of the Secretary of Defense (2006–2009), a research associate at the Naval Postgraduate School (2003–2005), and a research assistant at the Henry L. Stimson Center (2001–2003).

C. Christine Fair is an assistant professor at Georgetown University's Security Studies Program in the Edmund A. Walsh School of Foreign Service. Fair obtained her Ph.D. from the University of Chicago, Department of South Asian Languages and Civilizations in 2004, and an M.A. from the Harris School of Public Policy in 1997. Prior to joining Georgetown University, she served as a senior political scientist with the RAND Corporation, a political officer to the United Nations Assistance Mission to Afghanistan in Kabul, and a senior research associate at the Center for Conflict Analysis and Prevention of the United States Institute of Peace (USIP). Her research focuses on political and military affairs in South Asia. She has authored, coauthored, and coedited several books including *Fighting to the End: The Pakistan Army's Way of War* (2014); *Policing Insurgencies: Cops as Counterinsurgents*, edited with Sumit Ganguly (2014); *Cuisines of the Axis of Evil and Other Irritating States* (2008); *Treading on Hallowed Ground: Counterinsurgency Operations in Sacred Space*, edited with Sumit Ganguly (2008); *The Madrassah Challenge: Militancy and Religious Education in Pakistan* (2008); and *Fortifying Pakistan: The Role of U.S. Internal*

Security Assistance (2006), among others. Fair has written numerous peer-reviewed articles covering a range of security issues in Afghanistan, Bangladesh, India, Pakistan, Iran, and Sri Lanka. She is a member of the International Institute of Strategic Studies, the Council on Foreign Relations, Women in International Security, and the American Institute of Pakistan Studies. She serves on the editorial board of *Current History, Small Wars and Insurgencies, Asia Policy, Studies in Conflict and Terrorism,* and *India Review.* She is also a senior fellow with the Combating Terrorism Center at West Point. Her publications are available at www.christinefair.net.

Daveed Gartenstein-Ross is a senior fellow at the Foundation for Defense of Democracies and an adjunct assistant professor in Georgetown University's security studies program. His academic work focuses on violent non-state actors in the twenty-first century. Gartenstein-Ross has contributed a decade of research, writing, and consulting on Afghanistan and Pakistan, including being volume editor of the book *The Afghanistan-Pakistan Theater* (2010) and frequently lecturing for military units preparing to deploy to Afghanistan. He is a Ph.D. candidate in world politics at the Catholic University of America and holds a J.D. from the New York University School of Law.

Karl Kaltenthaler is professor and director of research projects at the Ray C. Bliss Institute of Applied Politics at the University of Akron. He teaches and researches in the areas of comparative politics and international relations. His research focuses on public opinion, political psychology, terrorism (al-Qaeda and affiliates), and political economy. He has published three books and several journal articles in these areas. His research has been published in *International Studies Quarterly, Political Science Quarterly, Journal of Conflict and Terrorism, European Journal of Political Research, Journal of International Political Economy, European Union Politics,* and others.

Feisal Khan is an associate professor of economics at Hobart and William Smith Colleges in New York. He earned his B.A. and M.A. from Stanford University and his Ph.D. from the University of Southern California. His work on Islamic banking and finance and on economic development and governance in Pakistan has been published in academic journals and edited volumes. His current research on the Pakistani experience with Islamic banking is to be published as *Banking on Allah: Islamic Banking and the*

Quest to Make Pakistan More Islamic. His nonacademic experience includes extended stints in corporate banking (ANZ Grindlays Bank) and project monitoring and analysis (Aga Khan Rural Support Program) in Pakistan.

William J. Miller is director of institutional research and effectiveness and instructor of political science and public administration at Flagler College. His studies focus on campaigns and elections, public opinion toward public policy (domestic and international), and the pedagogy of political science. He is the editor of seven volumes on the Tea Party, Republican politics, redistricting, and political issues. His research appears in the *Journal of Political Science Education, Journal of Political Marketing, Studies in Conflict & Terrorism, International Studies Quarterly, Nonproliferation Review, Afro-Americans in New York Life and History, Journal of South Asian and Middle Eastern Studies, American Behavioral Scientist, Political Science Quarterly, PS: Political Science and Politics,* and *Journal of Common Market Studies.*

Aparna Pande is research fellow and director of Hudson Institute's Initiative on the Future of India and South Asia. A 1993 graduate of Delhi University, she holds a master of arts in history from St. Stephens College at Delhi University and a master of philosophy in international relations from Jawaharlal Nehru University. She received a doctorate in political science from Boston University. She wrote her dissertation on Pakistan's foreign policy. Her book *Explaining Pakistan's Foreign Policy: Escaping India* was published in 2011. She is currently writing a book on India's foreign policy.

Paul Staniland is assistant professor of political science and co-director of the Program on International Security Policy at the University of Chicago. His research focuses on civil war, international security, and state building in South and Southeast Asia. He is the author of *Networks of Rebellion: Explaining Insurgent Cohesion and Collapse* (2014) and has published in *Asian Survey, Civil Wars, Comparative Political Studies, Comparative Politics, India Review, International Security, Journal of Conflict Resolution, Perspectives on Politics, Security Studies,* and the *Washington Quarterly.*

Stephen Tankel is an assistant professor at American University and a nonresident scholar in the South Asia Program at the Carnegie Endowment for International Peace. His research focuses on terrorism, insurgency, the evolution of violent nonstate actors, and political and military affairs in South Asia. Tankel is also an adjunct staff member at the RAND Corporation, where he has contributed to research assessing jihadist ideology and decision making. Tankel has conducted field research on conflicts and militancy in Algeria, India, Lebanon, Pakistan, and the Balkans. He is frequently asked to brief government officials, analysts, and practitioners on issues relating to jihadist violence and on security issues related to South Asia. Tankel has written extensively on these issues, and his book *Storming the World Stage: The Story of Lashkar-e-Taiba* (2011) examines that group's ideological, strategic, and operational evolution since the 1980s within the context of developments in Pakistan, India, and Afghanistan.

Tara Vassefi is a researcher and education specialist for the Leadership and Development Education for Sustained Peace (LDESP) program based at the Naval Postgraduate School (NPS). Vassefi holds an M.A. from the University of St. Andrews (2009) and is currently pursuing her J.D. at the Washington College of Law at American University, where she is specializing in international law. The views expressed are her own and should not be attributed to LDESP, NPS, or the U.S. Department of Defense.

Sarah J. Watson is an Intelligence Research Specialist with the New York City Police Department. Her independent research interests include South Asian security and counterterrorism policy. Watson holds a J.D. from Yale Law School and a master's in security studies from Georgetown University. The views expressed here are her own and should not be attributed to the New York City Police Department.

Joshua T. White is deputy director for South Asia at the Stimson Center in Washington, D.C. He has spent extensive time in Pakistan and has held short-term visiting research fellowships at the Lahore University of Management Sciences, the International Islamic University in Islamabad, Pakistan's National Defence University, and the Institute for Defence and Strategic Analyses (IDSA) in Delhi. White graduated magna cum laude, Phi Beta Kappa, from Williams College with a double major in history and mathematics and received his Ph.D. with distinction from the Johns Hopkins School of Advanced International Studies.

Huma Yusuf is an award-winning journalist and columnist. She writes for Pakistan's *Dawn* newspaper and the *International New York Times*. She is a

Global Fellow of the Woodrow Wilson Center for International Scholars in Washington, D.C., and was the Pakistan Scholar there in 2010–2011. She has also conducted extensive media policy research for Open Society Foundations and BBC Media Action. She has won the All Pakistan Newspapers Society "Best Column" Award (2008 and 2010), the European Commission's Prix Natali Lorenzo for Human Rights and Democracy Journalism (2006), and the UNESCO/Pakistan Press Foundation "Gender in Journalism" Award (2005).

Index

Afghanistan: American support to government formation, 21; American withdrawal from, 11–13, 19, 46; as a major militant outfit, 41; Obama administration *vs* Bush administration, 6–7; pro-state Pakistani groups in, 46; as safe haven for militant groups, 45–47; as situational location for cross-border strikes, 46; tension between Taliban and non-Taliban forces in, 21

Afghanistan-Pakistan relationship: Afghan-Soviet War and, 284–86; demand for Pashtunistan, 19, 280–84, 292–93; Pakistan military presence in Afghanistan, 21; Pakistan's support for violent Islamist groups in Afghanistan, 287–90; post-9/11 era, 288–93; tensions in, 46, 282–83; violent nonstate actors (VNSAs), role of, 278–80, 290–93

Afghan Taliban, 2, 7, 20–21, 27, 33

Ahl-e-Hadith movement, 29, 33, 56, 58

Ahl-e-Kitab, 60

Ahmadinejad, Mahmoud, 236

al-Qaeda (AQ), 2, 33, 36, 39, 41–42, 61, 68, 76, 83, 102, 162, 223, 236, 279, 285

al-Qaeda Central (AQC), 45–46

Alverez, Luis, 116

Alvi, Awab, 157

anti-American sentiment in Pakistan, 206, 214, 221, 227–28; among Muslims, 230; analysis, 247–49; cultural aspects, 241; intensity of, 229; militant, 243–47; nationalist, 230–33; religious, 230–33, 241–43; Salafi beliefs, 245–47; sources of, 229; sovereign-nationalist views of United States, 236–41; survey data, 233–34;

United States as a hostile nation, 241. *See also* Pakistani views on Americans

anti-Shia agitation, 69, 171

army privileges in Pakistan: democracy, role in, 134–36; direct military rule, 134; legal, political, and institutional transformations, role in, 134; military leaders, importance of, 135; Musharraf's nine years, 137; provisional constitution order (PCO), 135; support for militants in Kashmir and U.S. drone program, 137

Authorization for the Use of Military Force (AUMF), 84

Awami National Party (ANP), 45, 145

Azhar, Maulana Masood, 34–35

Bhutto, Benazir, 2, 136, 138, 146, 148, 212

Bhutto, Zulfikar Ali, 283–84

bilateral security agreement (BSA), 10

blockading, 85

Bokhari, Meher, 161

Bolognani, Marta, 163

Brennan, John, 76

Bush, George W., 1, 3, 72, 178, 266

Caldwell, Dan, 108

Central Intelligence Agency (CIA), 72, 77

Central Treaty Organization (CENTO), 257

Charter for Democracy, 138

Chaudhry, Iftikhar Muhammad, 137, 139

Cheema, Umar, 162

China, 12–13, 228, 256, 270–72; agreement to keep Sino-Pakistani border secure, 268–69; economic support for Pakistan, 263–64; Free Trade Agreement (FTA) with Pakistan, 265; GDP growth rate of, 182;

China (*continued*)
investment in Pakistani infrastructure projects, 265, 267–68; Pakistan's view of, 264–65; policy of preserving Pakistan as a captive market for defense matériel, 268; Sino-Pakistani cooperation in the nuclear field, 264–66; Sino-Pakistani defense cooperation, 268; as a source of military assistance, 19; trade and diplomatic ties Pakistan, 258–59; Uighur issue, 269; weapons technology to Pakistan, 266
China Nuclear Energy Industry Corporation (CNEIC), 265
civilian maturity since 2008, 141–15; civil-military relations, 143; constitutional changes, role in, 143–45
"deconcentration" of power, 143–44; in elections, 141–42; institutions of governance, 143; in Pakistani politics, 145–48
Clinton, Bill, 1, 264
Clinton, Hillary, 7
Coalition Support Fund (CSF), 210
Coalition Support Funds (CSF) program, 3
coal reserves of Pakistan, 197n17
Composite Dialogue, 31
Corera, Gordon, 103
counterinsurgency and counterterrorism, 38, 72, 211–14, 225
cross-border raids, 38

Dadullah, Mullah, 33
Davis, Raymond, 8
Deobandi Jamiat Ulemae-Islam, 28
Difa-e-Pakistan Council (DPC), 14, 40, 56, 67, 69
Dobbins, James, 151
Dogar, Abdul Hameed, 137–38
domestic security issues of Pakistan, 13; balance of power between military and civilian rulers, 16; command and control threats to nuclear program, 16; consequences of, 15–16; jihadist insurgency, 27
drone program, 2, 151, 227; accuracy of strikes, 76; American and Pakistani interests for, 89–91; American domestic law and, 80–81; attacks on Pakistani Taliban, 77–79; background, 74–79; challenges, 82; consent of Pakistan's establishment to, 15, 88–90; estimates of civilian casualty rates, 75–76, 92n6; in

FATA, 84–87; future of, 89–91; human rights law and, 82–83; *jus ad bellum* justification, 80–2; *jus in bello* justification, 80–81; legal aspects, American, Pakistani, and international, 79–84; against militants in Pakistan's northwest, 15; as military-to-military cooperation between Pakistan and the United States, 77–79, 83; negative consequences for Pakistan's polity, 73; number of strikes, 75; under Pakistani law, 80–81, 84; Pakistan's civilian politicians' support for, 77; and Pakistan's internal security landscape, 15, 84–87; Rehman's death and significant repercussions, 78–79; Sharif's stance, 79, 92n3; signature strikes, 77; strikes in Pakistan, 2004–June 2013, 75. *See also* Federally Administered Tribal Areas (FATA); Pakistani militancy
Durand, Sir Henry Mortimer, 280
Durand Line, 280

economic challenges of Pakistan, 214; circular debt, 17; development of private power plants, 17; electricity blackouts, 180–86; external debt servicing, 188; major long-term problems, 179–80; retarding GDP growth and tax revenue, 180; Taxation Administration Reform Program (TARP), 191, 193; taxation system, 17; tax debacle in Pakistan, 187–89; tax reforms, 191–94. *See also* electricity debacle in Pakistan
Economic Support Funds (ESF), 211
electricity debacle in Pakistan: blackouts (load shedding), 180, 186; "circular debt" problem, 185–86; cost differential between hydroelectric and thermal, 183; economic growth and, 181; independent (privately owned) power producer (IPP) program, 183–85
electricity-generating capacity in Pakistan, 182–83
electorate of Pakistan, 145–48; on countries beneficial to Pakistan, 146–47; on relations with Kabul, 146; voting youth cohort, 146
Enhanced Partnership with Pakistan Act, 2009, 212
Excess Defense Articles (EDA), 210

Fareedia, Jamia, 35
Federally Administered Tribal Areas (FATA), 33, 72, 212; American drone strikes in, 84–87; American perspective, 90; based militants, 39; civilian casualty due to drone program, 75; colonial system for maintaining peace, 85; Frontier Crimes Regulation (FCR), 86–87; insurgent mobilization in, 211; legal regime in, 85–86; militant milieu of, 41–42; Pakistan's options to internal security threat, 87–89; regions, 85; social order in, 87
Feldman, Herbert, 178
Foreign Military Financing (FMF), 210
Friends of Democratic Pakistan (FoDP), 267
Frontier Crimes Regulation (FCR), 86

Ghazi, Abdul Rashid, 149
Gilani, Yousuf Raza, 139, 189
"Global War on Terror" (GWOT), 227
Gul, Hamid, 286
Gwadar seaport, development of, 265

Haqqani, Husain, 10, 141
Haqqani, Jalaluddin, 3, 30, 32–33
Haqqani Network (HQN), 7, 37, 39, 41–43, 45, 78, 83, 278, 291; as a "platform for operational development and force projection," 41–42
Harkat-ul-Jihad-al-Islami (HuJI), 29
Harkat-ul-Mujahideen-al-Alami, 34
Harkat-ul-Mujahideen (HuM), 29, 31, 34
Hayden, Michael, 77
Hippel, Frank von, 116
Hizbul Mujahideen (HM), 27, 29, 43, 55
Hizb ut-Tahrir, 112, 171
Hub Power Company, 183
hypocrites, 61, 68; Hafiz Saeed's treatment, 63; individual, 63; jihadists against, 61, 63–64; Maududi's interpretation, 64

ideological anti-American sentiment, 229
India, GDP growth rate of, 181–82
Indian Mujahideen (IM) network, 32, 44
India-U.S. civilian nuclear agreement, 266
Indo-Pakistan conflict/competition, 13–14, 228, 257–88
Indo-U.S. relations, 4
instrumental anti-American sentiment, 229
Inter-Ministerial Committee for the Evaluation of Websites (IMCEW), 165–66

internally displaced persons (IDPs) following drone program, 87–88
Inter-Services Intelligence (ISI), 8, 28, 31, 100, 162, 288–89; situational awareness of Afghanistan, 46; support to money and other goods to LeT, 40
Islamic movements, 56
issue-oriented anti-American sentiment, 229

Jaish-e-Mohammed (JeM), 29
Jamaat-e-Islami (JI), 56, 58, 62, 67–69; of the modernist tradition, 14
Jamaat-ud-Dawa (JuD), 14, 40, 57
Jamaat ul-Furqan, 34
Jamiat Ulema-e-Islam (JUI-S), 14, 56, 58, 68
JeM, 31, 34–35
jihadist movement in South Asia, 27–28
jihadists: against polytheists and hypocrites, 61, 63–64; significant commonalities in beliefs, 68–69; Surah at-Taubah, significance of, 58–60, 64
judiciary, Pakistani, 137–41; intervention in Qadri's incident, 140–41; judicial activism against PPP government, 138–39; lawyers' movement, 138–39, 148, 158–59; media censorship and control, 171; Memogate, 141; Musharraf's era, 137–38; National Reconciliation Ordinance (NRO), 138; role of facilitating subversion of representative institutions, 141; *suo moto* powers, 137; as ultimate arbiter of political integrity and morality, 141
Jundal, Abu, 171
jus ad bellum, 80–82
jus in bello, 80–81

Kaltenthaler, Karl, 8
Karachi Electric Supply Corporation (KESC), 180
Karamat, Jehangir, 139
Kargil conflict, 264
Karzai, Hamid, 10
Kashmir: India-centric militant groups and, 30–32; pro-state groups fighting in Pakistan, 37
Kashmir-centric military groups, 43–44
Katzenstein, Peter, 229
Kayani, Ashfaq Parvez, 3–4, 37, 138, 148, 150
Keohane, Robert, 229
Kerr, Paul, 116

Kerry-Lugar-Berman (KLB) bill, 212–13
Khalis, Yunus, 287
Khan, Abdul Qadeer, 103–4, 118
Khan, Ayub, 178
Khan, Feroz Hassan, 104
Khan, Imran, 17; emergence as a national
    politician, 139, 145–46; official Facebook
    page, 156–57
Khan, Muhammad Daoud, 282
Khyber Pakhtunkhwa Province (KPK),
    35–36, 46, 84–85, 87, 214
Kidwai, Khalid, 107, 110
Korengal Valley, 38

Laden, Osama bin, 9, 102, 133–34, 208,
    216–17, 236, 285, 287
Landau Network–Centro Volta, 107
Landay, Jonathan, 76–77
Lashkar-e-Jhangvi (LeJ), 29, 34–36, 45, 76,
    171
Lashkar-e-Taiba (LeT), 7–8, 27, 29, 31, 37,
    44, 55, 67–68, 70; attacks on TTP, 39;
    books and publications, 49n21, 59;
    ideology, 69; Kashmir-centric, 43; LeT-IM
    operations, 48n9; propaganda campaign
    against al-Qaeda and TTP, 39, 49n21;
    Saeed's lectures, 57–58; Surah at-Taubah,
    significance for, 58–60; use of social
    media, 171
law of armed conflict (LOAC), 79
Lewis, Jeffrey, 108
Living Under Drones, 80
Lucman, Mubashir, 161

Mahmood, Sultan Bashirud-Din, 101
Majeed, Chaudiri Abdul, 101
Maududi, Maulana, 63
McChrystal, Stanley, 6
media in Pakistan, 17; Associated Press of
    Pakistan (APP) news agency, 167; Baloch
    Hal, 168; Baluchistan, use of digital media,
    167–68; ban on Facebook and YouTube,
    169; capacity to effect change, 157–60,
    163–64, 172–73; class aspect of, 163–65;
    extremist groups' online presence, 170–71;
    Imran Khan's use of social media, 156–57;
    Internet-based communication, 165–66;
    Islamization policies, 169; 2007–2008
    lawyers' movement and, 158–59; main-
    stream media's credibility, 161; media

censorship and control, 166–72; mobile
    networks, 165; Musharraf's use of social
    media, 159–60; new vs old, 160–63; online
    censorship of websites, 167; online video-
    sharing, 170; Pakistani cyberspace,
    172–73; Pakistani firewall, plan for, 166;
    Pakistan Telecommunication Authority
    (PTA) and, 164; Pakistan Television
    Network (PTV), 167; process of licensing
    a 3G network, 164–65; pro-democracy
    movement, role in, 159; Progressive
    Papers Limited (PPL), 167; public
    perception, 160, 163; security issues and,
    162; SMS networks, role in anti-Musharraf
    activists, 159; social media, 17, 156–60,
    162–63; spread of new media technol-
    ogies, 157–58, 162–63, 172–73; television
    news channels, 160; use in education, 164
Mehsud, Baitullah, 39
militant anti-American sentiment, 230,
    243–47
military incursions, 34–36, 38
military operations: Operation Al Mizan, 34;
    Operation Enduring Freedom, 2; Oper-
    ation Rah-e-Nijat, 38; Operation Rah-e-
    Rast (Swat), 38; Operation Sher Dil, 38;
    Operation Zalzala, 39
military-to-military cooperation, 210;
    American focus on training and
    equipment, 213; Coalition Support Fund
    (CSF), 210; drone program, 77–79, 83;
    Excess Defense Articles (EDA), 210;
    financial aids, 3, 7, 212; Foreign Military
    Financing (FMF), 210; Obama strategy,
    213
Miller, William J., 8
Missile Technology Control Regime
    (MTCR), 266
Morozov, Evgeny, 165
Mubarakmand, Samar, 107–8
Muhammad, Nek, 74
Muhammad, Sufi, 29–30
Musharraf, Pervez, 1, 17, 72, 74, 107, 131,
    137, 148–50, 158, 178–79, 261; American
    and international support, 209; charges
    against, 149; economic aid received during
    period of, 211; Lal Masjid debacle, 211;
    legal woes of, 149–50, 211–12; military
    assistance and reimbursements during
    period of, 210; Pakistani militancy, 30–32,

34, 37; political strategy, 209–10; primary power base, 210; role in war efforts (international military campaign), 2; support for American aims in Afghanistan, 208–11; threat of impeachment and resignation, 148; U.S. support to, 2–3; U.S.-Pakistan relationship during period of, 30–32, 34, 37. *See also* U.S.-Pakistan relationship
Muslims and non-Muslims, 60–61, 67
Muttahida Qaumi Movement (MQM), 145
Muttahida Quami Movement, 45

Najibullah, Mohammad, 286
national income tax number (NITN), 189
nationalist anti-American sentiment, 230–33
National Reconciliation Ordinance, 2
National Transmission and Dispatch Company (NTDC), 181, 185
Nazir, Mullah, 39
New America Foundation, 74
Nikitin, Mary Beth, 116
noninternational armed conflict (NIAC), 83
nonstate actors, 38; Pakistan's nuclear program and, 99–101; violent, role in Afghanistan-Pakistan relationship, 278–80, 290–93
Northern Alliance, 3
nuclear risk, 105
nuclear risk, after 2014, 119–22

Obama, Barack, 5, 77–78, 83, 206, 213, 235–36
Omar, Mullah, 3
Organization of the Islamic Conference (OIC), 284

Pakistan: attempts for pan-Islamism, 259–60; campaign of ethnic cleansing, 11; civilian participation, 141–45; early 2000 status, 1; and Eighteenth Amendment of Constitution, 143–45; forms of military aid received, 210; 2013 general elections, 10–11; internal conflict, 83; International Monetary Fund (IMF)'s financial assistance to, 266–67; judiciary, 137–41; neglected minority populations of, 11; nuclear dangers, 99; peace process with India, 31; perceptions of its allies, 258; political parties of, 28; post 9/11 status,

1–2; privileges of army in, 133–37; security challenges of, 11–13; Sharif's regime, 131–32; U.S. conspiratorial activities in, 221; and U.S. presence in Afghanistan, 11–13. *See also* China; Saudi Arabia
Pakistan Counterinsurgency Fund (PCF), 213
Pakistani arsenal/nuclear program, 15–16, 116, 262; battlefield nuclear weapons, 117–19; development of tactical nuclear weapons, 152; estimates of arsenal, 105–6; expansion of, 121, 152; Saudi Arabian support, 262; Sino-Pakistani cooperation in the nuclear field, 264–66. *See also* Pakistan's nuclear weapons, safety and security of
Pakistani militancy, 14; Afghanistan-centric groups, 32–34; after 9/11, 30–37; attacks against Shia population, 29; cases of torture and extrajudicial execution in FATA, 87–88; Deobandi sect, 28–29; diversity of, 14; dynamics of, 40–42; Ghazi brothers' exhortations, 35–36; incursions into FATA, 34–36; India-centric groups, 30–32, 37; jihadist influence, 14; Kashmir-centric groups, 30–31; Lashkar-e-Taiba (LeT), 29; major crisis of, 210–11; during Musharraf era, 30–32, 34, 37; Operation Rah-e-Haq, or "Path of Truth," 36; Operation Rah-e-Nijat, 36, 38; Operation Rah-e-Rast (Swat), 38; Operation Sher Dil, 38; post–U.S. withdrawal from Afghanistan, 42–45, 222; pro-state and anti-state militants, 14, 37, 42; Punjabi militant groups, 29; recruitment efforts in India and terrorist operations, 31–32; revolutionary and sectarian loci groups, 34–37; role in Afghan insurgency by 2005, 33; safe haven in Afghanistan, 45–47; sectarian affiliation of militant groups, 28–29; security establishment and internal threats, 37–38; and security policy, 37–40; support for proxies, 40–41; support for Taliban in Afghanistan, 29–30. *See also* drone program; Federally Administered Tribal Areas (FATA)
Pakistan Institute of Legislative Development and Transparency (PILDAT), 142
Pakistani security establishment, 40; American aid, 215; concerns about U.S. and NATO drawdown, 42–45; support to LeT, 40

Pakistani views on Americans: of American hostility to Muslims, 243; on attacks on U.S. military, 244; attitudes toward Pakistan-U.S. cooperation, 239; attitudes toward the current U.S. government, 2007, 235; concern about military threat, 240; culture, 242; lack of confidence in American leadership, 235–36; opinion about raid for Laden, 238; opinion of drone attacks, 237; response to the question of identity, 242; of the United States as enemy or partner, 235; of U.S. dominance, 241. *See also* anti-American sentiment in Pakistan

Pakistan Muslim League–Nawaz (PML-N), 16, 131, 156, 164, 267

Pakistan Peoples Party, 3, 45; five-year tenure of, 142; legislative affairs of PPP-led government, 142

Pakistan Peoples Party (PPP), 267

Pakistan's nuclear weapons, safety and security of: A. Q. Khan's role in sensitive technology swaps, 103–4; battlefield nuclear weapons, 117–19; insider threats, dangers of, 101–6, 109–12; intelligence agencies, role of, 111; material protection, control, and accounting (MPC&A) regime, 105; material protection and accounting programs, 109; nonstate actors, role of, 99–101; nuclear risk associated with Pakistan's nuclear arsenal, 119–22; outsider threats, dangers of, 112–17; Pakistani state, steps taken by, 105; permissive action links (PALs), 105, 108–9; principal-agent challenges, 100; and readiness of forces, 106–12; risk of intrusion, 113–17; screening of staff, 110–11; Special Services Group (SSG) for, 112; Strategic Plans Division (SPD) and, 105, 107, 111, 114; tamper resistance strategy, 108; terrorist attacks and, 112–13; "two-man rule," 105, 109, 119; and Ummah Tameer-e-Nau (UTN), 101–2; from unauthorized detonation, 107–9

Pakistan Tehreek-e-Insaf (PTI), 17, 145, 156; social media frenzy of, 156

Palestine Liberation Organization (PLO), 284

Pande, Aparna, 121

Parliamentary Committee on National Security (PCNS), 142–43

Pashtunistan, Afghanistan's demand for, 19, 280–84, 292–93

Perkovich, George, 100

political polarization of Pakistan, 131

polytheists, Surah at-Taubah interpretations of, 61, 64, 67

Provincially Administered Tribal Areas (PATA), 87

Qadri, Mumtaz, 112, 172–73

Qadri, Tahir, 140

Quetta Shura Taliban, 33, 37, 43

Qureshi, S. M. M., 282

radical anti-American sentiment, 230

Rahman, Abdur, 280

Raymond Davis affair, 8, 215–16

Rehman, Wali ur, 78

religious anti-American sentiment, 230–33

revolutionary anti-American sentiment, 229

revolutionary jihad, 41

Riaz, Malik, 161

Riedel, Bruce, 5, 13, 105

Rubenstein, Alvin, 229

Saeed, Hafiz Muhammad, 14, 57, 59–61; on illegitimate participation of Pakistan's Islamic parties, 62; normative reading of at-Taubah, 61–63, 67; against Pakistani state, 61–63; treatment of hypocrites, 63

Sagan, Scott, 100

Saudi Arabia, 19, 122, 139, 228, 256–58, 267, 270–72, 285; assistance to Pakistan, 195, 258, 260; defense cooperation, 261–62; donations from wealthy individuals and charities to Pakistan, 262–63; role in Pakistan's domestic politics, 260–61; Saudi-Pakistani military alliance, 195; support for Pakistan's nuclear program, 262

secular doctrine, 45

Seng, Jordan, 113

Shafi', Mufti Muhammad, 58, 61, 64

Shah, Muhammad Zahir, 282–83

Sharif, Nawaz, 1, 11, 18, 20, 44–45, 77, 79, 91, 92n3, 131–32, 136, 139, 148, 150, 178, 261, 264; developments in civil-military relations, 151; expansion of nuclear program, 152; tax reforms, 191–94; *vs* General Raheel Sharif, 150

Sharif, Raheel, 150

Shura Ittihad-ul-Mujahidin (SIM), 39
Sipah-e-Sahaba Pakistan (SSP), 29
Smith, Donald, 229
social anti-American sentiment, 229–30
Soomro, Illahi Bux, 167
South Asia, 223
South Asia analytical community, 7
Southeast Asia Treaty Organization
  (SEATO), 257
Spain, James, 280, 282
SSP, 35
Student Islamist Movement of Indian
  (SIMI), 32
Sunni Islamic movements, 14, 56; pan-Sunni
  coalitions, 57, 70
Sunni organizations, 56–57
Surah at-Taubah: Ahmadi sect, treatment of,
  64; jihadists and, 58–60, 64; Lashkar-e-
  Taiba, significance for, 58–60; Maududi's
  interpretation, 63–64; Muslims and non-
  Muslims, significance for, 60–61; on Paki-
  stani state, 61–64; against polytheists and
  hypocrites, 61, 64, 67; preparations for
  Tabuk campaign, 64–5; subject-matter of,
  58–59; Sunni commentaries, 61; Sunni
  traditions and jihad beliefs, 67; vision of
  jihad, 64–66
Sustainable Development Policies Institute
  (SDPI), 146–47

Tafseer Surah at-Taubah, 57–58
takfiri ideologies, 68
Talibanization, 36
Taseer, Salman, 112, 172
tax debacle in Pakistan, 187–89; composition
  of tax revenue, 189; corruption in the FBR,
  190; general sales tax (GST), 189–91;
  impact of SRO283(1)/2011, 191;
  nonpayers of tax, 189; reasons for, 190; tax
  administration and collection process,
  187–88; tax-revenue-to-GDP ratio, 188;
  unimportance of personal income tax
  revenue, 189; untaxed sectors, 190; U.S.
  financial assistance following, 188, 197n22;
  wholesale and retail trade (W&RT) sector
  and, 192. *See also* economic challenges of
  Pakistan
Tehreek-e-Nafaz-e-Shariat-e-Mohammadi
  (TNSM), 29–30, 32

Tehreek-e-Taliban-e-Pakistan (TTP), 4, 36,
  55, 68, 70, 78, 89, 213–14, 290–91; attacks
  on, 39; connections to LeJ and SSP, 36;
  cross-border TTP strikes, 38; infrastructure, 38; peace negotiations with, 45
Tenet, George, 102
Tertrais, Bruno, 108

Ummah Tameer-e-Nau (UTN), 101–2
U.S.-led military alliances, 257
Usmani, Muhammad Taqi, 61, 64
U.S.-Pakistan relationship, 122, 143, 178–79;
  of 2013, 222–23; accountability on
  American flows toward Pakistan, 212;
  American outreach to Pakistan, 11–12;
  American Pakistan strategy since 9/11,
  207–17; American perspective, 3, 221;
  anti-Americanism as a factor, 18; bin
  Laden affair and, 133–34, 216–17; CIA's
  escalation of drone strikes, 9; counterterrorism cooperation, 211–14, 223; criticism
  of U.S. failures in Pakistan, 5; Davis affair
  and, 8, 215–16; following American
  drawdown from Afghanistan, 11–13, 19,
  46, 205–7; instants of failures, 9–10;
  Kerry-Lugar-Berman (KLB) bill, 212–13;
  mass public's attitudes toward United
  States, 18–19; during Musharraf regime,
  30–32, 34, 37; NATO ground supply
  routes, closing of, 9; Obama administration *vs* Bush administration, 6–7;
  Obama strategy, 213; Pakistan army's
  point of view, 4–5; Pakistan perspective,
  3–4, 220–22; PCNS's framework for
  restructuring, 143; political obstacles
  impacting, 214–17; post-2014, 217–24;
  raid for Laden's hiding place and, 9; reimbursements to Pakistan, 3, 7; sanctions on
  Pakistan since 1990, 208; shift in domestic
  political conditions and, 212; since 9/11,
  18, 205; since 2007, 3–4; strains in, 209;
  tensions in, 8; transactional relationship,
  223; U.S. assistance to Pakistan, 188,
  197n22; U.S. security assistance to
  Pakistan, 3, 7, 212; U.S. war in Afghanistan, Pakistan's assistance to, 2–3

Water and Power Development Agency
  (WAPDA), 180–81, 183

Waziristan, military incursion in, 30, 33–34, 36, 38, 45–46
White, Joshua, 85
white paper on South Asia and Middle East, 5–6

Zardari, Asif Ali, 16, 77, 138, 143, 189, 289
Zemin, Jiang, 264
Zia-ul-Haq, Muhammad, 135, 169, 286
Zimmerman, Peter, 108

Acknowledgments

The editors are deeply indebted to all of the authors who worked so hard on this volume. We are also thankful to the United States Educational Foundation in Pakistan (USEFP), which sponsored our author's meeting in 2012 in San Diego. In particular, many thanks go to Rita Akhtar of the USEFP, who believed in this project and believed that it would enhance the mission of USEFP. We are thankful to all who gave critical feedback to earlier versions of the essay. We are also thankful to Georgetown University's Edmund A. Walsh School of Foreign Service and the Security Studies Program, which subsidized the labors that went into this volume. We would also like to thank the two anonymous reviewers who gave sharp, firm, and insightful advice on how to organize the volume and revise the varied chapters. Finally, we owe much gratitude to the efforts of Bill Finan, who believed in this project. Despite the able advice and assistance of these helpful persons, the editors and the individual authors are solely responsible for any errors of fact or interpretation.